AF501886

Stereotypes and stereotyping in early modern England

Manchester University Press

Politics, culture and society in early modern Britain

This important series publishes monographs that take a fresh and challenging look at the interactions between politics, culture and society in Britain between 1500 and the mid-eighteenth century. It counteracts the fragmentation of current historiography through encouraging a variety of approaches which attempt to redefine the political, social and cultural worlds, and to explore their interconnection in a flexible and creative fashion. All the volumes in the series question and transcend traditional interdisciplinary boundaries, such as those between political history and literary studies, social history and divinity, urban history and anthropology. They thus contribute to a broader understanding of crucial developments in early modern Britain.

Stereotypes and stereotyping in early modern England

Puritans, papists and projectors

Edited by

Koji Yamamoto

MANCHESTER UNIVERSITY PRESS

Published by Manchester University Press
Oxford Road, Manchester M13 9PL

www.manchesteruniversitypress.co.uk

British Library Cataloguing-in-Publication Data
A catalogue record for this book is available from the British Library

ISBN 978 1 5261 1913 1 hardback

First published 2022

Typeset
by Cheshire Typesetting Ltd, Cuddington, Cheshire

Contents

Figures

Contributors

William J. Bulman (PhD, Princeton, 2010) is Professor of History at Lehigh University, Bethlehem, PA. He is the author of *Anglican Enlightenment: orientalism, religion and politics in England and its empire, 1648–1715* (Cambridge, 2015) and *The rise of majority rule in early modern Britain and its empire* (Cambridge, 2021), and he is the co-editor of *God in the Enlightenment* (Oxford, 2016) and *Political and religious practice in the early modern British world* (Manchester, 2022). He has also published a series of articles in journals including *Past & Present*, *Historical Journal* and *Journal of British Studies*.

William Cavert is Associate Professor of History at the University of St Thomas in Minnesota, where he teaches early modern European and environmental history. He is the author of *The smoke of London: energy and environment in the early modern city* (Cambridge, 2016) and subsequently translated into Chinese, and of other studies of London's coal consumption, air pollution and the cold winters of the Little Ice Age. His current research explores bounties on animals considered vermin, and associated programmes of agrarian improvement in early modern Britain and its empire.

Tim Harris is the Munro-Goodwin-Wilkinson Professor in European History at Brown University, Providence, RI. His books include *London crowds in the reign of Charles II* (Cambridge, 1987); *Politics under the later Stuarts* (Abingdon, 1993); *Restoration: Charles II and his kingdoms* (London, 2005), *Revolution: the great crisis of the British monarchy, 1685–1720* (London, 2006), and *Rebellion: Britain's first Stuart kings, 1567–1642* (London, 2014). The edited collections he has published include *Politics, religion and ideas in seventeenth- and eighteenth-century Britain: essays in honour of Mark Goldie* (Woodbridge, 2019, with Justin Champion, John Coffey and John Marshall). He edits the book series Studies in Early Modern Cultural, Political and Social History for Boydell Press.

Sandra Jovchelovitch is Professor of Social Psychology at the London School of Economics. Before coming to England, she trained as a psychologist in Brazil, where she actively participated in the process of deinstitutionalisation and restructuring of policies relating to the care of the mentally ill. Her research interests are both theoretical and applied, and she has published widely in the field of social representations, health, community and development in both English and Portuguese.

Peter Lake is the University Distinguished Professor of History and Professor of the History of Christianity, Divinity School at Vanderbilt University, Nashville, TN. From 1993 to 2009 he was Professor of History at Princeton. He is the author of eleven books, the most recent of which are *All hail to the archpriest: confessional conflict, toleration and the politics of publicity in post-Reformation England* (with Michael Questier) (Oxford/New York, 2019), *Gentry culture and the politics of religion: Cheshire on the eve of civil war* (with Richard Cust) (Manchester, 2020) and, on his own, *Hamlet's choice: religion and resistance in Shakespeare's revenge tragedies* (New Haven, CT, 2020). He is currently finishing a study of Laudianism, and three books including one with Michael Questier on life writing, memory and religious identity in the post-Reformation.

David Magliocco is an independent scholar. He held the position of Research Assistant Professor of History at Vanderbilt University, Nashville, TN. His thesis, funded by the Arts and Humanities Research Council and defended in January 2014, is entitled 'Samuel Pepys, the Restoration public and the politics of publicity'; it examined questions of publicity, agency and identity utilising the diary of Samuel Pepys.

Adam Morton is a Senior Lecturer in British History at Newcastle University. He is an historian of the English Reformation, and his research focuses on anti-popery and visual culture in the early modern period. He has written widely on those themes, and his publications include *The power of laughter and satire in early modern Britain* (Woodbridge, 2017), edited with Mark Knights; *Queens consort, cultural transfer and European politics c.1500–1800* (Abingdon, 2016), edited with Helen Watanabe-O'Kelly; and *Getting along? Religious identities and confessional relations in early modern England – essays in honour of Professor W. J. Sheils* (Abingdon, 2012) edited with Nadine Lewycky. He is currently preparing a collection of essays on civil religion and anti-popery in early modern Britain.

Bridget Orr is an Associate Professor in the Department of English at Vanderbilt University, Nashville, TN. She is the author of *Empire on the*

English stage, 1660–1714 (Cambridge, 2001) and *British Enlightenment theatre: dramatizing difference* (Cambridge, 2020). She is also editor of a special Pacific issue of *The Eighteenth Century: Theory and Interpretation* and has published many essays on Restoration and eighteenth-century drama and New Zealand, Maori and Pacific writing and film. Among other awards she has won fellowships from the National Endowment for the Humanities and the American Council of Learned Societies.

Kate Peters is a Senior College Lecturer in History at Murray Edwards College, Cambridge. She is the author of *Print culture and the early Quakers* (Cambridge, 2005) and a number of scholarly articles on Quakers and radical religion in the English Revolution. She is currently working on the politics of archives and record-keeping in the English Revolution.

Koji Yamamoto is Associate Professor of Business History at the University of Tokyo, Japan. He is the author of *Taming capitalism before its triumph: public service, distrust, and 'projecting' in early modern England* (Oxford, 2018), and has also published articles in *Historical Journal* and *English Historical Review*. He is a founder of the Japanese grassroots organisation Historians' Workshop, a platform for preparing Japan-based early-career historians for a global academic arena. His current book project is a history of the South Sea Bubble.

Acknowledgements

This book has taken a long time to finish. For patience and support I am grateful to all the contributors and everyone at Manchester University Press, especially Meredith Carroll. Peter Lake has been extraordinarily generous from the project's inception. I will fondly remember a number of calls we had across different time zones. I hope to pay forward the generosity, the insights and the enthusiasm that I received from him.

Many of the chapters were first presented in a two-day conference, 'Stereotyping in early modern British public spheres', held at the Senate House, the University of London, on 16 and 17 June 2014. The idea was to present early modern papers and invite response from social psychologists and sociologists interested in stereotypes and public attitudes. I thank the wonderful psychologist, Vlad Glăveanu, for co-hosting it. For generous support for the conference, I would also like to thank the Institute of Historical Research, University of London, the Society for Renaissance Studies (UK), the Department of History and the School of Arts and Humanities, King's College London, and finally COST Action IS1205 (Social psychological dynamics of historical representations in the enlarged European Union). As I complete the editorial process, I have drawn on the funding I received as a University of Tokyo Excellent Young Researcher.

Peter Lake and I also organised a related conference at the Huntington Library, 'Stereotypes and stereotyping in the early modern world' (19–20 April 2019). I would have been far less alert to wider issues of race, gender and occupation were it not for the discussions we had at the beautiful grounds of the botanical gardens. I thank speakers there for feedback, and especially Steve Hindle for generous support throughout.

For discussions, advice, friendship and inspirations, I would like to thank Martin Bauer, Steve Hindle, Rob Iliffe, Ludmilla Jordanova, Sandra Jovchelovitch, Sakiko Kaiga, Mark Knights, Bridget Orr and Brodie Waddell. Tim Harris and Lisa Hellman offered constructive feedback when I faced difficulties. I thank Shifra Diamond and Hiroyuki Komatsu for editorial assistance, John Firth for copyediting and Hannah DeGroff for indexing.

As this volume evolved, the themes related to stereotyping have taken on additional urgency as we have witnessed the British exit from the European Union, the election of Donald Trump as the 45th president of the United States and the rise of populist politics in countries including the United States, the United Kingdom, Hungary, Poland, Turkey, India and Japan. In editing the chapters for publication, I have tried to weave together early modern case studies in ways that enable us not only to make better sense of the period, but also to suggest that early modern experiences of stereotyping have surprising resonance in the twenty-first century. We can learn a great deal from the early modern past without being anachronistic.

Finally, I would like to thank Dr Yuko Nakamura. She has seen this volume coming to fruition, and our numerous conversations have prompted me to interrogate my own deeply held beliefs. Without her acuity, empathy and kindness, I would not have been able to realise how hard, and how rewarding, it is to confront and move beyond the stereotypes we hold about ourselves. For this and much more, I cannot thank her enough.

5th January 2022, Tokyo
Koji Yamamoto

Note on conventions

All works cited were published in London unless otherwise specified. The dates are given in the old style, but with the year taken to have started on 1 January.

Introduction: Rethinking early modern stereotyping in the twenty-first century

Koji Yamamoto and Peter Lake

Our choice of the gerund – stereotyping – is deliberate. By it we wish to direct our critical attention not only to the *contents* of any stereotypical representations, but also to the ways in which these representations were *put to use* in polemical exchanges, often appealing to existing prejudices and invoking ideologies. This volume of essays explores stereotyping as a form of contested practice embedded in various negotiations of power concerning spheres of life such as politics, religion, everyday life and knowledge production.

Stereotyping in early modern England calls for our scrutiny now because then – as now – stereotypes were pervasive and even affected the unfolding of events of profound consequence. In recent years, such events include two political upheavals of 2016: the British referendum on Brexit, and the American presidential election through which Donald Trump entered the White House, a property tycoon with no previous experience of political office. In both events, competing camps – including those self-styled defenders of progressive values – stereotyped the other as unacceptable parties perpetrating great wrongs to the countries which they were supposed to serve. In the process, a wide range of stereotypes were marshalled to orchestrate support and attack opponents – of immigrants, of African Americans, of conservative southerners, of incompetent bureaucrats, of metropolitan elites and of autocrats.[1]

Walter Lippmann, who helped define the term stereotype, would have considered this a uniquely *modern* phenomenon, modern in that its diffusion and impact supposedly rested on a range of modern mass media and the large literate audience consuming them.[2] Such views are no longer sustainable. Stereotyping has also been found across virtually every aspect of life during the early modern period.

In this volume, we define stereotyping as the attribution of certain characteristics to some category of person, institution, event or thing.[3] Shared by a large number of people, stereotypes usually have negative connotations.[4] We use stereotypes as a window into the early modern past because they shaped, and were shaped by, broader ideologies, prejudices and polemics. Take English stereotypes about patriarchy and Roman Catholics. Such early modern stereotypes were integral to wider ideologies like the divine rights of monarchy and the reformed Anglicanism. While closely tied to elaborate doctrines, stereotypical representations of failed patriarchs, unruly women and papists (i.e. those accepting the authority of the papacy) also reflected existing prejudices, embodying popular culture, that elusive 'mentality' of the population.[5] These highly charged stereotypes were often employed in Parliament, in law courts and in local parishes to sway opinion. As such, stereotyping was a key component of the broader manifestations of power across centre and peripheries. Practices of stereotyping played a critical role during the moments of intense political crisis, such as the unfolding of the Civil Wars in the 1640s and the so-called Exclusion Crisis between 1679 and 1681. Stereotypes also circulated widely beyond moments of crisis, shaping religious identities, fuelling political debates, picked up in theatre plays and disseminated via prints, woodcuts, manuscripts and oral gossip. Stereotypes thereby conditioned civic participatory politics, while also shaping knowledge about the self and influencing the advancement of learning about non-Christian faiths inside and outside Europe.

Here, then, is an unexpected overlap that will emerge from this volume: if societies in the early modern period and in the twenty-first century are both profoundly affected by stereotyping, would it be possible for historians of the early modern period to learn from social science research into present-day stereotypes, while at the same time offering useful insights into the dynamism of stereotyping based on early modern case studies? In 2012, Vlad Glăveanu and Koji Yamamoto edited a special issue of the journal *Integrative Psychological and Behavioral Science*, titled 'Bridging history and social psychology', in which five historians responded to psychologists' articles. They all questioned psychologists' depictions of 'traditional societies' as static and monolithic, and showed that uses of memories and representations in pre-modern societies have more similarities to modern-day practices than hitherto assumed by social scientists. In 2014, Mark Knights further explored the possibility for interdisciplinary engagements by paying critical attention to visual, linguistic and cognitive elements of historical stereotypes.[6] This volume complements these interventions by focusing on mobilisation and contestation – what people *did* with stereotypes.

This is a timely exercise. Traditionally, psychologists understood stereotypes as an 'automatic and inevitable consequence of categorization', a mental process required to 'simplify the cognitive tasks confronted by the social perceiver'.[7] As we shall see, more recent accounts have also begun to pay attention to how stereotypes are used in particular contexts, suggesting parallels with historians' turn toward practice and process. This volume invites readers to pursue further cross-fertilisation between history and social science, especially aspects of social psychology and sociology. We do this not because we wish to celebrate interdisciplinarity for its own sake. Rather, we urge historians and social scientists to keep crossing boundaries because doing so will render historical scholarship more analytically rigorous while making its findings open and freshly relevant to social scientists and broader audiences more interested in contemporary societies.

So far, stereotypes about religious faith, gender, race, poverty and other themes in the early modern period have tended to be studied separately. This is partly because scholars have not necessarily used the same terminology, but instead separately discussed representations and images in their respective subfields. Few accounts nowadays treat early modern stereotypes as mere myths or errors, or view those holding stereotypes as simply irrational. Even so, there still is a related tendency to suggest that those holding stereotypes were the victims of scare-mongering.[8] At worst, such approaches can lead us to reproduce the traditional psychological model and project it back on past societies. Doing so induces us to trivialise the agency of historical actors – to treat them as passive components with few other options but to process information through a series of simplistic stereotypes that derived from and lent legitimacy to the existing social order.

Instead of treating stereotyping as an inevitable cognitive propensity, we would do well to follow Peter Burke's dictum that images and representations are themselves events, and heed Roger Chartier's advice that the consumption of these images be studied as 'another production'.[9] Building upon these views, we suggest that stereotyping must also be examined as events with far-reaching repercussions, an integral component in so many negotiations of power as most notably studied by Susan Amussen, Michael Braddick, John Walter and Bernard Capp, among others.[10]

If we take this perspective and begin to bring together studies of early modern stereotypes often conducted separately, we can reveal the remarkable extent to which early modern actors – far from being irrational – were more capable of mobilising and contesting stereotypes than hitherto has been allowed. Crucially, close comparative scrutiny of stereotyping and its repercussions also enables us to explore a striking paradox: actors' attempts to refute and control the effects of stereotypes hardly led to their complete removal; rather the reverse. Efforts to confront stereotypes and control and contest their meanings often led to the escalation of polemics and conflict, and to the further reproduction of stereotypes and to their perpetuation. Stereotyping all too often bred more stereotyping. What does progress mean if stereotypes were so pervasive in the early modern period and beyond?

Early modern England: an overview for non-specialists

For this interdisciplinary engagement to flourish, we must ensure that our research is accessible to non-experts in the early modern period. A fuller introduction to seventeenth-century British politics and religion, and the role of stereotypes, will be provided by Tim Harris's chapter. The following paragraphs sketch some of the important themes about early modern England before turning to relevant historiographies and key interventions of this volume.

Early modern England, here defined for our convenience as between 1550 and 1750, witnessed a series of geopolitical, religious, economic and intellectual transformations. At the beginning of this period, England was a modest country on the periphery of Europe, having recently broken away from the Catholic church. Within two centuries, post-Reformation England became Europe's leading trading *entrepôt*, an emerging empire boasting expanding north American colonies with strong overseas trade, backed up by thriving industries at home.

In the process, inhabitants of the British Isles witnessed a series of upheavals. First was constant warfare abroad: the defeat of the Spanish Armada in 1588, the Thirty Years War which England joined in 1618, the three Anglo-Dutch Wars in the 1650s, 1660s and 1670s, the Nine Years War that followed the Glorious Revolution of 1688 and the ensuing War of Spanish Succession.[11] Though fought abroad, these wars nevertheless expanded government debts and put unprecedented fiscal pressures upon the population. These battles were mainly fought against Catholic countries, one of the factors that ensured the ongoing circulation of the anti-Catholic stereotypes like 'popery' discussed throughout this volume.

Inhabitants of England witnessed domestic turbulences too: the Civil Wars of the 1640s, the beheading of King Charles I in 1649, the republican experiments led by Cromwell and others, followed by the restoration of monarchy with the return of Charles II in 1660. Charles II's brother James was Catholic, and between 1679 and 1681 there was an attempt to exclude him from the line of succession – the Exclusion Crisis. In 1685, the succession of James as the Catholic king of a Protestant nation led to his expulsion only three years later, the so-called Glorious Revolution of 1688. The British Isles thus saw at least two revolutions and more political crises during this period. As we shall see, stereotyping was never directed solely against Catholics. Other types of stereotype also proliferated; studying them will help us to throw fresh light on many of these moments of profound social, political and religious crisis.

Despite successive political crises, early modern England also witnessed economic expansion and development.[12] By 1750, navigable rivers had been extended, the granting of patents to promote technology transfer became more common, new urban and rural industries had been set up and numerous schemes enhanced productivity in various sectors such as textiles, agriculture and mining. Regional economies became more specialised, and expanding networks of rivers, highways and ports turned them into something of an integrated national economy, which in turn was fuelled by incoming raw materials from colonies, to be processed and finished for re-exporting back to colonies as well as to European cities. Fruits of such expansion were never distributed evenly across social hierarchies or regions. There were a number of cold winters and bad harvests, and much dearth; poorer landless labourers were driven to starvation, and many flooded into expanding urban centres, especially London, only to suffer from contagious disease, dirty water and the thick smoke of coal burning, all of which kept infant mortality dangerously high. Hostility against foreign immigrants intensified, especially during the periods of hardship and depression.

And then there was a wave of intellectual experiments and transformations, often called the 'scientific revolution'.[13] This is the age that witnessed the diffusion of the telescope, the invention of the microscope and a series of discoveries by luminaries such as William Harvey of the circulation of blood, Robert Boyle of the weight of the air and Isaac Newton of the law of gravity. Historians of science, technology and medicine have now moved firmly beyond the study of their great discoveries. More recent works have instead explored how methods of biblical criticism and interest in alchemy provided templates for reforming 'natural philosophy'; they have unearthed how social practices surrounding 'credible witnesses' lent themselves to the staging of experiments, and the reporting of their results as 'matters of fact'.[14] Contemporary norms and expectations about status, gender and civility turned out to be as crucial as intellectual traditions. We can begin to see why historians of science and medicine therefore have long paid close attention to various stereotypes about the 'scholar', the 'quack', the 'empiric', the 'midwife' and the 'projector', all of which conditioned the production of knowledge in the early modern period.[15]

Early modern responses to this period of successive crises and profound change were far from impartial. Communications were so problematic that even appeals to impartiality lent themselves to polemics and the pursuit of power and authority. Peter Lake and Steven Pincus captured this well in their introduction to *The politics of the public sphere in early modern England* (2007):

> it was out of the need to navigate their way through the consequent welter of claim and counterclaim, plot and counter-plot, conspiracy and counter-conspiracy, that contemporaries developed standards and expectations about

> rational argument and proof, credibility and civility, even as their own political and discursive practices and manoeuvres continued to contravene, and perhaps even to subvert, those very standards.[16]

Such divisive exchanges were fuelled by the growing print industry, and from the 1570s also by commercial theatres in London and theatre companies touring across regions.[17] Early modern observers were aware of the danger. As Thomas Hobbes wrote in the immediate aftermath of the English Civil Wars, by the art of words 'some men can represent to others, that which is Good, in the likenesse of Evil; and Evill, in the likenesse of Good; ... discontenting men, and troubling their Peace at their pleasure'.[18]

Stereotyping was everywhere to be found because it was a vital part of such manoeuvres. Consider the case of religious stereotypes. 'Under the name of a puritan all our religion is branded', declared Sir Benjamin Rudyerd in November 1640, highlighting the profound impact of the image of the puritan that had begun to gain currency from the end of Elizabeth I's reign.

> Under a few hard word[s] against Jesuits all popery is countenanced, whosoever squares his actions by any rule either divine or humane he is a puritan ... he that will not doe whatsoever other men would have him do he is a puritan ... Mr Speaker let it be our special cares that those ways neither continue nor return upon us[.][19]

Unfortunately for Rudyerd (and perhaps unsurprisingly for Hobbes) stereotyping of this kind thrived, rather than declining, for the rest of the century. The image of the lawless, promiscuous Ranter pervaded interregnum England. From the late 1670s, images of nonconformists and popery played a vital role in the succession crisis surrounding the Catholic Duke of York; once he acceded to the throne as James II, the repealer movement of the 1680s faced strong public suspicion fuelled by deep-rooted stereotypes about popery (once again) and the perceived danger of arbitrary government. Stereotypes were not limited to the sphere of religious politics, however. Early modern England was replete with stereotypical representations, not only of the puritan and popery, but also of the poor, the foreigner, the monopolist, the projector, the woman, and even of the 'smoky air' due to increasing fossil fuel consumption. What unites the chapters in *Stereotypes and stereotyping in early modern England* is the close attention that each essay pays to the pervasive stereotypes of various 'others' that shaped the religious, political, economic and social life of early modern England. Rhetoric, polemics and prejudices had, and continue to have, a startling capacity to disrupt communication in the public sphere and affect private lives.

The present volume brings together essays that explore such a prevalence of stereotyping and does so with fresh conceptual tools. In doing this, we build on three broad areas of early modern historiography: mentality and popular culture; the turn towards 'practices' via the 'linguistic turn'; and studies responding to (and moving beyond) Jürgen Habermas's account of the public sphere. Each strand is rich and warrants closer scrutiny in its own right than is afforded here. What follows instead is a necessarily limited overview, which we hope nevertheless enables us to situate the conceptual thrust of this volume.

Historiography

Stereotypical representations have featured prominently in studies of early modern popular belief and 'mentality' since the early twentieth century. As Lucien Febvre declared in 1938, it was deemed vital for historians 'to establish a detailed inventory of the mental equipment of the men of the time, then by dint of great learning, but also of imagination, to reconstitute the whole physical, intellectual and moral universe of each preceding generation'. This was the context in which scholars of the Annales school set out to explore senses of time, food, comportment, popular belief and mentality in past societies. Historians of subsequent generations have studied stereotypes because these were also part of the 'mental equipments' (*outillages mentaux*) that informed experience and shaped social life.[20]

One prominent example building on this tradition is Bob Scribner's study (first published in 1981) of the popular visual propaganda for the German Reformation. Scribner's goal was to understand how 'visual propaganda' helped promote religious reform.[21] He argued that visual propaganda effectively exploited 'cultural stereotypes such as the opposition between darkness and light', stark dichotomies that their target audiences readily understood. For example, labelling 'the pope and his followers as spiritual wolves' devouring the innocent in the darkness of night made it possible for reformers to present themselves as the defenders of true religion, bringing brethren to the light of the biblical Word.[22] Such visual stereotyping enabled evangelical reformers 'to occupy the positive ground of saving belief'. In this account, 'the most observable feature' of their campaign was 'the presentation of a simple black-and-white contrast between the opposing views'. This depended on 'a process of simplification' and of 'reification' – the 'reducing [of] the complex issues involved in the Reformation to a number of discrete and easily identifiable symbols'.[23] This account views early modern religious life as being organised around a series of familiar, often dichotomous, symbols tapping into deep-held values, and even fears and prejudices.

This was a groundbreaking work in that it firmly integrated elements of popular culture and thereby established that the Protestant Reformation was much more than the history of great leaders in religion and politics. All the same, this approach risks treating stereotypes as monolithic, a kind of mentality that was pervasive among the otherwise diverse population. Such an impression of uniformity is carefully rejected in Stuart Clark's landmark study of early modern demonology. Clark argued that stereotypical representations of demonology were closely interwoven with a bundle of intellectual traditions such as natural philosophy and Aristotelianism.[24] His account urges us to consider witchcraft as something in dialogue, and often in creative tension, with these intellectual currents. This study reminds us that certain stereotypes and the manner of their mobilisation were often informed by ideologies – a set of doctrines, values and assumptions lending themselves to challenging or legitimating relations of power. *Pari passu*, certain stereotypes therefore became the virtual carriers of wider bodies of assumptions and principles in such a way as almost to have become ideologies in and of themselves. Clark's opus has shown that stereotypes were often shaped as much by these ideologies as by the popular beliefs studied by Scribner.

Yet, like Scribner's work, Clark's analysis also hinged upon the key feature of early modern culture and mentality – binary oppositions: '[i]f early modern thought was pervaded by dual classifications of things "positive" and things "negative", this was due in no small measure to the absolute primacy of the opposition between God and his adversary and its asymmetrical, yet complementary, character', such as the witch who represented the inversion of God and the social order He created.[25] According to Clark, this network of binary symbols lost its intellectual appeal once its governing logic of oppositions and inversions no longer looked natural or preordained, once what he called their 'linguistic instability' was laid bare through repeated religious polemics and rising natural philosophical enquiries. This is a rich argument. Yet it is true that this account focuses primarily on reconstructing what Clark calls the system of signs and symbolic structures.[26] Accordingly, this account tells us relatively little about dynamic aspects – how men and women put these signs to use to reproduce, sustain, question and eventually modify the system of beliefs. If we want to understand how stereotypes affect behaviour and change courses of events, then it is vital that we focus squarely upon such processes of stereotyping and examine individual and collective agency over those processes.

We find seminal works in this direction by the early 1990s. This owes partly to the evolution of the 'linguistic turn', the second theme with which this volume engages in addition to that of popular culture and mentality.[27] Admittedly, the linguistic turn is an amorphous concept, and it certainly includes the analysis of 'linguistic structures' exemplified by Clark's study of demonology. Yet, equally relevant here is the increasing appreciation of language and discourse as something open to creative subversions. Literary scholars like Jonathan Dollimore and Patricia Parker were alert to just such potentials and revealed how Shakespeare and other writers playfully inverted grammatical order, reversed plot lines, swapped social roles and even disrupted expectations of their audience in ways that questioned order, hierarchy and political status quo.[28] In an analogous fashion, by the 1990s it became increasingly common for historians to give greater attention to stereotypes in action. How were stereotypes put to use by a range of actors and disseminated to discrete or public audiences via scribal, print or visual media? In political and religious history, the analysis of anti-popery and anti-puritanism has become an important lens through which to explore both popular politics and religious polemics of post-Reformation England.[29] In social history, the complementary images of the 'deserving' and 'idle' poor have become paradigmatic for understanding the politics of poor relief.[30] In the history of science and technology, too, we have learned that natural philosophers such as Boyle and other Fellows of the Royal Society distanced themselves from 'mechanics' and 'artisans' in order to lend credibility to their own claims to truth and trustworthiness.[31]

The analysis of practice and mobilisation has become prominent also in studies of gender – one of the most important themes related to stereotypes. Maria Ågren and her team have taken seriously the analysis of performativity pioneered by Erving Goffman and Judith Butler: 'the idea that situated practice is fundamental to identities and social relations'. Applying this to social and economic history, Ågren's team has examined 'constitutive tasks', the kind of daily work activities undertaken by early modern Swedish women and men that gave rise to their individual and group identities.[32] Lisa Hellman's work on Swedish merchants in eighteenth-century Canton has likewise examined 'practices of group formation in relation to ethnicity, class and gender'.[33] Amanda Herbert has shown that female Quakers travelling to Ireland and the American colonies often 'resorted to early modern stereotypes of femininity [as a weaker sex] in order to solicit sympathy and empathy' from distant readers. Eleanor Hubbard has revealed that some women in London tried to present themselves to church courts deliberately as a 'whore' so that they could win divorce from an abusive husband refusing separation. Even the negative stigma attached to the whore could be tactically co-opted.[34]

These studies of gender, religion, poor relief and science are richly varied, and cannot be taken as a coherent body of scholarship. All the same, these works highlight scholars' linguistic turns moving towards the analysis of situated practices. They thereby invite us to move beyond the contents of given stereotypes towards their deployment in concrete local settings.[35] The analytic potential of such an approach is well articulated in Lake's analysis of anti-popery, published in 1989. Lake, too, began with Clark's idea of inversion and binary oppositions, this time between true (Protestant) religion and popery but his analysis moved far beyond describing the binary opposition as the 'symbolic structure', only slowly changing over time. On the contrary, in the run-up to the Civil Wars, Lake suggested, a loosely knitted group of puritans were able to 'lead bodies of opinion which in normal times could scarcely be called Puritan'.[36] Admittedly, the 'grounds for and intensity of their opposition to popery might vary considerably from group to group and individual to individual'; yet they were able to turn 'the "serial group" of the non-popish' into something of a temporary alliance thanks to their 'common opposition to popery'.[37] Notice that in this analysis the fear of popery and the Antichrist pertains not so much to the seemingly stable popular mentality, nor to a complex system of signs, as to the world of politics in which various groups and individuals vied to win greater support for their causes. Lake's underlying analytic move is succinctly summarised in a sequel published in 2006. The attention to anti-popery and anti-puritanism tells us 'a good deal more about the people doing the constructing and the labelling – what and who they hated, what they wanted, what they feared and what they hoped for – than it does about the persons being labelled'.[38] In other words, this account is already alert to the fact that stereotypical representations lent themselves to the formation of group identities, to the orchestration of diverse bodies of opinion for a particular cause and to the unfolding of political crises leading to the Civil Wars of the mid-seventeenth century. This is the direction that we want to take further.

Now we can see clearly why political and religious historians of early modern England were among those who came to question the notion of the public sphere as developed by Jürgen Habermas – the third historiographical element addressed in this volume. In his once-influential formulation, the public sphere was said to have first emerged in eighteenth-century Britain, a society dotted with lively coffee houses, awash not only with hot beverages but also with prints, periodicals and newspapers. It was argued that citizens were able to use these media and locales to scrutinise conducts and misconducts of the state. The eighteenth-century public sphere was depicted as something rational and idealistic.[39]

Early modernists know well that this rosy picture has been thoroughly revised, in terms of its chronology and its contents. As for chronology, Lake and others have shown conclusively that concerns about, and practices of, public politics came to maturity much earlier, certainly by the end of Elizabeth I's reign. Civic participatory politics evolved further during the 1640s and the 1650s, in the heat of the Civil Wars and the ensuing republican experiments.[40] Even more crucially, however, recent studies have demonstrated that early modern public discourse was far less rational. Mark Knights's works are especially important. He has shown that popular preconceptions and artful misrepresentations were in fact central to partisanship in the 'First Age of Party', and indeed to the early Enlightenment culture in eighteenth-century England more generally.[41] Political debates were very often 'intemperate, personalized, abusive, passionate, and ... traded printed accusations of lying and manipulation'.[42] The 'degradation of the public sphere was apparent at its very inception.'[43] This is why stereotyping in early modern England should be of interest to a broader audience beyond specialists of the period.

This broader audience includes social psychologists. For, having studied public opinion and attitudes, they too have come to question Habermas's notion of rational communication, as we see below. Psychologists' parallel critique of Habermas makes sense if we turn to the history of these disciplines. Though rarely noted by historians (or by social psychologists for that matter), the two fields have arguably evolved in tandem towards dynamic conceptions of culture and practice. This shared trajectory and perspective is most evident in Durkheim's notion of 'collective representations' and its legacy. For Durkheim, collective representations are produced and reproduced through events like religious rituals, and then come to have a life of their own. Irreducible to individual sense impressions, these representations help symbolise, express and interpret existing social relationships, thus motivating and inhibiting individual actions. Collective representations are accordingly central to social cohesion and constitute a central subject of Durkheimian sociology: 'collective psychology'.[44]

The concepts of collective representation and collective psychology inspired generations of scholars, both historians and psychologists. French historians including Lucien Febvre, Marc Bloch, Georges Duby and others set out to examine collective psychology of the past. The history of mentality discussed above emerged in this context, with the notion of 'popular mentalities' eventually taken up by Scribner's study of visual propaganda.[45] As historians in the French and Anglophone traditions later became critical of the underlying monolithic conception of culture, so too did social psychologists.[46] The most significant revision came from Serge Moscovici. His work has been significant for social psychologists because he proposed 'social representation' as a conceptual alternative to Durkheimian collective representations. Social representations are defined as representations that could be deployed by people of different positions in society in ways that affirm their entrenched beliefs and/or advance their own positions. Thus, in Moscovici's renowned study of the notion of psychoanalysis in the French press in the 1950s, he found that psychoanalytic idioms were used very differently by liberal newspapers, Catholic newspapers and Communist party propaganda. Psychoanalysis was co-opted in strikingly different contexts, essentially to confirm and advance the respective ends and positions of these presses. Particular social representations – such as of psychoanalysis – can hardly be equated with a widely shared belief. Rather, Moscovici's work urges us to pay closer attention to specific milieus in which representations were mobilised and put to use.[47]

Social psychological literature has evolved in ways that invite readers to explore the fundamentally pluralistic, dynamic and even contradictory nature of representations. This helps us understand why some scholars writing after Moscovici have (as have early modernists) questioned Habermas's notion of communication as potentially rational and transparent.[48] Like early modernists, some psychologists have now begun to explore representational practices as inherently plural and dynamic, open to manipulation and negotiation.[49] Some of them have turned to early modern studies as a field that is good to think with.[50] Given these striking parallels and comparable orientations, social psychology literature and some of their conceptual idioms represent useful, yet under-appreciated, tools for historical analysis. We shall accordingly draw on their conceptual idioms and do so without necessarily subscribing to all of their theoretical assumptions.[51] If we proceed with caution and critically engage with psychological literature, we might even be able to throw fresh light on some aspects of stereotyping and psychological dynamism that have been relatively under-theorised.

Unlike colleagues in psychology or sociology, historians have not yet developed comparative analyses of stereotypes or their repercussions during the early modern period. Instead, existing accounts have tended to be thematically or chronologically isolated. Lake's seminal studies of anti-popery (1989) and anti-puritanism (2006) have indicated the vitality and centrality of these prejudices by focusing on the Elizabethan and early Stuart periods. While Knights's 2011 monograph covered a wider range of subjects (such as gender, Grub Street journalism and the birth of the novel) within the five decades between 1670 and 1720, the Lake and Pincus volume has covered a longer chronology (*c.* 1550–1700) by focusing on politics and religion.[52] Few attempts have been made to juxtapose stereotypes in different contexts, say in religious and party politics and in discussions of urbanisation, political economy and European understanding of non-Christian faiths.

One important exception is the volume of essays, *Moral panics, the media and the law in early modern England* (2009) edited by David Lemmings and Claire Walker.[53] Under the rubric of 'moral panics', it has brought together a range of case studies from anti-Catholicism in the late sixteenth century, witch-hunts and the popish plot in the seventeenth, to legislations against forgery in the eighteenth century and anti-Jacobinism in the 1790s. Crucially, these case studies do not treat stereotypes involved as mere myths or errors, or view those holding stereotypes as simply irrational. These case studies have instead explored how various actors, including huckster writers and government-backed polemicists, helped incite latent fears and prejudices and thereby gave rise to legislative interventions. The volume is attentive to social processes involving the media, 'moral entrepreneurs' (stirring up popular anxieties) and ensuing governmental actions. Alexandra Walsham's elegant analysis of the Jesuit missions to England during the 1580s has taken a step further to acknowledge the remarkable agency of the Jesuits targeted by scare-mongering: the Catholic missionaries themselves co-opted the looming fear about them, and actively spread the idea 'that their first entrance to the country had greatly disturbed the English government and its subjects'.[54] Yet on the whole, the concept of moral panic lends itself more readily to the analysis of actors forging the panics and political authorities acting upon them. It is less well equipped to unpack the responses from reading publics or the likes of Jesuits who became the subject of the panic. Lemmings thus indicates that eighteenth-century polite readers may have been 'early victims of the "incapacitating anxiety" often associated with modern urban living', thus in need of 'scapegoating cultural enemies'.[55]

This view is dangerously close to the traditional psychological view of stereotypes mentioned above, in that the media and 'moral entrepreneurs' are held to be activating a quasi-automatic mental process of categorisation and scapegoating. It is also at odds with Knights's analysis of public appeals to reason in the incipient public sphere. Knights suggests that both Tory and Whig polemicists accepted and appealed to 'a notion of a polite, rational nation capable of discerning, judging and discounting irrational public discourse' in favour of more reasonable, balanced and moderate opinions.[56] Admittedly, 'the language of rational evidence was appropriated by the most rabid of partisans.' Even so, 'the more frequently it was invoked by partisans and by those who attacked partisanship, the more embedded an ideal it became and hence, ironically, a cultural restraint on party zeal.'[57] Reading Knights's works alongside Lemmings and Walker thus forces us to raise the following question. Why, despite the possible cultural restraint, did stereotyping and ensuing media frenzy come back again and again? It remains difficult to make sense of the resilience of stereotypes across time and different spheres of life without presupposing 'incapacitating anxiety' or similar, allegedly widespread, mentality. We still know relatively little about how concrete social processes of stereotyping led to more stereotyping, more contestation and further social divisions over time.

If we want to tackle these questions, we must scrutinise two underlying assumptions: firstly, that the mobilisation of negative stereotypes had predominantly harmful effects on society; and secondly, that stereotyping and attendant appeals to reason contained a cure to its own escalation. We can start by taking a closer look at how stereotypes were invoked alongside their inversions. For example, when attacking opponents as puritans or popish Antichrist, defenders of Anglican orthodoxy often lent legitimacy to their own cause by invoking the image of the defender of true religion.[58] This normative position-taking is crucial for our analysis because it often exposes those marshalling stereotypes to reasoned critique and even polemical backlash. Are promoters of 'true faith' living up to the exalted image with which they associate themselves? Are they not indulging in hypocrisy, or worse using the veneer of religion to promote tyranny over the church and state? Are self-styled promoters of true religion not Machiavellian Antichrists in disguise? By stereotyping puritans, defenders of the Anglican church thus exposed themselves to these searching questions which included stereotyping. Notice that a wide range of actors, puritans under attack, lay people in local parishes and even Anglicans themselves could pursue such scrutiny. By simultaneously reproducing images of true and false religion familiar to a wide range of actors, stereotyping could facilitate not only polemical debates, but also participatory politics.[59]

The implications are threefold. First, it is likely that appeals to reason were often themselves part of the polemical exchange, as Knights has suggested. Second, those contesting certain stereotypes were capable of marshalling the same or other stereotypes when occasion suited them. In such cases, responses to stereotyping could lead to further exchanges of stereotypes and escalation. Third, it is highly likely that stereotyping was not always simply harmful to society. Rather, stereotypes provided partial, yet powerful, frameworks for understanding and engaging with complex reality, and even taking political actions. Print, pulpit, the stage and other oral literate and peripheral media all took part in such sense-making practices, and often lent themselves to the escalation of stereotyping. Taken together, we suggest, the early modern politics of stereotyping points to what we call a *dialectics of stereotyping*: stereotyping was so foundational to social life, and yet so very liable to escalation, that collective engagements with stereotypes often ended up perpetuating or even accelerating the very processes of stereotyping. This explains why stereotyping then, as now, had such powerful impacts on society.

If we are to test these hypotheses, we must do more than go beyond the older accounts of stereotypes as indicative of shared mentality or of a system of signs. What we now need is to adopt a set of analytic idioms suitable for analysing stereotyping as a process, and to bring together local case studies so that we can start building a larger picture from the ground up and eventually arrive at broader conclusions about practices of stereotyping and their persistence in early modern England. This is the larger task to which this volume contributes.

Concepts and arguments

In the remainder of this introduction, we outline how the chapters in this volume adopt fresh analytic tools and jointly advance our understanding of early modern politics of stereotyping.

Stereotypes as 'false composites'

If we wanted to recover stereotyping as concrete processes, then we must first ask how far we can draw on older social scientific literature and portray stereotypes as fixed images or mere prejudice with which to simplify an otherwise complex world around us. Harris's opening chapter tackles this question by outlining religious and national stereotypes in early modern England. He acknowledges that racial and religious stereotypes were often fuelled by prejudices and ideologies. Yet there were further complexities, as Harris shows through a letter sent by an English army officer. In it the English officer described the enemy (Scottish men) as at once 'filthy' and 'barbarous' (thus stereotypical Highlanders), while also being 'develish' and 'puritanical Crue of the Scotch Covenant', thus invoking Presbyterians from the Lowlands. Here we have a typical example of what Harris calls a *false composite* – in this case a description which adeptly combines 'stereotypical characteristics supposedly evinced by different types of Scots but which were never [in reality] found together in one' individual. Historical evidence of such false composites enables us to make an important methodological point: our sources can rarely be treated as unproblematic reflections of prejudices or mentality. Rather, 'they are works of polemic designed to exploit existing stereotypes and latent prejudices', as Harris suggests.[60] Typical examples of such polemical uses would include accusing opponents of popery or sectarian puritanism in order to undermine them and dissuade a silent, moderate majority from supporting them.

False composites can also be found outside religious topics, for example in depictions of foreigners in sixteenth-century London, a thriving capital that attracted immigrant artisans as well as richer bankers and merchants enjoying royal patronage.[61] Guild members' petitions and pedlars' bills not only viewed these 'aliens' as a threat to their livelihood, but also mixed this accusation up with other kinds of allegation of criminality, immorality and privilege. In reality, it was clear that only a small minority of immigrants were powerful enough to enjoy protection by the Crown and by the City of London. Yet when immigrants were stereotyped as the 'alien', such a distinction was often elided, and they were depicted as crime-ridden, deceitful aliens who were impoverishing native inhabitants and still evading justice thanks to some perceived political privileges. This pattern of perception is being repeated today. For example, conservative Americans in Louisiana interviewed by the sociologist Arlie Russell Hochschild in fact viewed African Americans as a class of (potential) criminals that paradoxically enjoy privileged access to welfare benefits and even to the American Dream.[62] Stereotyping 'others' such as immigrants and African Americans as false composites makes it easier to stigmatise minorities while bringing together otherwise diverse 'in-groups'. More immediately for the purpose of this volume, the analysis of false composites and their deployment is important because it provides us with a departure point for subsequent chapters by alerting us to the complexity of seemingly simple stereotypes, and to the variety of uses to which they could be put.

Stereotypes as heuristic device

Even if we find powerful negative stereotypes of the Scots, the Irish or the alien immigrant, we must not suppose that stereotypes were weapons always wielded by the powerful against the subordinate. It is of course important to emphasise how racial stereotypes, for example, served colonial projects. In plantation societies in which slaves far outnumbered white inhabitants, emerging stereotypes presenting African slaves as property helped induce poor white labourers to 'define their interests as coincident with those of planters rather than slaves'.[63] Racial stereotypes thereby helped prevent cross-racial alliance at the bottom of the colonial hierarchy. Here is a classic example of stereotyping wielded against an out-group to forge an impression of coherent 'white' in-group identity.[64] At the same time, there are other, perhaps less well-explored, aspects of stereotyping such as explaining failure, displacing anxiety, revealing corruptions, encouraging scrutiny and even facilitating intellectual discovery. The three following chapters, written by Lake and Yamamoto, examine just such aspects – what we might call *heuristic functions* of stereotypes.

Chapter 2 (by Lake) focuses on the puritan stereotype as a case study and reappraises its virtually forgotten heuristic functions. Famously, studying Ben Jonson's *Bartholomew Fair*, the historian of Reformation England Patrick Collinson once argued that the puritan identity came into being 'by virtue of being perceived to exist, *most of all by their enemies*, but eventually to themselves and to each other' and that it was the writers close to the establishment who first used theatre plays to forge the negative image of the puritan.[65] The puritan stereotype was accordingly believed to have been created (like racial stereotypes) as a weapon for the powerful in-group to label and persecute an out-group. Lake's chapter challenges this account by looking closely at printed literature by George Gifford in the 1580s. Three decades before puritans were mocked in London theatres, the godly reformer Gifford in fact complained that his effort to adhere to tighter religious disciplines attracted mockery as being mere 'puritain'. Gifford himself elaborated the self-image in print in order to explain the lack of thoroughgoing Protestant Reformation around him. The popular reactions – even hostility – to the likes of him (again analysed by Gifford in print) cannot be taken as evidence of the inherent, timeless, conservatism of the English believers. Rather, as Lake suggests, it is indicative of a 'tense interaction between the claims of the godly and the (often frankly hostile or assertively indifferent) reactions thereto of their neighbours'.[66] Such neighbours' ridicule of Gifford as a puritan, he argues, was a sign of their reprobation. The puritan stereotype thus initially served the godly as a heuristic tool for understanding their own relative isolation, only to be co-opted against them later by their more powerful enemies. Lake's chapter forces us to recognise that the social function of a given stereotype can change dramatically depending on actors' positionality and the contexts of its mobilisation.

Yamamoto's Chapter 3 complements Lake's by focusing on another heuristic stereotype frequently associated with Jonson: that of the 'projector'. In the history of science, mercantilism and political economy, the image of the projector (what we would call an entrepreneur today) has recently attracted much attention, but historians in these related fields have rarely considered how the pioneers of commercial theatre plays active from the 1580s depicted the abuse of royal prerogative and other corrupt behaviours associated with the projector. Yamamoto's chapter reveals that Elizabethan history plays staged characters strikingly similar to projectors decades before Jonson developed the stereotype in the early seventeenth century. These earlier plays about monarchical excess and failure exposed proto-projectors' vices and their abuse of royal power in ways that were as unforgiving as Catholic attacks upon the Elizabethan regime. The Elizabethan history plays even invited the audience to detect corruptions and condemn the underlying insatiable appetite for power, profit and sex in ways that anticipated the mobilisation of the projector stereotype on the eve of the Civil Wars. Far from being invented singlehandedly by Jonson, the potent image of the projector emerged from existing efforts to discover corruptions symptomatic of the contradictions of rapidly commercialising society with an ambitious monarch heavily dependent on the collaboration and goodwill of both official and unofficial collaborators.

The ensuing Chapter 4, co-authored by Lake and Yamamoto, pushes the analysis by exploring how Jonson developed representations of the puritan and the projector in the 1610s. By elaborating on the two stereotypes, Jonson highlighted his mastery over two highly explosive topics. Also noteworthy is that Jonson staged these two characters *in comedies*, implying that both projecting and godliness represented ridiculous excess of ambition, greed and hypocrisy, and not so much real threats to the church and the state. Jonsonian stereotypes thus achieved what Harris calls *anxiety displacement*, thereby trivialising the remarkable extent to which royal finance in reality relied upon projecting, and the degree to which the voice of the godly and its suppression were central to the religious politics of the period.

Here it is worth remarking that the theatre was an emergent form of commercialised mass media, in direct competition with the popular pulpit for audiences, attention and esteem. This highlights the role of stereotypes in selling not merely opinions, political or ecclesiastical platforms, or rival claims to authority or status, but also actual commodities, in this case access to the theatre. The wholly commercial nature of the theatrical project also shows just how such competition for audience and market share not only led to the appropriation and intensification of existing stereotypes – stereotypes which, as in the case of anti-puritanism, had often been generated and deployed for quite other purposes – but also helped to develop entirely new ones. Here the standout example is what Jonas Barish famously called the anti-theatrical prejudice, which was rooted in a series of tropes and stereotypes going back to classical antiquity and was also inflected by the contemporary polemical conflict between the pulpit and the commercial theatre for popular attention and social and cultural esteem.[67]

Ben Jonson is important as he is a perfect example of the contradictory impulses in play here. In going after puritans he was taking down the enemies of the stage – the godly – while, through his image of the projector and his dupes, and in his famous prefaces and asides satirising the taste and discernment of his own audiences, also distancing himself from any taint of the market. Jonson thereby sought to identify and stage a series of extremes, between which he could then locate himself, and thus establish his claims to 'moderation'.[68] Here was no hack writer, desperate for a popular audience or court connection, but rather a distanced and moderate observer of human folly, a true poet, capable of instructing his contemporaries on the nature of vice and the path of virtue.[69] Nor was such elaborate self-positioning limited to Jonson, as we shall see in William Cavert's and Bridget Orr's chapters discussed below.

Thus, the three chapters by Lake and Yamamoto demonstrate that we cannot understand stereotypes only in terms of weapons for persecuting the minority. At the same time, stereotypes were generated and invoked in order to provide rationales for religious reform or the lack thereof, detect corruptions at the intersection between the political and economic spheres, facilitate political participation, highlight one's mastery over sensitive subjects and even displace anxiety about them by replacing real threats with comic relief. But even within these contexts, stereotyping did – and probably still does – contain seeds for further escalation. In other words, we need to explore not only the contents of any given stereotypes and their development, but also their mobilisation and responses to them, topics explored in depth by Chapters 5 and 6, by Kate Peters and Adam Morton respectively.

Contesting stereotypes

We argue that the set of notions developed by the sociologist Erving Goffman and his followers is highly relevant when studying responses to stereotyping. First, the notion of *stigma consciousness* is useful when describing those exposed to the threat of stereotyping.[70] Puritans, projectors, wives, widows, stepmothers and those receiving aid from a local parish, for example, were acutely aware of the danger of being stereotyped, and often tried to do something about it – pursuing what sociologists would call *coping strategies*.[71] A case in point is Peters's analysis of powerful stereotypes about the Ranters and the Quakers, groups of religious radicals who were both denounced for their alleged religious heterodoxy and moral and sexual deviance. These stereotypes were so powerful and prevalent that scholars have found it worth their while to treat them as so much social reportage, in the process, with A. L. Morton, either endorsing or, with J. C. Davis, refuting their accuracy. Thus, Davis has argued that the Ranters were little more than a myth, a product of a 'moral panic' that in turn called for the control and persecution of religious radicalism.[72] Historians and literary scholars have now challenged Davis's view and have shown that Ranters did exist albeit in less well organised form than A. L. Morton supposed.

The concept of stereotyping, Peters shows in Chapter 5, enables us to take an exciting step further by focusing on the *mobilisation* of the stereotypes about the Ranter and the Quaker and *contestations* of their veracity. Hostile accounts of the Ranters not only vilified Ranters themselves, but also stereotyped their alleged followers. Far from pushing for the unconditional rejection of the out-group, however, these accounts included a variety of responses from prosecution to toleration, from avoidance to rebuttal. Evidence regarding Quakers is even more telling. For Quakers were acutely aware of their bad name and tried to dispel this, for example by asking their opponents to provide evidence for their accusations, and thereby reducing generic stereotypes into deniable instances. Quakers were pursuing the coping strategy that was also adopted by women accused of 'whoredom'.

As Capp and Laura Gowing have shown, early modern women often challenged their adversaries in court 'by demanding to know *whose* whore she had been', likewise reducing the general accusation to deniable instances.[73] The case of Quakers thus suggests that, far from being indicative of a simple myth or a moral panic, stereotyping and ensuing responses tell us much (as in gender history) about the remarkable individual and collective agency in bringing stereotypes under control.[74]

Even more unsettling in terms of sociopolitical consequences is what we have chosen to call *counter-stereotyping*, a process whereby those prone to a given stereotype pick up its core contents and turn the accusation back on the accusers themselves. This concept allows us to bring together similar observations made in isolation. For example, we know that early modern women traded accusations, calling each other 'whore' as they sought to defend their reputation in and outside courts. Licensed physicians and 'irregular' medical practitioners likewise traded accusations of 'quackery' in all directions. Accusing the rival party of 'hoarding' and 'monopoly' was a standard practice when challenging projects for economic improvement.[75] Similar rhetorical practices are also found in the politics of religion. The defenders of the Anglican church who had been accused by puritans of being popish would in turn argue that these 'hot' puritans were themselves behaving in a 'popish' fashion, feigning true faith, undermining the English church and destabilising the Protestant monarchy, as all Jesuits would do.

We must be careful not to treat these cases as mere squabbles accidentally sharing similar rhetorical patterns. Something larger was at stake, as Morton's Chapter 6 suggests. It explores such a case of counter-stereotyping by focusing on a period of intense political crisis: the so-called Exclusion Crisis. By the end of the 1670s, Charles II was ageing and the royal succession was high on the agenda. His younger brother, the Duke of York, was a Catholic, however, and this created a heated controversy. Then came the popish plot of 1678, in which Titus Oates claimed to have 'discovered' a plot to assassinate Charles II and force the Catholic succession. Morton demonstrates that stereotyping and counter-stereotyping were central to the ensuing explosion of print polemics. Predictably, Whigs (who often had long-held puritan connections) drew on anti-popish stereotypes to denigrate the imminent Catholic succession as the coming of tyranny, persecution and bloodshed. Significantly, Tory royalists fought back, not by accusing Whigs of using stereotypes, but by arguing that Whigs/nonconformists (rather than Tories) were the true source of 'popery' because they were the ones who posed a greater risk to England's constitution by disrupting peaceful succession and questioning the existing church and state. Morton examines this royalist counter-stereotyping by focusing on the polemicist-in-chief, Roger L'Estrange. Polemicists like him were more than capable of thinking beyond existing stereotypes, and crucially expected their readers to do so as well. Perhaps this is hardly surprising given that men and women of different ranks were indeed trading accusations and challenging stereotypes in their everyday life.

Stereotypes, their uses and counter-uses, were therefore crucial for mundane social relations, for the promotion of health and economic improvement, and even for debating the nature and future of English church and state. Concepts like coping strategies and counter-stereotyping are useful for historical analysis because, we argue, adopting them enables us to move firmly beyond content analysis and start exploring rich processes of stereotyping, ensuing contestation and their repercussions that were central to the unfolding of events. Only by doing so can we begin to reappraise not only the remarkable agency of individuals in coping with particular stereotypes, but also the paradoxical resilience of stereotypes more broadly, something that we continue to find to this day.

Ambiguity, irony and subversion

In highlighting the (often unintended) escalation of stereotyping, we are not suggesting that stereotyping can be adequately understood in terms either of escalation or of containment. Another aspect worthy of our critical attention is the coexistence of contradictory explanatory frameworks about a single subject – what social psychologists would call *cognitive polyphasia*.[76] Stereotypes play an important role in the plurality of logics within society and within individuals. In early modern England, for example, youth represented at once a foundation for adulthood, industrious labour and mature Christian piety, and excess, idleness, lust and sin. Informed by Scripture and rooted in daily experience, such contradictory perspectives in turn informed impulses to control youth conviviality and play, regulate courtship and household relations, punish illicit sex and discipline the 'master-less' idle youth. Representations of youth thus operated as 'contested territory', as Paul Griffiths put it.[77]

By contrast, David Magliocco's Chapter 7 explores the plurality of logics within one wealthy individual: Samuel Pepys. We thus move from the world of print polemic (studied by Peters and Morton) to that of fashionable sociability and cultural distinction. In Pepys's diaries, Magliocco detects an exceptional frequency with which Pepys recorded all things French – music, language, clothing and people – with striking ambiguity. On one hand, French Catholicism was linked with absolutism and arbitrary government (as discussed by both Harris and Morton), and more generally with excess and the lack of moderation. At the same time, Frenchness was also associated with prestige, refined taste and distinction. It was possible for individuals like Pepys to embrace these contradictory stereotypes, invoking different aspects of them depending on context. Transnational interactions often gave rise to repulsion and ethnocentrism as well as to the emulation of the 'others'.

The rich, seemingly contradictory, dynamics of stereotyping can be further illuminated by looking at jocular, ironic, uses. The earlier chapter on Jonson by Lake and Yamamoto focused on how Jonson's comic rendering of the puritan and the projector helped deflate anxiety by *trivialising* the threat they posed to post-Reformation church and state. There was another scenario. If public audiences were urged to see beyond any given pejorative stereotypes (as Peters and Morton show), then it was also possible for early modern people to draw on stereotypes without necessarily accepting all of their pejorative connotations. Indeed, it was possible to allege that stereotypical representations (for example, of the Ranter) were totally absurd, and that those promoting them were utter hypocrites, those accepting them at face value no better than gullible fools. It was possible to invoke such stereotypes in ways that undermined their very validity. Such was the case explored by Cavert's Chapter 8 on stereotypical representations of London's dirty, smoky air. The capital's population increased tenfold between the mid-fifteenth and the mid-eighteenth centuries. The growth of the city led not only to a larger number of opulent mansions, but also to the burning of coal in greater quantities that in turn polluted the air.[78] By the 1630s, the images of smoke and sin, of 'sin and sea coal', became a powerful metaphor for talking about sins associated with urban life, especially the excessive consumption of luxuries and the attendant pursuit of vanity and extramarital sex. One might expect such a trope to boost serious anti-urban critique. Strikingly, however, the image was taken up not only by those criticising urban immorality, but also by those embracing it as something inevitable. This inversion was accomplished in particular through comical depictions of those innocently subscribing to an extreme aversion to urban 'sin and sea coal'. Cavert presents several examples – many of them comedies – in which characters either positively thrive on urban immorality or hate urban 'sin and sea coal' so much that they end up becoming a gullible, parochial Englishman who also readily accepts all kinds of simplistic stereotypes – of the French, of popery and of the courtly life.

His analysis of the anti-urban stereotype does more than nuance the standard chronology of metropolitan imagination which is often said to have shifted from condemnation to celebration. The persistent image of 'sin and sea coal', drawn from across Caroline England and *The Spectator* of the early eighteenth century, reminds us of the possibility of knowingly accepting urban imperfections as a necessary evil consequent upon urban growth and economic improvement. Here, then, is another example of stereotypes facilitating *anxiety displacement*, but this time through *reductio ad absurdum*, rendering moral objections to urban growth hilarious and less threatening. Instead of escalating polemics or fuelling violence, the artful practice of stereotyping made it possible for early moderns to explore and even accept an urban identity that was highly ambiguous.

Stereotyping and the production of knowledge

Magliocco's and Cavert's chapters establish that the heuristic value of stereotypes was never confined to the political and religious spheres. Building on this perspective, the final two chapters of this volume go on to explore how stereotyping conditioned the production of identity and knowledge more broadly during the eighteenth century, the age of Enlightenment frequently associated with reason and progress. Orr's Chapter 9 does this by exploring the elaboration of new and existing characters in the theatre. At the heart of her analysis lies an insight into how identity and subjectivity emerge from one's negotiation with stereotypes: '[s]ubjectification *per se* ... depends on our being cast in gendered, raced, classed and sexual roles from our first appearance in the *theatrum mundi*'.[79] As earlier chapters have shown, men and women, much like professional actors and actresses, frequently negotiated, ignored or redefined the roles, expectations and stereotypes cast upon them. Orr demonstrates that the theatre of the long eighteenth century is important because it was a 'laboratory of subjectification', a venue in which 'its dependence on stock types and stereotyping' was used in order 'to model the process of differentiation from norms by which individuality is in general achieved'.[80] Thus, the commercial stage did much more than produce and circulate new stereotypes (as indicated by Lake and Yamamoto in their earlier chapters). On the stage the audience found dramatic struggles with social, political, racial and gender stereotypes, in other words heightened comic and moralised versions of their own experience, anxieties and aspirations. Creative engagement with stereotypes was therefore central to theatre's capacity to attract and retain genuinely popular, socially heterogeneous, audiences. Orr shows this was how the theatre continued to play a pivotal role in developing and disseminating new stereotypes, giving rise to a wide range of stock characters and even national identities.

The process of stereotyping was foundational also in the production of knowledge about nature, God and non-European civilisations. As Rob Iliffe has suggested, English natural philosophers of the late seventeenth century often alleged that their Continental rivals were given to too much talking and the uncritical adoration of ancient authorities. Stereotyping Cartesian philosophy as idolatry and labelling Spinoza's method atheism profoundly shaped the range of scholarly methods that could be taken up with respectability. It was against such stereotypes that Fellows of the Royal Society defined their experimental methods and presented themselves as defenders of truth in a superior 'Land of *Experimental Knowledge*'.[81] Such boundary-drawing exercises were hardly limited to English philosophers, as shown by recent works by Yoshi Kato, Han van Ruler and Kuni Sakamoto. Descartes' mechanical philosophy challenged conventional views of God and divine will, and hence was accused of promoting heresy. In order to avoid this accusation, his Continental followers accordingly found it prudent to omit certain controversial elements of Cartesian doctrines while emphasising other aspects – clear examples of *coping strategies* to avoid stigmatisation. Such coping strategies conditioned wider philosophical debates to such an extent that indifference to the danger of being stereotyped was crucial for Spinoza's radicalism.[82] The role of stereotyping in the entangled evolution of natural, moral and political philosophies on the eve of the Enlightenment represents a promising field of enquiry.

How did European practices of stereotyping condition their encounter with non-European civilisations? Huiyi Wu and Thijs Weststeijn have shown that eighteenth-century French writers understood aspects of Chinese philosophy and Japanese Buddhism by comparing them to Spinoza's radical philosophy: 'otherness within Europe gives meaning to the otherness of an extra-European reality'.[83] William Bulman's Chapter 10 enriches this line of enquiry by asking how post-Reformation religious stereotypes discussed elsewhere in the volume provided a fertile ground for understanding non-Christian faiths. By the mid-seventeenth century, the detection of religious deviance associated with popery and puritanism – such as imposture, priestcraft, enthusiasm and fanaticism – became a powerful template not only for understanding Christian sects, but also for making sense of other world religions such as Judaism and Islam. In the writings of the diplomat Paul Rycaut and others, oriental non-Christian religions were no longer explained in terms of diabolical operations but explored as different forms of religious deviance that could destabilise society. Anti-popery and anti-puritanism became useful focal points because, for travel writers and learned authors debating English and Islamic societies, these notions provided a yardstick for debating which groups in England or Ottoman Turkey or elsewhere were engaged in practices that fuelled religious intolerance and sectarian violence, thus ultimately tending to the destruction of church and state. The Enlightenment understanding of non-Christian faiths owed much more (than hitherto accepted) to well-established post-Reformation stereotypes. Orr's and Bulman's chapters, alongside works by intellectual historians like Iliffe, thus warn us against equating the age of Enlightenment with the march of reason and progress. The production of knowledge and identity in the age of Enlightenment owed much to the process of stereotyping and ensuing negotiations.

Why early modern stereotypes now?

We believe that bringing together these early modern case studies has civic as well as scholarly implications today. Collectively, this volume enables us to understand why stereotypes were so very pervasive in early modern England. Far from being tools merely to simplify complex realities or to persecute out-groups, stereotypical representations were elaborated, put to use, contested and subverted with surprising inventiveness in plays, print polemics, travel writings, songs and petitions, and in places like parish churches, meeting houses, busy theatres and in Westminster. In the process, stereotypes provided a powerful framework for explaining religious tensions, encouraging participatory politics, inciting laughter, displacing anxiety and making sense of gendered self-identity and of religious 'others'. Stereotypes were so very versatile and pervasive that even attempts to bring them under control often led to more stereotyping. It is therefore hardly surprising that even the advancement of knowledge in the age of Enlightenment hinged heavily upon stereotypes and their mobilisation.

In this volume, we have chosen to bring together studies loosely related to politics, religion, economy and knowledge production. This is partly because the editor's research interests cut across, but rarely go beyond, these areas. Accordingly, many important subjects are not given systematic attention – stereotypes related to gender, occupation, race and colonial slavery, to mention but the most notable omissions. It is possible that, while those who were labelled puritans, papists or projectors produced plenty of written responses, as for themes like gender and colonial slavery, those liable to stereotyping left far fewer 'ego documents' in their responses. Accordingly coping strategies in these areas would have to be recovered somewhat differently.[84] We hope that the case studies contained in the present volume will provide us with a series of reference points for future comparison and for developing a more comprehensive account of early modern practices of stereotyping.

As for civic implications, we hope that bringing together early modern cases of stereotyping carries more than an antiquarian interest today. Doing so enables us to raise an even larger question about the nature of progress in relation to stereotyping. Proponents of liberal progress have nowadays suggested that religious superstition will soon go away, prejudices will be gradually removed and rational scientific knowledge will ultimately triumph over vulgar errors and 'identity-protective cognition'.[85] The underlying assumption of progress seems to derive from a daring hope of ameliorating the society in which we find ourselves. This is a laudable ambition. But if stereotyping persisted before the advent of the Enlightenment, if the Enlightened projects of learning and science also drew heavily on stereotypes, and if stereotyping continues to persist to this day, it is vital that we face such evidence and scrutinise our assumptions. What does progress stand for in relation to stereotyping?

We can rephrase the question: have we outlived the dialectics of stereotyping that is documented through the early modern case studies collected in this volume? Or are we left with no other option but to keep reproducing stereotypes as we combat what is deemed blatant racism, bigotry, misogyny and hypocrisy in our world? At its very best, historical investigation has the potential to refine our everyday assumptions by connecting the past and the present while avoiding undue anachronism. To begin with, we can start questioning the powerful assumptions that stereotypes are inherently negative and that they can be gradually removed like vulgar errors and superstition. Moreover, once we focus squarely on social processes of stereotyping, we no longer have to rely on preconceived notions of human nature or cognition to explain why stereotyping persists over time. We can avoid viewing stereotyping as a fixed *cause* affecting social interactions. Stereotyping and its pervasiveness can instead be laid open to analysis and empirically examined as a *result* of rich, yet often divisive, social interactions. Only by shifting our perspectives and treating stereotyping as socially constructed and sustained can we begin to understand, from the bottom up, why stereotypes have been so difficult to eradicate.[86] We believe that future hopes of mitigating stereotypes and their adverse consequences rest on such empirical investigations.[87] Early modernists working in libraries and archives have the potential to challenge and possibly even transform our assumptions about the turbulence of the twenty-first century, a point to which we shall return at the end of this volume.

We would like to thank Tim Harris, Sandra Jovchelovitch, Brodie Waddell, Shaun Yajima and an anonymous reviewer for valuable suggestions.

Notes

1 Social scientists offering relevant reflections include Arlie Russell Hochschild, *Strangers in their own land: anger and mourning on the American right* (New York, 2016) and Jan Werner-Müller, *What is populism?* (London, 2017; originally published 2016).

2 Walter Lippmann, *Public opinion* (New York, 1997; originally published, 1922). Michael Pickering has likewise suggested that 'as process and practice, stereotyping is endemic to modernity': Michael Pickering, *Stereotyping: the politics of representation* (Basingstoke, 2001), p. xii.
3 The minimal working definition presented here draws on Henri Tajfel, 'Cognitive aspects of prejudice', *Journal of Biosocial Science*, supplement 1 (1969), 173–91, p. 177; David J. Schneider, *The psychology of stereotyping* (New York, 2004), pp. 29–30. As Yamamoto's discussion (Chapter 3) makes clear, in some cases the attribution of deviant behaviours becomes prevalent first, before a character is invented to give a name to the wrongdoer. Practices of stereotyping can therefore precede the production of a character-based stereotype.
4 The literature on stereotypes is vast. Useful overviews include Mark Knights, 'Historical stereotypes and histories of stereotypes', in Cristian Tileagă and Jovan Byford (eds), *Psychology and history: interdisciplinary explorations* (Cambridge, 2014), pp. 242–67, esp. pp. 242–50; Charles Stangor (ed.), *Stereotypes and prejudice: essential readings* (Philadelphia, PA, 2000). Social, moral, educational and epistemological dimensions are explored in Lawrence Blum, 'Stereotypes and stereotyping: a moral analysis', *Philosophical Papers*, 33 (2004), 251–89; Claude M. Steele, *Whistling Vivaldi: how stereotypes affect us and what we can do* (New York, 2010); Endre Begby, *Prejudice: a study in non-ideal epistemology* (Oxford, 2021).
5 The history of mentality will be discussed in the Historiography section in this introduction.
6 Vlad Glăveanu and Koji Yamamoto, 'Bridging history and social psychology: what, how and why', *Integrative Psychological and Behavioral Science*, 46 (2012), 431–39; Knights, 'Historical stereotypes', pp. 243–7. See also his article in the 2012 special issue: Mark Knights, 'Taking a historical turn: possible points of connection between social psychology and history', *Integrative Psychological and Behavioral Science*, 46 (2012), 584–98.
7 See Lorella Lepore and Rupert Brown, 'Category and stereotype activation: is prejudice inevitable?', *Journal of Personality and Social Psychology*, 72 (1997), 275–87, p. 275; Galen V. Bodenhausen, 'Stereotypes as judgmental heuristics: evidence of circadian variations in discrimination', *Psychological Science*, 1 (1990), 319–22, p. 319.
8 For an older account, see J. C. Davis, *Fear, myth and history: the Ranters and the historians* (Cambridge, 1986), esp. ch. 5. See also our discussion of the book on 'moral panics' edited by David Lemmings and Claire Walker, on pp. 12–13.
9 See Peter Burke, 'Presenting and re-presenting Charles V', in Hugo Soly (ed.), *Charles V, 1500–1558, and his time* (Antwerp, 1999), pp. 393–475, at p. 393; Roger Chartier, *Cultural history: between practices and representations*, trans. Lydia G. Cochrane (Cambridge, 1988), pp. 5, 41 (at p. 41).
10 Susan Dwyer Amussen, *An ordered society: gender and class in early modern England* (New York, 1993); Michael J. Braddick and John Walter (eds), *Negotiating power in early modern society: order, hierarchy and subordination*

in Britain and Ireland (Cambridge, 2001); Bernard Capp, *When gossips meet: women, family, and neighbourhood in early modern England* (Oxford, 2003).

11 Tim Harris (Chapter 1) provides a more detailed overview of the political history of the period.

12 The best introduction to the social and economic history of the period remains Keith Wrightson, *Earthly necessities: economic lives in early modern Britain* (New Haven, CT, 2000). For a thematic survey, see also Keith Wrightson (ed.), *A social history of England, 1500–1750* (Cambridge, 2017).

13 Steven Shapin, *The scientific revolution* (Chicago, 1998).

14 Steven Shapin and Simon Schaffer, *Leviathan and the air-pump: Hobbes, Boyle, and the experimental life* (Princeton, NJ, 1985); Lawrence M. Principe, *The secrets of alchemy* (Chicago, 2013); Rob Iliffe, *Priest of nature: the religious worlds of Isaac Newton* (New York, 2017).

15 Steven Shapin, '"A scholar and a gentleman": the problematic identity of the scientific practitioner in early modern England', *History of Science*, 29 (1991), 279–327; Roy Porter, *Quacks: fakers and charlatans in English medicine* (Stroud, 2000; originally published, 1989), pp. 15–24; Margaret Pelling with Frances White, *Medical conflicts in early modern London: patronage, physicians, and irregular practitioners, 1550–1640* (Oxford, 2003), pp. 137–40, 186, 210–11, 277–95. Going well beyond these stereotypes, scholars are recovering how women, astrologers and projectors gathered knowledge and pursued their careers. See, for example, Elaine Leong, *Recipes and everyday knowledge: medicine, science, and the household in early modern England* (Chicago, 2018); Lauren Kassell, *Medicine and magic in Elizabethan London: Simon Forman: astrologer, alchemist, and physician* (Oxford, 2005); Koji Yamamoto, 'Medicine, metals and empire: the survival of a chymical projector in early eighteenth-century London', *British Journal for the History of Science*, 48 (2015), 607–37.

16 Peter Lake and Steven Pincus, 'Rethinking the public sphere in early modern England', in Peter Lake and Steven Pincus (eds), *The politics of the public sphere in early modern England* (Manchester, 2007), pp. 1–30, at p. 22.

17 On the rise of commercial theatres, see Chapter 3, pp. 89–90.

18 Thomas Hobbes, *Leviathan*, ed. Richard Tuck (Cambridge, 1991), pp. 119–20 (ch. 17, [87]).

19 Chetham's Library, Manchester, MUN Mun.A.6.17 (speeches, charges and petitions in the Parliament of 1640), p. 28.

20 Lucien Febvre, *A new kind of history: from the writings of Lucien Febvre*, ed. Peter Burke, trans. K. Folca (New York, 1973), p. 9. Two useful surveys are Chartier, *Cultural history*, pp. 21–4, and Peter Burke, *The French historical revolution: the Annales school, 1929–89* (Cambridge, 1990), esp. pp. 16–18, 22–4. See also discussion below, pp. 11–12.

21 R. W. Scribner, *For the sake of simple folk: popular propaganda for the German Reformation*, rev. edn (Oxford, 1994).

22 Scribner, *Simple folk*, pp. 58, 56.

23 Scribner, *Simple folk*, pp. 58, 242.

24 Stuart Clark, *Thinking with demons: the idea of witchcraft in early modern Europe* (Oxford, 1999).
25 Clark, *Demons*, p. 81.
26 Clark, *Demons*, pp. 6, 400.
27 Judith Surkis, 'When was the linguistic turn? A genealogy', *American Historical Review*, 117 (2012), 700–22.
28 Jonathan Dollimore, *Radical tragedy: religion, ideology and power in the drama of Shakespeare and his contemporaries* (3rd edn, Basingstoke, 2004; originally published, 1985), pp. 25–8; Patricia Parker, *Shakespeare from the margins: language, culture, context* (Chicago, 1996), ch. 1. See also Susan D. Amussen and David E. Underdown, *Gender, culture and politics in England, 1560–1640: turning the world upside down* (London, 2017), chs 3–4.
29 Tim Harris, *London crowds in the reign of Charles II: propaganda and politics from the Restoration until the Exclusion Crisis* (Cambridge, 1987); Peter Lake, 'Anti-popery: the structure of a prejudice', in Richard Cust and Ann Hughes (eds), *Conflict in early Stuart England: studies in religion and politics, 1603–1642* (London, 1989), pp. 72–106; Peter Lake, 'Anti-puritanism: the structure of a prejudice', in Kenneth Fincham and Peter Lake (eds), *Religious politics in post-Reformation England* (Woodbridge, 2006), pp. 80–97; Patrick Collinson, 'Anti-puritanism', in John Coffey and Paul C. H. Lim (eds), *The Cambridge companion to puritanism* (Cambridge, 2008), pp. 19–33; Jonathan Scott, *England's troubles: seventeenth-century English political instability in European context* (Cambridge, 2000); Alexandra Walsham, *Charitable hatred: tolerance and intolerance in England, 1500–1700* (Manchester, 2006).
30 Paul Slack, *Poverty and policy in Tudor and Stuart England* (London, 1988); Steve Hindle, *On the parish? The micro-politics of poor relief in rural England, c. 1550–1750* (Oxford, 2004).
31 Steven Shapin, *A social history of truth: civility and science in seventeenth-century England* (Chicago, 1994), pp. 86–101, 361–72.
32 Karin Hassan Jansson, Rosemarie Fiebranz and Ann-Catrin Östman, 'Constitutive tasks: performances of hierarchy and identity', in Maria Ågren (ed.), *Making a living, making a difference: gender and work in early modern European society* (Oxford, 2017), pp. 127–58, esp. pp. 127–8, 147–51, 155 n. 2 (quotation, p. 127). See also an important discussion by Laura Gowing, *Domestic dangers: women, words, and sex in early modern London* (Oxford, 1996), pp. 112–38 (on Butler at p. 125).
33 Lisa Hellman, *This house is not a home: European everyday life in Canton and Macao 1730–1830* (Leiden, 2019), pp. 24 (quotation), 25, 72–4, 255, 260–2.
34 Amanda E. Herbert, *Female alliances: gender, identity, and friendship in early modern Britain* (New Haven, CT, 2014), pp. 156–7, 167, at p. 156; Eleanor Hubbard, *City women: money, sex, and the social order in early modern London* (Oxford, 2012), pp. 173, 179, 182 (at p. 173).
35 The turn to practices is discussed in Nathan Perl-Rosenthal, 'Generational turns', *American Historical Review*, 117 (2012), 804–13. For an earlier statement, see Chartier, *Cultural history*, pp. 11–14, 37–45.

36 Lake, 'Anti-popery', p. 95.
37 Lake, 'Anti-popery', p. 96.
38 Lake, 'Anti-puritanism', p. 85.
39 Jürgen Habermas, *The structural transformation of the public sphere: an inquiry into a category of bourgeois society*, trans. Thomas Burger (Cambridge, MA, 1989; German original, 1962).
40 Peter Lake, 'The politics of "popularity" and the public sphere: the "monarchical republic" of Elizabeth I defends itself', in Lake and Pincus (eds), *Politics of the public sphere*, pp. 59–94; Jason Peacey, *Print and public politics in the English Revolution* (Cambridge, 2013).
41 Mark Knights, *Representation and misrepresentation in later Stuart Britain: partisanship and political culture* (Oxford, 2004); Mark Knights, *The devil in disguise: deception, delusion, and fanaticism in the early English Enlightenment* (Oxford, 2011). See also David Lemmings, 'Conclusion: moral panics, law and the transformation of the public sphere in early modern England', in David Lemmings and Claire Walker (eds), *Moral panics, the media and the law in early modern England* (Basingstoke, 2009), pp. 245–66, at pp. 246–7, 251, 264.
42 Mark Knights, 'How rational was the later Stuart public sphere?', in Lake and Pincus (eds), *Politics of the public sphere*, pp. 252–67, at p. 262.
43 Knights, *Representation and misrepresentation*, p. 223. Important articles building on earlier works by Knights, Lake and Pincus have appeared as a special issue of the *Journal of British Studies*. See Laura A. M. Stewart, 'Introduction: publics and participation in early modern Britain', *Journal of British Studies*, 56 (2017), 709–30.
44 Emile Durkheim, 'Représentations individuelles et représentations collectives', *Revue de Métaphysique et de Morale*, 6 (1898), 273–302, at p. 302; W. S. F. Pickering, 'Representations as understood by Durkheim', in W. S. F. Pickering (ed.), *Durkheim and representations* (Abingdon, 2000), pp. 11–23, at pp. 14–18.
45 Scribner, *Simple folk*, p. 13. For background, see Burke, *The French historical revolution*, pp. 14–20, 22, 24–30, 70–1, 75–6; Chartier, *Cultural history*, pp. 21–37; H. Stuart Hughes, *The obstructed path: French social thought in the years of desperation, 1930–1960* (New Brunswick, NJ, 2002; originally published, 1968), ch. 2.
46 On the centrality of Durkheim for sociologically minded social psychology, see Sandra Jovchelovitch, *Knowledge in context: representations, community and culture* (Hove, 2007), pp. 50–3, 90–3.
47 Serge Moscovici, *Psychoanalysis: its image and its public* (Cambridge, 2008; French original, 1961). See also Serge Moscovici, 'Notes towards a description of social representations', *European Journal of Social Psychology*, 18 (1988), 211–50.
48 Habermas suggests that 'anyone who systematically deceives himself behaves irrationally'. The social psychologist Sandra Jovchelovitch argues that the German philosopher fails 'to understand the multiple logics of human behaviour, the reasons behind our self-deceptions and illusions, the sorrows and the hopes that accompany them', leaving him 'cold to the complex rationality of human

desire'. See Jürgen Habermas, *The theory of communicative action: vol. 1 reason and the rationalization of society*, trans. Thomas McCarthy (Boston, MA, 1984; German original, 1981), p. 21; Jovchelovitch, *Knowledge in context*, p. 65.

49 Alex Gillespie, 'Social representations, alternative representations and semantic barriers', *Journal for the Theory of Social Behaviour*, 38 (2008), 375–91; Stephen Reicher, 'From perception to mobilization: the shifting paradigm of prejudice', in John Dixon and Mark Levine (eds), *Beyond prejudice: extending the social psychology of conflict, inequality and social change* (Cambridge, 2012), pp. 27–47.

50 See, for example, Sandra Jovchelovitch, 'Narrative, memory and social representations: a conversation between history and social psychology', *Integrative Psychological and Behavioral Science*, 46 (2012), 440–56; Vlad Petre Glăveanu, *Distributed creativity: thinking outside the box of the creative individual* (Cham, 2014); Susanne Bruckmüller et al., 'When do past events require explanation? Insights from social psychology', *Memory Studies*, 10 (2017), 261–73; Denis J. Hilton and James H. Liu, 'History as the narrative of a people: from function to structure and content', *Memory Studies*, 10 (2017), 297–309.

51 We are therefore being strategically eclectic when adopting theories for historical research. On this see Glăveanu and Yamamoto, 'Bridging history and social psychology', 431–9.

52 Lake, 'Anti-popery'; Lake, 'Anti-puritanism'; Knights, *Devil in disguise*; Lake and Pincus (eds), *Politics of the public sphere.*

53 Lemmings and Walker (eds), *Moral panics.*

54 See David Rowe, 'The concept of the moral panic: an historico-sociological positioning', in Lemmings and Walker (eds), *Moral panics*, pp. 22–40, esp. pp. 24–7; Alexandra Walsham, '"This newe army of Satan": The Jesuit mission and the formation of public opinion in Elizabethan England', in Lemmings and Walker (eds), *Moral panics*, pp. 41–62, at p. 54.

55 David Lemmings, 'Introduction: law and order, moral panics, and early modern England', in Lemmings and Walker (eds), *Moral panics*, pp. 1–21, at p. 16. See also Lemmings, 'Conclusion: moral panics', in Lemmings and Walker (eds), *Moral panics*, p. 264.

56 Knights, 'How rational', p. 258. See also Knights, *Representation and misrepresentation*, pp. 334, 337–43.

57 Knights, *Representation and misrepresentation*, pp. 343–8, at pp. 345, 348.

58 Lake, 'Anti-popery', pp. 73–7, 83, 89, 91–3.

59 Note, however, that stereotypes and their contents never in and of themselves determine how they are used.

60 See Chapter 1, pp. 46, 37.

61 This paragraph draws on Brodie Waddell, 'The Evil May Day riot of 1517 and the popular politics of anti-immigrant hostility in early modern London', *Historical Research*, 94 (2021), 713–35.

62 Hochschild, *Strangers*, p. 147. For background, see Theda Skocpol and Vanessa Williamson, *The Tea Party and the remaking of Republican conservatism* (New York, 2012).

63 Susan Dwyer Amussen, *Caribbean exchanges: slavery and the transformation of English society, 1640–1700* (Chapel Hill, NC, 2007), pp. 174, 216, at p. 174. For a penetrating account of the emerging stereotypes of African women, see Jennifer L. Morgan, *Laboring women: reproduction and gender in New World slavery* (Philadelphia, PA, 2004), pp. 7–8, 36, 40, 46–9.

64 For relevant discussions in psychology, see Schneider, *Psychology of stereotyping*, pp. 229–64, esp. p. 242. Stereotypes can even become institutionalised and shape the systems of persecution and criminal justice. We find this happening in post-Emancipation America, as in medieval Europe. Compare Khalil Gibran Muhammad, *The condemnation of blackness: race, crime, and the making of modern urban America* (2nd edn, Cambridge, MA, 2019); R. I. Moore, *The formation of a persecuting society: power and deviance in western Europe, 950–1250* (Oxford, 1987).

65 Patrick Collinson, 'Ben Jonson's *Bartholomew Fair*: the theatre constructs Puritanism', in David L. Smith, Richard Strier and David Bevington (eds), *The theatrical city: culture, theatre and politics in London, 1576–1649* (Cambridge, 1995), pp. 157–69, at p. 158 (italics added).

66 See Chapter 2, p. 79.

67 Jonas A. Barish, *The antitheatrical prejudice* (Berkeley, CA, 1981), chs 1–4.

68 Ethan H. Shagan, *The rule of moderation: violence, religion and the politics of restraint in early modern England* (Cambridge, 2011).

69 For background, see Peter Lake with Michael Questier, *The Antichrist's lewd hat: Protestants, papists and players in post-Reformation England* (New Haven, CT, 2002), pp. 425–620; Barish, *Antitheatrical prejudice*, ch. 5.

70 The classic analysis of stigma is Erving Goffman, *Stigma: notes on the management of spoiled identity* (Englewood Cliffs, NJ, 1963). The concept of stigma consciousness is developed by E. C. Pinel, 'Stigma consciousness: the psychological legacy of social stereotypes', *Journal of Personality and Social Psychology*, 76 (1999), 114–28. For a related notion of 'stereotype threat', see Steele, *Whistling Vivaldi*, pp. 152–69.

71 The notion is borrowed from Miriam Heijnders and Suzanne Van Der Meij, 'The fight against stigma: an overview of stigma-reduction strategies and interventions', *Psychology, Health & Medicine*, 11 (2006), 353–63.

72 Davis, *Fear, myth and history*; A. L. Morton, *World of Ranters: religious radicalism in the English Revolution* (London, 1970).

73 Capp, *Gossips*, p. 190 (quotation); Gowing, *Domestic dangers*, p. 77.

74 For further examples of what we call coping strategies, see Hubbard, *City women*, p. 192; Helen Smith, *Grossly material things: women and book production in early modern England* (Oxford, 2012), pp. 141–3; Sara Mendelson and Patricia Crawford, *Women in early modern England* (Oxford, 1998), pp. 164, 175; Koji Yamamoto, *Taming capitalism before its triumph: public service, distrust, and 'projecting' in early modern England* (Oxford, 2018), ch. 3, esp. p. 106.

75 Hubbard, *City women*, p. 182; Capp, *Gossips*, p. 203; Porter, *Quacks*, pp. 161–71; Kassell, *Medicine and magic*, pp. 81–2, 84, 117, 119, 121–2; Yamamoto, *Taming capitalism*, p. 150 n. 93–n. 94.

76 Jovchelovitch, *Knowledge in context*, pp. 69–70.
77 Paul Griffiths, *Youth and authority: formative experiences in England, 1560–1640* (Oxford, 1996), pp. 18–19, 45–8, 54–61, 174–5, 232–4, 400–1.
78 William M. Cavert, *The smoke of London: energy and environment in the early modern city* (Cambridge, 2016), pp. 22–5, 35–7.
79 See Chapter 9, p. 266.
80 See Chapter 9, p. 281.
81 Robert Iliffe, 'Foreign bodies: travel, empire and the early Royal Society of London, Part II', *Canadian Journal of History*, 34 (1999), 23–50, at p. 40. See also David S. Sytsma, *Richard Baxter and the mechanical philosophers* (Oxford, 2017).
82 A useful overview is Yoshi Kato and Han van Ruler, 'Confessional clamour and intellectual indifference: religion and philosophy in the wake of Descartes's new method', *Church History and Religious Culture*, 100 (2020), 133–43, esp. pp. 134, 138–9. Followers of Descartes were concerned especially at the danger of being accused of anti-trinitarianism – the denial of the Trinity. See Yoshi Kato and Kuni Sakamoto, 'Between Cartesianism and orthodoxy: God and the problem of indifference in Christoph Wittich's *Anti-Spinoza*', *Intellectual History Review* (2020), doi.org/10.1080/17496977.2020.1852373. On Spinoza, see Yoshi Kato, 'Foreshadowing Spinoza: Johannes Clauberg on God and miracles', *Church History and Religious Culture*, 100 (2020), 234–54. We thank Dr Kato for a helpful discussion. For a comparable case study of 'Hobbism' as a stereotype and its impact on the development of political philosophy, see Jon Parkin, 'Straw men and political philosophy: the case of Hobbes', *Political Studies*, 59 (2011), 564–79.
83 Huiyi Wu, *Traduire la Chine au XVIIIe siècle: les Jésuites traducteurs de textes chinois et le renouvellement des connaissances européennes sur la Chine (1687–ca. 1740)* (Paris, 2017), pp. 268–70, 282–4, 287, at p. 287, our translation; Thijs Weststeijn, 'Spinoza *sinicus*: an Asian paragraph in the history of the radical Enlightenment', *Journal of the History of Ideas*, 68 (2007), 537–61, pp. 537–8.
84 On the problematic 'violence' and 'silence of archives', see Marisa J. Fuentes, *Dispossessed lives: enslaved women, violence, and the archive* (Philadelphia, PA, 2016); Nadine Akkerman, *Invisible agents: women and espionage in seventeenth-century Britain* (Oxford, 2018), esp. pp. 83–8, 109–10. We have engaged with scholars working on gender, occupation, race, colonial disease and slavery by organising a two-day conference in April 2019 on 'Stereotypes and stereotyping in the early modern world' at the Huntington Library.
85 Stephen Pinker, *Enlightenment now: the case for reason, science, humanism, and progress* (London, 2019; originally published, 2018), pp. 7–14, 355–60, 377–81. Pinker's trust of data underplays the key role *judgement* plays when interpreting them. See Jerry Z. Muller, *The tyranny of metrics* (Princeton, NJ, 2018). For a more reliable account of the Enlightenment, see John Robertson, *Enlightenment: a very short introduction* (Oxford, 2015).

86 The conceptual thrust of this volume thus builds on many research works in the humanities and social science that have explored culture, knowledge and markets as socially constructed and historically embedded. We have drawn inspiration in particular from Adrian Johns, *The nature of the book: print and knowledge in the making* (Chicago, 1998), esp. pp. 19–20; Mary Poovey, *A history of the modern fact: problems of knowledge in the sciences of wealth and society* (Chicago, 1998); Mark Bevir and Frank Trentmann, 'Markets in historical contexts: ideas, practices and governance', in Mark Bevir and Frank Trentmann (eds), *Markets in historical contexts: ideas and politics in the modern world* (Cambridge, 2004), pp. 1–24.

87 Notice that this is not to exclude the possibility of cognitive patterns shaping human interactions. Our point is that historical conditions might shape cognitive practices as much as the other way around. On the mutual constitution of psychological experience and historical contexts, see Bruckmüller et al., 'When do past events require explanation', p. 270.

1

Religious and national stereotyping and prejudice in seventeenth-century England

Tim Harris

King James VI of Scotland was known to have had a stormy relationship with the Scottish Presbyterian clergy. Sometime before moving south to become king of England in 1603, so it was said, he happened to hear a sermon by a Presbyterian minister who began railing from the pulpit against king, church and state. Taken aback, James commanded the preacher 'either to speak sence, or come down'. Unfazed, the preacher 'saucily' replied: 'I say Man, I'le nowther speak sence, nor come downe'.[1]

This anecdote appears in a manuscript commonplace book held in the collections of the British Library. Little is known about the provenance of the book, except that it dates from the later seventeenth century, but the collector was seemingly writing down things he had heard or read – 'Apothegms ancient and modern' he styled them – so we can presume that this tale of King James's encounter with the Presbyterian cleric was in more general circulation. Some nineteenth- and early twentieth-century historical works related the story as if true (without citing any sources), though they disagreed over whether the sermon had been delivered in Edinburgh or St Andrews and whether the king in question was James VI and I (*r*. 1567–1625) or James VII and II (*r*. 1685–88). One confidently named the preacher as the Edinburgh minister Robert Bruce (1554–1631).[2] What we can say for certain is that our commonplacer was in the business of collecting things he found amusing. On the page immediately preceding the anecdote about King James he wrote of 'a certain Man that was exceeding fat, and corpulent, yet alwayes rode upon a very leane Horse'; when people 'ask'd him the reason thereof', he explained this was because 'he fed himself, but trusted others to feed his horse'.[3] Thus the story about King James and the preacher was clearly a joke, though a joke that might have been based on an event that had actually happened. It was at a certain level a joke at the expense of the Scots, as the mocking of the Scottish accent makes clear,[4] and it embodies a stereotype of the Scots, or rather of a particular type of Scottish clergyman. The stereotype reflects a prejudice, suggesting as it does that English people tended to prejudge people based on their accent.

However, the joke is more particularly anti-Scottish Presbyterian than it is anti-Scottish. The Scottish Presbyterians, who had rebelled against the new prayer book imposed on the Scottish Kirk in 1637, were widely blamed by the English in the later seventeenth century for having caused the Civil War that broke out in 1642 and led ultimately to the downfall of Charles I. Allegations of refusing to respect royal authority could equally well be made against the English puritans, and indeed were. The joke, we might suggest, relies on an English royalist association of a particular strand of Protestant religiosity with hostility towards monarchy. The joke arguably tells us less about English attitudes towards the Scots than it does about the political and religious anxieties of the era, with humour serving as a form of anxiety displacement – though the joke does not work unless you can read the minister's remark in a Scottish accent. Moreover, if the joke is in some respects anti-Scottish, James VI and I himself was a Scotsman, and was sometimes satirised by English critics for the thickness of his Scottish accent. It was, of course, perfectly possible to express contempt for Scottishness and at the same time support particular individuals who were Scottish. Later in the century, for instance, the republican poet John Ayloffe became so disillusioned with the restored Stuarts, whom he denigrated as 'this stinking Scottish brood', that he joined the rebellion in Scotland led by the Scottish Earl of Argyll against the newly crowned James VII and II in 1685.[5] Scotophobia in seventeenth-century England was clearly more complex than a straightforward and undiscriminating antipathy to all those who hailed from Scotland. Yet to offer such reflections is perhaps to over-intellectualise. The story about King James and the Presbyterian minister was just a joke, after all. On the previous page our commonplacer recorded a witty anecdote at James VI and I's expense: 'King James was a Prince, that allwayes esteem'd Soldiers the Worst of Men, and the most formidable to his Person; for when a certain Lord newly come from the Warrs abroad, desir'd the honor to Kiss his Majesties hands, the King told him, That he fear'd he would bite it, and therefore bad that he should be mufled'.[6]

It has long been recognised that human beings have a propensity to stereotype – to develop oversimplified ideas of the characteristics which typify a person or a group – because of the way they categorise in order to make comprehensible the complexities of their world.[7] Stereotypes are often negative, but not invariably so; there can be positive stereotypes, and stereotypes that carry a mixture of negative and positive connotations. It is particularly common to stereotype those who are seen as being in some way outsiders to a group or society. The early modern English certainly tended to stereotype foreign nationals. Take these observations recorded in a commonplace book from *c.* 1669–77: 'The French loves every where/The

Spaniard loves well/Itallian knows whoome to love/The German knowse not how to love'.[8] Or these from a commonplace book from the late 1650s: 'The German tongue is fit to command, the Italian to make Love, the French to buy and sell, and the Spanish to move mercy'.[9] The English thought character and temperament were shaped not just by nationhood, but also by climate. This same commonplacer recorded the view that '[t]he Northern man being hot within', because living in a colder climate, was 'more courageous, taller and stronger than the southern, whose inward heat' was 'drawn out and dispersed into the outward part by the fervent heat of the sun', making the southern man 'lesse able (though more sensuall) to the act of generation than the northern man'.[10] Yet the seventeenth-century English stereotyped a whole range of out-groups, not just foreigners or those who lived overseas, but also those who were seen in various ways as outsiders within English society: from various types of religious nonconformist (Catholics, puritans, Protestant dissenters) through to marginalised groups such as suspected witches, vagrants and the poor.

We have a considerable body of scholarship on English prejudice towards and stereotyping of foreigners and religious minorities in the early modern period. Indeed, it is virtually impossible to write about the political upheavals of seventeenth-century England without addressing in some way the issues of religious and national stereotyping and prejudice. We are deeply familiar with how, at moments of political crisis in the seventeenth century, rival polemicists sought to exploit popular fears and prejudices in an effort to mobilise mass support for a given cause: one thinks of the work on anti-Catholicism and anti-puritanism on the eve of the English Civil War, or on anti-popery and Francophobia during the Exclusion Crisis, though we also have much valuable scholarship on English attitudes towards the Irish, Scots, Welsh, Dutch, the Jews and the Turks.[11] These are themes I have explored extensively in my own research.[12] Here I want to stand back from my own work and that of others and offer some more general reflections on stereotyping and prejudice in early modern England. I shall start by raising some broader conceptual and methodological questions. What is the relationship between stereotyping and prejudice? Are stereotypes purely projections, or do the stereotyped influence the stereotype in some way? And how do we study stereotyping and prejudice historically: what do the sources at our disposal actually tell us, can they be taken at face value and how do we handle humour and jokes when the author may or may not have been trying to be serious? We shall see that our sources rarely offer straightforward reflections of given stereotypes and prejudices; more often they are works of polemic designed to exploit existing stereotypes and latent prejudices in an effort to mobilise opinion behind a particular agenda.[13] I shall then proceed to examine how seventeenth-century controversialists and polemicists sought to harness and manipulate popular stereotypes and prejudices for partisan ends, focusing in particular on Scotophobia, anti-puritanism and anti-popery. We shall learn that these phobias were not straightforward prejudices but in fact multivalent and complex cultural phenomena. They were rarely unambiguous, and were frequently contested, capable of being used for radically different ideological purposes at different times and even competing ideological purposes at the same time.

Conceptual and methodological issues

Stereotyping invariably involves prejudgement based on the stereotype. Thus stereotyping and prejudice are clearly related – but in what way, precisely? For instance, an antipathy towards Catholicism was widespread in seventeenth-century England, and this 'prejudice' (if that is what it was) was based to a certain extent on stereotyping: that all Catholics were at heart traitors and rebels and that Catholicism was a superstitious, idolatrous and persecuting religion which upheld tyranny in the state. However, different types of Protestant could be anti-Catholic in different ways – and their anti-Catholicism might lead them to very different political and religious viewpoints. In short, English Protestants who were prejudiced against Catholics were not all responding to the same stereotype. Yet was anti-Catholicism in early modern England really a prejudice? Was it an irrational fear and hatred either of Roman Catholics or the Roman Catholic religion? Or was it a reasoned, even intellectualised, condemnation of what Protestants took to be a politically dangerous, false religion, and in that respect a reflection of distinctive political and religious values – in short, a species of ideology?[14] The issue becomes even more complicated once we remind ourselves that the real concern for the seventeenth-century English was popery. Anti-popery and anti-Catholicism did overlap, but they were distinct. In fact, it surely makes sense to see anti-popery as both a prejudice and an ideology. We might even say it was several discrete ideologies. It was based on both irrational fears and prejudices, as well as being an intellectualised position. The ideology was so powerful precisely because it appealed to the emotions.[15]

It is a commonplace that stereotypes tell us more about those doing the stereotyping than about the stereotyped. At the same time, the stereotype must have some credible link to reality – or, at least, must be an intelligible way of representing the stigmatised other within a given culture – otherwise the stereotype could never take hold in the first place. The stereotyped inevitably shape the stereotype to some degree: by how they act in real life or react to being stereotyped (and whether their reactions serve to mitigate or reinforce the stereotype). The degree to which the stereotyped might shape the stereotype can thus be related to the extent to which the stereotyped is a known or an unknown entity. Is a stigmatised out-group feared because people feel they know what they are like? Or is the fear purely a projection, a fear of what society imagines the unknown other to be like? Most people in seventeenth-century England would have encountered actual Catholics, puritans or Quakers. They were likely also to have encountered Scottish, Welsh and Irish people. The nature of that encounter could vary in intensity and in significance from place to place and over time. There were pockets of the country with untypically high concentrations of Catholics: the area around St Giles-in-the-Fields in London, for example, or parts of Lancashire in the north-west. There were other parts of the country where one would be far less likely to encounter an actual Catholic.[16] Many who lived in the north-east of England would have been deeply familiar with the Scots, but people's experience there of the Scots would be different in the 1630s, when the Scots remained north of the border (by and large), in 1640, when the Scots captured Newcastle upon Tyne following victory against Charles I in the second Bishops' War, or during the mid-1640s, when Scottish forces were waging a military campaign in the north in alliance with the English Parliament against Charles I. By contrast, most English people were unlikely ever to have seen an actual Jew or Turk, though Londoners might have done in the later seventeenth century.[17]

However, this issue is more complicated than it might seem. People who did not know real Scots or real puritans, say, could be 'taught' to fear what Scots or puritans were represented as being. People could get on well with their actual Catholic neighbours but nevertheless despise what they thought popery stood for. What Londoners thought of Irishmen in their midst could be vastly different from their view of the unknown, ethnically different (Gaelic) Irishmen in Ireland.[18]

Social psychologists have observed that stereotypes and prejudices often emerge out of the need 'to construct, maintain, and defend specific self-images and to avoid the aversive feelings that could result from threats to the self', thus leading to the projection of threatening or undesirable attributes onto other individuals or groups – another form of anxiety displacement.[19] In seventeenth-century England it was common to stigmatise hated out-groups by alleging that they were guilty of violating society's moral norms. Yet this phenomenon also highlights the difficulties in trying to draw distinctions between the 'known' and the 'unknown' other. It did not matter what puritans, for instance, were really like, or whether you did know real puritans, because the stereotype is a projection – it is about an imagined other – and people might embrace the projection, even of groups with whom they were familiar. They might see in real-life puritans the personality traits which the stereotype had taught them to perceive.[20] The presence of the stereotyped in one's midst could certainly affect the psychodynamic of stereotyping. Some people might come to recognise that real puritans were not as they were represented. The more familiar, or closer to home, the stereotyped out-group was, the greater the likelihood that this stereotype might be effectively contested. Yet sometimes the activity of real puritans might seem to offer confirmation that they really were as they were imagined.[21]

What we can say with confidence is that stereotyping in seventeenth-century England – and distancing from the stigmatised other – did *not* function to promote social or national cohesion. It did not serve to promote a sense among the people of England that they were all English (not Scottish, Welsh, Irish or European), and all Protestant (not Catholic, Jewish, or Muslim), and thus united. Even the most cursory look at how stereotypes were articulated and mobilised in this culture shows that stereotyping divided the English among themselves.

So how do we study this phenomenon historically? We have no shortage of sources across a variety of media (printed, manuscript, visual and performative) reflecting on religious and national stereotyping and prejudice in seventeenth-century England: treatises, pamphlets, newspapers and mock travel literature; handwritten libels, rhymes, poems and verse songs; graphic satire; sermons, speeches and alehouse talk; stage plays; riots and demonstrations; even street theatre and pageantry. Can we approach this material as social psychologists would, and endeavour to deconstruct a given stereotype or prejudice into core versus peripheral concepts, identifying those that remained constant over time and distinguishing those that were mutable, dropped in and out of focus, or waxed and waned in significance? To a certain extent we can, and we should. There were certain core elements to the anti-puritan stereotype that were repeated over and over again: puritans were consistently seen as proud, hypocritical, ignorant, uncharitable, gluttonous, dissembling, given to acts of sexual indiscretion, disrespectful of authority and a divisive presence in local communities.[22] Central to anti-Catholicism was the view that the Catholic faith encouraged superstition, idolatry, treachery and rebellion. We could likewise identify, perhaps, core elements in the stereotyping of national groups: the French, Spanish, Scottish, Welsh or Irish.

Yet a difficulty lies in the fact that our historical sources are not equivalent to the types of survey, questionnaire or observational situation that social psychologists can deploy or replicate. Much of the material we have from the seventeenth century was polemic or propaganda, produced with the intention of shaping or swaying opinion, and thus of creating a prejudice rather than reporting it. In representing the threat of Catholicism or popery in a particular way, polemicists necessarily had to appeal to people's prejudices and assumptions, and what they said or wrote must to some degree have reflected what people believed. Yet propagandists often sought to appeal to prejudices and assumptions in such a way as to redirect them in the service of a particular cause. The challenge for the historian, then, is determining the extent to which a given work of polemic reflected existing core beliefs or instead what the polemicist hoped he could persuade people to believe.[23] Insofar as the polemic proved persuasive, the polemicist would inevitably shape the stereotype; he or she might also reshape it by highlighting certain elements that before were only peripheral and making them central to the core, or by adding further elements and in the process helping to develop new stereotypes – as Peter Lake and Koji Yamamoto illustrate in chapters 2 and 4 on stereotypes of the puritan and the projector below. The problem is that in seventeenth-century England this process of production, reproduction, contestation and redefinition was going on all the time.

A further difficulty relates to how to read tone and intent in sources that were produced over three centuries ago. Some of our material appears fairly straightforward. Take, for instance, this report of an Anglican sermon delivered in 1681, in which the cleric describes Catholicism as 'that silly, that foolish, that cruell Religion, a Religion which changes soe many of its professors into blood sucking leeches ... a Religion that joys in murthers by retayle'.[24] It seems clear where our cleric stood, and he was likely to have been saying the types of thing his congregation were used to hearing and probably believed themselves. However, how do we treat sources that were intended to be funny? Humour might serve a number of functions. One would be to enhance the appeal of a particular work, reinforcing (or redirecting or even creating) a stereotype as people were having a good laugh.[25] Humour could be a form of anxiety displacement, a coping mechanism in a society under intense stress, or 'displaced or sublimated aggression'.[26] Sometimes humour could be merely frivolous and light-hearted, albeit nevertheless building upon – and thus shedding insight into – a widely held prejudice. 'A man being asked what was the Church of Rome like', records one jestbook from 1685, answered, 'I think her as like my Wife as any thing ... she commands what she pleases without regard of either God or man, and then curses all the Family to Hell if they give not present Obedience'.[27] At other times humorous works could be making deadly serious points: one thinks of the visual satires directed against Archbishop Laud in 1641, calling for the Archbishop's execution, or royalist anti-puritan polemic of 1641–2, as the nation was dividing to go to war – much of which material was also quite funny (and intentionally so).[28]

Yet knowing how to read the humour present in our sources is not as straightforward as we might imagine. Humour does not always translate across cultures (even cultures that share the same language) and tone does not always come across in writing (especially when being read hundreds of years later). Is there a risk that we can misread some of the stereotyping we encounter? For instance, Owen Felltham's *Brief character of the Low Countries* of 1652, a popular work that went through several editions, indulges in some vicious anti-Dutch stereotyping for sixty pages: their country was 'the buttock of the World, full of veines and bloud, but no bones in't'; you could not walk down the road in the Low Countries 'without the hazard of drowning'; '[t]he people are generally Boorish'; '[y]ou may sooner convert a Jew, than make an ordinary Dutch-man yield to Arguments that cross him'; 'the Scythian-Bear could nere have been more savage' – it goes on and on. However, Felltham had written the work much earlier (probably in the mid- to late 1620s), and although it did circulate in manuscript Felltham regarded it 'among his *puerilia*', a 'piece too light for a prudential man to publish', and based on limited observations, given that he had only been in the Low Countries for three weeks. The first part of the work was merely 'joculary and sportive', but because the latter part, which was serious, went on to praise the Dutch for being an industrious, chaste, valiant, virtuous and diligent people, Felltham and his publisher thought the characterisation of the Dutch was in 'no way injurious to the people'.[29] Doubtless Felltham was trying to engage readers by offering them both utility and delight. He might also have been using humour as anxiety displacement, minimising the threat that the positive accomplishments of the Dutch might be perceived to represent by poking fun at the people first. Having said that, the work nevertheless does reflect and perpetuate a stereotype. Moreover, it first appeared in print at the time of the first Anglo-Dutch War (1652–4) and was reprinted, under a new title *Batavia; or, the Hollander display'd*, in 1672, the year of the outbreak of the third Anglo-Dutch War (1672–4), so the text was subsequently appropriated in support of the foreign policy objectives of the Republic and the restored monarchy.[30]

There was a tradition in early modern England of writing mock travel narratives in which, while relating his travels, the author would set out to say as many humorous things as possible about the country he was visiting and its inhabitants. The way countries and their people were satirised in such works was often remarkably similar: there would be jokes about the physical landscape (urban and rural), climate, food, people (men and women) and culture. Sometimes the satire could be geographically specific. For instance, in its section on Scotland *The comical pilgrim* of 1722, a classic of the genre, highlighted the problems Edinburgh had with sanitation, with its multistorey residences built on a hill: 'such a Place of Nastiness was not to be found upon Earth', the author bemoaned, 'having a Dung-Tub at the

Head of every Pair of Stairs in their Houses, which are 14 or 15 low Stories high', which were 'emptied a-nights on Peoples Heads without any respect of Persons', so that the whole city was 'scented with the excellent Perfume of Scotch Civit Cats'. However, often the insults were generic. Foreign food is terrible. Foreign women are all whores. 'Here is every Day an Autumn among the Women' in Scotland, our *Comical pilgrim* opined, since 'for a Noggin of Brandy they will fall as thick on their Backs as the Leaves in St James's Park do in September'. He also believed it was doubtful there was 'any such Thing' as a virgin in Ireland 'after she's in the Teens'.[31] The satire here is formulaic. It is questionable how much it really tells us about what English people genuinely thought about the national types being satirised. (One might even argue that the satire was directed in part against the English, mocking the way they stereotyped others.)[32] We often find exactly the same joke being made about different peoples: a joke about a Welshman elsewhere becoming a joke about 'an ignorant country fellow', or a joke at the expense of the Irish elsewhere being related as a joke about the Welsh.[33] In such instances, otherness is invoked simply as a device to set up the joke.

So how do we read the famous satire attributed to Sir Anthony Weldon, supposedly penned when Weldon accompanied King James VI and I on his progress to Scotland in 1617? Scotland, we are told, was a country

> too good for them that possesse it and too bad for others to be at charge to conquer it; the ayre might be wholesome but for the stinckinge people that inhabit it; the ground might be more fruitfull had they the wit to manure it; the beasts are generally small (women onely excepted) of which sort there are none greater in the World. There is greate store of fowle as fowle houses, fowle linnen, fowle potts and dishes, fowle trenchers and napkins, fowle sheetes and shirts ...[34]

Seventeenth-century Englishmen seemingly found this hilarious. The tract was already in its fourth edition by 1626 and was regularly republished over the course of the century. We find it copied out in a number of commonplace books.[35] A version of it was appended to Felltham's *Batavia* of 1672. Other writers stole the joke, as did our *Comical pilgrim* of 1722.[36] Yet although the joke seems specific to Scotland, it could also work for Ireland. The author of *Mercurius Hibernicus* of 1645, after having spoken of the plentiful rivers and abundance of fish, fowl and beasts in Ireland (which the natives were not putting to good use), later realised he had missed a punning opportunity and wrote: 'I told you before that they had a great store of foule and beasts, for so they have, for there is foul Dishes, foule Vessels, foule Houses, foule Linnen, and foule Sowes; but the beasts are generally small, the Women excepted'.[37] The wide circulation of Weldon's joke clearly lent English people a framework for thinking about Scotland and the

Scots, and perhaps also points to the way that English people predisposed to a negative view might have thought about their neighbours to the north. Yet the fact that the joke proved transferable meant that it could also lend the English a framework for thinking about other countries they regarded as backward. Thus deciphering precisely what the joke reveals about English attitudes towards Scotland and the Scots is not as straightforward as we might imagine. A closer reading of Weldon's tract, in fact, suggests that the real bite of the work was its attack on Scottish Presbyterianism.

Besides, Weldon's was not the only view of the country of Scotland prevalent at the time. John Speed produced a more favourable description of Scotland in his atlas *The theatre of the empire of Great Britain* of 1623, which went through numerous editions and appeared in an abridged edition in 1627. Speed described Scotland as 'faire and spacious', 'furnished with all things befitting a famous Kingdome; both for Ayre and Soyle, Rivers, Woods, Mountaines, Fish, Fowle, and Cattle, and Corne so plenteous, that is supplyeth therewith other Countryes in their want'; he thought 'the people' there 'of good feature, strong of body, and of courageous minde, and in warres so venturous'.[38] One might suggest that satires like Weldon's worked because they were satirising familiar *positive* representations, or at least because they were satirising the genre in which positive representations had appeared.[39]

Multivocal representations and false composites

Our sources, then, are problematic and need to be interpreted carefully. Historians cannot approach their material in quite the way that social psychologists analyse their data, but then our enterprises are different. What might appear to be problems with the sources are, for historians, their strength. It is the very ambiguity and complexity of the sources that enable us to generate meaningful historical insight. They reveal that the stereotypes and prejudices we are examining were in fact multivalent and multivocal representations, reflecting to a certain extent attitudes and assumptions that were embedded in popular culture, but also the agendas of polemicists and controversialists who were seeking to mobilise them and to redirect them. Even mere jokes can reveal latent attitudes and assumptions – attitudes that might not have been particularly discriminating (in the sense that the same prejudice could easily shift from one group to another), but which could be capable of becoming quite powerful once mobilised, especially at times of heightened stress or politico-religious crisis. Our sources further show that attitudes and assumptions about foreigners or religious minorities were continually contested. And although we are dealing in part with stereotypes and prejudices that could remain fairly stable, even though contested – the stereotype of the puritan, for instance, persisted for quite some time even though not all would have embraced it – we are once again reminded that we are dealing with much more: with articulations of particular political and religious positions and beliefs – in short, with ideologies.

Seventeenth-century English representations of foreigners or religious minorities were often compound constructs, not typically *a* stereotype but rather a cluster of discrete stereotypes, which might come to be blended in varying ways in people's minds, depending on context. Let us take Scotophobia, for example. There were several types of distinctive Scots stereotype.[40] There were the ancient inhabitants of Scotland, seen as barbarous and uncivilised, who were even alleged to have practiced cannibalism.[41] Then there were the Highlanders – supposedly the descendants of the ancient Scots – who spoke the Irish language, wore Irish apparel and were 'rude and unruly'. These were a people quite distinct from the Lowlanders, who used 'the English language and apparaill' and who were thought to be 'more civil'.[42] The stereotype of the Highlander was embraced by Lowland Scots: James VI and I, for instance, thought the Highlanders of the Isles 'alluterly barbares, without any sort or shew of civilitie'.[43] However, there was also an image of the Scots in general, that is, the inhabitants of the political entity that was Scotland, foreign nationals who prior to 1603 had often been at war with the English – an enemy other, still not to be trusted, whether Highlanders or Lowlanders. In the eyes of the English, the Scots' *national* character was shaped by the fact that they lived in an economically impoverished country with a cold climate. Antipathy towards Lowland Scots increased following the union of the crowns in 1603 as James VI and I brought a number of his countrypeople with him to London and gave them titles and places at court. Hence emerged the English stereotype of the 'beggarly Scot'.[44] Furthermore, following the Reformation in Scotland, which had been forged in opposition to the Crown rather than by it (as had been the Reformation in England), there emerged the image of the Scot as a Presbyterian (again, overwhelmingly Lowland Scots) and all which that entailed – a hostility towards the English episcopalian system of ecclesiastical government and support for resistance theory. This image of Scottish Presbyterians became even more firmly entrenched as a result of the political and religious upheavals of the seventeenth century, when the first to resist the Stuarts were the Scottish Covenanters.[45] Along with these various negative stereotypes, the English also embraced positive stereotypes of the Scots, as being brave and hardy, and thus valiant soldiers,[46] although of course such characteristics in the inhabitants of a potentially hostile neighbouring country could be sources of fear rather than admiration.

Social psychologists style the tendency to harbour different, and at times contradictory, modes of thinking about the same issue *cognitive polyphasia*. Here, of course, I have been talking about a collective – the English, in general – so such contradictions are perhaps to be expected. But it is important to recognise that individuals are also prone to cognitive polyphasia – as David Magliocco explores in Chapter 7 on Samuel Pepys's quite contrasting attitudes towards the French.[47] With regard to Scotophobia, it was not just that different types of English people held different views of the Scots – though they did. It was that an individual's thinking about the Scots could be logically inconsistent or even muddled.

Certainly the English had a tendency to lump together, in a somewhat indiscriminate manner, all the things they had learned to believe were undesirable about the Scots. In his pro-Union treatise of 1605–7 the Scotsman Sir Thomas Craig noted how '[s]o long as the two countries were enemies, nothing that was Scottish ever found favour with our neighbours', and that the English tended to asperse 'the Scots as uncivilised, wild, and barbarous'. When he visited England at the time of the Union negotiations, he observed how English children would play at being 'English and Scots' in mock fights – rather like children in the twentieth century might have played at cowboys and Indians. One Englishman told Craig that the reason why the English had never conquered Scotland was because Scotland 'was of too little worth to tempt England to retain', and that Scotland 'owed her security solely to her cold climate, her poverty, mountains, and bogs'. When attending a service at St Paul's Cathedral, Craig was treated to a 'wild and virulent sermon' condemning the Scots as 'poor, lying, and prone to all manner of treachery'.[48]

Indeed, there was a tendency for the English to blur or conflate discrete stereotypes of the Scots, leading to the creation of a *false composite* – an image of the Scots that drew on stereotypical characteristics supposedly evinced by different types of Scot, but which were never found together in any one Scottish person. Note, for instance, how in June 1639 the English officer Captain Thomas Windebanke wrote a letter to his father explaining how English troops sent to Berwick to fight the Scottish Covenanters at the time of the first Bishops' War kept their spirits up

> with the hopes of rubbing, fubbing, and scrubbing those scurvy, filthy, durty, nasty, lousie, ytchy, scabby, shitten, stinking, slovenly, snotty-nos'd, logger-headed, foolish, insolent, proud, beggerly, impertinent, absurd, grout-headed, vilainous, barbarous, bestiall, false, lying, rogueish, divelish, long-ear'd, short-hair'd, damnable, Atheisticall, puritanical Crue of the Scotch Covenant.[49]

Or note, too, how a verse satire from that same year mocked the Scots' claim to be fighting a 'holy war', since 'Religion all the world can tell/Amongst

High-landers ne're did dwell'.[50] In such remarks we see images of the Scots as barbaric and uncivilised, Highlanders, foreign nationals, enemy others and Presbyterians all blurred into one, a composite affixed also to Scots who would have been Lowlanders. The label 'Scot', in other words, possessed broad resonances, with the potential to invoke in the mind of someone predisposed to be hostile towards the Scots a cluster of negative associations about the peoples of Scotland. It is, of course, difficult to demonstrate a hidden subtext empirically, though Windebanke's letter perhaps provides an example of someone making explicit what was often a buried implication. The fact that royalist polemicists sometimes qualified their Scotophobic diatribes by insisting that they were thinking of only certain types of Scot – the 'perfidious' ones – and pretended to chastise the rashness of those 'fools' who would 'lay the blame upon the Nation totall', further suggests that contemporaries recognised the broader resonances that the negative stereotype of the Scot had the potential to carry.[51]

The construction of false composites is quite common in stereotyping: it can be found also in representations of the immigrant, for example.[52] What we have noted with regard to Scotophobia might be thought of as the 'everything bar the kitchen sink' approach: while condemning the Scots, one might as well invoke all the negative stereotypes one could think of. Yet discrete stereotypes could also be conflated more tactically, for instance by polemicists deliberately seeking to make it seem as if the undesirable traits associated with a particular subgroup applied to a broader group of people who were being targeted for attack.

Anti-puritanism is here a case in point. As noted above, there was a generalised negative stereotype of the puritan as hypocritical, proud, gluttonous, unchaste and uncharitable, which made the puritan appear contemptible and ridiculous but not necessarily the object of fear. More threatening were the radical puritans, the separatists. However, the potential for slippage was always present, since the separatist was a type of puritan, and the stigmatisation of the separatist could easily encourage the view that all puritans were equally bad. In the late 1580s, for instance, the canon of Westminster Richard Bancroft (later Bishop of London and Archbishop of Canterbury) deliberately sought to tar Presbyterians and separatists with the same brush in his propaganda war with 'Martin Marprelate' and the English Presbyterians.[53] On the eve of the Civil War, supporters of Charles I sought to build up support for the Crown by exploiting fears of radical sectarians, whom they represented as a threat to the rule of law, the social hierarchy and gender norms. At the same time, they deliberately blurred the distinction between separatists and moderate puritans. Typical in this regard was John Harris's *The puritanes impuritie: or, the anatomie of a puritane or seperatist* of 1641, which spoke of 'these Seperatists alias Puritanes'.[54] Yet moderate puritans were equally alarmed about the rise of the sects in 1641–2: Henry Parker styled separatists 'the dregges of the vilest and most ignorant rabble'; Edward Reynolds accused them of falling 'into the phrenzie of Schisme and prophanenesse'.[55] This was why the anti-sectarian card was such a powerful one for supporters of Charles I to play, since it had the potential to appeal to the moderate middle ground and thus to dislodge people from their previous support for Parliament's reformist agenda. All puritans were damned by association.

Mobilising and contesting stereotypes

As these last remarks indicate, political and religious polemicists often sought to exploit latent prejudices and preconceptions in order to mobilise support for a particular cause. It was a tactic that could prove extremely effective: note the efforts of the Whigs to rally support for their campaign to exclude the Catholic heir from the succession during the Exclusion Crisis, which initially met with considerable success. Yet such attempted mobilisations rarely went uncontested – as indeed they were not during the Exclusion Crisis.[56] In studying stereotyping we must also pay close critical attention to the various responses to such stereotyping, therefore. People did not always buy into the polemic: they did not necessarily believe of the stigmatised out-group what propagandists and polemicists urged them to believe. Furthermore, rival propagandists and polemicists often sought to construct competing representations, in order either to negate popular antipathy towards a stigmatised out-group or to channel such antipathy to the service of an alternative politico-religious agenda.

By way of illustration, let me start by returning to Scotophobia. Many English people simply did not embrace the negative view of the Scots propagated by supporters of the government in 1638–40, either because they were so disillusioned with the religious and political policies of the Caroline regime that they were willing to support anyone who could mount an effective challenge to it (my enemy's enemy is my friend), or because they positively identified with the reforming agenda of the Scottish Covenanters. The Northamptonshire puritan lawyer Robert Woodford saw the Scottish revolt as divine judgement upon the English nation and repeatedly expressed his support for the Scots' efforts to carry out 'the worke of reformacon'.[57] Others saw the Scots as delivering England from 'the persecuting Arch-bishop'.[58] The parliamentarian reformers of 1640–2 were strong supporters of the Scots, and brought the Scots into the war against Charles I in 1643 with the Solemn League and Covenant.

Yet how people in England felt about the Scots at any given time or in any given place was affected by changing circumstances and realities on the ground. In the political crisis of 1640, it was easy to welcome the Scots as deliverers, especially in the more southern parts of England, but even initially in the north-east, which the Scots occupied following the defeat they inflicted on Charles I's forces at the battle of Newburn in August 1640. During the Civil War, however, depredations by Scottish troops in the north of England caused many in that area to turn against the Scots.[59] Anti-Scottishness became a key defining feature of royalism during the first Civil War.[60] However royalist authors, while denigrating the Scots in general terms as a people, often qualified their remarks, as mentioned above, by insisting they did not mean all Scots – there were 'honest men and knaves in every Nation' – but only those who were rebels against Charles I (i.e. the Presbyterians).[61] Amongst those who backed Parliament against Charles I, Independents and sectarians disliked the Scottish alliance and the commitment to establish Presbyterianism in England if Parliament won the war, without the liberty of conscience that Independents and separatists so desired. There were Scotophobes, in other words, on both sides during the English Civil War. Scotophobia in England grew more complicated in the late 1640s. Royalists had to modify their views when Charles I allied with the Scots and started the second Civil War in 1648. This in turn resulted in an upsurge of anti-Scottish sentiment amongst supporters of Parliament, especially the Independents, and even more so after 1649 following the Scots' opposition to the regicide and their decision to declare for Charles II.[62] Anti-Scottish polemic from the late 1630s through to the 1650s repeatedly drew on anti-Scottish stereotypes, and the propaganda would not have had the effect it did unless the stereotypes drawn upon were embedded in this culture. Yet it is clear that Scotophobia was not simply a prejudice against the Scots. It was a multifaceted and multivalent ideology. Anti-Scottish polemic was used to articulate distinctive, and differing, politico-religious agendas – agendas that were continually contested by others of a different politico-religious persuasion.

Let me conclude by looking at anti-popery. What popery meant was fiercely contested, with it taking on different meanings for different types of Protestant. As the royalist cleric Edward Symmons put it in 1643, 'there be more points of Popery then one'; Symmons listed eleven.[63] English Protestants, to quote Anthony Milton, were 'able to deploy multiple modes of anti-Catholic polemic'.[64]

Anti-popery was built, to a certain extent, upon the stereotyping of a religion: Catholicism was seen as a superstitious, idolatrous and persecuting faith. Yet it was a religion with startling political implications, so far as English Protestants were concerned, since the Catholic church held that the Pope, not the king, was the head of the church and that he could depose heretical rulers, whilst Catholics believed in resistance theory. English Protestants' views of Catholicism were further shaped by history: the persecution of English Protestants under Mary Tudor (1553–8) and of Protestants on the Continent during the French wars of religion (notably the St Bartholomew's Day massacre in Paris of 1572), the papal bull excommunicating Elizabeth I of 1570 and the various Catholic conspiracies and rebellions during Elizabeth's reign, the threatened invasion by the Spanish Armada in 1588, the gunpowder plot of 1605, the assassination of Henri IV of France by the fanatical Catholic François Ravaillac in 1610 and the Irish rebellion of 1641. English people were brought up anti-Catholic, and anti-Catholicism was reproduced over the generations through instruction and commemoration.[65] Parents might teach their children what to think of Catholicism. Protestant clergymen saw it as their duty to offer guidance to their parishioners about the importance of avoiding the errors of popery. The state introduced annual commemorations for deliverance from Catholic conspiracies, such as the Armada and the gunpowder plot, which were in turn celebrated in the street with bonfires and firework displays.[66] Every year on 5 November sermons delivered up and down the land reminded English Protestants that the Catholic religion was 'Rebellion' and its practice involved the 'murthering of soules and bodies'.[67] So deeply entrenched in English culture was this stereotype of the Catholic religion and its adherents that it was possible to attack Catholicism obliquely, without mentioning it by name, confident that others would grasp the allusion. For instance, in early 1687, a few months after James II had issued a ban on anti-Catholic preaching, Dr Thomas Ken, Bishop of Bath and Wells, delivered a sermon at Whitehall on the blasphemies, superstitions, perfidy and spirit of the scribes and Pharisees, knowing full well 'that all the auditory understood his meaning of a parallel between them and the Roman priests'.[68]

However, this fear of Catholicism tended not to translate into an antipathy towards ordinary, individual Catholics. Although there were quite a few anti-Catholic riots at times of political crisis in the seventeenth century, the targets of these tended to be symbols of the Catholic religion (such as Catholic chapels), foreign Catholics (such as Catholic ambassadors resident in London), or Catholic or crypto-Catholic courtiers who were seen as responsible for unpopular government policies in church and state.[69] Even the most stridently anti-Catholic preachers stressed that their ire was directed not against Catholics as people, but against their religion: 'not the men, but the Errors'.[70]

Furthermore, the fear of popery was often related to concerns about what other English Protestants were doing. Puritans tended to see popery within the Church of England. Indeed, the term puritan was coined originally to refer those who wanted to purify the established Church of England of all remaining relics of popery, such as the use of the sign of the cross in baptism or kneeling for communion. When Archbishop William Laud in the 1630s urged strict ceremonial conformity to the Book of Common Prayer, beautified the churches with stained glass windows and golden ornaments on the communion table and encouraged churches to place their communion table 'altar-wise' at the east end and to rail it in, this was 'popery' to many puritans and even mainstream Protestants, even though such Protestants who accused Laud of promoting popery were well aware that the Archbishop was not a Catholic.[71]

Yet to English Protestants popery also meant refusing to acknowledge the royal supremacy, rebelling against one's lawful sovereign, resistance theory and seeking to undermine the established Protestant church in England. For this reason, the charge of popery was frequently levelled by defenders of the king and the established church against their puritan and parliamentarian critics – countering a stereotype with another stereotype, in a sense, though one could debate which stereotype came first. Accusing opponents of popery was a tactic pursued by defenders of the Crown from the time of the Covenanter revolt in Scotland of 1638–40 and throughout the 1640s, through the Civil Wars and up to the regicide, in an effort to build up popular support for Charles I – with some, albeit limited, success.[72] It was a tactic pursued by Tory supporters of Charles II against the Whigs during the Exclusion Crisis in the late 1670s and early 1680s, with a considerable degree of success, as I have argued extensively in some of my previous work.[73] It is also a theme which Adam Morton explores in Chapter 6 below.

Social psychologists have long observed how difficult it is for a propagandist to run counter to people's deeply held prejudices.[74] If the puritans in 1640–1, or the Whigs in 1679–81, had been successful in turning public opinion against the government by playing on people's fears of popery, it was unlikely to have been an effective counter-strategy for the government simply to insist that the fear of popery was unfounded. What pro-government propagandists chose to do instead was try to appeal to people's very fears of popery, but in such a way as to redirect these in the service of their cause. Thus the effort to control stereotypes and their meanings led to the escalation, rather than the reduction, of stereotyping – a not uncommon phenomenon, as Lake and Yamamoto note in their Introduction.

It would be wrong to think the Anglican royalist strategy was purely opportunistic, however, or that it was insincere. It was not that the puritans framed a stereotype and Anglican royalists *invented* an alternative to counter it. Rather, they *mobilised* an existing stereotype. Accusing puritans of acting on popish principles had been a staple feature of anti-puritan polemic from Elizabethan times onwards. Bancroft had done this in the aftermath of the Marprelate controversy.[75] James VI and I frequently compared papists to puritans, accusing both of wanting to make kings but 'dukes of Venice'.[76] Both Lord Chief Justice Heath and Archbishop Laud made the comparison at the Star Chamber trial of the puritan William Prynne in 1634.[77] A manuscript satire of 1638 described the puritans as 'the Jesuits of the English Church', albeit not genuinely 'of our Church', since they were 'as farre in opinion from the Church of England ... as the Papists bee'.[78]

It was therefore not opportunism when royalist propagandists accused puritans of acting on popish principles in 1641–2: this was something always believed by the types of people who identified with the vision of government in church and state promoted by those who championed the cause of Charles I on the eve of the English Civil War. Furthermore, it was indeed the case that both the Covenanters in Scotland and the puritans and parliamentarians in England, in justifying their forcible resistance to Charles I's government, utilised arguments that had first been developed by Catholic resistance theorists, and in particular by Jesuits.[79] Royalist polemicists of the 1640s made the allegation that the parliamentarian-puritan position was popish time and time and time again. As Sir Robert Filmer succinctly put it, 'the only point of Popery is the alienating and withdrawing of Subjects from their obedience to their Prince, to raise Sedition and Rebellion', and so 'Popery and Popularity agree in this point'.[80] The charge of popery against the enemies of Charles I was so widely made that parliamentarian authors found it necessary to try to refute it.[81]

Within the parliamentarian alliance, different Protestant interests accused each other of popery. Independents accused Presbyterians of popery for persecuting people for their religious beliefs. Presbyterians accused Independents and sectarians of popery for developing king-killing theories and supporting the regicide in 1649. Cavaliers likewise thought Presbyterians, Independents and the sects guilty of popery for the self-same reasons.[82] This is why anti-popery was a species of ideology. More accurately, it was several distinct ideologies, reflecting discrete conformist Anglican (episcopalian), puritan, Presbyterian, Independent, sectarian – even separate Baptist and Quaker – religio-political values and agendas.

Once these ideologies became entrenched, they proved particularly robust and resilient. Anti-popery, and the types of argument found in anti-popish polemic, did not change much over the course of the seventeenth century. What changed was the historical context, which structured how relevant, poignant or effective a particular strand of anti-popish polemic was likely to be at any given moment. For example, from the 1670s onwards, with the growing international threat posed by France (which had risen to replace

Spain as the dominant Catholic power in Europe) and the prospect of a Catholic heir succeeding to the English Crown – and especially after the revelations of the supposed popish plot in the summer of 1678 – there did again appear to be a genuine threat to the security of the Protestant religion in England. Likewise, as France began to rescind the liberties formally granted to its Protestant inhabitants from the late 1670s and early 1680s, and French Huguenots started arriving in England as they fled persecution in their homeland, the idea that Catholicism was a persecuting religion and therefore that a future Catholic king of England would also probably persecute his Protestants, as had the last Catholic ruler in England Mary Tudor, seemed all the more credible. The specific arguments that the Whigs made against popery in the late 1670s and early 1680s were not in themselves particularly new; it was the context that gave them such powerful purchase at this time.[83]

The same might be said about the way the Tories sought to turn the charge of popery against the Whigs. Their arguments were not new: they were exactly the same as those developed by supporters of the Crown against the puritans and parliamentarians in the 1640s, although they had not been new then either. What was new in the late 1670s and early 1680s was that what previously had merely been a prediction of what could potentially happen had since come true. The puritans *had* rebelled against the king, in the 1640s, and they had gone on to destroy the Church of England, execute Charles I and set up a republic. They had achieved everything that the Pope, ever since the Reformation, had tried but failed to achieve. There was thus now a history to which Tories could appeal which made their arguments more compelling, and which helps explain why the Tories were more successful in playing the anti-popery card in the early 1680s than their Cavalier predecessors had been in the 1640s. As one Tory writer complained in 1681, the Whigs 'under the notion of crying against Popery and Arbitrary Government, would pull down the King and the Bishops, and set up a Common-wealth again'.[84] 'What is term'd Pop'ry?', asked a Tory rhymester: 'To Depose a King. What's true Presbytery? To Act the Thing.'[85] 'The Papists they would Kill the King', noted a Tory balladeer, 'but the Fanaticks did'.[86] The Tory invocation of this line of anti-popish rhetoric proved remarkably successful, and helped rally public support for the Crown in opposition to Exclusion. The government's success in turning the charge of popery against the Whigs and nonconformists was not the only reason for the defeat of the Exclusionist movement: there were other dimensions (ideological and political) to the Crown's efforts to negate the challenge of the Whigs.[87] The point to emphasise here, though, is that the power, purchase and persuasiveness of a particular polemical construct, or stereotypical representation, was determined not solely by the stereotype itself, but also crucially by the context in which it was deployed.

Conclusion

This chapter has sought to explore some of the conceptual and methodological problems involved in the analysis of religious and national stereotyping in seventeenth-century England. Although the drive to stereotype, we have been taught, comes from the need to categorise and simplify in order to make sense of a complex world, in fact stereotypes were themselves complex cultural constructions. They were multivalent composites that blended different concepts and even at times discrete stereotypes that may or may not have been internally consistent. Moreover, the sources at our disposal are themselves far from straightforward, and it is not always easy to tell the extent to which they reflect culturally embedded stereotypes or a given author's ideological agenda. Accounts which, on the surface, seem to reflect what the seventeenth-century English thought of the Scots, puritans or Catholics, say, might be telling us not only what a particular author thought of the Scots, puritans or Catholics, but also what he hoped he could persuade others to believe. Thus, our sources are frequently polemically charged and ideologically laden.

Nor do the stereotypes we have been looking at reveal, in any uncomplicated way, the prejudices of the seventeenth-century English. It is true that contemporaries did prejudge based on existing stereotypes – they saw in stigmatised out-groups behaviours which the stereotype had taught them to perceive. But Scotophobia, anti-puritanism and anti-Catholicism (and anti-popery as well) were also ideologies, reflections of distinctive political and religious outlooks and opinions. How one saw the Scots (or Catholics or puritans) was dependent upon context (temporal and geographical): they could be feared, loved or ignored to varying degrees depending on circumstances. Furthermore, stereotypical representations were frequently contested, precisely because such representations were recognised as being polemically motivated. As we have seen, many in England refused to buy into the negative representation of the Scots by government supporters in 1638–40 because of their own disagreement with the government's political and religious agenda. The contesting of stereotypes was facilitated by the fact that they were often composites: thus Tories during the Exclusion Crisis could rebut Whig anti-Catholicism by appealing to different aspects of the anti-Catholic stereotype. The seventeenth-century English might well have been prejudiced against foreigners and religious minorities. But a study of national and religious stereotyping – of how polemicists sought to manipulate stereotypes in the service of a particular cause and why they thought doing so was likely to be an effective strategy in mobilising opinion out-of-doors – tells us about so much more than just the prejudices of the English or what they thought of outsiders.

As the chapters in this volume variously attest, such a study also tells us what they thought of each other, why they disagreed so much amongst themselves and what was at stake during this century of political and religious upheaval.

Notes

1 British Library, Additional MS 63,783, fol. 11 (hereafter cited as BL, Add. MS). The Library Catalogue dates the work 'after 1655–*c.* 1700'.

2 The story is recalled in Robert Jamieson, *Cyclopaedia of religious biography: a series of memoirs of the most eminent religious characters of modern times* (London, 1853), p. 72; Andrew Kennedy Hutchison Boyd, *Twenty-five years of St Andrews, September 1865 to September 1890 … in two volumes* (London, 1892), vol. 1, p. 82; Edward John Hardy, *How to be happy though civil: book on manners* (New York, 1910), p. 279. Jamieson clearly believed that the incident actually happened, with the sermon being delivered in St Giles Kirk, Edinburgh by Bruce. Boyd thought the sermon was delivered in St Andrews. Hardy believed the story was about James II. Bruce did deliver a number of fiery sermons criticising the king in the 1590s: James Kirk, 'Bruce, Robert (1554–1631)', *Oxford Dictionary of National Biography* (Oxford, 2004), hereafter cited as *ODNB*, doi.org/10.1093/ref:odnb/3756 (accessed 7 July 2021).

3 BL, Add. MS 63,783, fol. 10^{v}.

4 Variants of 'nowther' are found in medieval English and at a later date in the north of England, but by the early modern period it was mainly a Scottish usage. See *Oxford English Dictionary*, 'nouther'; *Dictionary of the Scottish Language*, 'nowther', www.dsl.ac.uk/entry/dost/nowther.

5 John Ayloffe, 'Britannia and Raleigh', in George deForest Lord et al. (eds), *Poems on affairs of state: Augustan satirical verse, 1660–1714* (7 vols, New Haven, CT, 1963–75), vol. 1, p. 234; Warren Chernaik, 'Ayloffe, John (*c.* 1645–1685)', *ODNB*, doi.org/10.1093/ref:odnb/937 (accessed 7 July 2021).

6 BL, Add. MS 63,783, fol. 10^{v}.

7 My thinking here has been influenced by Walter Lippmann, *Public opinion* (New York, 1922); Gordon W. Allport, *The nature of prejudice* (Cambridge, MA, 1954); Henri Tajfel, 'Cognitive aspects of prejudice', *Journal of Social Issues*, 25 (1969), 79–97; Douglas W. Bethlehem, *A social psychology of prejudice* (London, 1985); C. Stangor and M. Schaller, 'Stereotypes as individual and collective representations', in C. Neil Macrae, Charles Stangor and Miles Hewstone (eds), *Stereotypes and stereotyping* (New York, 1996), pp. 64–82; David J. Schneider, *The psychology of stereotyping* (New York, 2004); Mark Knights, 'Historical stereotypes and histories of stereotypes', in Cristian Tileagă and Jovan Byford (eds), *Psychology and history: interdisciplinary explorations* (Cambridge, 2014), pp. 242–67.

8 BL, Add. MS 47,113, fol. 14.

9 BL, Add. MS 27,419, fol. 37^{v}.

10 BL, Add. MS 27,419, fol. 36. See Margaret T. Hodgen, *Early anthropology in the sixteenth and seventeenth centuries* (Philadelphia, PA, 1964), ch. 7.

11 The relevant historiography is too extensive to be listed here. Works relevant to my argument will be cited in the following notes.

12 Starting with my first book, *London crowds in the reign of Charles II: propaganda and politics from the Restoration until the Exclusion Crisis* (Cambridge, 1987).

13 This point is also discussed in the Introduction, above, pp. 1–2, 15–16, 19–21.

14 Peter Lake, 'Anti-popery: the structure of a prejudice', in Richard Cust and Ann Hughes (eds), *Conflict in early Stuart England: studies in religion and politics 1603–1642* (Harlow, 1989), pp. 72–106.

15 Tim Harris, 'Anti-Catholicism and anti-popery in seventeenth-century England', in Evan Haefeli (ed.), *Against popery: Britain, empire and anti-Catholicism* (Charlottesville, VA, 2020), pp. 23–50. See also the discussions in this volume, pp. 105–7, 199–200, 314 below.

16 John Miller, *Popery and politics in England 1660–1688* (Cambridge, 1973), pp. 13–14, 24.

17 See Nabil I. Matar, 'Muslims in seventeenth-century England', *Journal of Islamic Studies*, 8 (1997), 63–82; and Nabil Matar, *Turks, Moors and Englishmen in the age of discovery* (New York, 1999), ch. 1, who suggests that people across England were more familiar with actual Muslims than we might imagine.

18 Tim Harris, 'Hibernophobia and Francophobia in Restoration England', *Restoration: Studies in English Literary Culture, 1660–1760*, 41 (2017), 5–32.

19 Leonard S. Newman, Tracy L. Caldwell, Brian Chamberlin and Thomas Griffin, 'Thought suppression, projection, and the development of stereotypes', *Basic and Applied Social Psychology*, 27 (2005), 259–66, p. 259.

20 Patrick Collinson, 'Ben Jonson's *Bartholomew Fair*: the theatre constructs puritanism', in David L. Smith, Richard Strier and David Bevington (eds), *The theatrical city: culture, theatre, and politics in London, 1576–1649* (Cambridge, 1995), p. 157. The tendency of people to see the stereotype which they have been taught to believe in has long been documented by social psychologists. See Eunice Cooper and Marie Jahoda, 'The evasion of propaganda: how prejudiced people respond to anti-prejudice propaganda', *Journal of Psychology*, 23 (1947), 15–25.

21 Peter Lake and Isaac Stephens, *Scandal and religious identity in early Stuart England: a Northamptonshire maid's tragedy* (Woodbridge, 2015), show that the negative stereotype of the puritan was based to a certain extent on how puritans actually behaved (e.g. pp. 99, 125, 145, 355).

22 Tim Harris, '"A sainct in shewe, a devill in deede": moral panics and anti-puritanism in seventeenth-century England', in David Lemmings and Claire Walker (eds), *Moral panics, the press and the law in early modern England* (Basingstoke, 2009), pp. 97–116; Peter Lake, 'Anti-puritanism: the structure of a prejudice', in Kenneth Fincham and Peter Lake (eds), *Religious politics in post-Reformation England: essays in honour of Nicholas Tyacke* (Woodbridge, 2006), pp. 80–97; Peter Lake with Michael Questier, *The Antichrist's lewd hat:*

Protestants, papists and players in post-Reformation England (2002), sections 4 and 5; Lake and Stephens, *Scandal and religious identity*, pp. 112–13; Knights, 'Historical stereotypes', pp. 242–67.

23 R. W. Scribner, *For the sake of simple folk: popular propaganda for the German Reformation* (Cambridge, 1981), p. 8; Harris, *London crowds*, pp. 97–8.

24 Folger Shakespeare Library (hereafter cited as FSL), V.a.403, p. 138.

25 The seventeenth-century journalist Marchamont Nedham, in his prospectus from June 1650 for his periodical *Mercurius Politicus*, explained 'the designe of this Pamphlett being to undeceive the People, it must bee written in a Jocular way, or else it will never bee cryed up': Joad Raymond, 'Marchamont Nedham', in Laura Lunger Knoppers (ed.), *The Oxford handbook of literature and the English Revolution* (Oxford, 2012), p. 385.

26 Keith Thomas, 'The place of laughter in Tudor and Stuart England', *Times Literary Supplement* (21 January 1977), 77–81; David Cressy, *England on edge: crisis and revolution 1640–1642* (Oxford, 2006), p. 346; Peter Burke, *Varieties of cultural history* (Cambridge, 1997), p. 78.

27 *London jests: or, a collection of the choicest joques and repartees* (London, 1685), p. 125.

28 Helen Pierce, 'Anti-episcopacy and graphic satire in England, 1640–1645', *Historical Journal*, 47 (2004), 809–48; Bernard Capp, *The world of John Taylor the water-poet*, pt 2 (Oxford, 1994); Cressy, *England on edge*, chs 10, 15; Tim Harris, *Rebellion: Britain's first Stuart Kings, 1567–1642* (Oxford, 2014), pp. 417–19, 464–73.

29 Owen Felltham, *A brief character of the Low-Countries under the States; being three weeks observation of the vices and vertues of the inhabitants* (London, 1652), sig. A4, and pp. 5, 7, 26, 27, 37–8; Maarten Ultee, 'Review article: The riches of the Dutch seventeenth century', *The Seventeenth Century*, 3 (1988), 228–9; Ted-Larry Pebworth, 'Felltham, Owen (1602?–1668)', *ODNB*, doi.org/10.1093/ref:odnb/9269 (accessed 7 July 2021).

30 The book was first published in 1652, although a pirated edition had appeared in 1648 under the title *Three moneths observations of the Low Countries, especially Holland*, in which the text is slightly different. Felltham himself was an Anglican royalist and can hardly be regarded – as Simon Schama characterised him – as a Cromwellian propagandist. Simon Schama, *The embarrassment of riches: an interpretation of Dutch culture in the Golden Age* (New York, 1987), pp. 44, 51, 238, 258, 265–7, 295, 375–9.

31 *The comical pilgrim; or, travels of a cynick philosopher* (London, 1722), pp. 56, 57, 92.

32 The discussion of Wales in *The comical pilgrim* is a reproduction of William Richards, *Wallography: or, the Britton describ'd* (London, 1682), a tract which some scholars have seen 'as quietly subverting the convention of ethnic character writing and pricking the complacency of English readers': John Kerrigan, *Archipelagic English: literature, history, and politics 1603–1707* (Oxford, 2008), p. 38; Michael Roberts, '"A witty book, but mostly feigned": William Richards' *Wallography* and perceptions of Wales in later seventeenth-century England', in

Philip Schwyzer and Simon Mealor (eds), *Archipelagic identities: literature and identity in the Atlantic Archipelago, 1550–1800* (Aldershot, 2004), pp. 153–65.

33 [Humphrey Crouch], *England's jests* (London, 1687), pp. 41–2, tells the story of 'an ignorant Countrey Fellow' who arrives in London and needs to change money and, seeing a large monkey at a stall, gives it half a crown; getting nothing back, he complains to the owner of the shop: 'I gave your Son half a Crown to change, and he will not give it me again, but Laughs at me'. We see the same joke about a Welshman in *The life and death of Sheffery ap Morgan, son of Shon ap Morgan* [London, 1683], pp. 6–7 (though here the Welshman mistakes the monkey for the shopkeeper's 'aged Father'). A joke at the expense of the Welsh circulating in Cambridge in the mid-1620s (BL, MS Sloane 1489, fol. 48): 'an English man and a Welshman arguing which had the richer land the Englishman said he knew a place in England so rich, that throwe a staffe in a field at night, and it would be so overgrowne by morning that one could not see it: the Welshman answered, that was nothing, for put a brave English horse in one of their fieldes at night, he could not be seene in the morning' – appears in *Bogg-witticisms: or, dear joy's commonplaces* [London, 1682?], 44 (#28) as a joke at the expense of the Irish (here set as a dialogue between a French footman and an Irish footman, with their respective speeches written in the appropriate national accents).

34 [Sir Anthony Weldon], *A discription of Scotland* ([Netherlands], 1626), p. 3. For a discussion of whether the attribution to Weldon is correct, see Joseph Marshall and Sean Kelsey, 'Weldon, Sir Anthony (*bap.* 1583, *d.* 1648)', *ODNB*, doi.org/10.1093/ref:odnb/28988 (accessed 7 July 2021).

35 For example: FSL, V.a.345, pp. 38–42; FSL, V.a.402, fols 13–19.

36 *Comical pilgrim*, p. 53.

37 *Mercurius Hibernicus: or, The Irish Mercurie* (London, 1645), pp. 4, 5.

38 John Speed, *England, Wales, Scotland and Ireland described and abridged* ([London?], 1627), sig. X2[v]. Broadside ballads also portrayed more positive images of Scotland and its people: Adam Fox, 'Jockey and Jenny: English broadside ballads and the invention of Scottishness', *Huntington Library Quarterly*, 79 (2016), 201–20.

39 Certainly, *A discription of Scotland* was satirising a genre that was popular at the time, such as the deadly serious Barnabe Rich, *A new description of Ireland: wherein is described the disposition of the Irish whereunto they are inclined* (London, 1610).

40 *Cf.* Fox, 'Jockey and Jenny', pp. 201–2, though my typology differs slightly from his. The English similarly held various stereotypes of the Irish: Harris, 'Hibernophobia and Francophobia'.

41 Roger A. Mason, 'The Scottish Reformation and the origins of Anglo-British imperialism', in Roger A. Mason (ed.), *Scots and Britons: Scottish political thought and the Union of 1603* (Cambridge, 1994), p. 185; Arthur H. Williamson, 'Education, culture and the Scottish civic tradition', in Allan I. Macinnes and Arthur H. Williamson (eds), *Shaping the Stuart world, 1603–1714: the Atlantic connection* (Leiden, 2006), p. 34.

42 William Camden, *Britain, or a chorographicall description of the most flourishing kingdomes, England, Scotland, and Ireland, and the ilands adjoyning*, trans. Philémon Holland (London, [1610]), 'Scotland', p. 5; BL, Add. MS 37,719, fol. 156. *Cf.* John Cramsie, *British travellers and the encounter with Britain, 1450–1700* (Woodbridge, 2015), p. 345.

43 *Political writings: King James VI and I*, ed. Johann P. Sommerville (Cambridge, 1994), p. 24 (from *Basilicon Doron*, written 1598). Highlanders and Lowlanders felt mutual disdain for one another: Kerrigan, *Archipelagic English*, p. 38.

44 Jenny Wormald, 'Gunpowder, treason, and Scots', *Journal of British Studies*, 24 (1985), 159–60; Pauline Croft, 'Libels, popular literacy, and public opinion in early modern England', *Historical Research*, 68 (1995), 277; Alastair Bellany, *The politics of court scandal in early modern England: news culture and the Overbury Affair, 1603–1660* (Cambridge, 2002), p. 170; Kerrigan, *Archipelagic English*, p. 94; J. O. Bartley, *Teague, Shenkin and Sawney: being an historical study of the earliest Irish, Welsh and Scottish characters in English plays* (Cork, 1954), p. 88.

45 Fox, 'Jockey and Jenny', pp. 202–4; Mark Stoyle, *Soldiers and strangers: an ethnic history of the English Civil War* (New Haven, CT, 2005), pp. 73–90, 142–8; David Scott, 'The "Northern gentlemen", the Parliamentary Independents, and Anglo-Scottish relations in the Long Parliament', *Historical Journal*, 42 (1999), 347–75; David Scott, 'The Barwis affair: political allegiance and the Scots during the British Civil Wars', *English Historical Review*, 115 (2000), 843–63; Tim Harris, *Restoration: Charles II and his kingdoms, 1660–1685* (London, 2005), pp. 241–4.

46 Speed, *England, Wales*, sig. X2^{v}; Sir Thomas Craig, *De Unione Regnorum Britanniae tractatus*, ed. and trans. C. Sanford Terry (Edinburgh, 1909), p. 277; *Tom Tell Troath* ([Holland?], [1630?]), p. 7; James Harrington, *The commonwealth of Oceana* (London, 1656), sig. B2.

47 See Chapter 7. On cognitive polyphasia, see Introduction, p. 21.

48 Craig, *De Unione*, pp. 242, 354, 356, 393.

49 The National Archives, SP 16/424, fol. 110.

50 Cambridge University Library, MS Add. 22, fol. 104^{v}; *Choyce drollery: songs and sonnets*, Joseph Woodfall (ed.) (Boston, Lincolnshire, 1876), p. 394.

51 John Taylor, *The impartialest satyre that ever was seen* (London, 1652), p. 6.

52 Brodie Waddell, 'The Evil May Day riot of 1517 and the popular politics of anti-immigrant hostility in early modern London', *Historical Research*, 94 (2021), 713–35.

53 Joseph Black, 'The rhetoric of reaction: the Martin Marprelate tracts (1588–89), anti-Martinism, and the uses of print in early modern England', *Sixteenth-Century Journal*, 28 (1997), 712. For Bancroft's anti-puritanism, see also Patrick Collinson, *Richard Bancroft and Elizabethan anti-puritanism* (Cambridge, 2013).

54 John Harris, *The puritanes impuritie: or, the anatomie of a puritane or seperatist* (London, 1641), p. 2.

55 [Henry Parker], *A discourse concerning puritans*, 2nd edn (London, 1641), p. 55; E[dward] R[eynolds], *Eugenia's teares for Great Brittaynes distractions* (London, 1642), pp. 20, 27.
56 Harris, *London crowds*, chs 5, 6, 7.
57 *The Diary of Robert Woodford, 1637–1641*, ed. John Fielding (Camden Society, 2012), 5th series, vol. 42, pp. 295, 327 (quotation), 361; Lake and Stephens, *Scandal and religious identity*, pp. 226–31, 234–6.
58 Richard Culmer, Junior, *A parish looking-glasse* (London, 1657), p. 4.
59 Scott, 'The Barwis affair'; David Scott, 'Motives for king-killing', in Jason Peacey (ed.), *The regicides and the execution of Charles I* (Basingstoke, 2001), pp. 138–60; Stoyle, *Soldiers and strangers*, esp. chs 4, 7.
60 Kerrigan, *Archipelagic English*, pp. 164–6.
61 John Taylor, *The causes of the diseases and distempers of this kingdom* (London, 1645), p. 6, margin. *Cf.* anon., *A discourse discovering some mysteries of our new state* (Oxford, 1645), p. 15; anon., *A new dialogue; or, a brief discourse between two travellers* (London, 1648), p. 5; Taylor, *Impartialest satyre* (London, 1652), p. 6.
62 Stoyle, *Soldiers and strangers*, pp. 142–8; Scott, 'Barwis affair'; Sarah Barber, 'Scotland and Ireland under the Commonwealth', in Steven G. Ellis and Sarah Barber (eds), *Conquest and union: fashioning a British state, 1485–1725* (Harlow, 1995), pp. 203–5; Sarah Barber, 'The people of northern England and attitudes towards the Scots 1639–1651: "the lamb and the dragon cannot be reconciled"', *Northern History*, 35 (1999), 93–118; Henry Reece, *The army in Cromwellian England, 1649–1660* (Oxford, 2013), p. 132.
63 Edward Symmons, *A loyall subjects beliefe* (Oxford, 1642), pp. 85–9 (quotation, p. 85).
64 Anthony Milton, 'A qualified intolerance: the limits and ambiguities of early Stuart anti-Catholicism', in Arthur F. Marotti (ed.), *Catholicism and anti-Catholicism in early modern English texts* (Basingstoke, 1999), p. 88.
65 Social psychologists call this the sociocultural/social learning model: Diane M. Mackie, David L. Hamilton, Joshua Susskind and Francine Rosselli, 'Social psychological foundations of stereotype formation', in Macrae, Stangor and Hewstone (eds), *Stereotypes and stereotyping*, pp. 41–78; Melinda Jones, *Social psychology of prejudice* (Upper Saddle River, NJ, 2002), pp. 91–4.
66 David Cressy, *Bonfires and bells: national memory and the Protestant calendar in Elizabethan and Stuart England* (London, 1989), chs 7, 9.
67 *Prayers and thankesgiving to be used by all the kings majesties loving subjects, for the happy deliverance of His Majestie, the Queene, Prince, and states of Parliament, from the most traiterous and bloody intended massacre by gunpowder, the 5 of November 1605* [London, 1606?], sig. D2v; Edward Symmons, *A vindication of King Charles* ([London], 1648), p. 69; [Henry Hammond], *Of resisting the lawfull magistrate upon colour of religion* ([London], 1647), p. 33.
68 Cited in Brent Sirota, *The Christian monitors: the Church of England and the age of benevolence, 1680–1730* (New Haven, CT, 2014), p. 51.

69 Tim Harris, 'London crowds and the Revolution of 1688', in Eveline Cruickshanks (ed.), *By force or by default? The Revolution of 1688* (Edinburgh, 1989), pp. 44–64; Tim Harris, *Revolution: the great crisis of the British monarchy, 1685–1720* (London, 2006), pp. 290–306; Milton, 'Qualified intolerance'; John Walter, *Understanding popular violence in the English Revolution: the Colchester plunderers* (Cambridge, 1999).

70 Matthew Newcomen, *The craft and cruelty of the churches adversaries, discovered. In a sermon preached at St Margarets in Westminster, before the honourable House of Commons assembled in Parliament. November 5, 1642* (London, 1643), p. 62; Huntington Library (hereafter Hunt. Lib.), EL MS 7732, 'Answers to quaries touching the Covenant'.

71 Harris, *Rebellion*, pp. 300–21; Anthony Milton, *Catholic and reformed: the Roman and Protestant churches in English Protestant thought, 1600–1640* (Cambridge, 1995), pp. 60–92.

72 Harris, *Rebellion*, pp. 392–3, 468; Harris, 'Anti-Catholicism and anti-popery'.

73 Harris, *London crowds*, chs 6, 7; Harris, *Restoration*, pp. 237–52, 263–92.

74 Cooper and Jahoda, 'Evasion of propaganda'.

75 Richard Bancroft, *A sermon preached at Paules Crosse, the 9 of Februarie, being the first Sunday in the Parleament, anno 1588* (London, 1588[/9]), pp. 52, 79, 81, 90, 94; Mary Morrissey, *Politics and the Paul's Cross sermons, 1558–1642* (Oxford, 2011), pp. 208–13.

76 James I, *An apologie for the Oath of Allegiance ... together with a premonition* (London, 1609), p. 44; in Elizabeth Read Foster (ed.), *Proceedings in Parliament, 1610* (2 vols, New Haven, CT, 1966), vol. 2, p. 103; David Calderwood, *The true history of the Church of Scotland* (Edinburgh?, 1680), pp. 784–5.

77 Hunt. Lib., HM 80, fols 23[v], 50.

78 Hunt. Lib., HM 60666, 'A new ballad called the Northampton-shire high constable', fol. 21[v]; Lake and Stephens, *Scandal and religious identity*, p. 84.

79 Quentin Skinner, *The foundations of modern political thought* (Cambridge, 1978).

80 Sir Robert Filmer, *The anarchy of a limited or mixed monarchy* (London, 1648), sig. A3[v].

81 William Bridge, *The wounded conscience cured, the weak one strengthened, and the doubting satisfied* (London, 1642[/3]), p. 32.

82 Miller, *Popery and politics*, pp. 85–6; Harris, 'Anti-Catholicism and anti-popery'.

83 Harris, *London crowds*, ch. 5; Harris, *Restoration*, ch. 3.

84 *Plain dealing; or, a second dialogue between Humphrey and Roger* (London, 1681), [p. 1].

85 *Interrogatories; or, a dialogue between Whig and Tory* (London, 1681).

86 'The downfal of the good old cause', in Nathaniel Thompson (ed.), *A choice collection of one hundred and eighty loyal songs* (London, 1685), p. 13.

87 Harris, *Restoration*, chs 4, 5.

2

On thinking (historically) with stereotypes, or the puritan origins of anti-puritanism

Peter Lake

In this chapter I want to talk about puritanism as a stereotype and about anti-puritanism, a discourse organised around that stereotype as an ideology, by which I mean a way of looking at the world and explaining what has gone wrong with it and what to do about it. Anti-puritanism provided a narrative, or series of narratives, about the recent past, the present and immediate future, a narrative that identified the villains and heroes of the piece. It thus provided a way of ordering experience, and of explaining things; of making appeals for support, and generating agendas for change and plans for action. A product of the post-Reformation in England, the stereotype of the puritan and the ideology of anti-puritanism that accreted around it might be thought to offer a perfect opportunity to study the development of a stereotype from its first inception, until, by the early eighteenth century, it morphed into something else.

It has long been a commonplace that the word 'puritan', and the stereotypes and ideologies that attended it, were a product of people who did not like the things being evoked or described by the term. This was a concept developed, not by the people subsequently known as puritans, but rather by their enemies. Thus, the conventional account sees 'puritan' as a pejorative term, a moniker, and an identity, to which no one would lay claim, not at least until very late in the game. As I hope to argue below none of this is quite right.

In the received account, the origins of anti-puritanism are threefold. They are to be found first in the polemical response to puritan arguments for further reformation, arguments which culminated in the Presbyterian movement for root and branch ecclesiastical reform, the conformist response to which produced massive, and sometimes abstruse, works of formal polemic written by ambitious clerical defenders of the ecclesiastical status quo: men like John Whitgift, John Bridges, Richard Bancroft, Matthew Sutcliffe, Richard Hooker. Starting in the 1570s, this move reached its culminating point in the 1590s, with the final official push against the puritan movement.[1]

While they might draw upon, these highly wrought polemical texts could not be collapsed into, the second source of anti-puritan animus which can be found in an altogether more demotic, 'popular' and spontaneously hostile set of responses to the evangelical efforts of a certain sort of rigourist puritan preachers and their lay followers and backers. Thirdly, it has been argued that these two long-standing forms of anti-puritan thought and feeling came together in an outburst of pamphleteering and popular theatrical performance provoked by the Marprelate tracts of the late 1580s, the result of which was the instantiation of the figure of 'the puritan' within the cultural scripts and political imaginary of post-Reformation England.

The Marprelate tracts were short, sharp pamphlets of remarkable vituperative energy and satiric bite that not only made the Presbyterian case for further reformation in the most uncompromising of terms, but also subjected the ecclesiastical authorities to a quite unprecedented series of *ad hominem* assaults. The Martinist assault provoked a series of responses written by denizens of proto-Grubbe street, like Thomas Nashe, Anthony Munday and John Lyly. These were produced at the behest of Richard Bancroft, Whitgift's right-hand man, subsequently to be Bishop of London and then Archbishop of Canterbury, and thus represented an official, or pseudo-official, recourse to popular pamphleteering, a use of the puritans' own propaganda methods, against the puritan cause.[2]

For all the emphasis on hypocrisy and self-interest that underpinned his analysis of the support base of the Presbyterian programme, even Richard Bancroft had concentrated his very considerable polemical energies on the puritan movement and the Presbyterian platform, rather than on the image of the puritan as a social type or what became known as a 'character'. Indeed, as Patrick Collinson liked to insist, Bancroft rarely used the word puritan. According to Collinson it took the pamphlet replies to Marprelate to connect the popular stereotype of the puritan as a Pharisaical hypocrite and blowhard to the arguments about the nature of the puritan movement and the Presbyterian platform to be found within the formal polemic.[3]

On the back of the anti-puritan offensive of the early 1590s, it was thus the pamphlet press and the popular stage that combined to produce the stereotype of the puritan as an upwardly mobile, proud, presumptuous and utterly corrupt hypocrite, the most famous theatrical examples of which are, of course, Falstaff, Malvolio in *Twelfth Night* and Angelo in *Measure for Measure*.[4] The sins which afflict these figures – greed, gluttony, lust and social ambition – are of the most obvious and (mostly) carnal sort, while their pretensions to piety and biblically inflected modes of speech serve merely as blinds behind which these hypocrites can pursue their own quintessentially carnal ends.

The result of all this, Collinson claimed, was that 'puritanism' was, in effect, the 'invention' of the pamphlet press and the popular stage. It was a chimera, a stereotype, of the most factitious and crude sort, cooked up by the media of the day at the prompting of the most anti-puritan wing of the Elizabethan establishment. Collinson's claims in this regard were part of a more general attempt on his part to collapse modes of piety and practice conventionally labelled 'puritan' into the mainstream of English Protestantism, a manoeuvre rendered all the easier if the stereotype of the puritan was both a relative latecomer and the invention of professional anti-puritans like Bancroft and their creatures amongst the play- and pamphlet-writing classes.[5]

These claims were the occasion of a certain scholarly debate, or, as Collinson once put it in a classically Collinsonian, both self-deprecating and pointed, put-down, a storm in a teacup; a scenario in which he was the cup and I (among others) the necessarily diminutive and ridiculous storm. My main objection to Collinson's contention was then, and remains now, that the stereotype of the puritan as Pharisaical hypocrite was *not* merely an invention of the stage, a product of a largely factitious polemical exchange, with specifically contingent political causes, albeit one with serious and, from Collinson's perspective, malign long-term cultural (and therefore political) consequences. Rather, it had far deeper roots in myriad local encounters between various sorts of self-consciously godly professors of true religion and their less-than-zealous neighbours, in the course of which the notion of 'the puritan' as a hypocritical busybody, a holier-than-thou *arriviste*, an avatar of social division and social control, had emerged.[6] As such the emergent notion or image of 'the puritan' represented something more like a caricature, an (admittedly both malign and mischievous, and often grotesquely overdrawn) exercise in sociological generalisation and category formation, which, certainly by the 1590s, was feeding off existing and readily recognisable forms of behaviour, both ascribed and owned identities.

Thus, despite Collinson's claims to the contrary, while I do not think that the likes of Falstaff, Zeal-of-the-Land Busy or Ananias the deacon were the result of value-free exercises in social reportage, conducted in the back streets and churches of post-Reformation England, I do think that the modes of scripturally infused discourse, the snippets of puritan-speak put into their mouths by Shakespeare and Jonson, were intended to recall to members of the audience patterns of speech and modes of diction that they had indeed heard coming spewing out of the mouths of what I still think we can call real puritans. It was only because that was the case that the audience's attention could be obtained and the jokes be made to work.[7]

This is not to argue that, as a both ascribed and owned identity, an identifiable mode of behaviour and affective style, the notion of the puritan or of puritanism was not discursively constructed and continually contested, but merely that those processes of construction and contestation took place in myriad social interactions, interpretative and vituperative moves and counter-moves, over the course of the twenty or thirty years before the literary spats of the 1590s. In this chapter I want to illustrate and develop that contention by arguing that the stereotype of the puritan and its defining other, the image of the so-called ungodly or the profane, was first elevated to the level of printed discourse and formal argument in the writings, not of the enemies of the godly and their hangers-on and clients amongst the play- and pamphlet-writing classes, but rather in the printed works of the puritans themselves. In short, I want to claim that, at the level of formal, printed discourse and literary contrivance, the stereotype of the puritan was at least as much the creation of those being stereotyped as puritans as it was of their conformist and literary enemies.

In making that case, and in setting it in the appropriate historical and historiographical contexts, I hope I might also be making some contribution to the collective discussion of what stereotypes are and what ideological work they can be taken to be doing.

The birth of the anti-puritan stereotype, or Atheos tells it like it is

To make that case I want to turn to one text in particular, George Gifford's famous tract of 1581, *A briefe discourse of certaine points of the religion which is among the commo[n] sort of Christians, which may bee termed the countrie diuinitie.*[8] Gifford was, for a time, vicar of Maldon in Essex. Deprived during the subscription crisis of 1584, he was later reinstated as town preacher there. Gifford was up to his neck in the Presbyterian movement, serving as the leading light of the Braintree conference and attending various of the clandestine national synods held by the movement throughout the 1580s. On the outs with the ecclesiastical establishment, he yet remained very well connected with the lay elite. He dedicated *A briefe discourse* to Lord Rich and was well regarded by both Burghley and Leicester. He served as a chaplain in the latter's expeditionary force to the Low Countries, ministering there to the dying Sir Philip Sidney. Thus, he survived the collapse of the classis movement and the repression of the early 1590s unscathed and died still in post at Maldon. He was the author of a series of dialogues and pamphlets exploring what he presented as the beliefs of the common folk who made up his flock.[9] His tracts on witchcraft have attracted particular attention, and led to Alan Macfarlane describing him as something like 'a Tudor anthropologist'.[10] More recently his views on the 'country divinity of the people' have proved central to the work of revisionist historians of the Reformation and post-Reformation like Christopher Haigh.

The text in question takes the form of a dialogue between a godly minister, called Zelotes, and one of his parishioners, called Atheos, and contains at its heart a fully realised version of the stereotype of the puritan as proud, preening, Pharisaical hypocrite. This comes spewing out of the mouth of Atheos and is then amplified by the commentary of Zelotes. Here is the puritan as hypocrite and busybody, as 'busy controller'.[11] 'Precise puritans do find fault where there is none; you condemn men for every trifle.'[12] The puritans were 'curious precise fellows, which will allow no recreation'.[13] Despite their pretensions to be animated by 'the spirit', they were presented as grasping aspirants for status and power – 'many of your spiritual men will never be satisfied'.[14] They were 'great scripture men' who, while they pretended to almost superhuman levels of sanctity and learning, were in fact no better, indeed very often a good deal worse, than their neighbours. 'None will deceive a man sooner than they; they will speak a man fair before his face and be ready behind his back to cut his throat.' 'They can say very well, but their deeds are as evil as other men's, for who is more covetous than they.'[15]

Puritans were singular and divisive. 'They will not do as their honest neighbours do, they will be wiser than their betters', and were always 'busy in checking every man'.[16] 'Ever meddling in small matters', they could not keep their nose out of other people's business.[17] 'You precise puritans do find fault where there is none.'[18] But 'holy as ye would seem to be', the puritans had more than enough faults of their own.[19] However, for all that, Atheos alleged, you 'see not your own [sins] but other men's'.[20] Accordingly, Atheos enjoined the godly to 'pull the beam out of your own eye. If every man would look to himself there should not be such finding of fault with other.'[21]

The puritans' spiritual pride and hypocrisy was matched by their 'presumption',[22] which reached its apogee in their claim that 'they know they shall be saved. I think they would make themselves Gods.'[23] 'Men will say they know God hath chosen them. How can they tell ... Did ever God tell them that they are elected?'[24] But while they arrogated salvation to themselves, they preached 'damnation to the people'.[25] 'Nowadays there is nothing among many of ye but damnation, damnation.'[26] 'They would drive men to despair and bring them out of belief with the fear of damnation.'[27]

The origins of these noxious habits of thought, and the entirely counter-productive preaching style such assumptions produced, were predestinarian. 'They meddle with such matters as they need not, as election and predestination. What should such matters be spoken of among the people. They make men worse.'[28] For 'if a man be chosen for to be saved, let him do as evil as he can, he shall not be damned; and if a man be appointed before he be born to be damned, let him do never so much good, he cannot be saved, and therefore when ye teach this doctrine ye were even as good tell the people that they may live as they lust.'[29]

Obsessed with preaching, the puritan clergy would not shut up, but rather ran at the mouth in the pulpit in myriad 'flying sermons',[30] all delivered more or less extemporaneously without proper preparation. As for their followers, they were forever gadding after sermons, often travelling as much as four or five miles to hear the right sort of preacher. They claimed to be doing this 'to learn to know God', but in fact they did it out of 'vainglory', to set themselves apart and make themselves feel special.[31] But while 'they talk much' they were no better than the rest of us.[32] 'These men are full of the spirit. These are precise fellows, these are holy saints, these think themselves God's fellows', 'better than all other men'. They were 'overfull of the spirit, over precise'.[33] 'They make themselves more holy than they be.'[34]

The result of all this was division and disorder. Confronted by a range of dissentient clerical voices, and different preaching styles, the godly called upon the people to 'try the spirits'; in other words, 'every man is for to judge whether the preacher speak true or false'.[35] This was a recipe, if not for disaster, then at least for division, and predictably enough, now whole towns 'are even divided one part against another since they had a preacher'. Asked who or what was to blame for such ructions Atheos answered 'I think the fault must needs be laid upon the preaching, because they were agreed before that came'.[36]

Such broils were driven on by 'young rash heads and troublesome fellows', newly arrived in the ministry and anxious to make a name for themselves,[37] and by their lay, sermon-gadding, busybody followers. Puritans were opposed to their governors in church and state. Hating bishops, they regularly disobeyed their prince. Defending a reading ministry, Atheos asks 'are not men allowed which are but readers, even by the learnedst in the land. Do ye find fault with the bishops? Or are ye one of those which do not allow of bishops?'[38] 'Are there not many which count themselves very holy, and yet break the queen's law?'[39]

We have here nearly all of the central features of the anti-puritan stereotype of the godly that would persist through the period down to the Civil War and beyond. While in the dialogue it is portrayed spewing out of the mouth of that ordinary punter in the pew, Atheos, it was in fact being introduced into the realm of public discourse defined by print by a leading puritan divine. Here is proof positive that the stereotype of the puritan existed years before the reaction against Marprelate. Indeed, here, in the early 1580s, we have 'puritan' being embraced as a term of self-description.

For, on the other side of the argument, its use as a term of opprobrium is being identified as perhaps the defining characteristic of the ungodly, the profane or the wicked.

> If there be any man which hath a care to know God and seeketh after his word, and will not commit those beastly sins which overflow in all places, then you, which cannot abide to have God's word set forth, devise a number of lies and slanders against them, calling them puritans, rascals and many other such like. On the contrary part, let a man be a common drunkard, a dicer, an ignorant beast which hath no knowledge of God ... he is an honest man.

Notably, Gifford defines the term 'honest' men as those who 'liveth as the most do'.[40]

All of which explained the extreme hostility with which the ungodly responded to the charitable reproofs of their godly neighbours. As Zelotes told Atheos

> ye know not that which the lord commandeth in sundry places, that we should admonish, and reprove one another, if any do amiss [and yet] ye cannot abide to be admonished, when ye commit any naughty thing ... When a man doth, after a godly manner, admonish ye, he is by and by a busy meddler, what hath he to doe, he shall not answer for you. And because ye may not do what lewdness ye list uncontrolled, ye say it was never merry since every man might read the scriptures.[41]

If, no matter how 'foul' or 'beastly' the relevant 'vice', 'crime' or 'sin' might be,[42] a man's first response to any admonition was to 'stamp and stare like mad men', and declare himself 'at deadly hatred with' the person doing the 'admonishing',[43] then he had, *ipso facto*, outed himself as one of the ungodly, just as surely as his interlocutor had been identified as, in all likelihood, one of the godly. It was, after all, a signal work of 'charity to look unto others, and to convert them from their sin, if they can',[44] and, therefore, a central characteristic of the godly to admonish their fellow Christians 'after a godly manner',[45] 'according as God commandeth',[46] and an equally certain sign of an 'obstinate' member of the ungodly to resent the hell out of them for so doing.

Such behaviour marked the opponents of the godly as agents of the devil himself. 'For those which do take part with those wicked men, and rail upon those which are godly, do fight under the same standard and seek to uphold the kingdom of the devil, labouring for to overthrow the gospel and to banish God's word.'[47] 'The more careful a man is to be holy to the lord, the more he is disdained and disliked, which doth evidently show that such as you are led by the devil.'[48] 'So long as a man is void of religion and maketh profession of no more than they do; so long, although he be full and swarm with great vices, he is an honest man, but let him follow the word and be careful to amend, then there is no lewder fellow upon earth, divers slanders be raised, things shall be reckoned up which he did seven years ago, and now they hate him like a dog.'[49]

All of which explains the seeming paradox that the anti-puritan stereotype is to be found first achieving both fully rounded literary expression and the apotheosis of print, not in the works of the puritans' enemies, still less (as Collinson would have it) in some anti-Martinist squib, but rather in text authored by a leading puritan divine. Gifford's book was intended to be an entirely recognisable representation both of the sorts of thing that were regularly being said about puritans, and of the attitudes and assumptions regularly being displayed by puritans, both in this book and in real life. In a staggering display of precisely the sort of self-righteousness and presumption of which their enemies were coming so vehemently to accuse the puritans, Gifford clearly thought that his account of the image of 'the puritan' and of the uses to which that image was put, would be so self-evidently malign, or as he put it in the dialogue, so self-evidently 'atheistical', popish and demonic, that merely by putting these things on the printed page he could identify the enemies of the puritans as the wicked or the profane and vindicate the puritans as what they took themselves to be; that is to say, as simply 'the godly'; personifications of true religion, the spreaders of saving knowledge and gospel light amongst a populace sunk into ignorance and irreligion by the combined efforts of the devil and his agent, Antichrist.

Moreover, as the logic of his own argument demanded that he should, Gifford owned the term puritan as a description of his own position, if, that is, that position were rightly understood.

> I abhor the error of the Catherists or puritans, I confess that I am loaden with corruptions: if that be your meaning, to charge me with that opinion, which is wicked and devilish. But if ye take the name puritan for one which hath more care to obey God than the common sort, and therefore laboureth to keep himself pure and unspotted of the world (as Saint James speaketh), then look to it, that ye be not found among those which revile not men but God. If ye mean by precise men, those which are so scrupulous, as to make sin where there is none, as your words doe plainly shew, then do I utterly renounce that name for to be called precise, and I disallow such fond persons, whosoeuer they bee. But I know you mean those which walk precisely as Saint Paul willeth, and doe take heed to their ways: not condemning men, but admonishing them, not in trifles, but in weighty matters: although you count them trifles. The commandments of God (at the least some of them) are but trifles with you. You see not, nor consider, how great the Lord God is, and therefore ye dare affirm divers sins done against him to be but trifling and small, ye measure not sin with a true measure, when ye do measure it after the rule of a man. Ye do not know wherefore there is eternal death threatened against

every small sin: ye marvel at that, because ye are blind and cannot judge how great he is, whose will is disobeyed.[50]

Thus are decades of nonsense talked about 'puritan' being simply a term of abuse that no one would own or admit refuted by the simple expedient of reading the sources and returning the use of the word by the puritans themselves to the context provided by the stereotyping, inversionary discourses in which it was first developed and deployed.

On taking texts seriously, not literally

In large part by ignoring that discursive context, historians have managed to make something of a mess of interpreting texts like Gifford's and thus have missed the ideological work that the notion of the 'puritan' was doing for a variety of contemporaries, including the puritans themselves. In discussing the resulting confusions and elisions I shall be dealing most obviously with certain central strands in the recent historiography of post-Reformation England. But as an effect of that discussion I shall also, I hope, be commenting on the ways in which historians might best exploit the stereotypes generated by contemporaries to make sense of their own concerns and experience as genuinely historical evidence, as well as literary and cultural tropes.

On one hand Christopher Haigh has cited Gifford's account, along with that provided by another Essex puritan minister, Arthur Dent in his *Plain man's pathway to heaven,* to prove just how unpopular Protestantism was with the people. This is part of his larger revisionist project to demonstrate that the English Reformation had no longer-term or deep structural causes, met no deep-seated ideological or spiritual needs, but was rather a function of the entirely contingent course of high Tudor politics. Because of this, as an attempt to change the religion of the mass of the people, the Reformation was more or less doomed to fail. Haigh in effect equates Gifford's puritanism with Protestantism *tout court* and uses Atheos's consistent rebuffs of Zelotes's arguments, and indeed Zelotes's own claim, for instance, 'that where there is one of these towns which are forward, there bee five which are not',[51] to prove that the people did indeed prove impervious to the rigidly predestinarian rigourism being peddled by the godly. This was true, such texts imply, even in areas like Gifford and Dent's Essex or Josias Nichol's Kent, where Protestantism was supposedly strong, let alone in places like Haigh's own more conservative, indeed Catholic-riddled, Lancashire.[52]

In response, others have argued that, for all of his distaste for the puritans and his claims that they simply could not engage with the religion of the people, Haigh is in effect placing enormous interpretative faith in the comments of the godly about that religion. Noting the centrality to the puritans' view of themselves, and of the world, of a rigid, binary opposition between the godly and the ungodly, such historians have argued that the polarities inscribed in Gifford's and Dent's accounts were seriously overdrawn and tell us at least as much about the nature of the puritans' own views as they do about the nature of contemporary social reality. In other words, such puritan jeremiads are not literally to be believed.

Others, drawing on the evidence of certain sorts of cheap print – on murder pamphlets and other cheap, sensationalised and providentialised pamphlets and plays – have argued that even a heavily predestinarian and providential form of Protestantism might, under the right circumstances, have achieved considerable traction with at least elements of the people, that is to say, with the social groups beneath the landed, mercantile and professional elites.[53]

Others still, most notably Alec Ryrie, have pushed such arguments further.[54] Observing that most early modern English people probably regarded themselves as neither simply godly nor profane, but rather a bit of both, they have sought to assimilate the resulting middle ground to a consensual Protestant mainstream, stretching virtually without change from the 1520s to *c.* 1640. This is to collapse puritanism into Protestantism, but not in order, with Haigh, to characterise the resulting, narrowly predestinarian, word- and sermon-based style of piety as a failure, but rather to identify a consensual, emotionally intense, prayerful Protestantism as a raging success. We have gone here something like full circle, returning within thirty years to a version of the Protestant triumphalism against which Haigh and the other revisionists were (quite rightly) reacting in the 1970s.

While one might not agree with everything that the likes of Christopher Haigh ever said, the best way to respond to revisionism is not (with Alec Ryrie) simply to act as though it had never happened. Indeed, with its stably consensual post-Reformation Protestant mainstream replicating almost perfectly Eamon Duffy's equally Panglossian (and consensual) account of pre-Reformation Catholicism,[55] Ryrie's work seems to me to be an object lesson in how not to respond to revisionism. We are in danger, in short, of another outbreak of Catholics and Protestants, and indeed of intra-Anglican polemicising, of the sort which used to dominate the historiography of the English Reformation. This, to me at least, is decidedly not an advance.

Mere Christianity – Atheos style

One way to respond to both Haigh and Ryrie is to return to George Gifford. Throughout his tract Gifford tried very hard to characterise the positions he attributed to Atheos as atheistical and popish, indeed as in effect satanic, since they represented precisely the sort of subtle, serpentine and apparently commonsensical arguments devised by the fiend, throughout human history, to obstruct the progress of true religion. But what Gifford actually portrayed was, in effect, an alternative version of Christianity, of the role of the clergy and of the nature of the Christian community; one that, while it was deeply antipathetic to his own style of Protestant rigourism, was arguably just as much a product of the somewhat episodic course of the English Reformation as his own style of piety.

Atheos is committed to a vision of social unity based on various forms of sociability and recreation that are viewed by Zelotes as simply sinful. He values clergymen who do not preach, or if they do, do not preach 'damnation' in the style of the puritans, but rather seek to preserve peace and good neighbourhood amongst their flock, eschewing the disruptive admonitions of petty offences. Such a minister goes along to get along, joining his parishioners in the harmless recreations of the ale bench or May game. 'He will seek for to make them friends for he will get them to play a game or two at bowls or cards and to drink together at the ale house. I think it a godly way.'[56]

As for his personal piety, Atheos is no moral incompetent. 'I can tell when I do well and I can tell when I do evil.'[57] He trusts that 'God will not require more at my hands than I am able to do',[58] and takes comfort from his own efforts 'to live honestly, serve God and think no man any harm'.[59] 'I thank God I can bring many to testify that I am an honest man and always have been.'[60] 'I am no thief, no murderer, nor traitor, I pay every man his own. I think this is God's bidding.'[61] In terms of formal religious profession he asks, 'what should unlearned men', that is to say, 'plain country men, plough men, tailors, and such other', 'meddle farther than to say the ten commandments, the Lord's prayer and the articles of faith'?[62]

But his is no simple works theology. He knows that he is a sinner, as are all men, even, perhaps especially, the puritans, and takes comfort from the fact that, in a fallen world, the best that anyone can do is 'repent, call for mercy and believe'.[63] 'Because Christ shed his blood for us I look for to be saved by him, what would you have me more?' 'I trust I believe as well as any scripture man of them all.'[64] He believes, because the bible told him so, that at 'what time soever a sinner doth repent him of his sin, God will forgive him'.[65] 'If a man be sorry and ask God forgiveness is he not even as good as those which are the most precise; the mercy of God must save all, and what would you have a man care for more than to be saved?'[66] Indeed, on this basis, he claims to have as 'good a faith and as good a soul to Godward as the best learned of them all'.[67]

Over against the strenuous, predestinarian, scripturally infused piety of the puritans, he opposes a vision of Christian profession based on the discharge of social duty and the maintenance of good neighbourhood, described under the rubric of 'love', a quality he ascribes to a golden age before the rise of puritan preaching. 'Now there is no love, then they lived in friendship and made merry together; now there is no good neighbourhood, now everyman is for himself, and we are ready to pull one another by the throat.'[68] Later, he writes,

> If a man labour all the week truly and honestly, and upon the Sabbath day come to the church and make his prayers, shall we say God regarded not his prayer, because he doeth not understand what he prayeth: his intent is good, he doth his good will: he hath a wife and children to provide for, he must follow the world, and let preaching go, or else he shall beg: and so long as he doth hurt no man, but dealeth uprightly: I think God doeth require no more at his hands. Such as have naught else for to doe, let them seek for knowledge.[69]

There is, of course, more than an element of caricature at work here. For Gifford is constructing a stereotype of the works righteousness of the ungodly against which the true godliness of the puritan can emerge, and by which the truth of the positions being pushed in the dialogue by Zelotes about the nature of true faith, the real terms upon which salvation is offered by a perfectly just and perfectly merciful God to sinful humanity, can be vindicated.

But just as with Gifford's evocation of the stereotype of the puritan, so here we can, I think, detect claims, indeed patterns of speech, that Gifford had heard and committed to memory and out of a pastiche of which he had constructed his account of the 'country divinity'. Certainly, in his *Plain man's pathways to heaven*, Christopher Haigh has gone to great lengths to corroborate the attitudes ventriloquised by Gifford, and his fellow Essex minister Arthur Dent, by trawling through and source-mining vast quantities of church court records. It is not clear to me that church court records provide any more direct or unfiltered access to contemporary social reality than the printed tracts produced by the likes of Gifford, but the fact that so many echoes and parallels can be found between a range of very different sources certainly confirms that for all its highly wrought constructedness there might be more than a grain of truth in Gifford's account of 'the country divinity'.

Being Protestant, Atheos style

Haigh's aim in thus corroborating the findings of the likes of Gifford and Dent was a way of confronting his critics and defending his own views about the inherent conservatism of the people, about what he terms elsewhere 'the continuity of Catholicism in the English Reformation'[70] and thus about the inherent unpopularity of Protestantism and the failure of the Reformation. But it would be a mistake to view the position attributed by Gifford to Atheos as anything like Catholic, or even, in any simple sense of the word, 'conservative'.

To begin with Catholicism, Atheos was portrayed as having absolutely no truck with the pope or with popery. 'I defy popery as much as the best of ye all.'[71] 'What tell ye me of the pope. I care not for him. I would both he and his dung were buried in the dunghill.'[72] Not only does he oppose the pope and popery now, he denies that even under Mary he had ever committed idolatry, for while when papists 'bowed unto images' they 'put devotion in it, I meant no such thing, but to be obedient to law'.[73] 'I never put any trust in images, nor thought they could do me any good.'[74] 'So long as I did keep my conscience and heart to God, I trust I did well.'[75] As Gifford noted, this position was designed to allow a certain Nicodemite conformity to a variety of even overtly Catholic or popish outward forms, which meant that, if things changed and 'it go with the laws of princes' to do so, those espousing such views could and almost certainly would conform again to popery. 'For ye use popish reasons to excuse your falling from God by idolatry, and whereby a man may easily see that you are ready unto it again if time served.'[76]

But the works theology that Gifford attributes to Atheos – Zelotes at one point remarks that 'I perceive you are a free will man, one of those that think by natural understanding to conceive of the mysteries of God' – bears none of the characteristics of Catholicism.[77] There is no trace of purgatory, of the cult of the saints, of the necessity for intercessory prayer or spiritual sacrifice. That is to say, all of the central defining marks of pre-Reformation Catholicism identified by Eamonn Duffy and others are notable only for their complete absence from Atheos's position. His hopes for salvation are located entirely outside anything resembling a Catholic economy of grace or penitential cycle.

At one point Atheos does exclaim that 'I pray God I may have time to repent at the end', but Zelotes does not seek to assimilate that sentiment to popery, merely observing that 'this reason' should be termed 'the porter of hell, for it openeth even the widest gate, that a thousand may go in on a rank'.[78] Again, there may be a trace of the Catholic distinction between damning and venial sin in Atheos's distinction between really serious sins, such as theft, murder or treason, and minor infractions, which he calls 'small matters' and Zelotes disgustedly describes as 'swearing, railing, talking in your filthy ribaldry, singing foul and beastly songs, these and such like are your petty faults'.[79] Again, when Atheos is admonished by Zelotes for swearing 'by my faith' he dismisses the practice as a mere peccadillo – 'I am not so precise as to make any account of swearing by my faith'. For Zelotes however it is an offence against the majesty of God and the cause of true religion.[80]

Admittedly, at times, Atheos cites approvingly the doings of his 'forefathers'. Of those that were not learned, he asks 'what should they do otherwise than their fathers before them. I knew some of their fathers, honest men, and never troubled themselves that way.'[81] In the face of Zelotes's unyielding denunciation of idolatry, Atheos responds that 'if you say true, then all our forefathers should be condemned, because they did worship images. I doubt not but God was as merciful unto them as he is unto men now. I think they pleased God better than we do now. Let us not stand so much in our own light.'[82]

Evidently, while happy enough to repudiate the pope and all his works, Atheos is much less willing condemn the doings of 'our forefathers' whom he tends to assimilate to a golden age of good neighbourhood and Christian love, far preferable to the fractiously divisive present. But he makes no attempt to assimilate or associate that lost golden age with Catholicism, locating it rather in a hazy period before the likes of Zelotes came on the scene. Thus while anything but hot Protestant, such views fall well short of anything that we, or more importantly for our purposes Gifford, felt comfortable calling overtly or simply Catholic.

Zelotes is certainly anxious to tar Atheos with the brush of popery, observing at one point that he is as 'crammed as full of popish dross as you can hold',[83] but, in fact, the position Atheos actually espouses locates his hopes of salvation in his own faith, the power of Christ's sacrifice and the mercy of God in Christ. Indeed, his insistent claims that since all men are sinners, all that anyone can do is have faith, repent and beg for divine mercy might be taken to represent a sadly watered-down internalisation of justification by faith alone, and certainly a repudiation of anything remotely resembling a Catholic theology of works.[84]

To all this can be added Atheos's excoriation of the puritans' disobedience to the prince and opposition to the bishops and his own repeated expressions of dutiful submission to authority. When Zelotes remarks that 'I know there be many which care not for the pope, but yet believe much of his doctrine. They be those which we call atheists, of no religion, but look whatsoever any prince doth set forth, that they will profess', Atheos replies that 'I think that is good, ought we not to obey our princes, and would ye have us to take upon us for to be wiser than they and their councilors?'[85]

Atheos is thus an avowedly loyal member of the English national church; a strident opponent of the pope and all his works, for all his nostalgia for a lost golden age of good neighbourhood and love, and for all his deference to his forefathers, he never associates such views with the old religion, or regrets the religious changes of Elizabeth's reign. Rather he restricts himself to rabid expressions of hostility to puritans. Atheos, then, is a certain sort of protestant, albeit not of a kind to gladden the heart of the likes of Gifford, or of his alter ego Zelotes or indeed of historians like Alec Ryrie whose version of the 'Protestant mainstream' excludes even Richard Hooker, let alone poor Atheos and his ilk.

Enter the 'church papist'

In thus excluding this strand of opinion from the magic circle of Protestant rectitude described in his book, Ryrie is in fact following a lead provided by Gifford himself. For in 1582, a year after he published *A briefe discourse*, Gifford produced another *Dialogue betweene a Papist and a Protestant, applied to the capacitie of the vnlearned.* In the dedicatory epistle he observed how 'some do wonder how it should come to pass that among us there should be so many which, being born since the gospel was restored to this land, are so zealously addicted unto popery, which they never did know'.[86] Just what sort of 'popery' was at stake became evident in the opening pages of the book, where Gifford explained that, while there are 'papists which will not come at the church', there were others 'which can keep their conscience to themselves and yet go to church'; indeed, he proceeded to finger his notional popish interlocutor as one such.

When the 'papist' asks Gifford's 'Protestant' just how he could tell that many of those attending the services of the national church were indeed papists – 'how can ye tell what is in men's conscience, you judge very deeply' – Gifford's mouthpiece outlines the characteristics and opinions that defined such people as 'papists':

> Some of them will not stick to maintain such popish opinions, as they know there is no great danger of law for. The simple sort ... speak of a merry world when there was less preaching, and when all things were so cheap that they might have xx eggs for a penny. Other there be that never name papists but Catholics, and if ye reason with them, they do but for argument's sake, not that they say so, but the Catholics say so. Another sort there are, and those are as pestilent as can be, for to the end they may do the greater mischief, they are protestants, but yet if any preacher do zealously beat down popery, he doth rail, he is choleric, he is uncharitable, and so they devise all means possible to disturb him. These and such like are the notes to discern a church papist.[87]

These last were, of course, precisely the opinions and propensities attributed in the previous dialogue to Atheos, now removed from the category

Protestant, which designation Gifford even now tells us many of the owners of such views proudly claimed for themselves and redistributed under the heading of 'church papist'.

What Gifford was doing here was eliding a series of positions that were anything but the same; those who on a particular topic might take what he regarded as a Catholic position; others who reacted to the divisions and aridities of the present religio-political scene with a nebulous nostalgia for a lost golden age before religion got difficult, divisive and demanding, whenever such conditions were taken to have pertained; and lastly those who resented and resisted the rigorously anti-popish preaching of a certain sort of Gifford-style puritan preacher. None of these groups were formally Catholic, nor did they necessarily overlap. Certainly none would have fitted within the category of *church popery* as Gifford's Catholic contemporaries were then starting to deploy it, to denote a group they also called schismatics, that is to say, people who maintained that they remained Catholic in heart and profession, but who also claimed that they could retain that status in the eyes both of God and man, and still go to the heretical services of the national church, at least enough to escape the penalties for recusancy. Those were the people whom the Jesuit missionaries Campion and Parsons had been hoping to convince of the error of their ways, and, by reconciling them to the church of Rome, convert from church popery to recusancy. On this account, while church popery was a term coming into currency at about the same time on both sides of the confessional divide, it did not denote a stable religio-political position or identity. Rather, it meant different things to different people, and operated, particularly on the Protestant side of the equation, as an ideologically and polemically constructed boo-word designed to play up the extent and pervasiveness of the Catholic threat at a moment when the puritans, dislike of whom united all of the groups being excoriated and elided by Gifford, were coming under massively increased pressure from at least parts of the Elizabethan establishment. This means that it is a mistake to take the increasing prevalence of the term to mean the rise of a particular religious identity or strand of opinion. We are dealing here with an ideological construct, developed and deployed for specific purposes, by different groups, each responding to the same politico-religious conjuncture – crudely the multiple and overlapping religious, political and dynastic crises of the early 1580s – in order to further their own particular factional or ideological interests and agendas. As ever, context – and the basic questions of who was doing what to whom, and why – matter enormously. Consequently, leaving the politics out in favour of a mode of cultural analysis that effortlessly spans 'the post-Reformation period' nearly always obscures a good deal more than it reveals.[88]

Quite remarkably, in the dedicatory epistle to his tract, Gifford admitted that the people whom he was grouping together under the moniker 'church papists' were a direct product of Protestant preaching.

> True it is, that our ministry doth fight against them, but yet in such sort that it doth greatly increase them. Seeming and pretending to tread upon those cockatrice eggs for to break them, and so destroy utterly the viperous generation, when as indeed they sit upon them, and so hatch the broods of this evil kind and bring them forth in great plenty. For behold a number cry out against popery and proclaim utter defiance in speech, but their doings are such that for every one which they convert to the gospel, they cause an hundred to revolt, to be hardened in their errors or to fall into flat atheism.[89]

Conventionally enough, Gifford proceeded to lay the blame for all this firstly on 'ambitious' pluralists and non-residents, 'not caring who feed the flock so they may come by the fleece', and secondly on the admission into the ranks of the parish clergy of 'a rout and swarm' of unpreaching ministers, 'not only unlearned idols, which have mouths and speak not', but also 'riotous dicers, gamesters, quaffers, quarrellers, adulterers and such like'.[90] Here are Atheos's 'godly' agents of social unity and Christian 'love' being redescribed as unlearned impostors, louts and hooligans, the very source of the ignorance and obstinacy with which the likes of Atheos met the strenuous evangelism of Gifford and his ilk.

That Gifford chose in 1583 to describe those attitudes as a form of 'church popery' and to blame this on his variously defective – either unlearned or ambitious – colleagues in the ministry was almost certainly a function of the political and polemical conjuncture of that crisis year, when the avatars of the puritan movement like Gifford were attempting to resist Whitgift's drive for conformity with a renewed insistence on the need for a common front against the popish threat – now considerably expanded to include the likes of Atheos and his mates on the ale bench – and a renewed assault on the unpreaching ministers that made up so much of the manpower of the national church.[91] Hard as Gifford tried, in *A dialogue betweene a Papist and a Protestant,* to blame Atheos on the activities of the wrong sort of minister and to type his views as a form of popery, on the evidence of *A briefe discourse* it is difficult not to conclude that Gifford was quite right that the nexus of attitudes attributed to Atheos were indeed a product of the realities of the post-Reformation English church, and that the style of ministry to which they represented a response, indeed against which they represented a reaction, included his own zealously strenuous style of ministry. When Gifford himself tells us that Atheos's style of Christianity was a product of people 'born since the gospel was restored to this land', who thus 'never did know popery', and that many of the people espousing such views proclaimed themselves 'Protestant', I think we can believe him, and them. His move, made between 1581 and 1583, to redescribe them as 'zealously addicted unto popery', effected through his coinage of the neologism 'church papist', perhaps deserves to be regarded with somewhat greater scepticism. Certainly, the ascribed identity as 'church papists', conferred on them by Gifford, seems to be a function of the ascribed identity as a 'puritan', conferred by them on Gifford and his ilk. This was a move made in the very particular political and polemical circumstances of the early 1580s, designed to move Gifford's local adversaries entirely beyond the pale of Protestant respectability and to vindicate puritans like Gifford as stalwarts of all order in church and state.

But turn-around is fair play, and if Gifford's and Ryrie's refusal to admit such people within the magic circle of Protestantism will not wash, neither will Haigh's tendency, on precisely the same grounds, to assimilate such views not merely to the inherent conservatism of the people, but to what he has memorably termed the 'continuity of Catholicism in the English Reformation'. For what we have here is nothing like simple conservatism, nor any sort of continuity. Rather, as Gifford himself more than implies, we should see the position espoused by Atheos as a response to the course of religious change over the past fifty years and thus as a tribute to the very considerable impact, if not the success (certainly as the likes of Gifford or Haigh or indeed Ryrie would define it) of the Reformation. The result is a version of mere Christianity collapsed into the discharge of everyday social obligation and the duties of good neighbourhood. It is a position that would enable the holder of such views to negotiate without risk the switchback changes of the mid-Tudor years, changes which many Catholic and Protestant contemporaries either hoped or feared were by no means done with by the 1580s. It was also a position that would enable its bearers to resist the claims of the various sorts of Christian rigourist to be found on both sides of the confessional divide. Moreover, the central doctrinal or pietistic claims attributed by Gifford to Atheos represented a watered-down version of Protestant doctrines of justification by faith and were legitimated by an overt repudiation of the pope and all his works and attended by elaborate protestations of obedience to the Protestant authorities in church and state.

Thus the position ascribed to Atheos was not so much a product of the changeless rhythms of popular belief, the timeless essence of English Christianity, untouched by the activities and attitudes of extremist minorities like the puritans, but rather of a tense interaction between the claims of the godly and the (often frankly hostile or assertively indifferent) reactions thereto of their neighbours.[92] Indeed, we might argue that the provocation of such a style of piety in reaction to their own rigourism was one of the most important of puritanism's effects on the post-Reformation religious scene. Far from the theatre creating 'puritanism', as Patrick Collinson would have it, might we not be dealing here with the creation, by the insurgent effects of puritanism, of the sort of 'popular Anglicanism' that the likes of Ian Green and Christopher Marsh tend to equate with the inherently moderate and timeless, indeed the positively Hobbit-like, instincts of what J. J. Scarisbrick once called 'English folk'.[93] Neither timeless nor moderate – in its anti-puritanism it was viscerally extreme – this strand of opinion would appear to be the other side of Collinson's tense relationship between the godly and their neighbours and sometime enemies, and as such perhaps one of the most important effects of the English Reformation, and in particular of the activities of the evangelical avant garde of that Reformation, the puritans. My claim here is that all this emerges only if we take stereotypes, like those being formulated and manipulated by Gifford, seriously as ways of thinking about and interpreting the world and as forms of historical evidence.

In the context provided by the post-Reformation Protestant national church, not only does talk of a Protestant mainstream that omits all mention of the strands of opinion represented by Atheos make no sense whatsoever, but if we factor that strand of opinion in to the analysis, it gives new salience to the notion of the puritan and puritanism as a crucial analytic category – a salience that Collinson has used the term's status as a polemical and literary construct, if not altogether to deny, then certainly to underplay, and Ryrie altogether to elide.

Conclusion

But Collinson was, of course, quite right to insist that the modes and models of anti-puritanism set in the late sixteenth century played a central, at times determinative, role in the cultural and religious politics of what we might term the long seventeenth century. The tensions between the godly and the ungodly, and the central, albeit highly ambiguous and contested, role played therein by the figure of 'the puritan', continued to dominate the puritans' view of themselves. Over the succeeding decades the course of anti-puritan polemicising and stereotyping revealed the extent to which the hostile view of the godly attributed by Gifford to his local enemies in 1581 had effectively prefigured subsequent developments. Myriad polemicists and hacks depicted the puritans as proud, ambitious, divisive and overbearing hypocrites, who used their entirely spurious claims to superior godliness, and their starkly bipolar, predestinarian view of the world, both to further their own sinful purposes and to construct a position of privilege and power for themselves, in ways that threatened not merely the harmony of local society, but all order in church, state and society.

As we watch the godly use the ungodly to construct their own position, reproducing as they did so both their own stereotype of the ungodly and the ungodly's stereotype of them, in what seems to me to be a classic exercise in group identity formation,[94] we need to retain a healthy perspectival relativism, and realise that both the godly's view of their enemies and their enemies' view of them were equally plausible, albeit equally overwrought, descriptions of what appeared to those involved to be social reality. For what, when viewed from the inside looking out, appeared to be godly prudence and mutual edification, conducted in the face of a hostile world, looked very different when viewed from the outside looking in. Just like Falstaff, far from being more virtuous and godly than the rest of us, the puritans were a good deal more sinful than the average Christian precisely because of their propensity to use a merely outward pretence of piety to mask their own sinful natures and corrupt purposes.

Certainly, we will get nowhere if, with Alec Ryrie, we simply dismiss such images, and the processes of mutual identity construction of which they formed so central a part, as so many chimeras, mere 'preachers' talk', so polemically motivated and literarily (over)wrought, that they conceal rather than reveal what was *really* going on. Nor will we get much further if, with Christopher Haigh, we simply believe them. Rather, as I have tried to argue, such materials are far from being irredeemably polemical expressions of self-interested political and personal animus that over time ossified into ideal types so crude and schematic as to have nothing to tell us about the real nature of post-Reformation experience or events. Rather, read aright, that is to say, set in the discursive political and cultural contexts which produced them and into which they were, in turn, designed to intervene, we can get rather a lot out of stereotypes.

Indeed, I would argue that if we marginalise or dismiss such polemically constructed images, caricatures and ideal types as expressions of mere prejudice, we will never be able to understand the fraught and contested ideological landscape of post-Reformation England. Indeed, *horribile dictu*, we might even be left with the (entirely false) choice between Ryrie's and (in certain moods, although not in others) Collinson's consensual 'religion of Protestants' on one hand, and Christopher Haigh's and Christopher Marsh's seamless web of popular conservatism and mere Christianity on the other. And almost anything would be better than that.

Notes

1 For those exchanges see Peter Lake, *Anglicans and puritans? Presbyterianism and English conformist thought from Whitgift to Hooker* (London, 1988).

2 Joseph L. Black (ed.), *The Martin Marprelate tracts: a modernized and annotated edition* (Cambridge, 2009); Joseph L. Black, 'The rhetoric of reaction: the Martin Marprelate tracts (1588–89), anti-Martinism, and the uses of print in early modern England', *Sixteenth Century Journal*, 28 (1997), 707–25; Joseph L. Black, '"Handling religion in the style of the stage": performing the Marprelate controversy', in Jane Hwang Degenhardt and Elizabeth Williamson (eds), *Religion and drama in early modern England: the performance of religion on the Renaissance stage* (Farnham, 2011), pp. 153–72. See also Peter Lake with Michael Questier, *The Antichrist's lewd hat: Protestants, papists and players in post-Reformation England* (London and New Haven, CT, 2002), pp. 509–56.

3 Patrick Collinson, 'Ecclesiastical vitriol: religious satire in the 1590s and the invention of puritanism', in John Guy (ed.), *The reign of Elizabeth I: court and culture in the last decade* (Cambridge, 1995), pp. 150–70; see also Patrick Collinson, 'The theatre constructs puritanism', in David L. Smith, Richard Strier and David Bevington (eds), *The theatrical city: culture, theater and politics in London 1576–1649* (Cambridge, 1995), pp. 157–69. Perhaps Collinson's best discussion of this topic, which can scarcely be bettered for its acuity and subtlety, is to be found in a little-known lecture given at the William Andrews Clarke Memorial Library: Patrick Collinson, *The puritan character: polemics and polarities in early seventeenth-century English culture* (Los Angeles, 1989).

4 On Falstaff's puritanism see Kristen Poole, *Radical religion from Shakespeare to Milton: figures of nonconformity in early modern England* (Cambridge, 2000), ch. 1, and Peter Lake, *How Shakespeare put politics on the stage: power and succession in the history plays* (London and New Haven, CT, 2016), ch. 14; on Angelo see Lake with Questier, *The Antichrist's lewd hat*, ch. 15.

5 The *locus classicus* for this attempt is Patrick Collinson, *Religion of Protestants: the church in English society, 1559–1625* (Oxford, 1982).

6 These were claims that, elsewhere in his *oeuvre*, Collinson was only too ready to make himself. Indeed, they constitute a position that Collinson himself has good claims to have originated. On this topic, as well as on a good many others, taking issue with Collinson means appealing from one aspect or tendency within his writing to another. *Cf.* Collinson, *The puritan character*. For something like his final position see Patrick Collinson, 'Anti-puritanism', in John Coffey and Paul C. H. Lim (eds), *The Cambridge companion to puritanism* (Cambridge, 2008), pp. 19–33. See also Peter Lake, 'Anti-puritanism: the structure of a prejudice', in Kenneth Fincham and Peter Lake (eds), *Religious politics in post-Reformation England: essays in honour of Nicholas Tyacke* (Woodbridge, 2006), pp. 80–97.

7 Lake with Questier, *The Antichrist's lewd hat*, ch. 14. *Cf.* Chapter 4 by Lake and Yamamoto in this volume.

8 I have used the following edition: George Gifford, *A briefe discourse of certaine points of the religion which is among the commo[n] sort of Christians, which*

may bee termed the countrie diuinitie (1582). The pages are numbered on one side only so the letter 'a' is used to denote the obverse side of the page.

9 See Brett Usher, 'Gifford, George (1547/8–1600)', *Oxford Dictionary of National Biography* (Oxford, 2004). See also Timothy Scott McGinnis, *George Gifford and the reformation of the common sort: puritan priorities in Elizabethan religious life* (Kirksville, MO, 2004).

10 Alan Macfarlane, 'A Tudor anthropologist: George Gifford's *Discourse* and *Dialogue*', in Sydney Anglo (ed.), *The damned art: essays in the literature of witchcraft* (London, 1977), pp. 140–55.

11 Gifford, *A brief discourse*, p. 2.

12 Gifford, *A brief discourse*, p. 76.

13 Gifford, *A brief discourse*, p. 3.

14 Gifford, *A brief discourse*, p. 5.

15 Gifford, *A brief discourse*, p. 10a.

16 Gifford, *A brief discourse*, p. 17.

17 Gifford, *A brief discourse*, p. 18.

18 Gifford, *A brief discourse*, p. 76.

19 Gifford, *A brief discourse*, p. 78.

20 Gifford, *A brief discourse*, p. 19.

21 Gifford, *A brief discourse*, p. 64.

22 Gifford, *A brief discourse*, p. 22; see also pp. 23 and 36.

23 Gifford, *A brief discourse*, p. 20.

24 Gifford, *A brief discourse*, p. 61.

25 Gifford, *A brief discourse*, p. 1.

26 Gifford, *A brief discourse*, p. 34.

27 Gifford, *A brief discourse*, p. 75.

28 Gifford, *A brief discourse*, p. 24a.

29 Gifford, *A brief discourse*, p. 59.

30 Gifford, *A brief discourse*, p. 49a.

31 Gifford, *A brief discourse*, p. 44a.

32 Gifford, *A brief discourse*, p. 26a.

33 Gifford, *A brief discourse*, p. 27.

34 Gifford, *A brief discourse*, p. 28.

35 Gifford, *A brief discourse*, p. 55.

36 Gifford, *A brief discourse*, p. 46a.

37 Gifford, *A brief discourse*, p. 48a.

38 Gifford, *A brief discourse*, p. 63a.

39 Gifford, *A brief discourse*, p. 83a.

40 Gifford, *A brief discourse*, p. 17a.

41 Gifford, *A brief discourse*, pp. 18–18a.

42 Gifford, *A brief discourse*, p. 65a.

43 Gifford, *A brief discourse*, p. 5a.

44 Gifford, *A brief discourse*, p. 65a.

45 Gifford, *A brief discourse*, p. 18a.

46 Gifford, *A brief discourse*, p. 65.

47 Gifford, *A brief discourse*, p. 17.
48 Gifford, *A brief discourse*, p. 19a.
49 Gifford, *A brief discourse*, p. 47a.
50 Gifford, *A brief discourse*, pp. 76a–7.
51 Gifford, *A brief discourse*, p. 43.
52 Christopher Haigh, *The plain man's pathways to heaven: kinds of Christianity in post-Reformation England, 1570–1640* (Oxford, 2007); Christopher Haigh, 'The taming of Reformation: preachers, pastors and parishioners in Elizabethan and early Stuart England', *History*, 85 (2000), 572–88; Christopher Haigh, 'The Church of England, the Catholics and the people', in Christopher Haigh (ed.), *The reign of Elizabeth I* (Basingstoke, 1984), pp. 195–219.
53 Lake with Questier, *The Antichrist's lewd hat*, section 1; Alexandra Walsham, *Providence in early modern England* (Oxford, 1999).
54 Alec Ryrie, *Being Protestant in Reformation Britain* (Oxford, 2013).
55 Eamon Duffy, *The stripping of the altars: traditional religion in England, 1400–1580* (London and New Haven, CT, 1992).
56 Gifford, *A brief discourse*, p. 2.
57 Gifford, *A brief discourse*, p. 31.
58 Gifford, *A brief discourse*, p. 32.
59 Gifford, *A brief discourse*, p. 31a.
60 Gifford, *A brief discourse*, p. 16a.
61 Gifford, *A brief discourse*, p. 12a.
62 Gifford, *A brief discourse*, pp. 29–30a.
63 Gifford, *A brief discourse*, p. 70a.
64 Gifford, *A brief discourse*, p. 20.
65 Gifford, *A brief discourse*, p. 67.
66 Gifford, *A brief discourse*, p. 66.
67 Gifford, *A brief discourse*, p. 6a.
68 Gifford, *A brief discourse*, p. 5.
69 Gifford, *A brief discourse*, p. 72.
70 Christopher Haigh, 'The continuity of Catholicism in the English Reformation', *Past & Present*, 93 (1981), 37–69.
71 Gifford, *A brief discourse*, p. 38a.
72 Gifford, *A brief discourse*, p. 22.
73 Gifford, *A brief discourse*, p. 40a.
74 Gifford, *A brief discourse*, p. 13a.
75 Gifford, *A brief discourse*, p. 40a.
76 Gifford, *A brief discourse*, p. 38a.
77 Gifford, *A brief discourse*, p. 31.
78 Gifford, *A brief discourse*, p. 66.
79 Gifford, *A brief discourse*, p. 19.
80 Gifford, *A brief discourse*, pp. 63a–4 (and also pp. 76a–7).
81 Gifford, *A brief discourse*, p. 18.
82 Gifford, *A brief discourse*, p. 41a.
83 Gifford, *A brief discourse*, p. 38a.

84 *Cf.* Michael P. Winship, 'Weak Christians, backsliders and carnal gospelers: assurance of salvation and the pastoral origins of puritan practical divinity in the 1580s', *Church History*, 70 (2001), 462–81.
85 Gifford, *A brief discourse*, p. 22.
86 I have used the following 1583 edition: George Gifford, *A dialogue betweene a Papist and a Protestant, applied to the capacitie of the vnlearned* (1583), sig. q3^{r}–[q3^{v}].
87 Gifford, *A dialogue*, sig. A2^{r}–[A2^{v}].
88 *Cf.* Alexandra Walsham, *Church papist: Catholicism, conformity and confessional polemic in early modern England* (Woodbridge, 1993), ch. 5, esp. pp. 100–6.
89 Gifford, *A dialogue*, sig. q4^{r}.
90 Gifford, *A dialogue*, sig. q4^{r}–[q4^{v}].
91 On the politico-religious climacteric of 1583–4 see Patrick Collinson, *The Elizabethan puritan movement* (London, 1967), pt 5, and Peter Lake, *Bad Queen Bess? Libels, secret histories, and the politics of publicity in the reign of Queen Elizabeth I* (Oxford, 2016), chs 5–7.
92 As, for instance, Christopher Marsh would have it. See Christopher Marsh, *Popular religion in sixteenth-century England: holding their peace* (Basingstoke, 2008).
93 Marsh, *Popular religion*; Ian Green, *Print and Protestantism in early modern England* (Oxford, 2000), esp. chs 1 and 10; J. J. Scarisbrick, *The Reformation and the English people* (Oxford, 1984).
94 See Peter Lake, '"A charitable Christian hatred": the godly and their enemies in the 1630s', in Christopher Durston and Jacqueline Eales (eds), *The culture of English puritanism, 1560–1700* (Basingstoke, 1996), pp. 145–83, now considerably expanded in Peter Lake and Isaac Stephens, *Scandal and religious identity in early Stuart England: a Northamptonshire maid's tragedy* (Woodbridge, 2015), ch. 3.

3

History plays, Catholic polemics and the staging of political economy in Elizabethan England

Koji Yamamoto

> But what is a Projector? …
> Why, one that projects ways to enrich men, or to make 'hem great, by suites, by marriages, by undertakings[.]
>
> Ben Jonson, *The Devil Is an Ass* (1:7, 9–12)[1]

The stereotype of the projector played a leading role in the politics and political imaginary of the early Stuart period and beyond. As a literary character, it reached full expression first in the plays of Ben Jonson, most notably *The Devil Is an Ass* (first performed in 1616). Political and economic historians have shown that, in real life, projectors such as Giles Mompesson and William Anys often enjoyed close ties with the successive royal courts of James I and Charles I, and procured numerous grants for monopolies and other privileges that proved highly controversial. Such men, and the character they embodied, were the villains in Parliamentary debates of 1601, 1621 and 1624.[2] When Charles I's personal rule finally collapsed and gave rise to the Long Parliament that opened in November 1640, its members swiftly condemned 'all Projectors and Monopolists whatsoever; … or that do receive, or lately have received, any Benefit from any Monopoly or Project'.[3] The accusations against those projectors and monopolists working for the king and his evil counsellors were central to the political thinking of those who took up arms against the king. Such accusations even fed into the emergence of the Leveller ideology. Projectors and the wrongs perpetrated by them fuelled the constitutional crisis of the mid-century.[4]

Existing accounts (my own included) have tended to trace the figure of the projector back to Jonson's *Devil Is an Ass* quoted at the beginning of this chapter.[5] As we shall see, however, monopolies and other forms of legal and economic policy proved highly controversial by the late 1570s, just at a time when commercial theatres began flourishing in London. Though rarely noted by scholars, texts and performances under Elizabeth addressed these issues head on, in effect offering penetrating accounts of projectors and their vices before the invention of the term. To demonstrate, this chapter concentrates on three Elizabethan history plays that deal most extensively with proto-projectors: George Whetstone's *Promos and Cassandra* (printed 1578), *Thomas of Woodstock* (composed by an anonymous author, 1591–5?) and Thomas Heywood's *First and Second Parts of King Edward IV* (printed 1599).

Some readers might suppose that in order to avoid censorship and punishments plays like these avoided obvious allusion to present politics. This chapter shows the direct opposite was the case: analyses contained in these plays were so politically trenchant as to be comparable to the critique of the Elizabethan regime penned by its sworn enemies: persecuted Catholic minorities. These plays were in some respects even more radical than Catholic writings, especially in highlighting the monarch's culpability, and in stressing the capacity of humbler men and women to judge such matters of state. By the time the Long Parliament condemned 'all Projectors and Monopolists', humbler members of society had indeed adopted the stereotype to question royal policies, just as it had been acted out in Elizabethan plays. Catholic polemics, I argue, can serve as a fresh parameter for evaluating the Elizabethan plays, their latent radicalism and the projector stereotype subsequently elaborated by Jonson.

Revisiting these Elizabethan history plays in context is a timely exercise. While historians studying post-Reformation politics and social relations have taken plays very seriously, there have been fewer comparable reappraisals by scholars interested in early modern economy and state formation.[6] The early modern concept of 'projecting' is now attracting critical attention from across disciplines, including political and legal historians, and historians of the financial and scientific revolutions.[7] Yet few accounts have gone further to trace precursors of the character of the projector. Economic criticism has thrived among literary scholars, but these studies rarely link these history plays explicitly with the rise of controversial projects in the period.[8] By revisiting the Elizabethan history plays we can learn more about the shaping and reshaping of norms, expectations, suspicion and anxieties, something so foundational to economic as well as religious and political relationships.

The main purpose of this chapter, then, is to improve our empirical knowledge about early modern projects and earlier discourses about them. At the same time, this chapter also paves the ground for the next one, co-authored with Peter Lake. While this chapter delineates the political concerns and discursive materials from which the figure of the projector emerged, the next chapter explores the very process of literary construction in the plays of Ben Jonson and other texts of the early Stuart period. They can be read as a pair, two halves of a larger cumulative argument about the origins, construction and deployment of a stereotype in early modern

England. These chapters thereby contribute to illuminate how a powerful new, character-based, heuristic stereotype came to emerge from existing *practices* of stereotyping, the collective effort to discover problematic behaviour and characterise it based on widely held assumptions.

Socioeconomic context and its moral consequences

Before turning to the plays, we need to sketch the socioeconomic conditions and attendant cultural contradictions, broad contexts that shaped both projectors' activities and the terms of praise and blame out of which that stereotype was subsequently made.

Let us start with how things were supposed to work. In 1578 Ferdinando Pulton, a lawyer attached to Lincoln's Inn, published *An abstract of all the penal statutes* then in force. Penal statutes were a body of laws dealing mostly with social and economic issues, under which a convicted offender was to pay a penalty to the Crown. Pulton explained that 'our Princes' had developed these legal codes 'with a fatherly care' so that subjects 'would do the parts of good Children, and obediently observe those ordinances'. The volume showed magistrates and the population 'how to rule, and how to obey'.[9]

Reality was far from such paternalistic ideals because of a series of social and economic dislocations. In the second half of the century England's population grew from 3.1 to 4.2 million. Meanwhile a steady inflow of American silver triggered rapid inflation without a matching rise in real wages.[10] Rural inhabitants were hit especially hard, and many younger siblings left their homes to search for opportunities, giving rise to vagrancy, the wandering of the able poor 'with no settled habitation, occupation or obvious means of support'.[11]

Economic and social polarisation followed.[12] While a huge number of poor people and labourers suffered from stagnant wages and rising prices, more prosperous groups, including 'middling sorts of people', benefited from greater disposable income and trading activities. Houses of local notables became larger, and increasingly were fitted with plaster ceilings, glazed windows and fireplaces with chimneys for increased comfort. Coal consumption grew nationally. The import of wine, currants, raisins, spices increased. Alehouses grew in number too, where those better off enjoyed drinks and showed off their wealth; these sometimes provided lodging for wandering migrants. The sheer scale of commercialisation also led to a steep rise in civil litigation relating to debts and contracts.[13]

At a more modest social level, a vibrant trade in consumer items like linen napkins, gloves, buttons and lace developed thanks in part to extensive and expanding networks of peddlers crisscrossing markets, inns and alehouses. Carried in the peddlers' sacks were also cheap print, including one-sheet ballads and short pamphlets of various sorts. Indeed, the number of printed books and pamphlets grew: according to the *English Short Title Catalogue*, 1,607 titles appeared during the 1550s including reprints and new editions. The number grew to 2,087 for the 1570s, and 3,030 for the 1590s.[14]

Contemporary observers were not necessarily aware of structural causes for these changes, as we now are. They instead focused on people's greed, covetousness, envy and pride. Thus there were two distinct, but related, exhortations about the threat of the tramping poor, the sturdy beggar and the masterless youths on one hand, and corrupt influences of luxury, lust and conspicuous consumption on the other. Yet there were simultaneously more celebratory accounts of the burgeoning prosperity of England, with commentators like William Harrison viewing material wealth and splendour as a sign of national glory and divine blessing.[15]

Nowhere were these contradictions starker than in London, the prime example and engine of the changes surveyed above. Between 1520 and 1600 its population jumped from 55,000 to a staggering 200,000.[16] Luxury and exotic goods flooded into London which boasted the Royal Exchange, newly established in 1565. However, London was also a site of great poverty, exacerbated by the mass migration from the provinces. In fact, the number of those punished as vagrants in London's Bridewell prison rose from 84 for 1559–60, to 188 for 1576–7, and 504 for 1600–1, at a rate greater than the growth in London's population.[17] Thus London was alternately celebrated as the new Troy, the jewel in the crown of an England endowed with unprecedented levels of wealth, and vilified as an epitome of corruption, disorder and ill-gotten wealth, with its alleyways awash with poverty, deprivation, bought sex, theft and criminality.[18]

The commercial theatre was integral to this development. London's first 'public amphitheatre', the Red Lion, opened in 1567, followed by a second permanent public playhouse, The Theatre, in 1576. One estimate suggests that at least 50 million visits to playhouses were made between 1565 and 1642 (when Parliament closed all the theatres), some enjoying plays for as little as a penny a visit.[19] These plays circulated not only as performances, but also as printed pamphlets. Theatres' influence also reached beyond the metropolis, thanks to many touring companies, with the leading company of the time The Queen's Men operating throughout its history without a permanent London base.[20] Critics saw the thriving theatre as an epitome of corruption, a place where a socially and sexually mixed audience could watch depraved stories of lust, tyranny and various sorts of moral deviance and crime acted out before them. By contrast, its defenders promoted it as a school of virtue where precisely such behaviours could be exposed as the crimes and sins that they were. Elizabethan plays and theatres thus embodied both the rapid commercialisation and underlying contradictions of the period.

Elizabethan state and its critics

The onset of inflation, commercialisation and social dislocation was 'matched in scale and pace by state formation, the extension of royal policy through law into communities'.[21] We thus return to Pulton's world, in which Parliament and the Privy Council passed statutes and proclamations often with utopian aspirations. Sumptuary laws and related royal proclamations were passed to restrict popular consumption of expensive clothing. The Statute of Artificers of 1562 was meant to control the labour market and wage rates. Because these measures did not bring expected results, more legislation followed. An act of 1571 set penal measures against vagrants, and also required a compulsory levy at the parish level for local poor relief. An act of 1576 then ordered houses of correction to be established in every county for vagabonds, ready to set them and other 'idle poor' to work on weaving, rope-making and other forms of labour.[22] The same regulatory impulse came to invade the sphere of religion, as a series of recusancy statutes were passed in order to enforce regular church attendance on recalcitrant Catholics and to impose a variety of fines and mulcts upon defaulters (on this see Chapter 4).

Parliaments regularly updated these statutes, and royal proclamations called for their stricter enforcement, to accomplish which the Elizabethan regime had perforce to rely on private individuals and licensed commissioners acting as informers. A great deal of discretionary power was placed in their hands. They were expected to support local under-sheriffs and bailiffs in disciplining the idle poor and vagrants, judiciously administering penal laws and punishment. In return for upholding social order, these willing collaborators and informers were promised a proportion of the fine levied from convicted offenders. This was a dangerous arrangement: the delegated authority became a hotbed for blackmail, extortion and corruption, the opposite of Pulton's paternalistic ideal.[23]

These problems grew worse as the reign went on. Admittedly, the new book of customs passed in Mary's reign created some extra revenues. Yet neither customs rates nor assessments for the subsidy rose to keep up with inflation.[24] This meant that much of the nation's new wealth was not available to the government as a source of tax revenue. The resulting fiscal pressure got worse after 1585 owing to the war with Spain, which put unprecedented demands on royal finance, at least by Elizabethan standards.

Desperate to fund the war, with the inflation diminishing the value of fixed revenues, the Crown turned to the delegated powers of the prerogative, and again to informants. Penal statutes became a source of extra-Parliamentary revenue, and their number grew to such an extent that, by 1603, Pulton's *An abstract* had been through at least eight editions.[25] Elizabeth's government also resorted to various sorts of patent and monopoly, which enabled courtiers to collect fees from those engaging in areas of economic activity that had not been touched by previous regulations.

These patents and monopolies authorised by the Crown turned out to be just as controversial. A good example are the patents to discover 'concealed crown lands'. These grants authorised patentees to search for lands owned by the Crown, most often seized from the monasteries, that had then passed inadvertently or covertly into the hands of private landowners. If Crown ownership could once be proved, the owner of such 'concealed crown lands' had to pay rents to the Crown retrospectively, or face confiscation. Ostensibly a way to increase the estate (and ensuing revenues) of the Crown, the discovering of the concealed lands became a cheaper way of rewarding royal servants. Unsurprisingly, the activity led to all sorts of abuse because patentees (and their syndicates) were again entitled to a slice of the profits. Anyone threatened with such proceedings also had every incentive to pay bribes to have the problem go away.[26] Sometimes a single enterprising individual could be involved in many of these activities in pursuit of power and profit, as exemplified by Sir Arthur Heveningham of Norfolk. Men like Heveningham procured controversial (but lucrative) patents and used their local standing to support other patentees and suppress dissent while denying accusations of corruption.[27] John Shakespeare, the father of William, was pestered by informers, and by the 1580s had his reputation and credit ruined because of costly lawsuits.[28] Pulton's *An abstract* was in fact managed through a monopolistic patent, which was in turn disputed by several claimants. Even the ideal message of law and harmonious order was subject to the controversial delegation of royal authority.[29]

These situations attracted criticisms in Parliament and elsewhere. Yet, in order to put theatre plays in proper context, we must take a look at the most uncompromising of these critiques, which came from dissident Catholics. These can be found throughout the reign, starting in the 1570s with the *Treatise of treasons* (1572), going through *Leicester's commonwealth* of 1584 and culminating in clandestine publications written in response to the anti-Catholic proclamation of 1591, including *A humble supplication* and the series of tracts attacking William Cecil.[30] Catholic tracts are important as a benchmark because Catholics were especially vulnerable to the machinations of the Elizabethan regime as the recusancy laws and related proclamations exposed them to the hostile attentions of spies, informers and legal officers, sometimes leading them to imprisonment, torture and execution. Crucially, not only did Catholic authors lament severe persecutions meted out on fellow believers, they also argued that the Catholic experience was only a more extreme form of the wrongs done to the queen's subjects at large.

For example, in 1591 at the height of dearth and high prices exacerbated by the machinations of informers and commissioners, Robert Southwell, an English-born Jesuit missionary, sent a long letter to Antwerp, reporting the condition of English subjects. 'It is straunge', he observed, 'to see how God maketh the whole realme to tast[e] of the same scourage that Catholikes are wronged with'.[31] The queen was being misled by her corrupt advisers; law was bent to favour the powerful. New taxes and fines were introduced to enrich the few. Poor tenants, by contrast, were undone by ruthless landowners. Trades and livelihoods were obstructed by new monopolies. The general suffering was such, argued Southwell, that there were reasons for the regime to 'make so many outcryes against Catholiks' to flare up 'imaginary feares of a few disarmed priests' and thereby 'draw men's considerations [away] from greater miseries and general calamities that hang daily over the whole realme'. England was no better than a tyranny led by evil counsellors.[32]

The idea that English subjects had been oppressed as heavily as a religious minority belonged to a current of Catholic polemics against Elizabeth and her counsellors such as Cecil, Leicester and Walsingham, something that was dispersed as manuscripts, printed on the Continent and smuggled across the English Channel. Such views were damaging to the legitimacy of the Protestant monarchy, and the regime accordingly did what it could to repudiate them and suppress their circulation.[33] We might therefore assume that these condemnations came mainly from oppressed individuals like Southwell and their collaborators. Surprisingly, however, judgements as critical as these were also made available to a broader audience through commercial plays, especially history plays as discussed below.

Abusing the royal authority in the king's absence

George Whetstone's *The right excellent and famous historye, of Promos and Cassandra* was published in 1578, the year in which Pulton's collection of penal statutes appeared.[34] Like other history plays *Promos and Cassandra* takes place in a real-life setting, and uses it to explore the corruptibility of power. In doing so, it suggests striking parallels between the staged past and the present, far beyond what was afforded by the image of harmonious social order. While the play is conventionally studied as a source for

Shakespeare's *Measure for Measure*, surprisingly little has been made of it in relation to wider questions about delegated authority and projecting.[35] In a broad survey of political communication, Barbara J. Shapiro concluded of early modern dramas that 'it was often unclear what the message was other than the obvious message that tyranny was to be condemned as were evil advisors and corrupt courts'.[36] We shall see that the plays discussed below went far beyond the obvious. *Promos and Cassandra*, for one, offered a vivid reconstruction of the machinations of the early modern state, and did so well before Jonson wrote about projectors, and also before the grievances attendant upon monopolists and patentees reached a climax in the 1590s.

Set in an imaginary town in Hungary, the play's story unfolds around the fate of a 'young Gentleman named *Andrugio*' (sig. [A iv]) who sleeps with his future wife before marriage. In the king's absence, the magistrate Promos revives a dormant statute against adultery and, under this law, Andrugio is sentenced to death. Andrugio's sister Cassandra – 'a very virtuous, and beautiful gentlewoman' (sig. [A iv]) – steps in to win Promos's leniency and save Andrugio. However, this attempt to save her brother's life goes wrong when Promos is so taken by Cassandra's beauty that he seduces her in return for commuting Andrugio's sentence. The ironies here are considerable and highly topical for the early modern audience since in the opening scene, Promos tasks himself 'to reform abuse' in the king's absence (sig. [A iv^{v}]) and does so by reviving a forgotten law against adultery. Alleging abuses and proposing to discover and 'reform' them were paradigmatic methods for promoting projects in post-Reformation England.[37] Many of the monopolies and patents discussed above were in fact justified on this ground. This reforming rhetoric remained prominent and problematic under the early Stuarts too, as summed up by a satirical pamphlet against projectors: 'he ... search[es] out the abuses of every Place, Profession, and Mystery whatsoever, next his greatest study is to propose the faire outside of a reformation'.[38] The play explores how Promos's 'faire outside of a reformation' lent itself to the gratification of his own lusts, a problem of pretended reformation that would continue to plague English society in coming decades.

But this is just the beginning of the chain of sins, a downward spiral of lust, corruption and murder upon which Promos is now launched. Having slept with Cassandra, Promos realises that saving Andrugio's life could undermine his reputation as an even-handed doer of justice (sig. e ii). But sending him to the gallows would be to break the promise he has made to Cassandra. Here, in the crucial monologue that opens Act 4, Scene 2, Promos comes up with a series of self-serving excuses: it was the 'rage of love' that drove him to swear an oath to win her over – 'Well, what I said, then lover-like I said'. Now what Promos calls 'the game' takes a different turn; he becomes more concerned with his own reputation as a deputy: 'Now reason says, unto thy credit look:/And having well, the circumstances weighed, /I find I must, unswear the oath I took' to Cassandra. He then shows a momentary gnawing of conscience: 'but double wrong, I so should do Cassandra' – by raping her *and still* sending her brother to the gallows. Even so, Promos persuades himself that, as the king's deputy, in effect the bearer of princely power, he can transcend ordinary moral standards: 'my might, commandeth right ... And thus shall rule, conceal my filthy deed' (sig. e ii). Here the play reveals a wrongdoer's psychological operation: the abuse of royal authority was justified by a series of self-serving reasonings.

Nor does the rot stop with Promos. From the outset, his subordinates are presented as 'parasites' and 'promoters', profiting as Promos does from the privatised regulation of markets and social order. Promos's man Phallax is described as a 'pettifogger' (sig. B iii), a derogatory term for the humbler law officers who played a critical role in these controversial exercises in the 'discovery' and 'reformation' of abuses. Phallax declares his intent: 'promote all faults, up into my office,/Then turn me loose, the offenders to fleece' (sig. [C i^{v}]). Thus when the prostitute Lamia is presented to him by his underlings, Rapax and Gripax, Phallax sends them away with the words 'myself will search her faults if any be' (sig. [D iv]). At that point, he lets Lamia off in return for her sexual favours, explaining that '(through love) this grace the Judge [i.e. Phallax] doth show'. Thus, 'love with love ought to be answered' (sig. [D iv]). Phallax thus extracts Lamia's sexual favour; Lamia would thenceforth be allowed to carry on with her brothel while all the others are shut down, thus achieving a *de facto* monopoly over prostitution in town. Being sent away from the scene, Gripax grudgingly makes the point: 'In such shares as this, henceforth I will begin,/For all is his, in his claws, that cometh in' (sig. [D iv]).

Monopolies and other projects caused much harm precisely through this kind of shady transaction. Parliament passed an act to 'redress disorders in common informers upon penal statutes' in 1576, just two years before the publication of the play. It set penalties on financial settlements reached between parties without the prior consent of the court, an indication of the pervasive reliance upon, and problems caused by, men like Phallax. Complaints about 'promoters' reached the Privy Council too.[39] A manuscript proposal submitted three decades later to Sir Julius Caesar is pertinent here as it describes the broader legal chicanery of which an informal settlement (or 'composition') was a part.[40] According to this proposal, offenders like Lamia first strike a deal with officers like Phallax under which the officers proceed to file a lawsuit against the offender before a given court, but they do so deliberately upon weak grounds and do not submit evidence or take any further action. Such a tactical procedure could delay or even prevent future *bona fide* lawsuits from being considered by that court. Colluding with promoters (as Lamia did) therefore became something of an insurance, whereby the supposed promoters of reformation were turned into agents for evasion. The proposal submitted in 1607 to Caesar was designed to prevent problems of this kind. Instances of these collusions were arguably hard to detect, let alone to eradicate. As the Jesuit Robert Southwell put it, 'in the lawes there is no justice used, sutes being more caryed with favour then right, and rather overruled by authoritie then law ... al things being governed by bribes and partialitie'.[41] The problems persisted up to the eve of the Civil Wars.[42] *Promos and Cassandra* is significant on this count because, as early as 1578, we see the playwright staging the underlying problem for all to see.

Lamia continues her business uninterrupted, entertaining Phallax's friends at her brothel; impressed with her 'success', Lamia's male servant Rosko decides to emulate her, battening off one Grimball who lusts after Lamia's maid (sigs [f ii^{v}–f iii^{v}]). Thus corruption spreads down through the food chain of enforcement, in the end enveloping even the humble companion of a brothel keeper, a process that *Promos and Cassandra* lays bare while locating the source of the problem in the precarious symbiosis involving public authority, law officers and their private collaborators. The play thus cloaks in the story of sexual predations a fundamental problem of early modern governance, something that attracted Catholic condemnations, troubled the Elizabethan Privy Council and exercised statesmen like Caesar under James I.

Tyranny and fiscal exaction

In *Promos and Cassandra*, the corruption starts *because the king is absent*. The wrongs perpetrated by Promos, Phallax and the like are redressed and the upright social order restored when the king Corvinus and his judicious adviser Ulrico return to the city (sig. [I iv]). In contrast, the Elizabethan England denounced by Catholic dissidents was governed *in the presence of* the monarch and her advisers and courtiers. The anonymous play *Thomas of Woodstock*, published in the first half of the 1590s, engaged head on with the issue: it offers an uncompromising analysis of tyranny and fiscal exaction on a par with Catholic critiques of the Elizabethan regime.[43] We now explore these radical elements that would later characterise the projector stereotype and its appropriations.

Set in Richard II's reign, *Thomas of Woodstock* draws on the well-known trope of a king surrounded by evil counsellors – in this case Bagot, Bushy,

Greene and the master manipulator Sir Robert Tresilian. Tresilian is described as 'that sly machiavel' (1:1, 63), just as Cecil was accused by Catholics of practising Machiavellian manipulations.[44] The others are young men, favourites of the equally young king, who curry favour by playing on his susceptibility for conspicuous consumption. Set against these flatterers are the king's uncles, who represent a more virtuous older generation. Chief amongst them is the main protagonist Thomas of Woodstock. Woodstock is a plain, virtuous statesman capable of sympathising with the plight of commoners. A stark contrast is drawn throughout the play between Woodstock and the king's (mostly young) evil counsellors.

A central marker of this difference is conspicuous consumption, something that was currently spreading outside the theatre as discussed above. Richard is in his early twenties and marries Anne early in the play (1:3). The wedding is extravagant and marked by sumptuous dress. Even Woodstock is forced to put on elaborate garb which, he bitterly complains, departs from his usual plain style (1:3, 83–4). He prefers plain dress because sartorial extravagance could require him to 'raise new rents', '[u]ndo my poor tenants', dismiss servants and 'sell more land' and even 'lordships' (1:3, 104–7). His plain style thus reveals acute awareness of adverse consequences of conspicuous consumption. The play shows that what Woodstock refuses to do to his tenants and servants, is done by the king and corrupt counsellors to the entire kingdom.

Prospects of discords and disturbances are visible from the beginning. We learn that '[t]he commons murmur 'gainst the dissolute king' (1:1, 157). One reason was that he has been resorting to forced loans to fund his and his flatterers' extravagance (1:3, 146–7). To ease fiscal burden upon 'the needy commons', the virtuous Woodstock proposes to distribute the 'rich and wealthy prize' recently won on the high seas by the Lord Admiral (1:3, 143). Richard has already given it all away to his minions, however. Woodstock and the uncles are enraged; Woodstock dismisses Richard's minions as mere 'cankers' eating away the fruits of hard-won military victory (1:3, 155). This scene carried a clear resonance when it was staged in the 1590s. Contemporary Catholic polemics repeatedly condemned the Privy Councillors for sheer 'opulence' and wasteful consumption.[45] They indeed charged Cecil and his underlings with siphoning off money and getting spectacularly rich while oppressing the public and defrauding the monarch. One author sarcastically remarked that if the money levied from poor subjects failed to fill 'the Queenes cofers', then 'the Lord *Trecherer* [*sic*] I trust ca[n] give her majestie and the realme good accomptes of them'.[46] By staging fourteenth-century corruption, the play thus provided commentaries on corrupt councillors that echoed uncompromising critiques of the Elizabethan regime at the time.

Richard defies his enraged uncles by appointing his favourites, Greene and Bagot, respectively as Lord Chancellor and Lord Keeper of the Privy Seal (1:3, 181–8). In the next scene, the king assembles his newly reconstituted council with Tresilian. Richard annuls the statutes introduced under the Protectorate (2:2, 184–5) and dissolves Parliament (2:2, 213). He also passes orders to enlarge Westminster Hall 'only [to] serve us for a dining-room', to 'have money to buy new suits' and 'devise some new' fashion (2:2, 196, 201–2, 206, 208).

Because of this orgy of opulence and conspicuous consumption the realm is plunged into a downward spiral of increasing oppression, corruption and tyranny. Desperate for money, and having denied themselves the traditional source of supply by closing Parliament, the king and his minions resort to prerogative power in order to squeeze more revenue from the subjects. Tresilian puts forward a scheme for 'blank charters', a device forcing subjects to subscribe their names to a blank parchment, with the amount of their 'voluntary loan' to be subsequently decided at the royal pleasure. 'O strange, unheard-of vile taxation' (3:2, 67) is the comment of one of the royal uncles on this practice. Catholic polemics at the time in fact argued that Elizabeth's councillors had imposed upon English subjects 'great & grieveous exactions' including '[f]orced benevolences' with 'huge masses of mony [being] raised by privy seales', that is, by means not approved by Parliament.[47] The search for extra-Parliamentary revenues continued well into the reign of Charles I, giving rise to a large number of projects based on monopolistic patents.[48] The play thus paralleled Catholic critique in showing how parasitical flatterers could abuse the king's authority to introduce arbitrary fiscal imposition without Parliamentary approval. Uncannily, it anticipated the fiscal exploitation of prerogative power that fuelled the constitutional crisis of the 1640s.

In *Thomas of Woodstock*, the people's response to such fiscal exactions is extremely adverse but the play shows how even dissent could be turned into yet another source of royal revenue, not to mention allowing corrupt agents of the regime to line their pockets in the process. Authorised by the Privy Council, and under Tresilian's direction, Nimble, Fleming and Crosby are sent to the market town of Dunstable in Bedfordshire to collect subscriptions to the blank charters (3:3). There, they discover that 'there are strange songs and libels, cast about the marketplace against my Lord Tresilian and the rest of the King's young councillors' (3:3, 27–30). Nimble immediately comes up with a scheme to turn this situation into ready cash. They should, he suggests, 'shadow [i.e. conceal] ourselves and write down their speeches' (3:3, 40). Three local men, Farmer, Cowtail and Butcher, are returning from a market, gossiping about the king's new councillors occupying 'honester men's places', and about 'strange tidings' about new taxes (3:3, 70, 56). Apprehended, they are first forced to sign and seal a charter and then arrested for libel as 'privy whisperers' speaking against royal councillors (3:3, 102–55).

What happens next captures how subjects could use songs to criticise tyranny. A schoolmaster enters, reciting to a servant two songs of his own making: if 'well searched' they are 'little better than libels', but their meaning, he explains, is well concealed (3:3, 166–8). The two songs are thinly disguised criticisms of Tresilian, other advisers and the blank charter, and yet both end in 'God bless my Lord Tresilian', a phrase that could be quoted if questioned about the song and its intent. They are presently arrested 'for most shameful treason' by Nimble and Ignorance, who are listening to the songs (3:3, 215–25). Nimble then proceeds to arrest for 'whistling treason' anyone reciting the same popular refrain, with or without libellous intent (3:3, 240–3).

The scene thus vividly portrays the mechanisms by which popular dissent was produced and covertly disseminated via songs, a key medium through which the projector stereotype was later appropriated in order to denounce corruption, as we shall see below.[49] The arrests of the schoolmaster and others for 'whistling treason' also highlight how the royal authority could be locally mobilised in most extreme and absurd ways to suppress signs of dissent and to squeeze fines upon the slightest of allegations. As Catholic writers argued, 'leuetenants and justices of shire' and their subordinates (like Ignorance) were 'so servilely subject that they go at every pursevant's commaundement to assist them and serve them in their offices'.[50] This was exactly what the play reveals on stage. The play's audience is told that in the end 13,000 blank charters have been signed and returned (3:3, 277–8), with 700 arrests having been made in the process (4:3, 8–10). True to the image of the greedy stateman, Tresilian later orders the money raised to be locked in 'my study' (4:1, 3–4).

Staging a monarchical breakdown

The discussion in the two preceding sections establishes, firstly, that the practices being exposed on stage bear a remarkable resemblance to some of the practices indulged by a variety of informers, intelligencers and flatterers working under Elizabeth and profiting from her royal authority. Even Tresilian's blank charters can be compared to the forced loans to which the Elizabethan regime resorted between 1588 and 1591 and again in 1597 in order to raise funds for the war effort during the 1590s.[51] Secondly, and equally crucially, we now know that these plays contained critical commentaries as pointed as those penned by dissident Catholics facing the threat of capture and execution. Remarkably, however, some of the Elizabethan history plays went further than the Catholic tracts, revealing the monarch's culpability and highlighting popular agency. These two elements are important because they later characterised the projector stereotype and its mobilisation.

As for the monarch's responsibility, the Catholic critique of the Elizabethan regime remained largely contained within what one might term the evil-counsellor mode, with the notable exceptions of Cardinal Allen's *Admonition to the nobility and people of England* (1588) – expressly written to accompany the Armada – and certain Latin tracts like Nicholas Sander's *De origine* (1585), which addressed mostly Continental audiences.[52] For the most part, the blame for the misgovernment of the country was placed on an evil clique amongst the queen's councillors – initially William Cecil and Nicholas Bacon, then the Earl of Leicester and his minions, and by the 1590s Cecil again, this time aided and abetted by his son, Robert. Accordingly, the queen herself was pictured as an innocent, if credulous, victim of those she trusted most.[53]

We can fully appreciate the explosiveness of *Thomas of Woodstock* in this context. In the play, rather than being seduced or simply misled by his evil counsellors, Richard is shown as repeatedly and enthusiastically acceding to, and at crucial moments, personally participating in, the most corrupt and reprehensible of his councillors' schemes. Thus, when Tresilian first proposes the blank charters, Richard moves 'to applaud thy wit' since, as he sees immediately, the scheme is a way to 'fill up our treasury,/Opening the chests of hoarding cormorants/That laugh to see their kingly sovereign lack' (3:1, 7–10). Again, when Tresilian and Greene come up with the dastardly plot to invite Woodstock to a court entertainment, capture him on the spot, send him to Calais and have him murdered there, Richard not only endorses the plan, but insists that he himself take a personal part in the masque under the cover of which the duke, his uncle, is to be abducted (4:1, 83–113). The young king is fully on board with fiscal exaction, and the kidnap and the killing of his virtuous uncle.

Thomas of Woodstock of course never addressed the present as did the Catholic tracts. For all its contemporary references, the play was simply staging 'history', leaving the application to the present entirely up to the judgement, courage and acumen of its audiences.[54] Having said that, it leaves its audience in no doubt that corruption, misgovernment and tyranny can emanate quite as much from the monarch as they do from evil counsellors. On this count, the play went much further than the bulk of the Catholic tracts which only allowed themselves tangentially, via hints and historical parallels, to implicate the queen in the persecution pursued by her councillors. Even the Grand Remonstrance of 1641 stopped short of attacking Charles I himself, focusing instead on his evil counsellors and those monopolists and projectors around them who collectively supported his personal rule without Parliaments. It was only after the king's execution in 1649 that apologists for the regicide came to highlight Charles's responsibility in the fiscal exaction and political oppressions.[55] *Thomas of Woodstock* is thus at once fascinating and disturbing: already in the 1590s it explored a downward spiral of arbitrary government, fiscal exactions and civil war, a dystopian scenario unfolding *outside* the theatre half a century later, in which projectors would play a pivotal role.

Highlighting popular political agency

Thomas of Woodstock was exceptional in depicting the tyrannical exercises of power plunging a nation into a civil war. Yet other history plays also went further than Catholic tracts in portraying the capacity of humble inhabitants to judge royal policies and political economy in ways that anticipated the participatory politics on the eve of the Civil Wars. Such elements of popular agency featured prominently in Thomas Heywood's *The First and Second Parts of Edward IV* (printed 1599), a play that went into six editions during his lifetime (1575–1641).[56]

Like *Thomas of Woodstock*, this play also revolves around a king over-confident in extending his prerogative power. Edward IV falls in love with Jane, the wife of London goldsmith Matthew Shore, and takes her to his court as a concubine. Jane then enters the stage 'ladylike attired, divers supplications in her hand ... and attended on by many suitors' (1:22). Here, she encounters one master Rufford, a proto-projector who requests a licence to export corn. Rufford approaches Jane and asks 'Mistress I fear you have forgot my suit?' She replies sternly: 'O, 'tis for a licence to transport corn/From this land, and lead to foreign realms,/I had your bill, but I have torn your bill' (1:22, 61–4). Notice that sending corn abroad was a highly sensitive topic in the 1590s, a time of severe dearth in England as is well documented by social and economic historians.[57] In fact, in 1595, 1596, 1597 and 1598, Elizabeth's government issued orders and proclamations designed to ensure stable provision of grain, preventing grains from being hoarded, exported or processed into starch (which was used during washing to keep ruffs and linen cloths crisp). One proclamation even prohibited the feeding of dogs with grain.[58] Given these developments, Jane's response takes on an added significance. Having torn up Rufford's bill, Jane declares: 'And 'twere no shame I think, to tear your ears,/That care not how you wound the commonwealth./The poor must starve for food to fill your purse' (1:22, 65–7).

Jane's confident pronouncement against the proto-projector is hardly surprising given what we now know about gender in the period. Conduct books often depicted wives as deputy magistrates in the governing of households, capable of instructing children and servants, managing estates and family businesses. Plays such as *The Merry Wives of Windsor*, *The Roaring Girl* and *Swetnam the Woman Hater* highlighted female agency in setting things right.[59] Such depictions were rooted in contemporary realities. Labouring women's legal testimonies suggest that their role combined 'production and consumption, and involved the protection of household assets as well as the generation of income', as Alexandra Shepard puts it. Women's household responsibilities were so significant that these 'validated their public interventions' during the Civil Wars, including petitioning Parliament and even criticising the emerging republican regime for some of its actions.[60] Women were involved also in the world of patenting and projecting. Some women in London and its suburbs earned a living by knitting stockings, making bone lace, making buttons and weaving points. They became involved in the production, overseen by projectors, of commodities that were relatively new to England and hence left untouched by guild regulations.[61] More dubious still, daughters of influential writers sometimes filed applications for patents to publish their fathers' books without necessarily completing the process – a tactical move that could help them (much like informers) to extract financial compensation from stationers anxious to continue their business undisturbed. Jane Yetsweirt, a widow of one of the patentees for Pulton's book of statutes, mobilised her contacts to claim her share in the publishing business, tactically drawing attention to 'her poverty, sex, and widowhood'.[62] *The First and Second Parts of Edward IV* is thus addressing an audience living in a dynamic society where women's seemingly 'domestic' activities interacted with exercises of royal patents, entrepreneurship and guild regulations. The play's audience is thus invited to learn that the wife of a London goldsmith is fully capable of passing just censure upon Rufford the proto-projector. What Shepard calls the 'moral authority' of early modern women encompassed grave matters of political economy.[63]

The kind of political literacy displayed by Jane is not unique to urban middling sorts. A surprising critique also comes in the same play from a humbler rural inhabitant, John Hobs a tanner of Tamworth. In an early scene, Hobs by chance meets the king Edward, who was travelling in disguise. Hobs falls into amicable conversation with him without knowing his true identity. The king, presenting himself as 'Ned', the confidant of the monarch, then suggests the tanner come to the royal court one day. Hobs shows no interest, to which the king gives a striking reply: 'Hast thou no suit, touching thy trade? To transport hides, or sell leather only in a certain circuit? ... To have letters patents'? (1:13, 72–4).

This is a significant scene in that it confronted the explosive question of royal patents, something that was drawing increasing public attention by the time the play appeared in 1599. Under Elizabeth's reign, patents began to be granted in large numbers in order to regulate particular industries promoting technology transfer from the Continent. By the end of the 1590s, at least 86 patents had been granted, many with exclusive privileges to import, produce, sell or issue licences.[64] One of these grants, for collecting customs on imported sweet wine, was given in 1589 to Robert Devereux the Earl of Essex, a rising favourite of Elizabeth. Grants like this one turned out to be deeply controversial as discussed above. Parliaments of the period did highlight related grievances, denouncing patentees (in general terms) as 'bloodsuckers of the commonwealth'.[65] Yet Members of Parliament could hardly deny that the queen was entitled to use her prerogative power and grant patents for rewarding her loyal subjects. Catholic dissidents were more vocal. In 1591, Southwell referred to the monopolies on wine, starch and playing cards and declared that '[t]here were never such devises heard of to get monye in England as are now ryfe'.[66] It is no accident that Thirsk called the period a 'scandalous phase' of projecting.[67]

The First and Second Parts of Edward IV puts on stage this highly sensitive topic, which Members of Parliament discussed with hesitation and Catholic polemics denounced. Being asked whether he would like to have a patent, Hobs the tanner responds with a rustic, yet sharp, criticism of the practice:

> I like not those patten[t]s! Sirrah, they that have them do as the priests did in old time: buy and sell the sins of the people. So they make the King believe *they mend what's amiss*, and, for money, they make the thing worse than it is. (1:13, 75–9, italics added)

Promos and Cassandra only lightly alluded to the reformation of alleged abuses, as discussed earlier in this chapter. In *Edward IV*, the tanner roundly condemns *both* monopolies *and* the pretended reformation of market abuses ('make the King believe they mend what's amiss'). The king then draws a lesson from the encounter: 'I see plain men, by observation ... Do gather knowledge; and the meanest life,/Proportioned with content sufficiency,/Is merrier than the mighty state of kings' (1:13, 98–102). Given the controversies around patents and monopolies, the tanner could appear both wiser and merrier than what Catholics viewed as a despotic government led by evil advisers.

Jane Shore and John Hobs – a goldsmith's wife and a rustic tanner – were not exceptional. *Thomas of Woodstock* portrayed the schoolmaster coming up with rhymes criticising the blank charter as discussed earlier. In *Promos and Cassandra*, we find humbler actors drawing on familiar principles to pass judgement comparable to that of wise rulers. The general theme is encapsulated by the king's statement on magistrates' exercise of power: 'If they their rule by conscience measure not,/The poore mans ryght is overcome by might' (sig. H ii). Cassandra, the 'gentle women', understood how this can happen. As she tells the king, she was forced to choose between 'Two evils' – either 'To see my brother put to death', or 'graunt his [Promos's] lewed request'. Then Promos broke the promise and arranged to kill her brother Andrugio 'with the spoyle of my good name' (sig. [k i^v]–k ii). Accordingly, the king orders Promos to marry Cassandra (to save her reputation) and be executed the next day. This royal intervention is commended by a clown: 'happy he ... Who checks the rytch, that wrong by might,/And helpes the poore, vnto his right' (sig. K iii). The same theme is echoed by Andrugio who narrowly escaped the gallows thanks to a relenting jailer: in his view, Promos 'maintained wrongs by might', his 'rule' being 'tyranny indeed' (sig. [L 1^v]). The underlying warning against might determining what is right and wrong was something repeated in advice manuals like *Myrroure for magistrates* (1559).[68] The play picks up this familiar theme and puts it into the mouths of the king; the clown, called 'such dunghill churles' (sig. [K iiii^v]); and the young victim of Promos's exactions.

The play even invites the audience to exercise similar critical scrutiny themselves. Theatre studies suggest that early modern theatregoers were not just passive; the audience were as visible to the players as the players were to the audience. Performers often directly addressed and made eye contact with the audience, reminding that they shared common knowledge about the world off-stage.[69] *Promos and Cassandra* made a similar move towards the end. While Promos narrowly escapes the gallows after Cassandra pleas for leniency, Phallax is banished from the city of Julio. He leaves the stage unrepentant: 'the best is, flattrers lyve everie where ... Yes, yes Phallax, knoweth whether to go'. His evocative farewell words might as well be directed to the audience: 'flattrers loves as lyfe, to join with lyers'. With this ends Part 2, Act 4 (sig. L iii). Where might these liars be found, flattering the rich and absolving the powerful of their corruptions? The closing lines are skilfully crafted to invite just such a question, encouraging the audience to look for similar corruptions in everyday life. Only then does the play proceed to the final Act 5, which rounds up the story with Promos saved from death in the final minutes.

Appealing to fears and prejudices

Elizabethan history plays thus staged in commercial theatres and made available via print what Elizabethan Parliaments only cautiously debated inside the chamber and what Catholics condemned in underground prints and letters. These plays even suggested that humbler sorts of people (including their audiences) were capable of passing their own judgements on these highly sensitive matters, contradictions at the heart of the emerging political economy of early modern England.

This is exactly what we find in subsequent decades. In about 1640, the London woodturner Nehemiah Wallington recorded in his diary that '[a]s wee in great misery in regard of the Church So we were in greate misery in regard of our Corrupted Judges ... As also projectors with their Letter pattens for all Stabel Commodities: As also Shipp mony & new corporations even to the undoing of many thousands.'[70] The woodturner considered projectors seeking patents to be a part of the larger misgovernment under Charles I. Equally crucially, the damages inflicted by projectors were considered real, as had been shown earlier by *Promos and Cassandra* and *Thomas of Woodstock*. This raises an important question about the political implications of these plays: did they serve as an ideal nursery of civic participatory politics? Walter Cohen once went so far as to argue that plays, especially those actually performed in public, 'automatically converted a heterogeneous and, it seems, largely popular audience into judges of national issues, a position from which most of its members were excluded in the world of political affairs'.[71] Can we agree with this view, and suppose that these history plays offered 'shrewd political instruction in the machinations of governors and superiors', thereby 'teaching intelligent mistrust' of the powerful as Chris Fitter has recently put it?[72] It is true that playwrights and defenders of the theatre expected plays to have didactic functions: to teach their audiences to love virtue and detest vices, to detect signs of tyranny and dangerous ambitions. Upon closer scrutiny, however, we find the plays under consideration appealing to familiar fears and prejudices while developing penetrating accounts of misgovernment.

In *Promos and Cassandra* the serial perversion of power linking Promos, Phallax and Lamia is couched in familiar themes of lust and greed, as discussed in 'Abusing the royal authority in the king's absence' above. Having slept with Phallax, Lamia alone is allowed to run a brothel in town, to 'set my Toyes to sale'. Having established a *de facto* monopoly over prostitution, she declares '[a]t hyest rate, my Toyes I value must' (sig. H iii). The 'raising of prices as they please' was one of the most common yet serious charges laid against monopolists in the period.[73] Perversion of this kind in reality owed much to the government's increasing debts, its fiscal arrangements and structural dependence upon officers like Promos and Phallax. Even so, the play's audience is induced to consider this complex issue in terms of personal appetite for money and sex. This is what psychologists would now call attribution bias.[74] In the play the root cause of corruption is attributed instead to well-understood themes of lust and greed, with an alluring scene of Lamia's brothel, where customers were welcomed by two prostitutes 'bravely apparelled'.[75]

The spectre of popery and Catholic invasions were also invoked to incite familiar anxieties, as we can see in *Thomas of Woodstock*. After Woodstock is dismissed from his position as regent, the king and his young advisers go on to devise a new attire, one that is heavily influenced by Catholic countries and their products: 'French hose [i.e. leg covering], Italian cloaks and Spanish hats', complete with 'Polonian shoes with peaks a handful long,/ Tied to their knees with chains of pearl and gold' (2:3, 91–3). Later in the play, as Richard plans to abduct and kill his uncle Thomas, he tells his flatterers to 'send unto the King of France for aid', presumably military aid, in case 'the commons should rebel against us', and proposes to relinquish the Continental forts of Guynes and Calais to the French (4:1, 120–4). These were variations on a familiar theme. The Spanish Armada was defeated only in 1588; the threat of Catholic invasion was all too real. Against this backdrop numerous pamphlets and playbooks of the period also warned against the danger of popery and Catholic influence – sometimes with erudition, sometimes with hostile laughter that appealed to paid audiences. As the Jesuit missionary Southwell complained, 'many poore printers and needy libellers make the best part of their living by our slaunders', with plays 'spiced with some quipp or jest against [Catholic] religion'.[76] Into this hostility towards popery and foreign influence partly fuelled by huckster writers, *Thomas of Woodstock* skilfully weaves the dramatic, highly topical, account of tyranny and misgovernment.

In short, the plays under consideration exposed delicate issues of royal policy and political economy, *both* by revealing perversions of justice and righteous rule, *and* by anchoring those stories onto everyday points of reference including deeply held fears about lust, greed, false religion and armed invasion, which were fully compatible with the commercial imperatives of the emerging theatre and print industries. Put differently, these plays were politically explosive in at least two ways: first, they encouraged popular judgement upon delicate issues of royal policy and political economy, and second, such judgement was driven partly by appeals to familiar fears and emotions. In fact, contemporary critics of the theatre denounced such plays precisely for these reasons. One such critic, Henry Crosse, highlighted how plays might 'breede contempt' of the powerful:

> [W]hen the faults and scandalls of great men, as Magistrates, Ministers, and such as hold publike places, shall be openly acted and objected to the sences, or faigned to bee replenished with vice and passion, it must needes breed disobedience[.][77]

Such popular engagement was deemed dangerous because plays directly appealed to emotions in the audience. According to Stephen Gosson, one of the most uncompromising critics of Renaissance theatre, plays were politically dangerous because they 'stirre vp affections, and affections are naturally planted in that part of the minde that is common to us with brute beastes'. Actors and playwrights 'studie to make our affections ouerflow, whereby they draw the bridle from that parte of the mind, that should ever be curbed ... which is manifest treason to our soules'.[78]

The Elizabethan history plays could be politically explosive, then, not so much because they fostered popular rational scrutiny of political authority or taught 'intelligent mistrust' (*pace* Fitter). Plays like these were considered dangerous because plotlines and actions were often designed to 'stirre up affections', in the process encouraging political engagements driven by stereotypical understanding of otherwise intricate matters of state.

Upon this precarious mixture depended the subsequent social circulation of the projector stereotype. A satirical Christmas carol circulating on the eve of the Civil War suggested that projectors build their fortunes and then 'jet in dancing and whooring', reminiscent of Promos and Phallax whom Whetstone depicted as driven by monetary greed as well as by sexual desire (see Chapter 4 for further discussion of this carol). As a Protestant reformer, John Dury found out to his frustration that would-be reformers like himself became a target of 'worldly mens derision & contempt', too often dismissed as 'a subtill projector & practitioner', or worse 'an inconsiderate & presumptuous foole'.[79] The figure of the projector could serve as a heuristic device for detecting what the Jesuit missionary Southwell earlier called 'greater miseries', identifying abusers and calling for reform. We find this in Wallington's diary and in the Commons's denunciations of monopolists and projectors. Yet at the same time, the projector stereotype also helped stir up suspicion and fuel existing prejudices, as indicated by the satirical carol and Dury's remark. In the Elizabethan history plays we already find both potentials for radical reform, and dangerous perils, stemming from civic participatory politics facilitated by the vibrant print and theatre industries. The Elizabethan history plays discussed here remind us that the projector stereotype did not emerge through idealised public uses of reason. Rather, the new stereotype that fuelled the constitutional crisis grew out of earlier, discursive practices that were driven by commercial imperatives and accompanied by a wider range of stereotypes about sexual excess, wasteful consumption and popery. Literary scholars have recently suggested that early modern plays helped cultivated their audience's 'emotional *habitus*'. The emotional *habitus* cultivated by the Elizabethan history plays, I suggest, had explosive political and economic repercussions throughout the seventeenth century.[80]

Conclusion

The powerful stereotype of the projector was never invented singlehandedly by Jonson. Rather, the thriving commercial theatres and printing industry under Elizabeth first provided a platform for creative *practices of stereotyping* – a collective search for an emerging pattern of problematic behaviour – and the identification of its causes based on an existing body of assumptions. Only then did a *character-based stereotype* of the projector come to be elaborated by a literary genius in the shape of Jonson. In revealing corruptions, these earlier texts turn out to be as uncompromising and politically explosive as Catholic attacks upon the Elizabethan regime.

This chapter establishes that the Elizabethan history plays discussed above are significant for studies of the early modern state and economy in general, and studies of projects and monopolies in particular. Three features stand out. Firstly, these texts adeptly exploited historical settings and exposed the mechanics of royal authority for all to see, especially how easily royal power could be abused when it is delegated down the social hierarchy in order to raise taxes and implement social and economic policies. These plays presented real-time reconstruction of the social and psychological processes involved that stirred up Parliamentary debates and exercised the Privy Council. Secondly, these history plays demonstrated that not only lesser officers but also corrupt royal advisers and even monarchs themselves could become complicit in the abuse of power if left unchecked. When that happens, as shown in *Thomas of Woodstock*, royal policies could disrupt everyday life, causing uprisings and even civil wars. Thirdly, and most importantly, the history plays under consideration indicated that humbler women and men could competently detect and pass judgement upon the perversion of royal authority (both at the top and down the social ladder). In endowing significant political agency on humbler sorts of people, the Elizabethan history plays discussed here may be considered more radical than the Catholic polemics. Yet I have also suggested that the kind of mixed-gender participatory politics staged by the plays cannot be celebrated as the politics of radical and rational critique. If we are to suggest that Elizabethan history plays highlighted aspects of popular political agency, then it was more like bounded political competence, a kind of emotional *habitus* fuelled by fear and prejudice as much as by normative expectations about right and reason. The subsequent condemnation of projectors and the unfolding of the constitutional crisis 'marked an intensification and appropriation of inherited discourse and practice rather than a sudden discontinuity', an inheritance which should now include Elizabethan history plays.[81]

Having established how politically dangerous these Elizabethan discourses were, we can now begin to explore, in Chapter 4, how Jonson's plays brought humorous elements to the fore, and thereby contained some of the more radical qualities prominent in the earlier writings – what Tim Harris in Chapter 1 calls *anxiety displacement*. Paradoxically, by developing the character of the projector, Jonson's plays also made it much easier for the broader population to identify and talk about the widespread problem via an identifiable perpetrator, thus paving the way for further reappropriation of the image and the escalation of stereotyping. In Chapter 4, we shall examine his plays as a key element in this dialectical process.

Recurring references to plays are given within the main text in parentheses. I thank Yuichi Tsukada, Genji Yasuhira, Maho Ikeda and the audience at the Huntington Library and the Historians' Workshop, Tokyo, for feedback. I owe special debts to Peter Lake for encouragement and suggestions. The idea for this chapter took shape when I held a postdoctoral position for Subha Mukherji's 'Crossroads of Knowledge' project in Cambridge, funded by the European Research Council (FP7/2007–2013) / ERC grant agreement no. 617849. I thank her for inspiration.

Notes

1 Ben Jonson, *The Cambridge edition of the works of Ben Jonson*, vol. 4, ed. David Bevington et al. (Cambridge, 2012), pp. 508–9.

2 Andrew Thrush and John P. Ferris (eds), *The House of Commons,1604–1629* (6 vols, Cambridge, 2010), vol. 5, p. 350; Thomas Cogswell, '"In the power of the state": Mr Anys's project and the tobacco colonies, 1626–1628', *English Historical Review*, 123 (2008), 35–64. For background see Linda Levy Peck, *Court patronage and corruption in early modern England* (London, 1990).

3 *Journals of the House of Commons*, vol. 2, p. 24.

4 Noah Millstone, *Manuscript circulation and the invention of politics in early Stuart England* (Cambridge, 2016), pp. 312–15; Alan Craig Houston, '"A way of settlement": the Levellers, monopolies and the public interest', *History of Political Thought*, 14 (1993), 381–420, pp. 385–7, 397–401; Koji Yamamoto, *Taming capitalism before its triumph: public service, distrust, and 'projecting' in early modern England* (Oxford, 2018), pp. 98–9.

5 J. M. Treadwell, 'Jonathan Swift: the satirist as projector', *Texas Studies in Literature and Language*, 17 (1975), 439–60, at p. 441; J. R. Ratcliff, 'Art to cheat the common-weale: inventors, projectors, and patentees in English satire, *ca.* 1630–70', *Technology and Culture*, 53 (2012), 337–65, at p. 343; Yamamoto, *Taming capitalism*, p. 82. The concept of 'project' and its rich connotations have been traced much further back in relation to alchemy, geometry, invention and international confessional conflict. See Vera Keller and Ted

McCormick, 'Towards a history of projects', *Early Science and Medicine*, 21 (2016), 423–44, at pp. 426–33; Yamamoto, *Taming capitalism*, pp. 3–6.

6 See Peter Lake, *How Shakespeare put politics on the stage: power and succession in the history plays* (New Haven, CT, 2016); Peter Lake, *Hamlet's choice: religion and resistance in Shakespeare's revenge tragedies* (New Haven, CT, 2020); Susan D. Amussen and David E. Underdown, *Gender, culture and politics in England, 1560–1640: turning the world upside down* (London, 2017), ch. 3; Andy Wood, 'Brave minds and hard hands: work, drama, and social relations in the hungry 1590s', in Chris Fitter (ed.), *Shakespeare and the politics of commoners: digesting the new social history* (Oxford, 2017), pp. 84–101.

7 Keller and McCormick, 'Towards a history of projects', pp. 424–6; Yamamoto, *Taming capitalism*, pp. 11–19.

8 This chapter therefore complements Valerie Forman, *Tragicomic redemptions: global economics and the early modern English stage* (Philadelphia, PA, 2008); Aaron Kitch, *Political economy and the states of literature in early modern England* (Aldershot, 2009); Stephen Deng, *Coinage and state formation in early modern English literature* (Basingstoke, 2011); David Landreth, *The face of Mammon: the matter of money in English Renaissance literature* (Oxford, 2012); András Kiséry, *Hamlet's moment: drama and political knowledge in early modern England* (Oxford, 2016). See also the editorial introductions to *Woodstock* and *Edward IV* cited below.

9 Ferdinando Pulton, *An abstract of all the penal statutes* (1578), [sigs] A iii, A iiii.

10 Jane Whittle, 'Land and people', in Keith Wrightson (ed.), *A social history of England, 1500–1750* (Manchester, 2017), pp. 152–73, at pp. 160, 166.

11 *Oxford English Dictionary*, 'vagrancy', n. 2.b. See also Steve Hindle, *The state and social change in early modern England, c. 1550–1640* (Basingstoke, 2000), p. 4; Paul Slack, *Poverty and policy in Tudor and Stuart England* (London, 1988), p. 93.

12 This and the following paragraphs owe much to Craig Muldrew, *The economy of obligation: the culture of credit and social relations in early modern England* (Basingstoke, 1998), pp. 18–21.

13 See C. W. Brooks, *Pettyfoggers and vipers of the commonwealth: the 'lower branch' of the legal profession in early modern England* (Cambridge, 1986), p. 51.

14 British Library, English Short Title Catalogue Online, http.//estc.bl.uk (accessed 25 November 2020). Figures are obtained by Advanced Search using date ranges of '1550->1559', '1570->1579', and '1590->1599'.

15 William Harrison, *The description of England*, ed. Georges Edelen (Ithaca, NY, 1968), pp. 46, 272, 284. See also the works cited in note 18 below.

16 Hindle, *The state and social change*, p. 41.

17 Ian Archer, *The pursuit of stability: social relations in Elizabethan London* (Cambridge, 1991), p. 239.

18 Paul Slack, 'Perceptions of the metropolis in seventeenth-century England', in Peter Burke, Brian Howard Harrison and Paul Slack (eds), *Civil histories: essays presented to Sir Keith Thomas* (Oxford, 2000), pp. 161–80, at pp. 162–4;

Peter Lake, 'From Troynouvant to Heliogabalus's Rome and back: "order" and its others in the London of John Stow', in J. F. Merritt (ed.), *Imagining early modern London: perceptions and portrayals of the city from Stow to Strype, 1598–1720* (Cambridge, 2001), pp. 217–49, at p. 223.

19 Muldrew, *Economy of obligation*, p. 20.

20 Scott McMillin and Sally-Beth MacLean, *The Queen's Men and their plays* (Cambridge, 1998), pp. 50, 65, 67, 170–88.

21 Malcolm Gaskill, 'Little commonwealths II: communities', in Wrightson (ed.), *Social history*, p. 91.

22 Slack, *Poverty and policy*, pp. 124–5.

23 M. W. Beresford, 'The common informer, the penal statutes and economic regulation', *Economic History Review*, new series, 10 (19), 221–38. See also John Strype, *Annals of the Reformation* (4 vols, Oxford, 1824), vol. 2, pt 1, pp. 313–4.

24 Conrad Russell, *The causes of the English Civil War* (Oxford, 1990), pp. 169, 172–4.

25 Beresford, 'Common informer', p. 222.

26 C. J. Kitching, 'The quest for concealed lands in the reign of Elizabeth I', *Transactions of the Royal Historical Society*, 5th series, 24 (1974), 63–78, esp. pp. 69–71.

27 A. Hassell Smith, *County and court: government and politics in Norfolk, 1558–1603* (Oxford, 1974), pp. 251–3, 261, 264, 275–6.

28 Glyn Parry and Cathryn Enis, *Shakespeare before Shakespeare: Stratford-Upon-Avon, Warwickshire, and the Elizabethan state* (Oxford, 2020), pp. 18–19, 87, 90, 95, 103, 108–14.

29 Helen Smith, *Grossly material things: women and book production in early modern England* (Oxford, 2012), pp. 141–3.

30 Thomas H. Clancy, *Papist pamphleteers: the Allen-Persons party and the political thought of the Counter-Reformation in England, 1572–1615* (Chicago, 1964); Peter J. Holmes, *Resistance and compromise: the political thought of the Elizabethan Catholics* (Cambridge, 1982); Peter Lake, *Bad Queen Bess? Libels, secret histories, and the politics of publicity in the reign of Queen Elizabeth I* (Oxford, 2016).

31 Robert Southwell to Richard Verstegan, December 1591, in Anthony G. Petti (ed.), *The letters and despatches of Richard Verstegan* (London, 1959), p. 11 (hereafter cited as 'Southwell to Verstegan').

32 'Southwell to Verstegan', p. 15. See also [Richard Verstegan], *A declaration of the trve cavses of the great trovbles* (1592), esp. p. 56. For in-depth accounts of the Catholic writings discussed in this chapter, see Lake, *Bad Queen Bess*, esp. ch. 14.

33 On the circulation of Catholic polemics, see Nancy Pollard Brown, 'Paperchase: the dissemination of Catholic texts in Elizabethan England', *English Manuscript Studies, 1100–1700*, 1 (1989), 120–43; Smith, *Grossly material things*, pp. 83–4. Key moments in Elizabethan politics unfolded in response to Catholic polemics against them. See Lake, *Bad Queen Bess*, pp. 89–93, 112–15, 155–232, 254–6, 312–21, 329–33, 410–11, 417–67.

34 George Whetstone, *Promos and Cassandra* (Edinburgh, 1910), no pagination. I have used the Tudor Facsimile Texts edition. I eagerly await a critical edition of this fascinating work.
35 Charles T. Prouty, 'George Whetstone and the sources of *Measure for Measure*', *Shakespeare Quarterly*, 15 (1964), 131–45; Peter Lake with Michael Questier, *The Antichrist's lewd hat: Protestants, papists and players in post-Reformation England* (New Haven, CT, 2002), pp. 701–11; John C. Higgins, 'Justice, mercy, and dialectical genres in *Measure for Measure* and *Promos and Cassandra*', *English Literary Renaissance*, 42 (2012), 258–93.
36 Barbara J. Shapiro, *Political communication and political culture in England, 1558–1688* (Stanford, CA, 2012), p. 132.
37 Yamamoto, *Taming capitalism*, pp. 70–2.
38 Thomas Brugis, *The discovery of a proiector* [1640?], sig. B 2.
39 18 Eliz.1 c. 5. See *Statutes of the Realm*, vol. 4, pt 1, p. 616; The National Archives, PC 2/11 fol. 129, 9 January 1577.
40 British Library (BL), Lansdowne MS 168/9, fol. 73, D. Hilles to Sir Julius Caesar concerning a project for levying penalties upon penal statutes, 4 May 1607.
41 'Southwell to Verstegan', p. 11. See also [Verstegan], *A declaration*, p. 59.
42 Samuel Rawson Gardiner (ed.), *The constitutional documents of the puritan revolution, 1625–1660*, 3rd edn (Oxford, 1906), pp. 206–7 (articles 43, 47).
43 I have used Peter Corbin and Douglas Sedge (eds), *Thomas of Woodstock, or King Richard the Second, Part One* (Manchester, 2002). The work only survives as a manuscript with no clear dating. Here I follow the majority of scholars who have dated its writing to the first half of the 1590s, including the editors of the 2002 Revels Edition that I have used. For an alternative dating, see Macd. P. Jackson, 'Shakespeare's *Richard II* and the anonymous *Thomas of Woodstock*', *Medieval and Renaissance Drama in England*, 14 (2001), 17–65.
44 [Verstegan], *A declaration*, p. 53. See also Lake, *Bad Queen Bess*, pp. 343, 349, 358; Clancy, *Papist pamphleteers*, pp. 167–77.
45 [Verstegan], *A declaration*, p. 55. See also Lake, *Bad Queen Bess*, pp. 79–80, 121–2, 137.
46 [Verstegan], *A declaration*, p. 60. See also 'Southwell to Verstegan', p. 14.
47 [Verstegan], *A declaration*, p. 60. See also Clancy, *Papist pamphleteers*, pp. 29–30.
48 Russell, *Causes*, pp. 175–8; see also Paul Slack, *Invention of improvement: information and material progress in seventeenth-century England* (Oxford, 2015), pp. 59–61; Yamamoto, *Taming capitalism*, pp. 73–7.
49 For rhymes against 'projectors' disseminated in manuscripts, see Thomas Cogswell, '"The symptomes and vapors of a diseased time": the Earl of Clare and early Stuart manuscript culture', *Review of English Studies*, new series, 57 (2006), 310–36.
50 'Southwell to Verstegan', pp. 8, 12–3, at p. 13. See also [Verstegan], *A declaration*, p. 56.
51 Michael J. Braddick, *The nerves of state: taxation and the financing of the English state, 1558–1714* (Manchester, 1996), pp. 85–6. On how loans were

'requested', see Richard Cust, *The forced loan and English politics, 1626–1628* (Oxford, 1987), pp. 31–5.

52 Clancy, *Papist pamphleteers*, pp. 16, 51–5; Holmes, *Resistance and compromise*, pp. 26–30, 135, 141–2, 152–60; Lake, *Bad Queen Bess*, pp. 144–5, 150, 257–8, 266–70, 273, 279, 305–7, 394–400.

53 Lake, *Bad Queen Bess*, pp. 72–8, 108, 126, 133, 136–8, 373–5.

54 Note that the play presents no clear victor and cannot be said to endorse outright resistance as a legitimate response to tyranny.

55 Gardiner (ed.), *Constitutional documents*, pp. 206–7; Thomas Cogswell, 'An accursed family: the Scottish crisis and the creation of the Black Legend of the House of Stuart, 1650–1652', audio recording, Distinguished Fellow Lecture, Huntington Library, 2015, https://archive.org/details/podcast_early-modern-history_an-accursed-family-scotti_1000428156795 (accessed 2 December 2020).

56 I have used Thomas Heywood, *The First and Second Parts of King Edward IV*, ed. Richard Rowland (Manchester, 2005).

57 Slack, *Poverty and policy*, pp. 48–50; John Walter, *Crowds and popular politics in early modern England* (Manchester, 2006), pp. 68, 74.

58 *A new charge giuen by the queenes commandement*; Paul L. Hughes and James F. Larkin, *Tudor royal proclamations*, vol. 3 (New Haven, CT, 1969), pp. 165–6, 169–72, 183–5, 193–5 (references to dogs on pp. 194–5).

59 See, for example, Amussen and Underdown, *Gender*, pp. 92–6, 98–100, 102.

60 Eleanor Hubbard, *City women: money, sex, and the social order in early modern London* (Oxford, 2012), pp. 113–14; Alexandra Shepard, 'Provision, household management and the moral authority of wives and mothers in early modern England', in Michael J. Braddick and Phil Withington (eds), *Popular culture and political agency in early modern England and Ireland: essays in honour of John Walter* (Manchester, 2017), pp. 73–89, at p. 84; Ann Hughes, *Gender and the English Revolution* (Abingdon, 2012), pp. 44–9, 54–61, 139, at p. 139.

61 Hubbard, *City women*, p. 198; Natasha Korda, *Labors lost: women's work and the early modern English stage* (Philadelphia, PA, 2011), pp. 20–5.

62 Smith, *Grossly material things*, pp. 141–3, 146.

63 Gendered accounts of political economy and projecting are emerging. Exciting new works include Misha Ewen, 'Women investors and the Virginia Company in the early seventeenth century', *Historical Journal*, 62 (2019), 853–74; Mabel Winter, *Banking, projecting and politicking in early modern England: the rise and fall of Thompson and Company 1671–1678* (Cham, 2022); Evan Bourke, '"I would not have taken her for his sister": financial hardship and women's reputations in the Hartlib circle', *Seventeenth Century*, 37 (2022), 47–64. These case studies can be paired profitably with an astute historiographical critique offered by Jane Whittle, 'A critique of approaches to "domestic work": women, work and the pre-industrial economy', *Past & Present*, 243 (2019), 35–70.

64 Yamamoto, *Taming capitalism*, p. 51 (n. 92).

65 T. E. Hartley (ed.), *Proceedings in the Parliaments of Elizabeth I* (3 vols, London, 1995), vol. 3, pp. 370–8, at p. 375.

66 'Southwell to Verstegan', p. 12.

67 Joan Thirsk, *Economic policy and projects: the development of a consumer society in early modern England* (Oxford, 1978), pp. 62–3; Yamamoto, *Taming capitalism*, pp. 70–3.
68 *A myrroure for magistrates* (1559), sig. [H iii^{v}].
69 Penelope Woods, 'Skilful spectatorship? Doing (or being) audience at Shakespeare's Globe Theatre', *Shakespeare Studies*, 43 (2015), 99–113, at p. 100; Evelyn Tribble, 'Affective contagion on the early modern stage', in Amanda Bailey and Mario DiGangi (eds), *Affect theory and early modern texts: politics, ecologies, and form* (New York, 2017), pp. 195–212, at pp. 204–5.
70 BL, Add. MS 21935, Nehemiah Wallington's diary, fol. 127.
71 Walter Cohen, *Drama of a nation: public theater in Renaissance England and Spain* (Ithaca, NY, 1985), p. 183.
72 Chris Fitter, 'Introduction: rethinking Shakespeare in the social depth of politics', in Fitter (ed.), *Shakespeare and the politics of commoners*, pp. 1–39, at p. 34.
73 See David Harris Sacks, 'The greed of Judas: avarice, monopoly, and the moral economy in England, *ca.* 1350–*ca.* 1600', *Journal of Medieval and Early Modern Studies*, 28 (1998), 263–307.
74 See D. T. Gilbert and P. S. Malone, 'The correspondence bias', *Psychological Bulletin*, 117 (1995), 21–38; Miles Hewstone, Mark Rubin and Hazel Willis, 'Intergroup bias', *Annual Review of Psychology*, 53 (2002), 575–604.
75 On the notable absence of 'constitutional arguments' and 'institutional solutions' in early modern dramas, see Shapiro, *Political communication*, pp. 134–5. On the entanglement of sexual and economic corruptions, see also William Cavert's discussion in Chapter 8.
76 Lake with Questier, *The Antichrist's lewd hat*, pp. 94–9, 349–51; George Peele, *The troublesome reign of John, King of England*, ed. Charles R. Forker (Manchester, 2011), pp. 61, 133, 179, 271–2; 'Southwell to Verstegan', pp. 4–5 (quotation).
77 Henry Crosse, *Vertues common-wealth* (1603), sig. P3–[P3^{v}].
78 Stephen Gosson, *Playes confuted in fiue actions* (1582), sig. f–[f^{v}].
79 Hartlib Papers, HP 1/9/5A, John Dury to?, 31 March 1634, www.dhi.ac.uk/hartlib (accessed 15 May 2021).
80 Ross Knecht, 'Emotional labour: Hamlet', in Katharine A. Craik (ed.), *Shakespeare and emotion* (Cambridge, 2020), pp. 167–80, at pp. 174–5; Tribble, 'Affective contagion', pp. 195–6; Yamamoto, *Taming capitalism*, esp. pp. 104, 125, 194–209.
81 Phil Withington, 'An "Aristotelian moment": democracy in early modern England', in Braddick and Withington (eds), *Popular culture and political agency*, pp. 203–22, at pp. 221–2.

4

Alchemists, puritans and projectors in the plays of Ben Jonson

Peter Lake and Koji Yamamoto

Let us start with a definition of terms.[1] A 'projector' was someone with a scheme for intervention in the social or economic life of the nation, purportedly to benefit the commonwealth. The scheme, or project, nearly always involved the delegation of the prerogative powers of the Crown to an individual or group who would then use those powers to regulate or control some aspect of national life with a view to enhancing economic activities, or maintaining order, and thus the general prosperity and well-being of England in general, and the revenues of the Crown in particular. Nearly always involved was the pursuit of private profit by the projectors and courtiers for the achievement of the public good.[2] We can see this principle in operation throughout late Elizabethan and particularly early Stuart government. It was not just about the patents and monopolies that caused so much discontent and controversy in the 1590s, as discussed in Koji Yamamoto's Chapter 3. This mechanism took on a greater prominence under the early Stuarts despite the hopes of reform that greeted the accession of James VI of Scotland to the English throne in 1603.[3] Even religious conformity was to be enforced through the same method: delegating royal power to enterprising servants of the Crown.

This chapter revisits Ben Jonson's plays within this broader chronology of post-Reformation England. We will examine three plays – *The alchemist*, *Bartholomew Fair* and *The devil is an ass* – all written and performed under James between 1610 and 1616.[4] They were all what have come to be known as 'city comedies', a genre which Jonson had done much to produce and refine. As such, they all staged a fallen world defined by commerce, greed and hypocrisy, a world in which a series of fools, buffoons, thieves, alchemists, puritans and projectors combine to swindle and outwit one another in search of money, status, food and sex.[5]

It is of course well known that Jonson's city comedies satirised alchemists, puritans and projectors.[6] We suggest we can gain fresh insights if we situate Jonson's characters in the longer-term politics of stereotyping from the late sixteenth century onwards. Building on Chapters 2 and 3, the first section of this chapter thus provides a broader set of contexts for revisiting these comedies: we show that projects for economic and fiscal improvement drew so heavily on the language of reformation for the public good, and religious policies (and oppositions to them) had such visible economic implications, that the economic and religious realms displayed striking similarities. To develop this perspective, we consider writings of the puritan Thomas Scott, in which we find him siding with godly reformation against court corruptions and nefarious projects. Jonson's comedies make sense precisely against these backdrops.

The remaining sections demonstrate that Jonson's comedies featuring the alchemist, the puritan and the projector can be read as wonderfully perceptive commentaries on the precarious symbiosis between private ambitions and public purposes – a volatile union that exercised monarchs, parliament men, Privy Councillors and Catholic polemicists alike, and had affected the religious, political and economic life of the nation at least since the 1570s. Jonson's comic energy was poured into showing how godly puritans (like Scott) could look like alchemists or projectors greedily pursuing money and status, and how the farcical get-rich-quick schemes of the projector resembled the fakery of puritan exorcisms. Laughing at these characters served to collapse any meaningful distinctions between puritans and projectors. In getting laughs in this way, Jonson was seeking not merely to turn an honest penny, but also to set himself apart from the corruption and popularity upon which his plays relied for much of their appeal. Thus contextualised, Jonson's plays reveal the remarkable creativity with which his characters engaged with some of the most fundamental tensions in post-Reformation church and state.[7] In so doing, his plays simultaneously offered comic relief from, and thereby diminished, the profound threat that both puritans and projectors posed to the status quo. His comedies thus promoted what Tim Harris in Chapter 1 of this volume has called *anxiety displacement*.

In the concluding section of this chapter, we assess broader repercussions of Jonson's drama for the early Stuart period. Ever since L. C. Knights, scholars have sought to combine literary analysis with political, religious and economic history; Jonson's plays have always played a prominent part in such studies.[8] The direction of analysis has tended to move from the sociopolitical, economic or religious context towards explication of the dramatic text, and from the dramatic text thus explicated to the contemporary social reality. We want to enrich this body of literature by highlighting the transformative agency of the theatre. The point here is not that the theatre simply 'invented' such stereotypes – Chapters 2 and 3 have laid such assumptions to rest.[9] Rather, we analyse how the popular stage fed off, refined and then recirculated a range of existing tropes and stereotypes and thus shaped social and political reality. We show just how literary interventions and their afterlives had a profound impact on the subsequent political and economic processes in the run-up to the Civil Wars. Those effects could be complex and even contradictory. The stereotype of the projector and the monopolist fed into dialectical processes, diffusing anxieties and legitimating the status quo, while also serving as flashpoints for anger, agitation and political escalation.

James I and projects for reforming religion, economy and finance

A departure point for our analysis is provided by the striking similarities between fiscal and religious policies, both of which were central to the post-Reformation English state. The figures we encounter below, such as Robert Cecil, Henry Spiller, William Cockayne, Arthur Ingram and Giles Mompesson, were variously involved in controversial religious and fiscal schemes, and Jonson was acquainted with some of these men. Reviewing the history of their exploits lays the groundwork for understanding Jonson's plays and the stereotypes he developed. Doing so will also prepare us for the discussion of Thomas Scott's puritan critique of projectors in the next section.

Let us start with the example of the farm of the Great Customs, a scheme initiated in 1604 by Lord Treasurer Robert Cecil to enhance or maximise royal revenue under James I. The Crown was devoid of a properly paid and structured bureaucracy, and of the financial means to acquire one, in order to collect the customs revenues that formed one of the most important sources of royal revenue. Accordingly, abuse and under-reporting were rife and the Crown, in desperate financial straits already, was forced to watch very large sums of potential revenue leech away. Cecil's scheme involved leasing the right to collect the customs to a cartel of merchants who, having bid competitively for the privilege, would then proceed to collect the customs themselves. The promoter's profit would be constituted by the difference between the amount they had paid the Crown and what they managed to collect. Being merchants, they would understand the technicalities of trade and accounting and be all too aware of the ways in which (other) merchants sought to avoid paying the full extent of what they owed.

The system would not work properly unless the bidding process for awarding the contract was rigorously conducted. This did not happen. Robert Cecil was in the midst of building Hatfield House, that ultimate prodigy house, which placed him under financial pressure. There were only limited numbers of merchants rich enough to undertake the task of collecting customs duties across different ports. As Lord Treasurer, Cecil accordingly proceeded to award the contract to some of his largest creditors.

Later, the control of Cecil's merchants was challenged (unsuccessfully) by the Earl of Northampton, who, hot in pursuit of royal service, wanted to replace Cecil's merchants with some of his own.[10] Here is a classic instance of the recruitment of private interest seemingly for the achievement of a public good.

We can find the same principles and problems unfolding within the enforcement of religious uniformity and the suppression of religious dissent, in this instance that of Catholics.[11] Here the key issue was how best to administer the recusancy laws and, in particular, how best to collect the fines that flowed therefrom directly into the coffers of the Crown. This problem provoked debates within the state and among its actual or wannabe agents. On one hand, there were those claiming that compounding for recusancy fines was the better bet. This involved exchequer officials approaching leading recusants and negotiating in effect a fee or fixed charge, which if paid regularly into the exchequer, would guarantee that the payer would no longer be subjected to the recusancy statutes. In a situation where the Crown was not actively 'persecuting', that is to say, not aggressively pursuing, imprisoning and intermittently executing Catholic priests, rich recusant families could purchase what was in effect a form of *de facto* toleration, or at least the right to exercise their religion within the privacy of their own households or estates. This method of enforcement would maximise the Crown's revenue, since a draconian application of the laws would merely drive many Catholics into at least outward conformity and thus prevent the Crown from collecting any fines from such people at all. This was in effect to delegate the regal power to suspend a statute to various agents of the Crown and, again, just as with the farm of the customs, the system depended on the negotiation of a just or proper price from each of the Catholics who were prepared to compound. Yet the chief advocate and agent for this method was Sir Henry Spiller, himself a crypto-Catholic. So there was a real danger of bribery undermining revenue collection.

Against this camp was another school of opinion demanding Catholics be squeezed to the full extent of the law. That way revenue would be maximised and the practice of Catholicism properly punished and disincentivised. Those who advocated this course often enjoyed special commissions under the Crown to seek out and mulct Catholics, powers which, as their critics within the administration and their Catholic victims both claimed, they roundly abused, running something like a protection racket and profiting personally from the sequestration of Catholic estates and the collection of fines. Here, then, was a classic instance of rival groups, each seeking to deploy and profit from the powers of the Crown, both claiming that their methods best served the interests of the commonweal (including here both the revenues of the Crown and the preservation of true religion). These competing groups also claimed that the practices of their rivals represented a form of corruption, that is to say the arbitrary use of public power for the corrupt pursuit of private profit.

Things began to spin out of control with the collapse of the Great Contract in 1610. This contract had been designed to grant an annual sum of £200,000 to the king in exchange for his feudal privileges and the power to impose new fiscal impositions. Despite Cecil's effort to promote it, the Contract was rejected by both James and Parliament. Then came the fiasco of the Addled Parliament in 1614. Far from aiding the parlous state of the royal finances, this Parliament was dissolved after only three weeks in a paroxysm of complaint about impositions and corrupt (Scottish) courtiers. By this time, James's court was also engulfed in a series of sex scandals. The most spectacular of these was the Essex divorce and the Overbury murder in 1613,[12] which were followed by lesser scandals like that involving Sir Thomas Lake and his wife and the eventual fall of the Earl of Suffolk. The latter had its gendered, sexualised, aspects, since a central feature of the case against Suffolk was the involvement of his wife in some of the most outrageous instances of greed and graft.[13] Amidst these court scandals mired with greed and sex was the swarm of projectors, promising to raise money by using the prerogative powers of the monarchy without having to rely on Parliament. There are myriad examples of such schemes littering the state papers, which still await their historian.[14]

Perhaps the best-known scheme of this period is the Cockayne project that took off in 1614, two years before the first performance of *The devil is an ass*. It was promoted by William Cockayne, a Lord Mayor of London, who persuaded James to give him the monopoly for England's main export trade: that of woollen cloth. The English cloth hitherto exported had been unfinished. Cockayne's plan was to dye and finish the cloth in England before it was shipped to the Continent and sold there at a higher price. This, he claimed, would employ the poor, stimulate the economy and greatly increase the Crown's customs revenues. However, the Dutch refused to cooperate, and it emerged that local textile workers lacked the expertise to actually finish the cloth. The cloth trade soon collapsed, causing a depression in the cloth-working areas of East Anglia from which they took decades to recover. Control of the trade was rapidly returned to the Merchant Venturers. As for Cockayne, he died in 1626 in possession of multiple country houses; leaving a rent roll of some £12,000 a year to his son, he was buried in St Paul's Cathedral, complete with a funeral sermon by John Donne.[15]

Not all 'projectors' operated at such distinguished social levels. Just below Cockayne, we might place Sir Arthur Ingram. Ingram bounced around between a money-lending business in London and his position as comptroller of the London Customs House. In 1615, he leased the Yorkshire alum business from the Crown and helped to manage the personal finances of the notoriously corrupt Earl of Suffolk. The 1630s found Ingram, an eager agent and ally of Thomas Wentworth who was the Lord President of the Council of the North, up to his neck in the composition for and collection of recusancy fines. By such means, and with the support of such powerful friends at court as Cecil, Northampton, Suffolk and later Wentworth, Ingram amassed a large, landed estate worth £6,000 a year and undertook an ambitious building programme at York and Temple Newsam.[16]

Ingram had an unsavoury enough reputation, but for a genuine bottom-feeder we must turn to Sir Giles Mompesson. One of Mompesson's most notorious ventures was his patent for the licensing of inns. The consumption of alcohol carried with it more than predictable concerns about drunkenness and disorder. In times of dearth, official efforts to control the grain supply often banged up against the demands of the brewing trade. While campaigns against tippling and the drive to regulate alehouses might carry with them a whiff of a 'puritan reformation of manners', they were also an expression of the more widespread concern (certainly not peculiar to puritans) to maintain order and protect the commonweal. The regulation and licensing of alehouses and inns usually fell to local justices of the peace. But in 1617 Mompesson gained a patent to license inns. He was given free rein to charge more or less what he liked provided four-fifths of the proceeds went to the exchequer. Mompesson proceeded to run something of a protection racket, charging exorbitant fees, reopening inns suppressed for riotous behaviour for the appropriate fee and entrapping various innkeepers and others for minor infractions of the rules. One of his agents was later accused of having persuaded an alehouse keeper to let him stay the night at his establishment, only the next morning to fine him for keeping an inn, not an alehouse. Mompesson thus became the poster child for court-centred corruption and, having been investigated by the Parliament of 1624, was driven into exile. His stay abroad did not last long. He was back in England by the 1630s, when he was at the centre of riots in the Forest of Dean, protesting at the enclosure of the royal forests there. At some point in the 1630s he came up with a scheme under which the branch of every tree in the royal forests would have the royal coat of arms stamped on it, the better to be able to prosecute people for making off with the king's timber. Mompesson, of course, was to have the patent for collecting the consequent fines.[17]

That might seem beyond parody, but projectors like Mompesson were on the rise after the collapse of the Addled Parliament in 1614. The collapse of the Parliament also led to heightened interest in an Anglo-Spanish match (a proposed marriage between James's son Prince Charles and Maria Anna of Spain), since it brought the prospect of fresh funds in the form of the dowry.[18] That interest was redoubled by the Bohemian crisis of 1618, when James's response to the onset of religious war in Europe was to double down on negotiations with Spain. The court thus became tainted also with popery and crypto-popery, with the Spanish ambassador Gondomar taking on the mantle of sinister Catholic evil counsellor when he replaced the Earl of Northampton after the latter died in 1614.

The 'puritan' critique and the critique of puritanism

By the end of the 1610s, then, James's court had been subject to a series of overlapping discourses of corruption centred on sex, greed and popery. Hence proceeded the nightmare vision conjured in Thomas Scott's infamous tract *Vox populi* of 1620.[19] This tract was a fictionalised account of a meeting of the Spanish council of state with Gondomar returning from England. Understanding Scott's uncompromising depictions of the 1610s at this point enables us to make better sense of a complex and contradictory position taken by Jonson early on.

In *Vox populi*, Scott used an imagined Spanish perspective to depict an English court full of self-seeking courtiers, papists, crypto-papists and various sorts of projectors, all seeking to bend the royal will to their own ends. According to Scott, such men used personal influence, flattery and graft to work their evil way up the court, abusing the prerogative powers of the Crown to the detriment of true religion and the rights, liberties and property of the subject. Fearing Parliamentary scrutiny of their nefarious designs, these men sought to persuade James that he both could and should rule through his prerogative, raising money through various schemes and projects rather than meeting his people in a Parliament. In fact, with the exception of the brief Addled Parliament in 1614, there had been no Parliament since 1610. Andrew Thrush has quite aptly termed the decade 1611–20, 'the personal rule of James I'.[20] On Scott's account, the absence of Parliament inevitably led to astronomical levels of corruption and popish and foreign influence, which blinded the king to the real nature of what was happening to his subjects and what was really at stake in the current conjuncture in Europe. For Scott, Parliament was an institution that had a permanent and necessary place in the working of monarchical government.[21]

The figure of the 'projector' played a prominent role in this argument. In 1620, Scott had preached an assize sermon at Norwich called *The projector, teaching a direct sure and ready way to restore the decays of the church and state both in honour and revenue*. There he conjured the figure of the projector, defined as those who 'propound some admirable project, how to raise great sums of money filling the exchequer, and those mountains aloft without draining the country bogs'. If Scott were such a projector, he had no doubt that he would be 'welcome to court and my message and person entertained with favour'. But Scott was precisely not *that* sort of projector; he was pushing an altogether different sort of project, one that would save both church and state. This was a war against sin to be waged by the minister and the magistrate using the established means and modes of doing justice, which were now reanimated by the political virtue and godly zeal of both governors and governed.[22] Scott conjured a world in which 'every man dares buy and sell, without fear of cozening, ... dares plant and plough and sow and reap and grow honestly rich'. This would be a blessed state of affairs, which Scott contrasted with England's current fallen condition.[23]

Whether or not Thomas Scott was a 'classical republican', he was indubitably a puritan.[24] In his tracts he put a good deal of time and energy into constructing himself as a moderate, but if we judge him by what he did as well as by what he said, Scott might be thought to have been something of a radical: a conviction Presbyterian with a relatively uncompromising vision of what a properly reformed commonwealth would look like. Either way, however we categorise him, he was driven into exile in the Netherlands for writing *Vox populi*. There he kept up a stream of commentary in a series of printed tracts until 1624. He was assassinated in 1626 by a deranged soldier who, even under torture, refused to admit that he had been suborned by the Jesuits.

The traditional whig accounts of James's reign followed the basic pattern laid down by Scott. These accounts describe James's court as a corrupt form of prerogative rule, saddled with an absolutist ideology and a profusion of corrupt courtiers and favourites. Over against that court was set a puritan opposition of precisely the sort conjured by Scott: an opposition in favour of parliaments and against all sorts of monopolies, patents, projects and projectors, and organised around a bluff, hot, Protestant ideology, favourable to the puritan godly and viscerally hostile to 'popery' in all its forms. On this view there was a simple, binary opposition between the figures of 'the projector' and the 'puritan'. The former epitomised court corruption and prerogative rule, the pursuit of private interests over public good and the 'privacy' of the court over the public service of the commonwealth, which could only be achieved by the virtuous action of 'public men', both in the conduct of local government and in Parliament. The ensuing patriot ideal, while often animated by a classical language of political virtue, was also equated with puritan godliness, with the commonweal being conflated with a vigorously Protestant, indeed, puritan, vision of true religion. Integral to that vision was an open-ended process of moral and spiritual reformation, with popery characterised as the master sin from which church and state must be protected, both at home and abroad.[25]

The impression of clarity disappears as soon as we take a closer look at how opposing labels like 'puritan' and 'projector' were actually put to use. As Johann Somerville has pointed out, if the language of political virtue and the commonweal was a mark of 'civic republicanism' and indeed of 'opposition' to the early Stuart regime, then James I himself must count as a 'republican' and a leading 'oppositionist', since James had serial recourse to precisely that language in legitimating his own rule. So too did a variety of projectors, whose whole pitch was based on the ways in which their projects would materially, and sometimes morally, benefit the commonweal. Those claims were open to contest of course, but it was rarely obvious which side was in the 'right'. The notorious Westminster soap monopoly active during the 1630s was justified as a means to achieve 'the reformation of abuses in making soap'.[26] The great trading companies – the Merchant Venturers and the East India Company amongst others – were all, in some sense, projects. They were monopolies reliant on the delegated prerogative powers of the Crown to manage trade, create profit and (purportedly) benefit both Crown and commonweal. Indeed, as Rupali Mishra and others have observed, the origins of English imperial political economy arguably lie in debates about the benefits and harms caused by such trading monopolies.[27]

Much the same sort of ambiguity surrounds the figure of the puritan. Always the heroes of their own story, in their own eyes the puritans were champions of true religion and therefore of the commonwealth, against popery, irreligion, ignorance, atheism and corruption, in both high and low places. It was enemies of the puritans in the state and particularly in the church who were pursuing their own private interests. In turn, bishops and their conformist hangers-on convinced the monarch that there was a puritan threat to order and monarchical authority and then told him (or her) that they were the best defence against the said threat. Seen from the puritan perspective, this was how bishops and their associates defended ill-gotten offices, wealth and power. These Anglican bishops were also hypocrites, telling the puritans that they too promoted further reformation although their hands were tied by the magistrate, a gesture displayed while (puritans alleged) they worked with the authorities to take down the godly.

But from at least the 1570s, and with increasing pace and intensity from the 1590s, there emerged an anti-puritan counter-discourse which reversed these claims, tainting the puritans with popularity and accusing them of pursuing their private interests against legitimate authority, canons and public determinations of the church.[28] In this view, puritans referred all to Scripture and then reduced the authority of Scripture to their own private opinion of what Scripture meant. They similarly used an appeal to the integrity of their consciences and the offence of their followers to legitimate all sorts of disobedience to the authority of both prince and bishop. By preaching divisive versions of the central doctrine of predestination, such puritans in effect divided the Christian community between the godly and the profane, and tended to equate the community of the godly (i.e. themselves) with the true church. Authority used to check their excesses became in their eyes a form of tyranny, indeed even of popish tyranny, wielded by the bishops, who, on some (Presbyterian and separatist) views of the matter, were themselves holders of an inherently Antichristian office. This rendered puritanism a form of rebellion waiting to happen. On this hyper-conformist view of the matter, it was the puritans (rather than those supporting the establishment) who were guilty of the true status- and wealth-grab as, through institutions and practices like the stipendiary lecture and the conventicle, they continually flattered and appealed to their lay supporters, thereby mobilising their support against the rightful rulers of church and state.

On this view, again, hypocrisy served as the defining characteristic of the puritans. The pursuit of the most overt and basic of private interests and drives – those centred on money, food, sex and wealth – were hidden or legitimated by the puritans' entirely false claims to an extreme piety and superhuman levels of godliness.[29] By the 1590s, these characteristics had coalesced into a stereotype which was established through a number of media – popular libels, cheap print, conformist propaganda and theatrical performance. As one person's corrupt project was another's improvement scheme, so one man's godly professor was someone else's Pharisaical hypocrite and sectary.

Ben Jonson on alchemists and puritans

Ben Jonson lived in the midst of the intensely contested and liminal cultural, political and social space defined by the figures of the projector and the puritan. As the leading author and dramaturge of the court masque under James I, Jonson was connected to, and heavily identified with, the court. Indeed, Jonson had what turned out to be the very considerable misfortune to have written a masque celebrating the ill-fated marriage in 1606 of Robert Devereux and Frances Howard. (Frances later played her part in the death of Thomas Overbury in 1613, which led to an intense court scandal and trial between 1615 and 1616.) Jonson also provided verses for an entertainment for Alderman Cockayne, whose project for exporting finished cloth was falling apart as Jonson was writing *The devil is an ass* (first staged in 1616). In that year, Cockayne dedicated a (now lost) play to James I, in which cloth dressers and others 'spake such language as Ben Jonson put in their mouths'.[30] On his way to Scotland in 1618, Jonson would be welcomed by the projector Sir Arthur Ingram in York and ride in a coach with him to meet the Archbishop of York.[31]

As John Creaser has pointed out, however, Jonson was much more than a creature of the court patronage. His friendship network included such outspoken critics of royal policy as Sir Edwin Sandys and John Hoskins.[32] Jonson was also up to his neck in the thoroughly commercial and popular world of the London stage and more than aware of the close connections between the commercial theatre and the hucksterish world of commerce, as well as the desperate search for an audience or a market to be achieved by pandering to popular taste and the follies of the people. These were precisely the characteristics of which the critics of the theatre (both puritan and non-puritan) accused the stage, and of which many anti-puritans, like Jonson himself, accused the puritans.

Implicated in both the court and the popular stage, Jonson as a poet also aspired to stay above them. As a number of critics have observed, this was neither a comfortable, nor even an entirely coherent, position. In this section and the next, we will show how Jonson used the figures of the alchemist, the puritan and the projector to negotiate this position in an attempt to establish an independent, corruption-free vantage point, above the polarities of contemporary debate and beyond the competing cries for popular attention and court patronage – a vantage point from which he could deliver his purging drafts of comic truth and commentary to both popular and elite audiences.

Much of the comic and dramatic energy humming through Jonson's city comedies is derived from the way in which Jonson guys, mimics and parodies various styles of iterative, even incantatory, speech, in the process rendering the key terms and turns of speech of his target groups both meaningless and, by the end, self-evidently absurd. Alchemy was the ultimate example of this sort of exalted secret language – a closed linguistic system or argot whose meaning was known only to adepts, but which could be used to mystify, impress and therefore gull susceptible, credulous or greedy outsiders.

Alchemists were also in many ways the first projectors. Certainly, the origins of the term had a distinct alchemical flavour: 'the project was a promise of alchemy like transformation, turning untapped resources (such as human ingenuity, dormant legislation or idle labour) into wealth, a process fuelled by another transmutation of private desires into public benefits'.[33] As the seminal researches of Glyn Parry have shown, the alchemist and magus John Dee had a remarkably sustained and not unsuccessful career as a sort of expert or projector under Elizabeth.[34] In the early Stuart period Cornelis Drebbel, the alchemist who invented both a perpetual motion machine and, as he claimed, the first submarine, represented almost an ideal type of the projector, full of schemes, constantly promoting his own reputation, looking for patrons both royal and merely rich.[35]

Jonson spends large swathes of *The alchemist* lovingly reconstructing and parodying the argot of the alchemist whom, in the characters of Face and Subtle, he presents as the ultimate con man. Here is Subtle instructing the hapless Abel Drugger on how best to lay out his shop to maximise his business:

> Make me your door, then, south; your broad side west;
> And on the east side of your shop, aloft,
> Write *Mathlai, Tarmiel* and *Barborat;*
> Upon the north part *Rael, Velel, Thiel.*
> They are the names of the mercurial spirits
> That do fright flies from boxes. (1:3, 63–8)

Here he is again, instructing Face on the next stage of their projection:

> Infuse vinegar
> To draw his volatile substance and his tincture,
> And let the water in glass E be filtered
> And put into the gripe's egg. Lute him well
> And leave him closed in *balneo*.

All of which elicits from the watching Surly the slighting comment 'what a brave language here is! Next to canting!' (2:3, 37–42). It is, Surly observes later in the same scene, 'a pretty kind of game/Somewhat like the tricks o'the cards, to cheat a man/With charming'. He continues:

> What else are all your terms,
> Whereon no one 'o your writers 'grees with other?
> Of your elixir, your *lac virginis,*
> Your stone, your med'cine, and your chrysosperm,
> ... Your sun, your moon, your firmament, your adrop[.] (2:3, 180–90)

The mimicry of modes of speech plays just as central a role in Jonson's unmasking of the godly as an essentially hypocritical crew of chancers and con men (and women). Here, in the same play, is Ananias the deacon denouncing the would-be gallant Kastril: 'they are profane, lewd superstitious idolatrous breeches ... avoid Satan! Thou are not of the light. That ruff of pride about thy neck betrays thee ... Thou look'st like Antichrist in that lewd hat' (4:7, 48–55). Here, in *Bartholomew Fair*, is Zeal-of-the-Land Busy in a more reflective, casuistical mode. The pregnant Win-the-fight has a longing to eat pig, and Dame Purecraft has turned to Busy to resolve this particular 'case of conscience' in such a way as to gratify that urge. At first, he demurs.

> The disease of longing, it is a disease, a carnal disease, or appetite, incident to women; and as it is carnal, and incident, it is natural, very natural. Now pig, it is a meat, and a meat that is nourishing, and may be longed for, and so consequently eaten; it may be eaten; and very exceedingly well eaten. But in the Fair, and as a Barthol'mew-pig, it cannot be eaten, for the very calling of it a Barthol'mew-pig, and to eat it so, is a spice of idolatry, and you make the Fair no better than one of the high places. (1:6, 39–45)

Pressed by Dame Purecraft to think again, Busy then reverses himself.

> Surely, it may be otherwise, but it is subject to construction – subject – and hath a face of offence with the weak, a great face, a foul face, but that face may have a veil put over it, and be shadowed, as it were; it may be eaten, and in the Fair, I take it, in a booth, the tents of the wicked. The place is not much, not very much. We may be religious in the face of the profane, so it be eaten with a reformed mouth, with sobriety and humbleness, not gorged with gluttony and greediness – there's the fear, for should she go there taking pride in the place, or delight in the unclean dressing, to feed the vanity of the eye or the lust of the palate, it were not well, it were not fit, it were abominable, and not good. (1:6, 55–64)

Then to avoid the sin of idolatry, which he clearly takes to be a sin of the eye, rather than of the heart, Busy proceeds to lead his flock through the fair towards the pig using only 'the famelic sense', in other words following their noses, looking neither to the right nor to the left. Peter Lake has argued elsewhere that this was not a dissection of puritan hypocrisy in general, but in fact followed very closely the casuistical logic of the puritan case in favour of conformity to ceremonies which they took to be offensive and even, under the wrong circumstances, unlawfully idolatrous. What we have here, therefore, is not merely a knock-about depiction of puritan hypocrisy, but a far more close-grained critique of attitudes and practices central to the puritan project.[36]

But this was not the only mode of puritan discourse that Jonson guyed in and ridiculed through the figure of Busy. In a more vituperative mood, Busy denounces the gingerbread stall as 'an idolatrous grove', maintaining that he will not be silenced by the complaints of the stall owner that he is disrupting trade (3:6, 77). Busy insists that his denunciations were no less than 'a sanctified noise. I will make a most loud and most strong noise, till I have daunted the profane enemy' (3:6, 83–4). Confronting the puppet Dionysius in a debate about the lawfulness of the stage, Busy proclaims '[t]hou art the seat of the beast, O Smithfield, and I will leave thee. Idolatry peepeth out of every side of thee' (3:6, 35–36). 'The place is Smithfield, or the field of smiths, the grove of hobby-horses and trinkets. The wares are the wares of devils. And the whole fair is the shop of Satan' (3:2, 32–4).

This is as close as we are likely to get to what a certain style of puritan spiritual ejaculation, a mode of extempore prayer and preaching, actually sounded like.[37] But be that as it may, this certainly is Jonson's rendition of puritan-speak, the mode of speech and self-presentation that marked the godly off from their contemporaries, and through which puritans, both clerical and lay, sought to ensnare their victims or, as they put it, to 'edify' both their flocks and one another. In putting the language of puritan preachers into the mouth of the plebeian blowhard and fraud Zeal-of-the-Land Busy, a baker from Banbury – a notoriously puritan town, whose preacher, William Whately (aka the 'roaring boy of Banbury') was known for his stentorian, denunciatory mode in the pulpit – Jonson was assimilating the mainstream puritanism of such famous town preachers and puritan bosses as Whately in Banbury, John White in Dorchester or Samuel Ward in Ipswich, with a strand of decidedly unrespectable, indeed plebeian, lay activism and hucksterism.[38]

While we have unpacked the telltale terminology and timbre of puritan discourse, the excellent editorial notes provided by Peter Holland and Bill Sherman for *The alchemist* assure us that Jonson was just as scrupulous in mimicking the alchemist's distinctive patter.[39] In one scene in *The alchemist*, as though to establish the equivalences between the two modes of speech and their (intended) obfuscatory, indeed delusory, effects on the unwary, Jonson brings the languages of alchemy and of puritanism together in an exchange between Subtle and Ananias the deacon. Having told Face to 'take away the recipient,/And rectify your menstrue from the phlegma/Then pour it o'er the Sol in the cucurbit,/And let 'em macerate together', Subtle turns to Ananias and asks, 'who are you?' When the reply comes, 'a faithful brother', Subtle asks 'What's that/A lullianist? A Ripley? *Filius artis*?/Can you sublime and calcify? Calcine?/ … Or what is homogene or heterogene?' Ananias responds that this is all Greek to him, and that since Greek was a heathen language ('all's heathen but the Hebrew') he wants nothing to do with it (2:5, 1–17). Subtle responds in kind, later delivering a blistering tirade to both Ananias and the pastor, Tribulation Wholesome, in which he details all of the signature hypocrisies and corruptions of the puritans: 'your holy vizard to win widows/To give you legacies, or make zealous wives/To rob their husbands for the common cause'. He turns next to the exquisite hypocrisy of puritan casuistry – the 'scrupulous bones' 'cast before your hungry [because fasting] hearers', 'as whether a Christian may hawk or hunt … Or have the idol starch about their linen'. Thence he proceeds to the puritans' seditious ways with their governors in church and state; their propensity

> to libel 'gainst the prelate
> And shorten so your ears against the hearing

Of the next wire-drawn grace. Nor, of necessity,
Rail against the plays to please the alderman
Whose daily custard you devour. Nor lie
With zealous rage, until you are hoarse. (3:2, 69–91)

Despite Surly's diatribes and their own scruples, not to mention Subtle's anti-puritan rant, the brethren persist in seeking the alchemist's services because their drive to turn base metal into gold and establish 'the discipline' outweighs all other considerations. This is an hypocrisy that Jonson stages both through Tribulation's persistent efforts to get the over-zealous Ananias to just shut up, and Ananias's elaborate casuistical effort to prove that, under the right circumstances, coining was perfectly legal.

Jonson on the projector (and the puritan)

Now, there are no puritans in *The devil is an ass*, and while a form of magic is used at the outset to establish both the cupidity and gullibility of the central protagonist Fitzdottrel, who enters seeking the service of a magician to conjure the devil in order to discover hidden treasure, the main source of performative linguistic fraudulence in this play is neither an alchemist nor a devil, but rather the projector Merecraft. The play's central scam involves a plan for fen drainage, or as Merecraft calls it, 'the thing … for the recovery of drowned land,/Whereof the Crown's to have his moiety/If it be owner; else the Crown and owners/To share the moiety, and the recoverers/T'enjoy the tother moiety for their charge'. The scheme was to run, Merecraft claims, 'throughout England' and would realise 'eighteen millions' (2:1, 45–51); more than enough, he explains, to buy Fitzdottrel a dukedom. After a brief discussion as to which title would be most appropriate, they settle, appropriately enough, upon the Duke of Drowned-lands (2:4, 15–23).[40]

Merecraft abounds with projects. He enters the action pulling one and then another out of a bag he carries with him, like so many rabbits out of a hat. It later appears he is engaged with Lady Tailbush

on a project for the fact and venting
Of a new kind of fucus – paint, for ladies –
To serve the kingdom, wherein she herself
Hath travailed specially, by way of service
Unto her sex, and hopes to get the monopoly
As the reward for her invention. (3:4, 49–54)

The fraudulence and absurdity of the project is underscored when Tailbush herself is completely taken in as Wittipol, posing in drag as 'the Spanish lady', sells her a ludicrous description of her own cosmetic concoction, 'th'*avagada*/And *argentata* of Queen Isabella', made up, he assures her, in a litany of absurdity and obscurity worthy of *The alchemist*, of

> your *alum scagliola*, or *Pol di pedra,*
> And *zuccerino*; turpentine of Abezo,
> Washed in nine waters ... make
> The admirable varnish for the face,
> Gives the right lustre; but two drops rubbed on
> With a piece of scarlet makes a lady of sixty
> Look at sixteen. (4:4, 27–39)

It is worth remarking here that the intense ridicule of the vogue for things Spanish and the fetishisation of Spanish-sounding terms and commodities that the figure of the Spanish lady allows, is almost certainly referencing and ridiculing trends set off around the court by the prospect of a Spanish match, a topic which was back on the political agenda in 1616 and, of course, was to remain there until the early 1620s. Once again – *except for the anti-puritanism* – we find Jonson addressing, in comic terms and modes, much of the polemical terrain occupied, only a few years later, in all earnestness, but also with more than a touch of satiric, fictionalised *sprezzatura*, by Thomas Scott.

Merecraft also has a scheme to establish what he calls an 'office of dependency'. This is 'a place/Of my projection too, sir, and hath met/Much opposition; but the state, now, sees/That great necessity of it, as after all/ Their writing and speaking against duels,/They have erected it'. This was a court to which recourse was to be had to settle quarrels amongst gentlemen, without recourse to duelling. 'They shall refer now hither for their process;/ And such as trespass 'gainst the rule of court/Are to be fined' (3:3, 62–74). But perhaps the two most perfectly formed of the projects contained in the play concern a toothpick monopoly and a project for 'the laudable use of forks'. As Merecraft explains to Lady Tailbush, he meant to offer the former to 'your ladyship on the perfecting of the patent'. It was a scheme

> for serving the whole state with toothpicks.
> Somewhat an intricate business to discourse, but
> I show how much the subject is abused,
> First, in that one commodity. Then what disease
> And putrefactions in the gums are bred
> By those are made of adult'rate and false wood!
> My plot for reformation of these follows:
> To have all toothpicks brought unto an office
> There sealed, and such as counterfeit 'em, mulcted.
> And last, for venting 'em, to have a book
> Printed to teach their use, which every child

> Shall have throughout the kingdom that can read
> And learn to pick his teeth by. (4:2, 38–51)

As for the latter, it was a project for 'the laudable use of forks,/Brought into custom here, as they are in Italy'. The aim here was 'th' sparing o'napkins', 'for 'twill be/A mighty saver of linen through the kingdom' and thus a means 'to spare washing', as well as a stimulus to industry in the manufacturing of forks. 'That should have made your bellows go at the forge, as his at the furnace', he tells Gilthead, who was to have had 'the making of all those/Of gold and silver for the better personages', while his mate Sledge was to have made 'those of steel for the common sort'. Merecraft brags that he has already 'dealt with the linen-drapers on my private,/By cause I feared they were the likeliest ever/To stir against, to cross it', and has already 'procured the signet for it' (5:4, 18–31).

We have here the typical language of the projector that had troubled England at least since the 1570s: the claims to pursue reformation in the market sphere for the common good and the interests of the subject, while raking in money both for the projectors themselves and for the Crown. Here, too, are the difficulties inherent in persuading the relevant authorities to give their assent and the need to buy off or suppress the various interest groups likely to be hurt by the scheme. And here, too, is the full gamut of types of project: for economic improvement – fen drainage; for the fostering of new products – the *fucus* and the fork patents; for the regulation of trade – the toothpick patent; and finally, for social regulation – the office of dependences. What we are seeing here, we argue, is more than topical commentary. As Yamamoto's Chapter 3 has shown, the Crown's chronic dependence on patents and the similar delegation of prerogative power provided inspirations for Elizabethan history plays to chronicle profound suffering and even a civil war. By staging Merecraft and Tailbush among others, by contrast Jonson transformed the same set of issues, through judicious exaggeration and accentuation, into satire, as the established figure of the puritan was joined on stage by the emergent one of the projector.

While *The devil is an ass* does not feature a puritan, there is an exorcism, a practice indelibly associated with the puritan godly. That spoof possession by the devil picks up the founding conceit of the play, which involves a junior devil Pug, who is determined to go to London to wreak havoc. Satan tells him he has no chance, such are the sophisticated levels of iniquity achieved by the current denizens of the city. Pug insists, is allowed his opportunity and thereupon is humiliated at the hands of the Londoners. The conceit reaches its apogee when Pug proffers his help to Merecraft and Fitzdottrel as they attempt to stage their fake possession and exorcism. This is intended to get them off the hook of the failed scam that has left them at the mercy of their intended victims. The claim is that Fitzdottrel has been given potions to enamour him of the Spanish lady, who, it turns out, is neither Spanish nor a lady, but his enemy Wittipol in disguise.

Now, as a real devil, Pug ought to know how to stage a possession, and accordingly he offers to

so advance
The business that you have in hand of witchcraft
And your possession, as myself were in you;
Teach you such tricks, to make your belly swell
And your eyes turn, to foam, to stare, to gnash
Your teeth together, and to beat yourself,
Laugh loud, and feign six voices[.] (5:5, 22–28)

However, his performance in the role of 'devil' has been so pathetic that the conspirators refuse his offer and hand him over to the constable to be hanged at Newgate, from which ignominious fate he is only rescued by the intervention of Satan himself (5:6).

Merecraft and Fitzdottrel then proceed to stage the possession in terms taken, not from the devil, but rather directly from the puritans. Or, to be more exact, from the practice of the notorious puritan exorcist John Darrell, whose activities in the 1590s had attracted the hostile attentions of Bishop Richard Bancroft, his attack dog Samuel Harsnett and the High Commission. Darrell had been imprisoned and removed from the ministry, and exorcism puritan-style had been, if not altogether suppressed, then certainly driven underground. Harsnett's case against Darrell was that his exorcisms were simple frauds, and Harsnett wrote an elaborate account of them as precisely that, a species of illusion, or legerdemain.[41] The issue was current in 1616 because of a recent case in Leicestershire when, on the accusation of one John Smith, a boy of 13, some nine women had been executed as witches, only for James I, visiting Leicestershire the following month, to unmask the boy as a fraud and thus save six more women from the hangman.[42] Thus Merecraft assured Fitzdottrel that ''tis no hard thing t'outdo the devil in;/A boy o'thirteen years old made him an ass/But t'other day' (5:5, 49–51).

Exorcism was, then, a practice of markedly and widely known puritan provenance, a point the play drives home in a passage directed by Merecraft to Fitzdottrel, as he instructs him how best to carry off the effects of possession.

It is the easiest thing, sir, to be done.
As plain as fizzling; roll but wi' your eyes,
And foam at th'mouth. A little castle-soap
Will do't, to rub your lips; and then a nutshell,

> With tow and touchwood in it to spit fire.
> Did you n'er read, sir, little Darrel's tricks,
> With the boy o'Burton, and the seven of Lancashire,
> Sommers at Nottingham? All these do teach it.
> And we'll give out, sir, that your wife has bewitched you. (5:3, 1–9)

It is worth noting here, that in this passage Jonson cuts out the middleman, not using Harsnett's unmasking of puritan fraud so much as the puritans' accounts of their own practice, in the case of Darrell's dealings with Thomas Darling, William Somers and the seven possessed children in the Starkey household in Lancashire. Clearly, for Jonson, what the puritans proffered as first-hand accounts of real possessions and exorcisms could serve as an instruction manual in how to reproduce what had always been simple sleights of hand. In order to work these effects, there was no need to consult or enlist the devil, at least not when the puritans were at hand.

There ensues a scene in which, at the prompting of Merecraft and his accomplice Everill – 'you do not tumble enough', '[w]allow, gnash!', 'give him more soap to foam with', 'act a little', 'speak, sir, some Greek if you can', 'your Spanish that I taught you' – Fitzdottrel acts out many of what were the commonly recognised, as it were Darrell-based, characteristics of the possessed person (5:8, 67, 67–9, 111, 115). He writhes, rants, foams at the mouth, his belly appears to swell. He claims that his wife, who has just entered the room, is tormenting him with pins and needles, and indulges in demonic-sounding gibberish – 'Yes, wis, knight, shite, Paul, jowl, owl, foul, troll, bowl' – in languages (Greek, Spanish and French) – that he is not supposed to understand (5:8, 109). This farrago of nonsense is brought to a close by the news, delivered by Shackles the keeper of Newgate to the otherwise entirely credulous justice Eitherside, that the real devil, i.e. Pug, has just been transported back to hell, leaving behind him only a foul smell and the body of the cutpurse, executed that very morning, which he has spent the day inhabiting. At that, Fitzdottrel comes clean and the play comes to a (very) rapid close.

The play thus ends with a series of discoveries – of the multiple projects and frauds of Merecraft, of the extreme folly and corruption of Fitzdottrel, and of a sham exorcism designed to cover all of that in the form of a classically puritan scam. Here is puritanism reduced from a free-standing form of hypocritical humbug, of both self- and other-directed deception and as such a real threat to order in church and state, to the status of an empty form, a mere script, to be appropriated by the real villains of the piece, in this case the projector (Merecraft) and his allies and (willing) victims (Fitzdottrel and Everill).

Theatre, pulpit and popularity

For the historian one of the great delights of Jonson's plays is the effort he puts into locating the action of his plays, and indeed his own metatheatrical interactions with the audiences of those plays, into a series of dense social, topographical, cultural and (albeit at one remove) political contexts. It is almost as if the first part of the work of contextualisation has been done for us. All we have to do is to recuperate and reanimate the contexts within which, and the perspectives from which, Jonson wanted his audiences to view his plays.

In the plays discussed above, Jonson was using actual or emergent stereotypes – here mainly the puritan, the projector and the alchemist/magician – to construct for himself a space of independent judgement; a space from which he could issue a stream of Olympian, but also broadly comic, commentary on the follies and corruptions to be found in the court, in the theatre and in the city – all arenas in which he was, in fact, a very active participant. If we take the polarities set up by the works of Thomas Scott, or indeed by the subsequent 'whig' accounts of the period that so closely mirrored Scott's works, then it becomes obvious that Jonson was seeking to rise above the emergent political tensions of the period by equating the puritan and the projector as risible threats to the status quo. No doubt the late Kevin Sharpe would have used Jonson's propensities in this regard to reject any interpretations of the period that rest upon the polarities and tensions being staged and, as he hoped, transcended by Jonson.[43] However, the very considerable efforts that Jonson put into refusing those polarities are anything but evidence that they did not exist. Rather, the extent of those efforts shows the strength of the polarising forces, the sometimes almost binary choices that Jonson was here trying to refuse. In doing so, he was decisively not seeking some sort of *via media*, some version of moderation as the golden mean. On the contrary, he was seeking to achieve an independence that was not defined by his position between various extremes but rather above the various vacuous and delusory pitches, the corrupt and ludicrous humours and impulses that, at least for Jonson, were coming to constitute the contemporary political, social, moral and religious scenes in the country, the city and the court. The sheer acuity of his moral judgement enabled him to see through all this and the force of his wit enabled him to unmask it.

Now, we do not have to assume that Thomas Scott gave his 1620 assize sermon the ironic title of 'the projector' because he had seen plays by Jonson, or indeed by anyone else. Scott was responding to the identifiable social and political phenomenon in the contemporary world with identifiable roots in the structures and limitations of the late Elizabethan and early Stuart states and the needs and opportunities provided by the English economy of the day. That is to say, there were people commonly called 'puritan', or some variant or synonym of the word, who defined themselves as the godly, or some cognate term, against the ungodly, one of whose defining characteristics was their propensity to call the *soi-disant* godly 'puritans', or some such pejorative name. Similarly, there were people pushing various projects of precisely the sort, and in precisely the terms, being guyed by Jonson. In short, we can no longer suggest the stereotypes were made up or simply 'invented' by the theatre.

But that, however, is not to deny that the commercial theatre had an increasingly important role to play in developing, disseminating and deepening the social reach and relevance of such stereotypes. In part, this was because many playwrights, Jonson *par excellence*, were remarkably sharp-eyed observers of the contemporary scene, dividing up the world into ins and outs, good and bad, heroes and villains, legitimating certain positions and claims while delegitimating others.

The underlying commercial drive for popularity is worth emphasising. Jonson's plays were particularly funny and controversial, and thus likely to attract popular audiences, precisely because those audiences could recognise central elements drawn from their immediate social experience and environment dynamically interacting in front of them. Playing with, and in the process developing and disseminating, a variety of stereotypes and a set of expectations around them, enabled Jonson to engage and retain the interest of the audience, and hence to make money from the plays, both as performances, and (sometimes) later as printed texts.

This point is perhaps best clarified by comparing the plays again with the pamphlets of Thomas Scott. As a pamphleteer, Scott mobilised and played with a number of contemporary stereotypes, including anti-popery. He played also with the anti-puritan stereotype by establishing the character of the puritan itself as a boo-word used by sinister elements to place moderate Protestants like him beyond the pale. Scott's works were also replete with the figures of the evil counsellor, the corrupt courtier, the duplicitous foreigner. None of these were strangers to the popular stage, but in his pamphlets, unlike the vast majority of the plays, they were deployed to make very particular political and ideological points. Since his pamphleteering activities drove him into exile, and even there put him at very considerable personal and political risk, it seems safe to conclude that Scott's motivations were political rather than commercial. But, given the highly contested views of contemporaries on the subject of 'popularity', his political motives only rendered his efforts to reach as wide an audience as possible differently illegitimate and, if anything, even more threatening.[44]

Precisely because Scott's political project turned on the popular appeal of his pamphlets, Scott can be found using some of the same literary devices and highly theatrical forms to achieve his aims. Hence the mixed generic forms that his pamphlets took. His first, most notorious exercise in the pamphleteer's art, *Vox populi*, was written complete with dialogue and stage directions. Just how readily this could be turned into drama is shown by Thomas Middleton's *A game at chess*, which draws heavily on Scott's tract. (This was a rare example of a clear political programme being promoted explicitly by a play.)[45] Later works by Scott and others writing in the same mode involved the recall of Raleigh's or of the Earl of Essex's ghosts, a debate held in heaven between the Tudors about the wisdom of current Stuart foreign policy and a variety of dialogues. Scott's *News from Parnassus* imagines a series of tableaux in which various princes from the present and recent past – the Spanish monarch Philip II, the Duke of Guises, the Duke of Alva among them – arrive at Parnassus and are there unmasked and punished before Apollo for their many crimes and deceits. Many of these texts came accompanied with vividly realised woodcuts and engravings. Although they shared many central characteristics with those genres, Scott's tracts were thus anything but bog-standard exercises in theological polemic or moral exhortation. Rather, they were highly wrought literary texts, designed to get and keep the attention of a mixed audience.[46]

For Jonson, the cash nexus and the need to get and keep a popular audience were a source of continual embarrassment which his plays address at a number of levels: satirising, indeed ridiculing, the critical capacities of the audience; asserting the independence of the author from the opinions of the vulgar, even as he asks for their favour; denying the very considerable contemporary resonance and reference of the plays while, in virtually the same breath, inviting his audience to make precisely such connections.[47] This was how Jonson put himself in direct competition with the puritan pulpit, which also claimed to be purging the contemporary social and political orders from sin and abuse. On the face of it, as ordained and beneficed ministers of the national church, puritan preachers had a far stronger claim to moral independence and spiritual authority than the thoroughly venal and commercialised denizens of the public theatre. In thus unmasking the godly as the hypocrites and con men that he claimed them to be, Jonson was attempting to outdo in the competition – explicitly so in the debate about the propriety of theatrical performance between the puppet Dionysius and the absurd figure of Busy, but implicitly throughout all his portrayals of the godly. And here Subtle's jibe in *The alchemist* (quoted above) about the puritans railing 'against the plays to please the alderman/Whose daily custard you devour' takes on renewed significance and satiric edge. On this view, therefore, the theatre was just one more populist 'project'. In its assault on puritanism, just as in the godly's assault on the theatre, each side was seeking to do down its most immediate rival for moral authority and 'popular' attention. Here is another indication that religious, political, economic and literary impulses were closely interwoven in ways that call for further investigation.[48]

Conclusion: Jonson and the early Stuart politics of stereotyping

To return, finally, to the topic of stereotypes and stereotyping, in the plays we have been discussing we find a certain sort of reportage, of parody, satire and ridicule, based on very close observation of immediately contemporary ways of being and speaking. This parodic or satirical reportage morphs into character-based stereotypes – that is to say, into memorable personae with relatively stable congeries of characteristics, of modes of speech and performance, which would be instantly recognisable to any contemporary observer or participant in the contemporary political or social scenes, based in either the court or the city. What we are watching, we submit, is the generation and circulation of stereotypes taking place, as it were, before our very eyes.

We can now begin to bring together discussions in this chapter and Chapter 3, and examine the broader politics of stereotyping during the Elizabethan and early Stuart periods. In both periods, we find what were identifiably the same phenomena being evoked, characterised and described through dramatic texts. The prerogative powers of the Crown were being delegated for ostensibly beneficent public purposes, only to be systematically abused for the pursuit of private ends. Those involved were not always private individuals, but sometimes were officers or instruments of the Crown, indeed in many cases 'magistrates' of one form or another. In the extreme scenario portrayed in the anonymous play *Thomas of Woodstock* (written during the 1590s), the main protagonists were the evil councillors led by King Richard II himself. As shown in Chapter 3, these Elizabethan history plays explored ensuing chaos without drawing on the projector stereotype; that stereotype had not yet coalesced when these plays were written. By contrast, in the texts examined here the analysis proceeded through just such a stereotype.

What functions did the emergent stereotype of the projector fulfil? What difference did the fully formed figure of the projector make? Asking these questions, we can finally bring together the findings presented thus far to make sense of a dialectical process of stereotyping at large, a process in which name-calling lent itself to the preservation of status quo, as well as to the escalation of criticism and stereotyping.

In the Commons' debates about monopolies in 1601, we already find an ardent search for evildoers, efforts for which the projector stereotype would soon provide a sharper focus. Monopolists and patentees had been causing grievances under Elizabeth (as discussed in Yamamoto's Chapter 3), but Elizabeth was known to be notoriously jealous of her prerogative, by which grants were issued to them. If alarmed and alienated by Parliamentary proceedings, the queen was likely to respond by vetoing proposed legislation, leaving the subject without redress and the parliament men engaged in a confrontation with a now enraged queen.

This was why the parliament men reserved their barbs mostly for the intermediaries, the middlemen, the holders of the patents and their agents, and the deleterious effects of these people's abusive activities on the localities and interests that the Commons took themselves to be representing. Queen Elizabeth's response, which culminated in her 'Golden Speech', was first to express shock and horror at these abuses (which, she claimed, had only just now come to her attention) and then to remove the offending patents and monopolies. In so doing, she was asserting rather than restricting, still less abandoning, her prerogative powers. This allowed the whole exchange to be glossed as an example of the queen's benign use of royal powers, the legitimacy of which everyone accepted, in response to her subjects' just grievances that had been brought to her attention by the diligence and pertinacity of her loyal parliament men. The episode of 1601 did not lead to a knock-down-drag-out fight between Crown and Commons, an unprecedented dispute about the nature and extent of the prerogative.[49] Instead, it ended as a textbook example of a righteous sovereign restoring order, as did Corvinus in *Promos and Cassandra* (printed 1578) discussed in Chapter 3. Notice that the nightmare scenario had already been imagined and staged: the precarious system had been stress-tested in *Thomas of Woodstock* to the point of dissolution by the machinations and depredations of King Richard II's evil counsellors, before being finally driven into a ditch by Richard himself. Of course, *Woodstock* tactfully ended well before the events that eventually deposed the king, but anyone with even a rudimentary knowledge of the history could draw their own conclusions. And anyway, soon enough there was Shakespeare's *Richard II* to fill in the gaps.[50]

The figure of the projector developed by Jonson streamlined and further enabled such precarious balancing acts. It did so by personifying and concentrating the structural tensions and abusive propensities at play here in the person of an emergent type. Thus the character of the projector emerged as a specialised subset of the evil counsellor, someone whose private ends and corrupt actions provided the polar opposite, even the defining other, of the properly public purposes of the Crown, the aggrieved subject and, when it was sitting, of Parliament itself.

Thomas Scott's writing is important once again as it highlighted the role of Parliament in the resulting politics of stereotyping. In his account, courts naturally attracted the most ambitious, self-serving and unscrupulous of persons unless they were held in check by Parliament. Since the very nature of royal power and of court life prevented the monarch from knowing first-hand the actual conditions under which his subjects lived, the resulting accretion of corruptions was taken as a structurally inevitable feature of personal monarchy. Earlier, plays like Thomas Heywood's *First and Second Parts of King Edward IV* (printed 1599) and Shakespeare's *Measure for Measure* (performed 1604, printed 1624) had addressed this underlying problem by featuring princes going underground or on a walk-about, where, in disguise, they were brought up against the true condition of their subjects.[51] Thus enlightened, when they cast off their disguise the rulers in question were able to redress their subjects' grievances and visit condign justice upon their oppressors with renewed insight and acuity. Whereas these plays staged processes of redress and reform through the essentially folkloric trope of the ruler passing disguised among his people, Scott envisaged this process being achieved through the institutional means of Parliament. For, by regularly calling Parliament, the monarch could gain a uniquely accurate picture of the condition of his realm and adjust his policies accordingly, restraining the corrupt propensities of the court and eradicating corruptions where necessary. The figure of the projector played a crucial role here, as the ultimate embodiment for many of the structural tensions, and consequently 'corrupt' practices inherent in the workings of the late Elizabethan and early Stuart church and state, court and economy.

Parliamentary scrutiny, and the deployment of the projector stereotype for discovering the abuse, is exemplified in its proceedings of 1621 against Sir Giles Mompesson. The parliament men denounced a number of culprits. Mompesson 'amongst others was a principal projector'.[52] The denunciation also spread outside Parliament, as in an engraving produced in 1621 for the popular market (see Figure 4.1). The image is a triptych, above which runs the banner headline 'A description of Giles Mompesson late knight, censured by the parliament'. In the first frame we see Mompesson, armed with his privy seal, extorting a poor female alehouse keeper. The caption above his head explains 'for greedy gain he thrust the weak to wall,/And thereby got himself the devil and all'. In the middle frame he is shown fleeing from the serjeant-at-arms into whose custody 'the parliament' has committed him, with a small devil fluttering over his left shoulder to encourage him on his way. In the final frame, now transformed into 'lame Giles', he is on crutches, hobbling into exile, with the caption reading in part 'those monopolies cursed be with shame,/Which have my reputation thus made

Figure 4.1 British Museum, Y,1.91, 'The Description of Giles Mompesson late knight censured by Parliament the 17th of March, Anno 1620' [1621].

lame/My honour, which hath turned to other styles,/From Sir Mompesson to poor lame Giles'.

Underneath the images, a series of other captions spells out the political moral. 'All you which monopolies seek for gains,/And fair pretences turn to other strains' were warned to 'example take by Giles Mompesson's fall'. 'See that you undertake/None other things but such as make/A benefit to commonwealth and king./Which will you wealth and honour bring.' 'For why you know our faithful king is bent/To give his faithful subjects all content ... By rendering justice unto great and small,/The small ones trip, the great ones down right fall./O what more needs a loyal subject crave/Than mercy, love and justice choice to have.' Thus, far from calling the legitimacy of the royal regime into question, Mompesson, presented in this print as the ultimate monopolist and projector, served as a vindication of the benignity of James's rule and of the corrective role of Parliament.[53] We are a long way here from the world of *Thomas of Woodstock,* or indeed of the Catholic polemics against the Elizabethan regime discussed in Yamamoto's Chapter 3.

The engraving thus epitomised the political hopes that animated the reforming efforts of the first half of the 1620s. As is well known, the 1621 Parliament impeached Sir Francis Bacon; the next one, of 1624, led to the downfall of Lionel Cranfield and passed the statute against monopolies. Viewed from the perspective of Thomas Scott, after years of dysfunction it must have seemed that the system was at long last working as it was supposed to, with the king, having turned his back on the Spanish match, working with Parliament to purge the realm of evil counsellors and corrupt courtiers, before turning against the popish and Spanish enemies.

That, of course, was not how things turned out. Even in the case of monopolies, a combination of loopholes in the law and the financial exigencies of the personal rule ensured that monopolies came back like gangbusters in the 1630s. If presented with the bare descriptions, it is hard to tell Jonson's parody of the toothpick or fork patents apart from Mompesson's genuine scheme (mentioned above) for stamping all the trees in the royal forests with the royal coat of arms. Likewise, there is an almost sinister resemblance between Merecraft's 'office of dependences' and the court of chivalry that was actually revived under Charles I's personal rule.[54]

That the figure of the projector had been rendered almost proverbial and faintly ridiculous by the comedies of Jonson and others ensured that this now well-established stereotype figured not merely in critiques of the regime's policies but also in legitimations of the Caroline peace. James Shirley's masque of 1634, *The triumph of peace,* featured in the brief antimasque a series of entirely ludicrous projectors, begging for patents to promote absurd schemes like a hollow horse bridle designed to so cool the horse that it never got tired. Rather than serious threats either to the commonweal or to the rights of the subject, projectors and their projects were presented as absurd phantasms easily dispelled by the sagacity of the king and the virtue of his lawyers and courtiers.[55] Here is a clear case of anxiety displacement being achieved at the expense of trivialising the entire situation.

It would be wrong, however, to suppose that projecting was treated by all as a source of anxiety that required deflating. It was possible to embrace projecting as a career. So did William Drake, a son of the famous navigator and pirate Sir Francis Drake. In his copious commonplace books, Drake noted his ideas about how to develop 'projects' – how to 'much stretch and inlarge my owne conceite and invention for matters of profit'. Meeting people, seeking advice, was important. So too was reading: '[d]iscourse much with able men … then to let my Imagination worke upon what I have discourse[d] of[,] then let my reading add strength and confirmation to both'.[56] Drake in fact noted 'Ben Johnson his Fox [*Volpone*] reade and let fancy worke and Enlarge upon Reading'.[57] *Volpone* (printed 1607) was another play that featured projects for defrauding others. More research is needed on the mental world of projectors, and in particular on Drake as the projector in the making.[58] But even this anecdotal evidence suggests that we cannot describe Jonsonian satire simply as a moral caution against projecting. Rather, we have to ask in what ways Jonson's and others' writings may have provided lessons and inspirations about how to become a better projector, while setting aside the structural problems of post-Reformation governance that the projector embodied.

This helps us understand why, despite the heated attacks in Parliament and elsewhere on projectors, the moral high ground of the public good and of reformation remained available to all kinds of individual. Accordingly, during the 1630s even more monopolies and projects, ranging from the soap monopoly to fen drainage, were imposed upon subjects under the banner of reforming abuses and pursuing the common good, with shades of the Duke of Drowned-lands coming to life. Indeed, the soap monopoly was rigorously enforced and opposing soap-boilers thrown into jail by the Attorney General William Noy, just at the time he was helping stage *The triumph of peace*. Two soap-boilers died while in prison.[59]

With the calling of the Short and Long Parliaments in the early 1640s, public discontents burst into serious political agitation, a rush of printed pamphlets and ultimately of Parliamentary action. In this context, the stereotype of the projector ceased to be the joke figure guyed in Jonson's *The devil is an ass* or pushed to the fringes of Shirley's masque. It rather became the organising image of a real assault upon the policies and practices of the Crown.

In a striking song printed late in 1640, monopolists and projectors were excoriated, and the Scots were in effect thanked for invading the country and thus enabling Parliament to bring these malefactors to justice – here associated with the papists, the bishops and 'Spain and the strumpet of Babylon':

> You jolly projectors, why hang you the head?
> Promoters, informers, what? are you all dead?
> Or will you beyond-sea frolick and play,
> With Sir *Giles Monpoison*, who led you the way?
> ... O how high were they flown in their floorishing hope
> With their patents for pins, tobacco and soap
> False dye and false cards, besides the great fyne
> They yearly received for enhaunting of wyne.
> The tide is now turn'd, let us drink th'other pot,
> And merrily sing; *gramercie good Scot.*[60]

While the Mompesson print (see Figure 4.1) had been a commodity, the equivalent of a commemorative mug, marking the triumph of royal justice and virtue and the Parliamentary way, now the figure of Mompesson, deliberately misspelt in the print version of the song as 'Monpoison', has returned to link the unfinished business of the 1620s with the crisis of the early 1640s. As treasonous in content as it was jocular in tone, this libellous ballad combined the satirical bite of *The devil is an ass* and *The triumph of peace* with the awareness of injustice and palpable tension captured by *Thomas of Woodstock* and the Catholic tracts of the 1590s. Now the familiar figure of the projector is being enlisted to call the legitimacy of the regime, in this case of the personal rule of Charles I, into radical question. Parliament is again presented as a legitimate channel for popular protest and resistance:

> The parliament saith we shall see better times
> Then let us not fa[i]nt as men without hope.
> An halter for traitours an hemp for the *Pope.*
> Let *Spaine* and the *strumpet of Babylon* plot
> Yet shall we be safe; *gra-mercie good Scot.*[61]

Here the optimism at the opening of the Long Parliament echoes that of the early 1620s.

But just like the Mompesson engraving, this ballad was a commodity as well as a piece of propaganda. There could scarcely be a better example of the liminal, intensely ambiguous nature and role of the stereotype. The stereotype Jonson helped develop became a heuristic tool for discovering and denouncing corruptions, while elsewhere displacing anxiety and providing a buttress for the status quo. It could drive popular oppositional passions and critique, all the while putting bums on seats in the theatre and selling engravings, woodcuts and pamphlets by the score.

Notes

1 Recurring references to plays are given within the main text in parentheses.

2 Vera Keller and Ted McCormick, 'Towards a history of projects', *Early Science and Medicine*, 21 (2016), 423–44; Koji Yamamoto, *Taming capitalism before its triumph: public service, distrust and 'projecting' in early modern England* (Oxford, 2018), pp. 1–9, 53–60.

3 R. C. Munden, 'James I and the "growth of mutual distrust": king, Commons and reform, 1603–1604', in Kevin Sharpe (ed.), *Faction and parliament: essays on early Stuart history* (Oxford, 1978), pp. 43–72. See also important forthcoming work by Nicholas Tyacke on a reforming petition presented to James I, at his accession, by a group of puritans.

4 Ben Jonson, *The alchemist* (1610), ed. Peter Holland and William Sherman, in David Bevington, Martin Butler and Ian Donaldson (eds), *The Cambridge edition of the works of Ben Jonson* (7 vols, Cambridge, 2012), vol. 3 (1606–11), pp. 541–710; Ben Jonson, *Bartholomew Fair* (1614), ed. John Creaser, in *Works of Jonson*, vol. 4 (1611–16), pp. 253–428; Ben Jonson, *The devil is an ass* (1616), ed. Anthony Parr, in *Works of Jonson*, vol. 4, pp. 465–609.

5 The pioneering work on the city comedy as a genre is Brian Gibbons, *Jacobean city comedy: a study of satiric plays by Jonson, Marston and Middleton*, 2nd edn (London, 1980).

6 Landmark studies include Leah S. Marcus, *The politics of mirth: Jonson, Herrick, Milton, Marvell, and the defense of old holiday pastimes* (Chicago, 1986); David Riggs, *Ben Jonson, a life* (Cambridge, MA, 1989); Julie Sanders, *Ben Jonson's theatrical republics* (Basingstoke, 1998). Important contextual works are collected in Julie Sanders (ed.), *Ben Jonson in context* (Cambridge, 2010). More recent studies have gone in different directions, but there are fascinating works exploring local histories and communities in and around London. See, for example, Adam Zucker, *The places of wit in early modern English comedy* (Cambridge, 2011); Kelly J. Stage, *Producing early modern London: a comedy of urban space, 1598–1616* (Lincoln, NE, 2018).

7 Few works that we know have approached Jonson's characters in this way.

8 From a vast and distinguished literature, see, for instance, L. C. Knights, *Drama and society in the age of Jonson* (London, 1937); Marcus, *Politics of mirth*; Lorna Hutson, 'The displacement of the market in Jacobean city comedy', *London Journal*, 14 (1989), 3–16; Douglas Bruster, *Drama and the market in the age of Shakespeare* (Cambridge, 1992); Jonathan Haynes, *The social relations of Jonson's theater* (Cambridge, 1992); Lars Engle, *Shakespearean pragmatism: market of his time* (Chicago, 1993); Jean E. Howard, *The stage and social struggle in early modern England* (London, 1994); Theodore B.

Leinwand, *Theatre, finance and society in early modern England* (Cambridge, 1999); Heather Easterling, *Parsing the city: Jonson, Middleton, Dekker, and city comedy's London as language* (New York, 2007); David Baker, *On demand: writing for the market in early modern England* (Stanford, CA, 2010).

9 *Cf.* Patrick Collinson, 'Ecclesiastical vitriol: religious satire in the 1590s and the invention of puritanism', in John Guy (ed.), *The reign of Elizabeth I: court and culture in the last decade* (Cambridge, 1995), pp. 150–70; see also Patrick Collinson, 'The theatre constructs puritanism', in David L. Smith, Richard Strier and David Bevington (eds), *The theatrical city: culture, theatre and politics in London, 1576–1649* (Cambridge, 1995), pp. 157–69.

10 Lawrence Stone, 'The fruits of office: the case of Robert Cecil, first Earl of Salisbury, 1596–1612', in F. J. Fisher (ed.), *Essays in the economic and social history of Tudor and Stuart England, in honour of R. H. Tawney* (Cambridge, 1961), pp. 89–116; Linda Levy Peck, 'Problems in Jacobean administration: was Henry Howard, Earl of Northampton, a reformer?', *Historical Journal*, 19 (1976), 831–58.

11 This and the next paragraphs draw on Michael C. Questier, 'Sir Henry Spiller, recusancy and the efficiency of the Jacobean Exchequer', *Historical Research*, 66 (1993), 251–66; Thomas Cogswell, 'Destroyed for doing my duty: Thomas Felton and the penal laws under Elizabeth and James I', in Kenneth Fincham and Peter Lake (eds), *Religious politics in post-Reformation England: essays in honour of Nicholas Tyacke* (Woodbridge, 2006), pp. 177–92.

12 On this see Alastair Bellany, *The politics of court scandal in early modern England: news culture and the Overbury affair, 1603–1660* (Cambridge, 2002).

13 See Roger Lockyer, 'Lake, Sir Thomas (*bap.* 1561–1630)', *Oxford Dictionary of National Biography* (Oxford, 2004), hereafter *ODNB*, doi.org/10.1093/ref:odnb/15903 (accessed 7 July 2021); Pauline Croft, 'Howard, Thomas, first Earl of Suffolk (1561–1626)', *ODNB,* doi.org/10.1093/ref:odnb/13942 (accessed 7 July 2021).

14 For overviews, see Linda Levy Peck, *Court patronage and corruption in early Stuart England* (London, 1990); John Cramsie, *Kingship and crown finance under James VI and I, 1603–1625* (Woodbridge, 2002). There has been no systematic study of monopolies or, indeed, of projecting under Elizabeth I and the early Stuarts. One exception is G. D. Duncan, 'Monopolies under Elizabeth I, 1558–1585', PhD thesis, University of Cambridge, 1976. Both of these topics have been too readily discussed, and to some extent dismissed, under the problematic heading 'corruption'. For an overview, see also Yamamoto, *Taming capitalism*, pp. 26–103, 141–6.

15 On the Cockayne project see Astrid Friis, *Alderman Cockayne's project and the cloth trade: the commercial policy of England in its main aspects, 1603–1625* (Copenhagen, 1927). See also the discussion in Menna Prestwich, *Cranfield: politics and profits under the early Stuarts: the career of Lionel Cranfield Earl of Middlesex* (Oxford, 1966), pp. 164–70.

16 For Ingram see Anthony Upton, *Sir Arthur Ingram, c. 1565–1642: a study of the origins of an English landed family* (Oxford, 1961) and Simon Healey,

'Ingram, Sir Arthur (before 1571–1642)', *ODNB*, doi.org/10.1093/ref:odnb/14414 (accessed 7 July 2021).

17 For Mompesson see Sidney Lee, 'Mompesson, Sir Giles (1583/4–1651x63)', rev. Sean Kelsey (2008), *ODNB,* doi.org/10.1093/ref:odnb/18932 (accessed 7 July 2021), and Yamamoto, *Taming capitalism*, pp. 99–102. We owe the story of the project concerning the royal forests to a seminar paper by John Nichols at what was then the Hurstfield seminar at the Institute of Historical Research in the late 1970s.

18 Prestwich, *Cranfield,* pp. 160, 178.

19 Thomas Scott, *Vox populi* ([London?], 1620).

20 Andrew Thrush, 'The personal rule of James I, 1611–1620', in Thomas Cogswell, Richard Cust and Peter Lake (eds), *Politics, religion and popularity in early Stuart Britain* (Cambridge, 2002), pp. 84–102; Andrew Thrush, 'The French marriage and the origins of the 1614 Parliament' in Stephen Clucas and Rosalind Davies (eds), *The crisis of 1614 and the Addled Parliament: literary and historical perspectives* (Aldershot, 2002), pp. 25–35.

21 On Scott see Peter Lake, 'Constitutional consensus and puritan opposition in the 1620s: Thomas Scott and the Spanish match', *Historical Journal*, 25 (1982), 805–25.

22 With his usual tact, Scott chose Phineas, and 'his zeal for the execution of justice', as his model justice of the peace (Phineas had pinned Zimri to the floor with his javelin for openly sleeping with a Midianite woman in the midst of the Israelite camp, thus calling down the judgement of God upon his people). The implications for the projected match between Prince Charles and a Spanish Catholic princess need hardly be mentioned.

23 Thomas Scott, *The projector, teaching a direct sure and ready way to restore the decays of the church and state both in honour and revenue* (London [Holland], 1623), various (quotations, pp. 18, 15, 10).

24 For a discussion of Scott as a civic republican, rather than a puritan, see Markku Peltonen, *Classical humanism and republicanism in English political thought, 1570–1640* (Cambridge, 1995), ch. 5.

25 See Peltonen, *Classical humanism and republicanism.* See also Richard Cust and Peter Lake, 'Sir Richard Grosvenor and the rhetoric of magistracy', *Bulletin of the Institute of Historical Research*, 54 (1981), 40–53; Richard Cust, 'The "public man" in late Tudor and early Stuart England', in Peter Lake and Steven C. A. Pincus (eds), *The politics of the public sphere in early modern England: public persons and popular spirits* (Manchester, 2007), pp. 116–43; Richard Cust, '"Patriots" and "popular spirits": narratives of conflict in early Stuart politics', in Nicholas Tyacke (ed.), *The English Revolution, 1590–1720: politics, religion and communities* (Manchester, 2007), pp. 43–61.

26 Yamamoto, *Taming capitalism*, pp. 70–3, 91–4 (quotation, p. 91).

27 Rupali Mishra, *A business of state: commerce, politics, and the birth of the East India Company* (Cambridge, MA, 2018).

28 This and the next paragraphs draw on Peter Lake, *Anglicans and puritans? Presbyterianism and English conformist thought from Hooker to Laud* (London,

1987), various but esp. pp. 101–44; Peter Lake, 'Conformist clericalism? Richard Bancroft's analysis of the socio-economic roots of Presbyterianism', in W. J. Sheils and Diana Wood (eds), *The church and wealth, studies in church history*, 24 (Oxford, 1987), pp. 219–29; Peter Lake, 'Anti-puritanism: the structure of a prejudice' in Fincham and Lake (eds), *Religious politics in post-Reformation England,* 80–97; Peter Lake with Michael Questier, *The Antichrist's lewd hat: Protestants, papists and players in post-Reformation England* (New Haven, CT, 2002), section 4. See also Peter Lake, 'Anti-puritanism as political discourse: the Laudian critique of puritan "popularity"', in Cesare Cuttica and Markku Peltonen (eds), *Democracy and anti-democracy in early modern England, 1603–1689* (Leiden, 2019), pp. 152–73.

29 For a sustained exercise in anti-puritan stereotyping from the 1630s, penned by that Ben Jonson wannabe Peter Hausted, see Peter Lake and Isaac Stephens, *Scandal and religious identity in early Stuart England: a Northamptonshire maid's tragedy* (Woodbridge, 2015), ch. 2.

30 Yamamoto, *Taming capitalism*, p. 86; Anthony Parr, 'Introduction', *The devil is an ass*, in *Works of Jonson*, vol. 4, pp. 467–76, at p. 470.

31 James Loxley, Anna Groundwater and Julie Sanders (eds), *Ben Jonson's walk to Scotland: an annotated edition of the 'Foot Voyage'* (Cambridge, 2015), p. 67.

32 John Creaser, 'Introduction', *Bartholomew Fair*, in *Works of Jonson*, vol. 4, 255–68, at p. 262.

33 Yamamoto, *Taming capitalism*, p. 5.

34 Glyn Parry, *The arch-conjuror of England: John Dee* (London and New Haven, CT, 2011).

35 Vera Keller, 'Cornelis Drebbel (1572–1633): fame and the making of modernity', PhD thesis, Princeton University, 2008.

36 Lake with Questier, *The Antichrist's lewd hat*, ch. 14, esp. pp. 586–7.

37 Lake with Questier, *The Antichrist's lewd hat*, pp. 602–4.

38 For details of the careers of Whately, Ward and White, see Jacqueline Eales, 'Whately, William (1583–1639)', *ODNB*, doi.org/10.1093/ref:odnb/29178 (accessed 10 July 2021); Margo Todd, 'Ward, Samuel (1572–1643)', *ODNB*, doi.org/10.1093/ref:odnb/28705 (accessed 7 July 2021); Rory T. Cornish, 'White, John (1575–1648)', *ODNB*, doi.org/10.1093/ref:odnb/29255 (accessed 7 July 2021). See also John Creaser, 'Jonson's *Bartholomew Fair* and Bancroft's *Dangerous positions*', *Review of English Studies*, 57 (2006), 176–84.

39 For example, see Jonson, *The alchemist* (1610), in *Works of Jonson*, vol. 3, pp. 606–10.

40 The best account of fen drainage both as project and improvement scheme is now Eric H. Ash, *The drainage of the fens: projectors, popular politics, and state building in early modern England* (Baltimore, MD, 2017).

41 By far the best account of the Darrell business is Marion Gibson, *Possession, puritanism and print: Darrell, Harsnett, Shakespeare and the Elizabethan exorcism controversy* (London, 2006). Now see Brendan C. Walsh, *The English exorcist: John Darrell and the shaping of early modern English Protestant demonology* (Abingdon, 2020). Many of the relevant texts are reprinted in

Philip C. Almond, *Demonic possession and exorcism in early modern England: contemporary texts and their cultural contexts* (Cambridge, 2004). On Harsnett see F. W. Brownlow, *Shakespeare, Harsnett and the devils of Denham* (Cranbury, NJ, 1993).

42 Marcus, *Politics of mirth*, p. 91.

43 Sharpe made suggestions of that sort about Jonson, and in his first book made precisely such a point by highlighting the friendship networks and political connections of Sir Robert Cotton, which by the way included Jonson himself. See Kevin Sharpe, *Sir Robert Cotton, 1586–1631: history and politics in early modern England* (Oxford, 1979).

44 On the difficulties surrounding the notion of popularity see Peter Lake, 'Puritanism (monarchical) republicanism and monarchy, or John Whitgift, antipuritanism and the "invention" of popularity', *Journal of Medieval and Early Modern Studies*, 40 (2010), 463–95; Peter Lake, 'From revisionist to royalist history; or, was Charles I the first Whig historian', *Huntington Library Quarterly,* 78 (2015), 657–81; Lake, 'Anti-puritanism as political discourse'; Richard Cust, 'Charles I and popularity' in Cogswell, Cust and Lake (eds), *Politics, religion and popularity in early Stuart Britain*, pp. 235–58; Cust, '"Patriots" and "popular spirits"'.

45 See Margot Heinemann, *Puritanism and theatre: Thomas Middleton and opposition drama under the early Stuarts* (Cambridge, 1980); Thomas Middleton, *A game at chess*, ed. T. H. Howard-Hill, The Revels Plays (Manchester, 1993) and T. H. Howard-Hill, *Middleton's 'Vulgar Pasquin': essays on A game at chess* (Delaware, 1995), but see also Thomas Cogswell, 'Thomas Middleton and the court, 1624: *A game at chess* in context', *Huntington Library Quarterly,* 47 (1984), 273–88.

46 See *Robert Earl of Essex his ghost*, according to the title page, 'printed in paradise, 1624', but included in Thomas Scott, *The workes of the most famous and reverend divine Mr. Thomas Scot* (Utrecht, 1624). For the ghost of Raleigh see Thomas Gainsford's tract *Vox spiritus*. The debate amongst the Tudors takes place in *Vox coeli, or news from heaven*, 'printed in Elysium, 1624', and likewise included in Scott's 1624 *Works*. For the dialogue form, see *A tongue combat lately happening between two English soldiers in a tilt boat of Gravesend, the one going to serve the king of Spain, the other to serve the States-general of the United Provinces.* According to the title page this tract was 'printed in London' and was also included in the 1624 *Works*. *News from Parnassus. The political touchstone taken from mount Parnassus, whereon the governments of the greatest monarchies of the world are touched* was 'printed at Helicon, 1622', but again included in the 1624 *Works*. There is an important study to be written about the use of visual media, woodcuts and more sophisticated engravings, in the propaganda wars waged in the early 1620s around the Spanish match, the threat of popery and monopolists, and the proper role of Parliament in the polity. For useful preliminary remarks see Alexandra Walsham, '"The fatall vesper": providentialism and anti-popery in late Jacobean London', *Past & Present*, 144 (1994), 36–87; Alexandra Walsham, *Providence in early modern England* (Oxford, 1999), pp. 256–64.

47 See Lake with Questier, *The Antichrist's lewd hat*, ch. 10.

48 In addition to Lake's and Yamamoto's Chapters 2, 3 and 4 in this volume, see also Lake with Questier, *The Antichrist's lewd hat*, chs 11–14, which explores related points at greater length.

49 See David Harris Sacks, 'The countervailing of benefits: monopoly, liberty and benevolence in Elizabethan England' in Dale Hoak (ed.), *Tudor political culture* (Cambridge, 1995), pp. 272–91.

50 On Shakespeare's *Richard II*, see Peter Lake, *How Shakespeare put politics on the stage: power and succession in the history plays* (London and New Haven, CT, 2016), chs 10 and 11.

51 See Chapter 3, p. 102 above, and Kevin A. Quarmby, *The disguised ruler in Shakespeare and his contemporaries* (Farnham, 2012). *Cf.* Anne Barton, 'The king disguised: Shakespeare's *Henry V* and the comical history', in Joseph G. Price (ed.), *The triple bond: plays, mainly Shakespearean, in performance* (University Park, PA, 1975), pp. 92–117. Also on *Measure for Measure*, see Lake with Questier, *The Antichrist's lewd hat*, ch. 15. In that play, the Duke goes into hiding to evaluate the project of puritan rule (which is personified by his 'precise' deputy, Angelo) by viewing the effects of Angelo's newly aggressive 'reformation of manners' upon the moral and political condition of the kingdom.

52 Wallace Notestein, Frances Helen Relf and Hartley Simpson (eds), *Commons debates 1621* (7 vols, New Haven, CT, 1935), vol. 2, p. 180 (see also vol. 6, p. 40).

53 The engraving refers to 'monopolies' and does not use the term 'projector' explicitly. But the identification was clear. When Mompesson came back to England and started enclosing parts of the Forest of Dean in 1631, it was reported that the 'foresters grieved with this attempt of his ... whom they termed to be an odious projector'. See Historical Manuscript Commission, *Manuscripts of the Earl Cowper, K.G., preserved at Melbourne Hall, Derbyshire* (3 vols, London, 1888–89), vol. 1, pp. 429–30.

54 Richard Cust, *Charles I and the aristocracy, 1625–1641* (Cambridge, 2013), ch. 3.

55 James Shirley, *Triumph of peace* (1634), pp. 7–8. On this and the following paragraphs, see also Yamamoto, *Taming capitalism*, pp. 94–7. Our account builds on Martin Bulter, *The Stuart court masque and political culture* (Cambridge, 2008), pp. 298–310.

56 University College London, Special Collection, Ogden MS 7/7, fol. 165. We thank Noah Millstone for the suggestion to read Drake's manuscripts.

57 Ogden MS 7/7, fol. 161. Elsewhere, Drake excerpted aphoristic statements from Jonson's *Sejanus* (printed 1605). See András Kiséry, *Hamlet's moment: drama and political knowledge in early modern England* (Oxford, 2016), pp. 208–9.

58 On Drake, see Kevin Sharpe, *Reading revolutions: the politics of reading in early modern England* (New Haven, CT, 2000). On projects in *Volpone*, see Vera Keller and Ted McCormick, 'Towards a history of projects', *Early Science and Medicine*, 21 (2016), 423–44, pp. 431–2.

59 Bulstrode Whitelocke, *Memorials of the English affairs* (1682), p. 20; *A short and trve relation concerning the soap-busines* (1641), p. 10.

60 National Library of Scotland, Adv. MS 33.1.1 [Denmilne], vol. 13, no. 69, *A new carrell for Christmasse made and sung at Londone* [n.d., 1640?].

61 *A new carrell for Christmasse.* For both the printed and manuscript texts of this ballad, see also Yamamoto, *Taming capitalism,* pp. 99–101; Noah Millstone, *Manuscript circulation and the invention of politics in early Stuart England* (Cambridge, 2016), pp. 303–4.

5

Ranter and Quaker stereotyping in the English Revolution

Kate Peters

In 1654, the fifth edition of Ephraim Pagitt's *Heresiography* was updated to include entries for Ranters and Quakers, advertised on the title page as the latest heretics. Quakers, the author stated, were the 'dregs of the common people'. Rejecting laws, magistrates and sacraments, 'honouring no man', and 'confining salvation within the circle of their own giddy uncleen heads', the Quakers' avowal of perfection and liberty was, the author claimed, a cloak for 'confusion and madness', 'resistance, not subjection'.[1] The Ranter, also 'an uncleane beast', was 'much of the make with our Quaker, of the same puddle … their infidelity, villanies, and debochements, are the same'.[2] The conflation of Ranters and Quakers into a shared stereotype of dangerous antinomian fanatic with murky social origins was a common trope: hostile puritan contemporaries Richard Baxter, John Bunyan and Thomas Collier all agreed that they were two of a kind.[3] This shared typology also endured for many years in historians' treatment of radical religion in the English Revolution, which emphasised the collective failure of social and religious radicalism, as well as the shared eccentricity and unpopularity of radical sectaries in the 1650s. In this analysis, the mystical antinomianism and challenging social behaviour of Ranters, Quakers and other sectaries placed them beyond constitutional politics, provoking significant popular hostility and official repression, while sensationalising them in print vastly overstated their actual significance, creating a single 'other' against which contemporaries could react in horror.[4]

Yet there are also important distinctions in the stereotyping of Ranters and Quakers. Significant in this respect is the work of Colin Davis, who argued in 1986 that the Ranters scarcely existed *beyond* the potent stereotype of deviance and madness: their image as a coherent and dangerous sect was deliberately cultivated by a hostile press in order to intensify public fears about religious liberty of conscience, but beyond the salacious printed stories there was little evidence of a collective or coherent group of Ranters. For Davis, Ranters were the invention of a short-lived 'moral panic' in 1650–1 and their significance as subversive deviants, challenging social and religious hierarchy, had been further distorted by Marxist historians seeking evidence of a radical revolution. Davis argued the power of the Ranter 'myth' had misled contemporaries and historians alike, famously claiming there was 'no Ranter movement, no Ranter sect, no Ranter theology'.[5] In contrast, the longer-term evolution of the Quakers into an established denomination, and the survival of their institutional records, placed their existence, and the development of collective Quaker belief and practices, beyond doubt.[6] Their careful self-fashioning in print from the early 1650s afforded clarity and coherence to the Quaker identity: indeed, it has been argued that the alacrity and vigour with which post-Restoration Quaker leaders publicly differentiated themselves from the antinomian enthusiasm of the Ranters served to exaggerate the Ranters' coherence and added further potency to the Ranter myth.[7] Thus, while Quakers mobilised successfully around their own stereotyping in order to assert their religious identity, Ranter stereotyping had been contrived by contemporaries as a heuristic device in order to mobilise against the perceived dangers of religious enthusiasm.

This paradoxical treatment of Ranter and Quaker typography, with both shared and antithetical functions, lends itself to further exploration in the context of a growing *corpus* of work that is beginning to explore the significance of radical print cultures, and through the lens of stereotyping as a distinct mode of mobilisation. In response to Colin Davis, historians and literary scholars focused largely on existential evidence for Ranters, emphasising the linguistic distinctiveness and polemical sophistication of Ranter writings, locating their beliefs within a broader, Continental mystical tradition, and noting the abundant circumstantial evidence that Ranters existed and moved within a networked community of like-minded people.[8] It is now clear that there were indeed Ranters, although not necessarily in a coherent sectarian structure. But there has been relatively little probing of the process by which hostile stereotypes of the Ranters were produced, nor of their broader political or historical significance. A growing *corpus* of work on the transformative nature of print culture in the English Revolution has stressed its centrality to a new participatory politics, while the work of David Como, Nigel Smith and Laurent Curelly has argued for the integration of 'radical' print politics into our understanding of the political and cultural revolution of the mid-seventeenth century.[9] Within this context, an exploration of stereotyping as a process in the construction of radical religious identities and the mobilisation of political responses offers a useful analytical framework. It allows us to explore the multiple representations of Ranters and Quakers, and the variety of ways in which these enabled political and religious mobilisation. Social psychology's stress on stereotyping as part of a normal cognitive process of ordering and simplifying the world, particularly important heuristically in times of crisis in which complex or challenging information must be processed and understood, is an important insight in response to Colin Davis's assertion that stereotypical projections of Ranters in print bore no relation to the existence of Ranters.[10] A stereotype, as 'an association of attributes with a certain group of people', can be understood to be the 'result of a normal and ubiquitous process', as Mark Knights has put it. As such, we can study stereotypes as socially meaningful and historically significant, without assuming that the underlying signified has been invented.[11] This chapter, building on the body of scholarship that has demonstrated the existence of Ranters, will therefore explore the complex processes by which Ranter and Quaker stereotypes were constructed, deployed, interpreted and contested. In so doing, it argues that stereotypes of both Ranters and Quakers constituted a meaningful and dynamic element of the cultural, political and religious landscape of the 1650s, beyond their more common depiction as marginal and alienating eccentrics. It focuses, first, on the wide range of audiences for whom Ranters (and their putative converts) were proposed as an 'out-group' and second, on the sophisticated strategies deployed by Quakers and commercial publishers seeking to define and control their collective identity. Finally, this chapter examines the distinct 'antinomian' episteme in which Ranter and Quaker audiences were urged in print and in public meetings to discern good from evil and truth from falsehood as a function of their spiritual inspiration. In so doing, I suggest that Ranters and Quakers proposed their own distinctive mechanisms for engaging with, and offering distinct interpretations of, abstract typologies of good and evil as part of a polemical debate between radical sects as they debated the nature of religious liberty. I argue that Ranters and Quakers alike were adept producers and navigators of their own stereotyping and that what is discussed in this volume as *stigma consciousness* was an integral feature of public debates about religious identity, truth and liberty of conscience.

The dynamics of Ranter stereotyping

The Ranters initially appeared in print as a literary sensation over the course of late 1649–50.[12] An important context was the passing of the Blasphemy Act in August 1650, the legislative culmination of Parliamentary concerns over the publications and preaching of 'Ranter' authors Abiezer Coppe and Laurence Clarkson in the early spring of 1650. Another legal context was the Adultery Act of May 1650, which sought to suppress the 'abominable' sins of fornication, adultery and incest.[13] Much of the anti-Ranter literature from October 1650 echoed the terminology and enforcement of this legislation, featuring reports of the breaking up of Ranter meetings by newly empowered magistrates. Journalists and publishers alike appeared to relish salacious reports of sexual and doctrinal misdemeanour, and of the wilful blaspheming, rowdy meetings and sexual license that featured in the examination and trials of Ranters. Davis's analysis of the anti-Ranter sensation focused almost exclusively on tracts produced in the immediate aftermath of the passage of the legislation between October 1650 and January 1651, largely the product of what he termed the gutter or 'yellow press'; and he identified a small handful of journalists, publishers or printers as key to the invention of the Ranter myth.[14] In reality, as we will see, a wide variety of publications throughout the 1650s concerned themselves with accounts of the new 'ranting' phenomenon. The sheer variety of printed accounts of Ranters that appeared over the course of the decade offered a range of stereotypes, indicating that Ranters were interpreted differently for different audiences in order to fulfil diverse political and commercial ends. The diversity of the stereotyping, I argue, far from suggesting that the Ranters were invented, indicates that they constituted a significant presence within post-revolutionary religious politics, and were presented as such to a number of different audiences – and presumably discussed by them.[15]

Ranters made good copy. The short, quarto pamphlets of the type which featured Ranters were profitable: quick and cheap to produce, they provided a useful source of short-term income to publishers and printers.[16] A number of publishing devices indicated the growing commercial importance of pamphlets to an increasingly sophisticated market in the years before the Civil Wars. Serial publications established a regular weekly market; pamphlet disputations locked readers into lengthy polemical exchanges; wondrous happenings and newsworthy events were reported as novelties for consumption. All of these commercial strategies were deployed on a vastly intensified scale in the political upheavals of the 1640s, to the extent that the nature of political engagement itself changed – domestic news, petitioning and rapid polemical exchanges all suggest an increasingly informed, mobilised and participatory readership that expanded exponentially over the course of the 1640s and 1650s. Central to this public politics was, as we shall see, stereotyping and various responses to it.

Many of the printed accounts of Ranters clustered around the moment of press 'sensation' in 1650–1 were clearly commercial publications. Many stressed the Ranters' novelty and topicality, often in the context of reporting arrests carried out under the new legislation. A number of tracts promised 'a discovery of the new Generation of Ranters'.[17] *The routing of the Ranters* announced them as 'a sort of people ... newly sprung among us, called Ranters alius Coppanites or Claxtonians', stressing their novelty and also, in referencing Richard Coppin and Laurence Clarkson, locating them within a 'Ranter' print culture – another commercial strategy.[18] Other pamphlets promised new or unique information. One complained that the many 'sundry Papers' on Ranters 'have been onely beating about the Bush, and have not discovered the Bird in its own nature'.[19] Another criticised a rival publication: 'many things are totally omitted, and other things minced and come short of the truth'.[20] The publication criticised, *Ranters of both sexes, male and female,* also denounced a competitor, 'written with too much haste, I know not by whom, with but few truths, which in this are more largely expressed'.[21]

A number of these commercial tracts bore eye-catching woodcut illustrations on their title pages, another commercial move to attract customers.[22] Some depicted salacious scenes of sex and drinking, others of rowdy Ranter meetings or their incarceration in prison, all compounding stereotypes of deviance, or of its restraint by the powers of the state.[23] The accompanying texts promised further details of Ranter license, referring to their 'dancing and revelling' or 'several kinds of musick, dances and ryotings'; and their alleged practice of 'lying with any Woman Whatsoever' – prurience presumably increasing their marketability, just as it attracted the attention of historians subsequently.[24]

Many of these tracts, as Davis and others noted, were produced by commercially prolific printers and publishers, underlining the broad market audiences at which lewd Ranter stories were directed. A handful were printed by the veteran printer-publisher Bernard Alsop, who had been in business for over forty years and was an experienced, indeed pioneering, producer of cheap print and news.[25] Alsop's output was polemically varied, balancing serious legal, religious and literary publications with news and other cheap, ephemeral tracts in ways that suggest his output was accessed by commercially broad audiences rather than one defined by religious or political ideologies. The publisher George Horton, similarly responsible for an ideologically eclectic output, and the printer 'J. C.', probably Jane Coe, both experienced producers of news, collaborated to publish a number of topical accounts of Ranters. The sheer variety of publications by figures such as Alsop, Horton and Coe makes it difficult to identify distinctive readerships for their commercial 'Ranter' publications, which must have weakened their capacity to construct Ranters as a meaningful 'out-group' in order to strengthen or motivate a particular 'in-group'; the variety of stereotypes deployed, however, underlines the breadth and diversity of the audiences open to interpretations of the new 'ranting' phenomenon.

Where it is possible to identify a broadly coherent market readership associated with a particular publisher, it becomes clear that different interpretations of the Ranters reflected different political concerns. Thus, *The smoke of the bottomlesse pit*, written by John Holland and printed for John Wright in late 1650, presented a serious account of Ranter doctrines.

Although little is known of Holland, John Wright was a substantial news and ballad publisher who produced over 400 extant titles during the 1640s and 1650s. He had been an official publisher to Parliament from 1642, as well as overseeing publications for the Council of the Army and London Common Council; he also published ballads and bestselling works of divinity.[26] Over the course of the 1650s, Wright produced a range of predominantly Presbyterian-leaning tracts that highlighted the multiple threats of Independency, Socinianism, Quakerism and Arminianism; he also published key works by Anthony Ascham and Francis Rous, justifying Presbyterian allegiance to the new commonwealth.[27] *The smoke of the bottomlesse pit* presented itself as a serious publication, promising 'a more true and fuller discovery' of the Ranters. The preface located its account of the Ranters within debates about religious toleration, emphasising that Ranters were best opposed through reasoned debate: spiritual enemies should not be battled with 'carnal weapons' but through argument, 'by the spirit of Christs mouth'.[28] Accordingly, the tract offered a considered account of Ranter principles in ways that stemmed from, and sought to encourage, polemical encounters with Ranters. A short account of Ranter principles on marriage offered no salacious details, but explained that Ranters rejected monogamy as a 'fruit of the curse' (of sin) from which they believed they were now free. Holland's style suggested the desirability of ongoing public disputes with Ranters: 'I did intend to ask them how we came to be freed from the curse, but I was prevented'.[29]

Other similarly definitional accounts of Ranters incorporated them into a well-established tradition of heresiography against which the true church had been founded and which, as Ann Hughes has argued, had been skilfully mobilised as a genre by the Presbyterian minister and polemicist Thomas Edwards in the 1640s.[30] In this context, the novelty of Ranters, stressed by some of the more salacious news tracts, was superseded by a narrative of millenarian timelessness. 'It hath beene the portion of Gods people, even in all ages, to be pestered with false prophets', wrote Raunce Burthall in a tract published for an Aylesbury bookseller, Stephen Dagnall – itself indicative of locally specific markets for anti-Ranter polemic. Burthall argued that the 'unreasonable practises' of the Ranters needed only to be 'named, and laid open to view' in order for 'reasonable men, to desert their wicked ways and societies'.[31] In these heresiographical narratives, Ranters were compared with other sects 'in former times, which came nearest in opinion and practise to them', from Donatists and other early Christian schismatics to the Family of Love, as well as historically specific heretics such as William Hacket and John Trask.[32] A number of these heresiographical works were produced by publishers with a known Presbyterian clientele. In 1651, the bookseller Michael Sparke published *The narrative history of King James*, which incorporated Ranters into a historical narrative of religious persecution.[33] This work 'revived' the story of the 1611 burning of Bartholemew Legatt and Edward Wightman for heresy, drawing attention to the legal instruments, the 'commissions and warrants', that had been used against Legatt and Wightman, who held the same 'old heresies' as 'our ranters'. The charges levelled against Wightman clearly resonated with those made against the Ranters. He had been accused of espousing 'the wicked Heresies' of early Christianity, 'Anabaptists, and other Arch-Hereticks',[34] as well as blasphemies specifically associated with Ranters; Wightman had claimed he was the Holy Ghost, believed in the mortality of the soul and that there should be no sacraments.[35] The parallels drawn by Sparke projected the Ranters as heretics and blasphemers, whose prosecution by the state was both necessary and legitimate; as Ian Atherton and David Como have shown, the burnings of Wightman and Legatt, at the order of James I and within machinery of the Church of England, had commanded widespread support in 1611.[36] Michael Sparke, a substantial publisher and active member of the Stationers' Company, worked with a group of publishers with well-established Presbyterian links; *The narrative history of King James* was thus a polemical nod towards the need for the punishment and restraint of dangerous blasphemous opinions.

Subsequent works published by Sparke suggest a more nuanced interpretation of the Ranters. In 1653, Sparke sold a work by the Jacobean separatist Henry Ainsworth, *The old orthodox foundation of religion*. The reprinting was in part a commercial gesture linked to political infighting within the Stationers' Company: Michael Sparke's son (now dead) had published its first incarnation, *The orthodox foundation of religion,* in 1641, and Sparke senior may have been asserting his rights to the title. But there was also a polemical edge, which incorporated Ranters into an agenda of broad religious cohesion. Sparke claimed he was republishing Ainsworth's doctrines 'for the profit or information of Presbyterians, Independents, Papists, Anabaptists, Arminians, Antinomians, Ranters, Quakers and Seekers' – a doctrinally eclectic audience.[37] In his address to the reader, Sparke hoped that Ainsworth's work would facilitate both a 'private search' and a 'publick Declaration' to overthrow the heresies of the day.[38] He lamented the delay in settling reformed religion 'according to the word of God, and the example of the best reformed Churches', and warned against the dangers of febrile religious disputes between men 'of the same Religion', an outcome that 'the Jesuites and their Confederates have projected'.[39] Ainsworth had been an irenic figure, reputed to have preserved discipline in his congregation against the religious discord of early separatism, and revisiting his doctrines may have seemed timely to Sparke who sought religious settlement in fractious times.[40] The decision to address his work rhetorically to all, from Ranters and papists to Presbyterians, also suggests a different deployment of the Ranter stereotype, not as deviant 'out-group', but framed within a putative model of religious comprehension. The agreement of doctrines was implicitly the proper route for religious settlement and the overthrow of heresy. Ranters, Seekers, Quakers, and all 'that desire to know Christ Jesus', were invited to reconsider Ainsworth as 'a pattern to a new reformation'.[41]

In similar vein, in 1653 Sparke also published a poem, *A new proclamation, or a warning peece*, which opened with a rhetorical address 'to the Ranters who goe up and down teaching men and women to embrace ungodliness and worldly lusts'.[42] The poem bemoaned at length the ruining of the national church, 'by schismes broken, and by Sects undone! O how they swarme!'[43] At the end it dismissed the Ranters specifically: 'No God, no good, no sin, no hell, no blisse, O tremble heaven, and hell, and earth at this!' Yet Ranters were posited as the recipients of this message, with power over their own reformation: 'And tremble Ranters, tremble at your state,/And see your sin before it be too late'.[44] In its rhetorical address to the Ranters, the author of *A new proclamation* implied a pervious wall between Ranters and 'the world', urging Ranters to come to their senses. This then was not presenting a binary account of Ranters as static out-group, but on the contrary positing an end to Ranting (as well as Quakers and Shakers). Ranters were thus assimilated into a polemic of religious orthodoxy; not as 'deviant' out-group, but to be persuaded into an irenic national church.

Other tracts that may have been intended for a more independent-minded audience suggested that the risk posed by the Ranters was their attractiveness to a gullible readership, and urged readers to be on their mettle. In the printer's address to the reader in the anonymous tract, *The Ranters creed*, James Moxon warned of the plausibility of the 'nonsensical Parables and Mysteries, which neither their Auditors or themselves understand'. Recalling the dangers of false prophets who '*creep into houses, leading silly women captive*', Moxon called on his readers to 'embrace the Apostles rule, *Believe not every spirit, but try the spirits whether they are of God*'. The pamphlet account that followed consisted of a series of apparently authentic transcripts of the examination of the followers of John Robbins, 'a blasphemous sort of people, commonly called Ranters', that Moxon 'exposed' to the view of the world, 'that their stupidity being manifest, their folly may be avoided'.[45] The transcribed examinations, which the tract claimed were taken before a Middlesex Justice called Thomas Hubbert on 24 May 1651 and presented without annotation or interpretation, effectively provided a narrative of the beliefs and practices of the 'Company of Ranters'. Robbins had proclaimed himself the Almighty and was recognised and worshipped as God by his followers; he had taken a married woman, Joan Garment, as his wife and it was widely claimed she was now pregnant with the son of God. As they were brought into court, the company was described 'clapping of their hands', 'skreeking', and crying out '*The glory of the Lord*'. Joshua Garment, one of Robbins's prophets and the husband of Joan, lay prostrate before Robbins 'and the women cast themselves down at his sides', Garment 'clasping his arms about the god's leggs' and crying out 'deliver us, deliver us'.[46]

Moxon's tract presented many familiar aspects of Ranting behaviour that both conformed to, and confirmed, contemporary and subsequent stereotypes of Ranters. Robbins's case was a real one, heard before the Middlesex bench and by the Committee for Examinations, and discussed in Parliament; the details of the trial and the pamphlet were shaped significantly by the terms of the Blasphemy and Adultery Acts. The case was widely publicised and discussed in print, and Moxon's transcripts appear to be authentic: this was a specific description of an actual prosecution. But Moxon's prefatory address in *The Ranters creed* presented a more abstract, and thus stereotypical, picture of Ranter *followers* as delusional and ultimately destabilising, the victims of a 'madness' that could infect others and should (by implication) be resisted.[47] In this analysis, it was not so much the Ranter Robbins as his followers and disciples that were characterised as a problematic 'out-group' for the benefit of Moxon's audience.

James Moxon's previous work as a printer and engraver suggests that much of his professional experience placed him in touch with publishers of radical works such as William Larnar, Giles Calvert and Henry Overton; he had printed books out of Rotterdam in the early 1640s and had printed army and Leveller material in 1647–8.[48] In addition to a clientele for his work as an engraver and producer of maps, many of Moxon's commercial contacts had links with radical markets, perhaps among army regiments and officers still on active campaign against the Scots and the royalist forces of Charles Stuart in the summer of 1651. In July 1651, Moxon also printed a serious account of a dispute held in Banbury between Richard Coppin, known at the time as a Ranter author and ringleader, and the minister and parishioners of Bampton, Oxfordshire; while not naming them as Ranters, the tract denounced a 'generation of men' who 'make it their business to resist the truth' and to worship the 'Great Idol' of 'sensual liberty'.[49] The political thrust of *The Ranters creed* highlighted the dangers posed by 'Ranter' false prophets to gullible audiences.

The range of stereotypes relating to the Ranters suggests not that they were caricatured as a marginal or deviant out-group to produce a unified reaction which would reject religious radicalism, but rather that they were a feature of broad-based discussion about the nature of religious settlement and the growing complexity of religious identities in the course of the 1650s. Printed accounts of Ranters stereotyped not just Ranters but also their putative followers, positing a range of political responses from prosecution to toleration, avoidance or rebuttal. Although Ranters featured as an 'out-group' in these accounts, this was a fluid identity, with a clear expectation of dialogue and persuasion, constructed in the context of ongoing public debates about the structure and discipline of a national church and the need to complete a thorough reformation.

Strategies of Quaker stereotyping

Quakers, who came to public attention a year or so after the Ranters, were depicted in strikingly similar ways to the latter, often in tracts produced by the same printers or publishers. Notably, one such tract, *The Quakers dream* (1655), reproduced on its title page the same woodcut illustration that had been used earlier in *The Ranters declaration* (1650). The images depicted open-air preaching and meetings featuring dancing, pipe smoking and sexually licentious behaviour, but the annotations and banners were altered to describe Quaker rather than Ranter practice (see Figures 5.1 and 5.2).

Beyond Nicholas McDowell's careful study of the polemical strategy in the Ranter author Abiezer Coppe's subversion of the 'mechanic preacher' stereotype, little evidence exists of Ranters collectively mobilising around, or contesting, some of the key typologies with which they were associated.[50] But there is abundant evidence allowing us to trace the ways in which Quakers appropriated and exploited the hostile stereotypes by which they were derided and, in particular, manipulated their own nickname to construct an equally hostile attack on their detractors. In this way, Quaker authors collectively adapted and exploited their stereotyping in order to present their opponents as an out-group defined by persecutory inclinations and by inability to discern the divine spirit by which Quakers, the 'in-group', were inspired. Drawing on Yamamoto's and Lake's suggestions, we can therefore begin to explore Quakers' collective *coping strategies* as they sought to control their own stereotyping as part of the mobilisation of their audiences in debates that, like those relating to Ranters, concerned religious liberty of conscience and the settlement of religion.

Quakers were unprecedentedly effective in marshalling their own printed pamphlets to consolidate a coherent collective identity and to challenge many of the religious and political opinions of their contemporaries. Like their puritan forebears, Quakers deployed print as part of a polemical

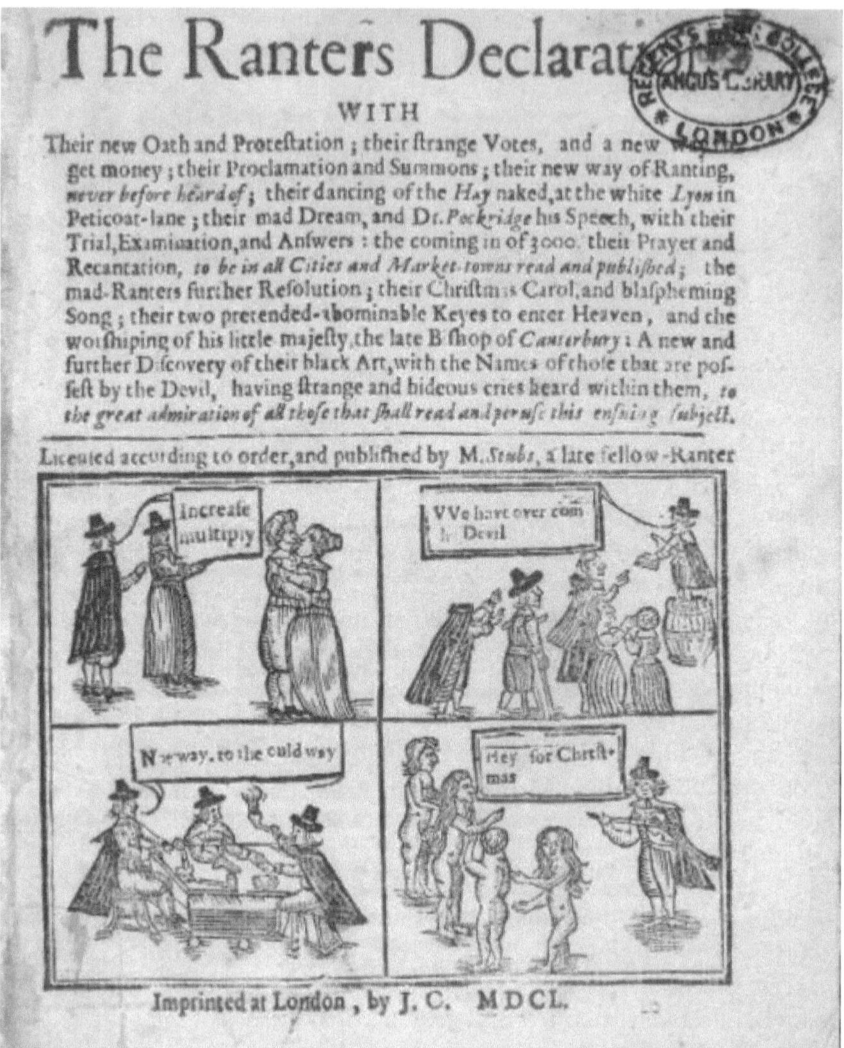

The Ranters Declarat[ion]

WITH

Their new Oath and Proteſtation ; their ſtrange Votes, and a new [way to] get money ; their Proclamation and Summons ; their new way of Ranting, *never before heard of* ; their dancing of the *Hay* naked, at the white *Lyon* in Peticoat-lane ; their mad Dream, and Dr. *Pockridge* his Speech, with their Trial, Examination, and Anſwers : the coming in of 3000. their Prayer and Recantation, *to be in all Cities and Market-towns read and publiſhed* ; the mad-Ranters further Reſolution ; their Chriſtmas Carol, and blaſpheming Song ; their two pretended-abominable Keyes to enter Heaven, and the worſhiping of his little majeſty, the late Biſhop of *Canterbury* : A new and further Diſcovery of their black Art, with the Names of thoſe that are poſſeſt by the Devil, having ſtrange and hideous cries heard within them, *to the great admiration of all thoſe that ſhall read and peruſe this enſuing ſubject.*

Licensed according to order, and publiſhed by M. *Stubs*, a late fellow-Ranter

Imprinted at London, by J. C. MDCL.

Figure 5.1 Regent's Park College Library, Angus Library 1.a.9 (b), *The Ranters declaration* (London: by J[ane]. C[oe]., 1650).

process through which they established their identity, differentiating themselves from other radical sectarian groups and challenging ministers and magistrates to acknowledge their rights to worship within the broadly tolerant religious framework of the commonwealth and Protectorate.[51] One of the most striking ways they did this was by redefining the negative image imposed upon them, that is, by appropriating and exploiting the

THE QVAKERS DREAM:

OR,

The Devil's Pilgrimage in England:

BEING

An infallible Relation of their ſeveral Meetings,

Shreekings, Shakings, Quakings, Roarings, Yellings, Howlings, Tremblings in the Bodies, and Riſings in the Bellies: With a Narrative of their ſeveral Arguments, Tenets, Principles, and ſtrange Doctrine: The ſtrange and wonderful Satanical Apparitions, and the appearing of the Devil unto them in the likeneſs of a black Boar, a Dog with flaming eys, and a black man without a head, cauſing the Dogs to bark, the Swine to cry, and the Cattel to run, to the great admiration of all that ſhall read the ſame.

London, Printed for *G. Horton*, and are to be ſold at the Royal Exchange in Cornhil, 1655.

Figure 5.2 Haverford College Quaker & Special Collections, William H. Jenks Collection BX7795 Q217, *The Quakers dream* (London: for G. Horton, 1655).

'Quaker' nickname. In his autobiographical *Journal*, George Fox claimed retrospectively that the term 'Quaker' had been coined by a Derby magistrate, Gervase Bennett, in October 1650, when Fox was tried for blasphemy (the proximity of this to the timing of the 'Ranter' sensation is telling). In a letter clearly written some years after the trial, Fox accused Justice Bennett of having begotten 'Reprochers scoffers and mockers through Every towne in the nation'; for 'thou was the first man that gave the children of god that name of quakers, and soe it was spread over the nation'.[52] Fox's claim was not strictly accurate, however, as references to Quakers predate this. Charles I's secretary of state, Sir Edward Nicholas, reported the ecstatic prophesying of a sect of women 'called Quakers' in Southwark in November 1647, in a letter detailing the Putney debates and agitation for religious liberty.[53] Quakers had also been referred to in print from 1647. The reliability of female prophesying by 'Quakers and Shakers' was discussed in an address to the army in late 1647, while in a 1648 pamphlet the naval officer Sir William Batten lamented the flourishing of 'Quakers' and other sects. In late 1649 the Fifth Monarchist John Spittlehouse had dismissed 'Quakers' as an insignificant group of Seekers.[54] In a printed account of a conference held in Warwickshire in August 1650, the minister Thomas Hall complained (with some legitimacy) of the many new sects, including 'Ranters, Seekers, Shakers, Quakers and now Creepers' that infected his region.[55] 'Quakers' had been discussed in print and in private intelligence as a dangerous sect from 1647: Fox's slightly disingenuous attempt to single out the significance of Bennet's intervention in October 1650 stemmed from the Quakers' project of appropriating their own stereotype as part of their own mobilisation.

The term 'Quaker' was appropriated by Quaker authors at a very early stage of their own pamphleteering. One of Fox's earliest extant broadsides, *An exhortation to you who contemne the power of God* (1652), included a lengthy discussion of 'Trembling and Quaking' as indicators of divine presence, citing key biblical passages in which Old Testament prophets and New Testament apostles had trembled in the presence of God. This scriptural justification of quaking was repeated in a number of subsequent publications: 'Moses quaked, David quaked, Jeremiah shaked ... and the rest of the holy men of God ... quaked and trembled as they who witness quaking now'.[56] Extended textual engagement with the allegorical significance of 'quaking' allowed Quaker authors to associate themselves with a range of abstracted ideological and polemical positions, as part of their own in-group identity formation. Quaking, they argued from Scripture, happened in those 'to whom the power of the Lord was made manifest', and thus signalled the immediacy and transcendence of the Quakers' spiritual experience as witnesses of God.[57] 'Search the Scriptures,' James Nayler instructed his readers, 'and you shall finde that the holy men of God do witness quaking and trembling, and roaring and weeping'.[58] Quaker authors maintained that the nickname had been coined by hostile detractors, who either did not, or could not, recognise the true significance of quaking, and who thus – even unwittingly – persecuted the heralds of the true church. Thus the failure of their opponents to discern or recognise the divine authenticity of quaking was presented as a counter-stereotype, indicative of their opponents' reprobation.[59] 'The world', Nayler declared, 'knows not the saints conditions'.[60] Denouncing those 'that scorne trembling and quaking', George Fox warned 'you are in the steps of your forefathers who persecuted the Apostles'.[61] Another Quaker, George Baiteman, refuted the accusation that quaking was 'counterfeit, or comes from the power of the Devill' by observing that his opponent could not have experienced 'the powring out of the Justice of God upon his soule … as hath made all his bones to quake', and, in a counter-stereotype, derided his ignorance as hypocrisy: 'I marvaile that such a one as he, who cryeth up the Scripture so high … should be so unacquainted with Gods dealing with some of his people in former time … [I]f he had lived in those dayes, he would have called *Moses* a *Quaker,* and that his trembling proceeded from the Devill.'[62]

Arguments such as these enabled a tactical redefinition of the Quaker stereotype. Persecution of quaking was presented as an allegory of biblical persecutions, confirming (for Quaker polemicists) the immanence of God's presence through time and the ongoing apocalyptic battle between the true and false church; as George Fox put it, 'now yee are the scoffers that are come in the last times whom they spoke of'.[63] By asserting the authority of Scriptural references to quaking, and implying their opponents' own understanding of biblical passages was flawed, Quaker authors countered accusations that Quakers denied the bible and were unlearned; and cast doubt on the biblical knowledge of their learned opponents. Ranter author Abiezer Coppe did the same thing.[64] '[S]ome scoffes at the power [of quaking] and call it of the Divell, and some persecute', wrote Fox, 'doe not you heere fulfill the Scripture and Christs sayings, who sayth if they kill you they thinke they doe good service, and yet you make a profession of Christs words, the Prophets and Apostles words, and calls yourselves Churches and ministers of the Gospell.'[65]

Contention over the spiritual authenticity of quaking was used to highlight the conflicting hermeneutics that distinguished the spiritual knowledge of Quakers from the 'worldly' learning of their opponents: quaking was abstracted as a uniquely spiritual experience that was incomprehensible to non-Quakers. James Nayler made a distinction between quaking, of which he said 'we owne it as that which the Lord hath said shall come upon all flesh', and other more salacious activities they were accused of by their detractors: 'grovelling upon the ground and foaming at the mouth' were 'slanders and lyes', 'inventions' of the puritan authors who wrote against the Quakers.[66] Critics of the Quakers were tellingly outraged that they made such a play on the significance of the nickname, arguing indignantly that the Quakers' claim that the moniker had been 'thrust upon them' was itself disingenuous: 'I could bring many instances ... to shew how they would make men believe they are greatly wronged when they are distinguished from other men by this term', complained Jeremiah Ives, a Baptist and former Leveller engaged in a protracted dispute with Quakers in 1656. For Ives, their exploitation of the nickname was a 'deceit'; 'they say Ishmael's Brood and the world calls them so, and yet they take paines to prove themselves so ... they are Lyers, in saying that they are Nick-named Quakers, when themselves say they witness quaking'.[67] Pagitt, more succinctly, observed, 'they owne the title of Quakers', 'a name imposed by themselves'.[68]

The appropriation and elaboration of the Quaker nickname translated, in print, to a literal stereotype – the word 'Quaker' – that served materially to advertise Quaker books to a commercial audience. Quaker authors initially used the word 'Quaker' paratextually, to signify both the prophetic status of the author and the unlawful persecution such status entailed. An early exponent was Richard Farnworth, one of the most prolific early Quaker pamphleteers, who styled an early tract as 'written by one whom the people of the world call Quaker, by name Richard Farnworth'; another promised the 'vindication of those whom the world calleth Quakers'.[69] This paratextual device first appeared in a series of five 'litle books' by Farnworth, printed in London in late 1652 or early 1653 as one of the earliest printing ventures. These may not have circulated in London: mainly octavo or duodecimo, they were distributed directly to sympathetic households in the north of England and were not acquired by the London bookseller George Thomason.[70] In these tracts, little visual emphasis was given to the word 'Quaker' (see Figure 5.3).

As shown in Chapter 4 by Lake and Yamamoto in this volume, under Elizabeth and James London commercial theatres helped to propagate stereotypes about puritans and projectors. Something similar happened in the world of print for the Quaker nickname. Indeed, it was contact with commercially savvy booksellers in London that appears to have led to the visual emphasis of the word 'Quaker' on title pages. Tracts published after February 1653 for the highly experienced radical London bookseller, Giles Calvert, emphasised the word Quaker on the title page of pamphlets: the type was much larger and the word increasingly dominated the title page, presumably a marketing device advertising Quaker books to a broad audience in Calvert's well-known radical bookshop, and beyond. Books that

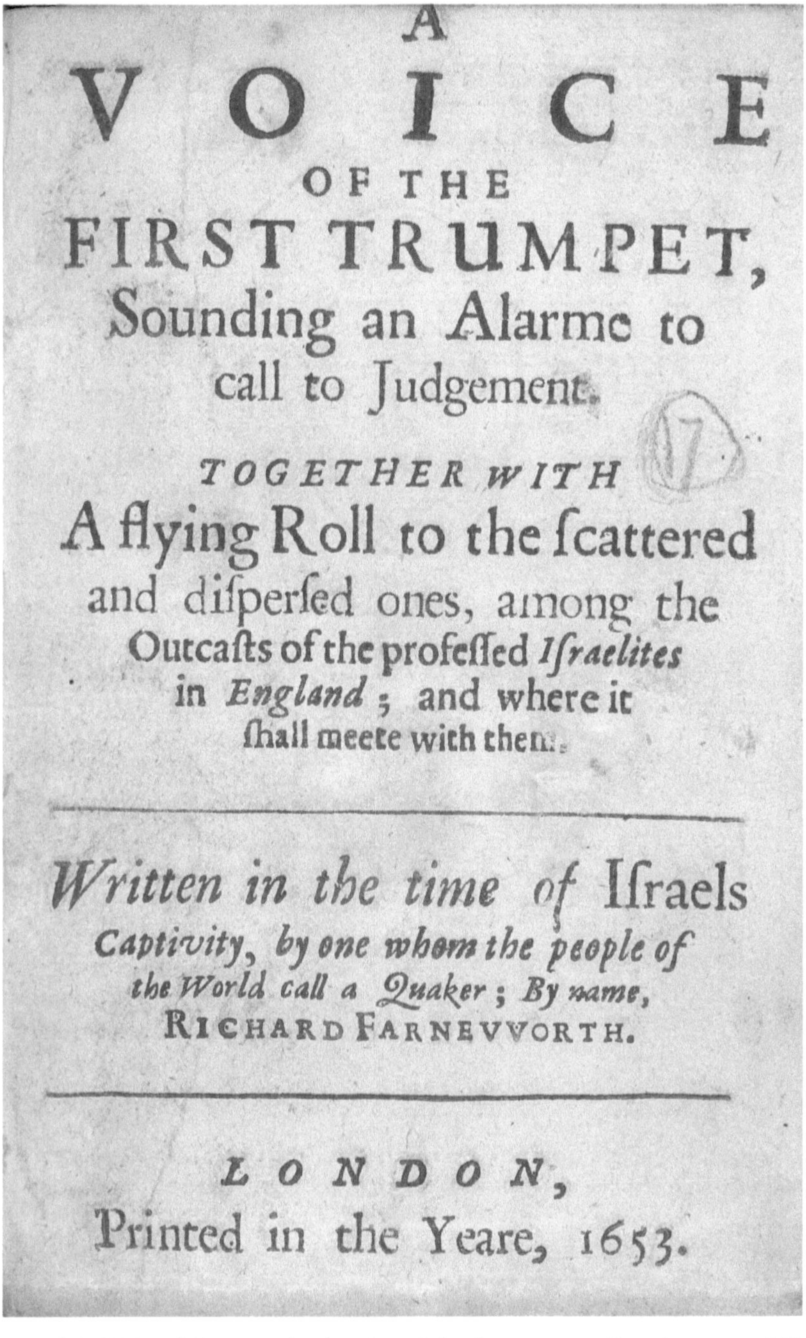

A VOICE OF THE FIRST TRUMPET, Sounding an Alarme to call to Judgement.

TOGETHER WITH

A flying Roll to the ſcattered and diſperſed ones, among the Outcaſts of the profeſſed *Iſraelites* in *England*; and where it ſhall meete with them.

Written in the time of Iſraels *Captivity, by one whom the people of the World call a Quaker; By name,* RICHARD FARNEVVORTH.

LONDON, Printed in the Yeare, 1653.

Figure 5.3 Richard Farnworth, *A voice of the first trumpet* (London: n.p., 1653, Wing STC F512B). All rights reserved by the copyright holder.

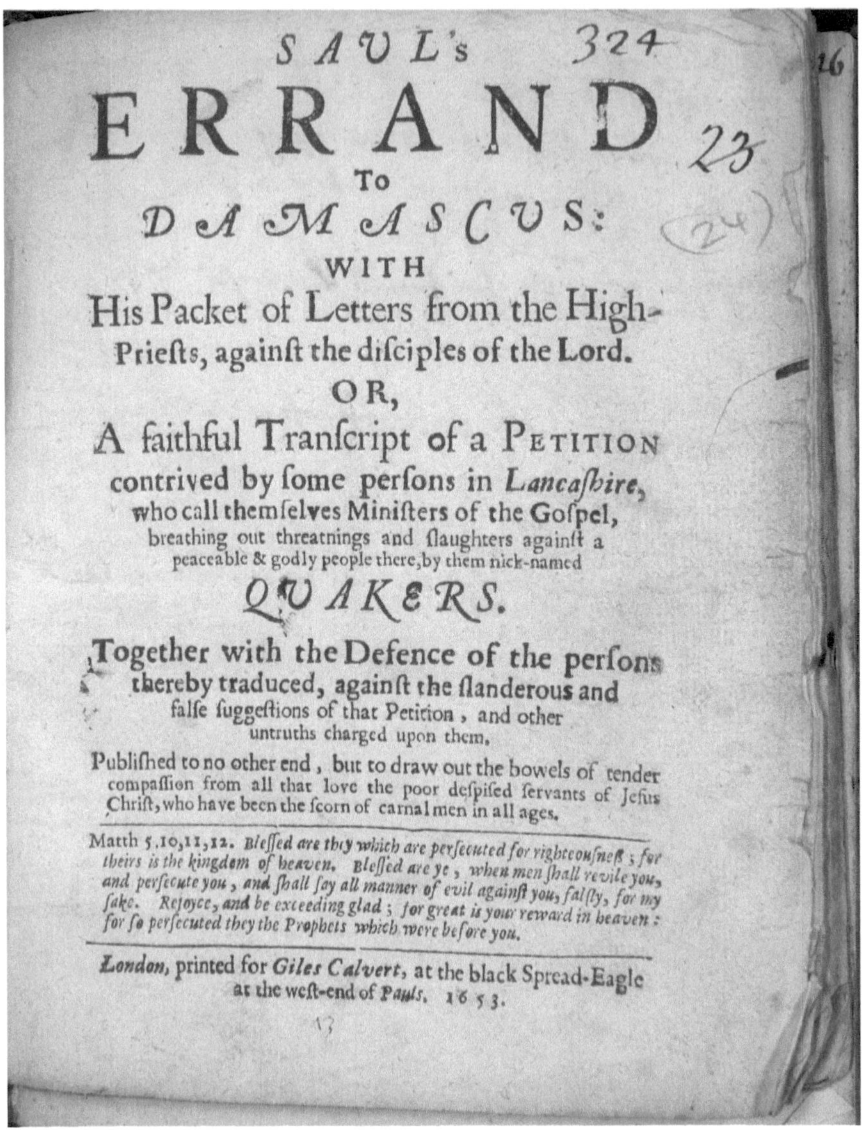

SAUL's

ERRAND

To

DAMASCUS:

WITH

His Packet of Letters from the High-Priests, against the disciples of the Lord.

OR,

A faithful Transcript of a PETITION contrived by some persons in *Lancashire*, who call themselves Ministers of the Gospel, breathing out threatnings and slaughters against a peaceable & godly people there, by them nick-named

QUAKERS.

Together with the Defence of the persons thereby traduced, against the slanderous and false suggestions of that Petition, and other untruths charged upon them.

Published to no other end, but to draw out the bowels of tender compassion from all that love the poor despised servants of Jesus Christ, who have been the scorn of carnal men in all ages.

Matth 5.10,11,12. *Blessed are they which are persecuted for righteousness; for theirs is the kingdom of heaven. Blessed are ye, when men shall revile you, and persecute you, and shall say all manner of evil against you, falsly, for my sake. Rejoyce, and be exceeding glad; for great is your reward in heaven: for so persecuted they the Prophets which were before you.*

London, printed for *Giles Calvert*, at the black Spread-Eagle at the west-end of *Pauls*. 1653.

Figure 5.4 Queen's College Library, Oxford, UU.b.1325(24), George Fox, *Saul's errand to Damascus* (London: for Giles Calvert, 1653). All rights reserved by the copyright holder.

were among the first to be circulated in London, from the spring of 1653, drew attention to their Quaker status, the earliest being *Saul's errand to Damascus*, acquired by Thomason on 12 March 1653 (see Figure 5.4).[71] Interestingly, the 'litle books' by Farnworth may have been less commercial, and they appear to have sold sluggishly: in 1654 the Quaker Thomas Aldam sent a consignment of them to George Fox to 'be spread abroad in the contry' by Quaker preachers, and explained that he still had plenty in storage in York, while of the larger more recent ones 'there is fewe to be had; but I have sent for more to London'.[72]

In addition, the Quaker epithet was used commercially to advertise anti-Quaker tracts to commercial markets, and thus to mobilise audiences around Quakers as an out-group. One such was John Gilpin's *The Quakers shaken*, which told of the author's brief brush with, and rejection of, Quakers in Kendal in 1653: its ostensible aim was to describe Gilpin's experiences 'so others may heare, and feare, and take warning by my example'.[73] Gilpin's tract thus provided an entertaining pastiche of Quaker belief and practice, emphasising key stereotypes: their denial of ministerial teaching and ordination, refutation of 'carnall' learning, and rejection of 'outward' family obligations in favour of their co-religionists. Gilpin's own experience of quaking was also explained as an 'imposture', the author concluding ultimately that his shaking and trembling had been inspired by a diabolical rather than a divine power. The whole account was presented in a tract which emphasised the word 'Quakers' on its title page.[74] A more erudite, heresiographical critique, *The perfect pharisee under monkish holiness,* presented a list of sixteen Quaker doctrines or 'positions', a list of their principles (not to salute anyone, not to give outward tokens of reverence to magistrates, parents or masters), and finally a consideration of their 'practices', including 'Quaking' and 'Rayling' (the evidence for which was borrowed from Gilpin's book). This work, too, emphasised the word 'Quakers' on its title page (see Figure 5.5).[75]

Both *The Quakers shaken* and *The perfect pharisee* used the Quaker moniker in large printed letters to identify Quakers as a deviant out-group and strongly suggest an implicitly polemic, anti-Quaker, market readership (although of course Quaker authors read, commented on and responded to both books). Both books were published simultaneously in London and in Gateshead, in Gateshead to be sold by William London, bookseller in Newcastle, and printed by Simon Buckley, who had been printer for the king in York during the 1640s.[76] As with Giles Calvert's typographical elaboration of the term Quaker, this appears to have been a commercially driven attempt to reach a presumptively anti-Quaker market, defined by its polemic dislike of, or curiosity about, Quakers. As with Ranters, then, there is evidence that commercially driven publishers and booksellers honed and exploited a Quaker stereotype in anticipation of an existing, non-Quaker, market readership for whom Quakers were projected as an out-group. Then, as now, collective negotiations and contestation over stereotypes took place in a dynamic environment that underlines the complex relationship between

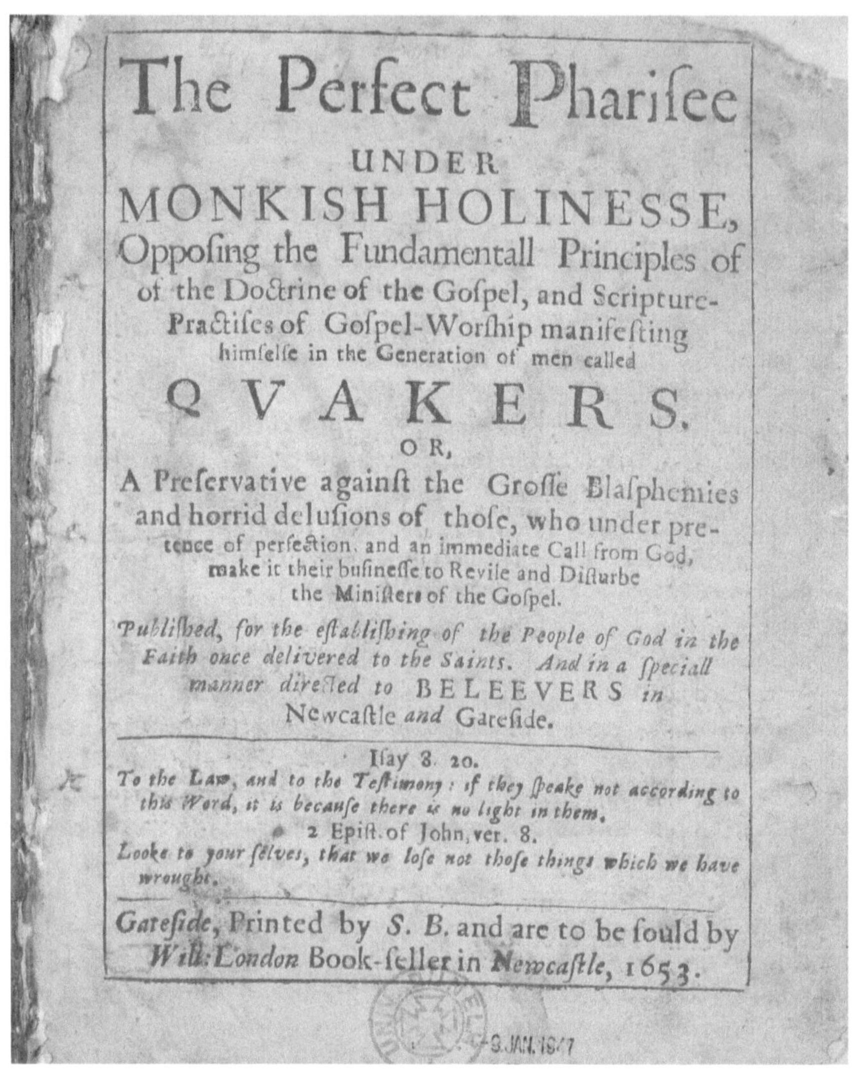

The Perfect Pharifee
UNDER
MONKISH HOLINESSE,
Oppoſing the Fundamentall Principles of
of the Doctrine of the Goſpel, and Scripture-
Practiſes of Goſpel-Worſhip manifeſting
himſelfe in the Generation of men called
QVAKERS.
OR,
A Preſervative againſt the Groſſe Blaſphemies
and horrid deluſions of thoſe, who under pre-
tence of perfection, and an immediate Call from God,
make it their buſineſſe to Revile and Diſturbe
the Miniſters of the Goſpel.

Publiſhed, for the eſtabliſhing of the People of God in the Faith once delivered to the Saints. And in a ſpeciall manner directed to BELEEVERS *in* Newcaſtle *and* Gateſide.

Iſay 8. 20.
To the Law, and to the Teſtimony: if they ſpeake not according to this Word, it is becauſe there is no light in them.
2 Epiſt. of John, ver. 8.
Looke to your ſelves, that we loſe not thoſe things which we have wrought.

Gateſide, Printed by *S. B.* and are to be ſould by *Will: London* Book-ſeller in *Newcaſtle*, 1653.

Figure 5.5 Special Collections, University of Durham, SB 0514, Thomas Weld, *The perfect pharisee under monkish holinesse* (Gateside, by S.B., 1653).

printed polemic, public debate and commercial calculation within the intricate politics of group identities.

As we have seen, much of the material published against Quakers in the 1650s shared similarities with printed attacks on the Ranters. Spurious, salacious accounts focused on their sexual depravity and blasphemy, and sought to titillate audiences; more serious heresiographical accounts attempted to catalogue, contextualise and interpret their principles and beliefs. Some of these printed attacks shared the same publishers and printers, and woodcuts, as earlier anti-Ranter works. George Horton, who had published a number of scurrilous works against the Ranters, published 'a new relation and further discovery' of the Quakers' 'trances, shakings, raptures, visions, apparitio[n]s, conflicts with Satan, revelations, illuminations, instructions in new divine mysteries, and seraphical divinity'; another related 'their several opinions and tenets, holding a community with all mens wives, either sleeping or waking; their strange doctrine, raptures, and inspirations' and further extrapolated the 'several sorts of Quakers; as Catharists, Familists, Enthusiasts, Mentatists, Valencians, & Libertins'.[77]

Quakers clearly made a conscious effort to contest the stereotyping in their own printed works. In 1655, Thomas Aldam, one of the earliest architects of Quaker use of print, confronted the journalist Henry Walker, the publisher George Horton and the printer Robert Wood about 'slanders and false reports' in their newsbook *The faithful scout* in 1655. In his printed account of the encounter with Walker, Horton and Wood, Aldam complained about the allegations, a specific one alleging an adulterous relationship between two leading Quakers, George Fox and Margaret Fell, and others more generic: that Quakers wore and exchanged ribbons, were secret papists and associated with witches.[78] The significance of wearing and exchanging ribbons was ambiguous and multifaceted, conflating a range of stereotypes that ultimately facilitated different polemical responses. Wearing ribbons was a sign of allegiance or association – Levellers and army regiments identified themselves with coloured ribbons; but the exchange of ribbons as favours could also suggest a sexual relationship, as that alleged between George Fox and Margaret Fell, or superstitious or idolatrous behaviour. Quaker authors criticised clergy wearing 'ribbons and cuffes and gaudy attire' as emblematic of their worldly greed and dedication to hierarchy, a sign that 'they are heady and high-minded men, for poore people bow to them in the streets, and call them Masters'.[79] An instance of early Quaker enthusiasm in Malton, Yorkshire, in July 1652, when Quaker shopkeepers burned lace and ribbons in a denunciation of worldly goods, had been discussed in print in 1653.[80] Some of the printed attacks on Quakers focused on the egalitarianism and enthusiasm implied by this incident: George Horton's tract, *The Quakers terrible vision; or the devils progress to the City of London* recounted the 'burning of their fine cloaths, points, and ribbons' by the Malton Quakers, who declared themselves 'abased by pride'. The significance of the ribbons was extended to include idolatory and demonology: 'compare these fellows burning of their ribbonds and silk, with Moses burning the molten Calf, Hezekiah breaking the brazen Serpent, and the burning of the Ephesian conjuring books in the Acts'.[81] The story then became generic. The title page of *The Quakers fiery beacon* (also published by George Horton) described the Quakers' use of 'inchanted potions, ribbons and bracelets'. The clergyman Donald Lupton's *The quacking mountebancke* alleged that 'they use Charmes, Spells and Incantations, by tying of Ribbons Laces Knots, and by giving some slight present' such that the recipient acted as though 'possessed and Frantick', abandoning clothing, families and estates. And William Prynne employed the reports of ribbons to argue that Quakers were Jesuits, who 'use inchanted Potions, Braclets, Ribons, Sorcery and witchcraft, to intoxicate their novices and draw them to their party'.[82] Other puritan commentators argued that the Quaker rejection of ribbons and other worldly goods was hypocritical, likened to 'a few outward observances, of casting off ribbons, not putting off the hat ... etc. ... whilest in the mean time they speak nothing of a work of regeneration and renovation in the heart'.[83] Richard Baxter argued that this was tokenism: 'Do you think that the salvation of the world doth lie upon this Doctrine? They come to preach down ribbons, and lace, and points, and cuffs: O glorious and excellent Doctrine, for children to make sport with!'[84]

Thus various and conflicting stereotypes could be, and were, invoked by their critics in response to the Quakers' public rejection of ribbons as they characterised them negatively for implicitly different audiences. In other publications Quaker authors and their opponents engaged polemically with these broader religious and social arguments. Yet Thomas Aldam's direct response to the journalists and their publishers is significant because it sought to refute the truth of the allegations on the basis of the scant evidence gathered by Walker, Horton and Wood. The strategy was rhetorically effective in inferring the empirical weakness of generic assertions made against Quakers. Aldam demanded evidence for the exchange of ribbons between Fell and Fox, as well as about another story of a 'gentlewoman' who allegedly wore ribbons and obliged her maid and husband to do the same: 'what is the name of this Gentlewoman, and the maid, and the name of her husband, the Country they dwell in, and what towne they dwell in, and the place where these things was done, and who saw it, and where they dwell?' Similarly, Walker was pressed for proof of the Quaker association with witches: 'mentione the names of those witches, ... that witch-craft may be found out, ... for witch-craft we deny'. George Horton and his printer Robert Wood were denounced in Aldam's tract for an over-reliance on third-party evidence when reporting a Quaker who 'went naked' in Smithfield. 'I said, Didst thou see it? He said no, but a lad told him ... that one went naked into Smith-field amongst the hay carts... To this many can witness against thee, that there was no hay carts there, for it was about 9 of the Clock at night.'[85]

As Mark Knights's discussion of stereotyping has shown, and as the example of the ribbons has demonstrated, generic or abstract language is effective in defining negative attributes of an out-group (as well as positive attributes of an in-group) because abstract descriptions are more static and enduring, and therefore more flexible, in shaping a stereotype.[86] In narrowing down the journalistic accusations of Walker and Horton to one-off events and casting doubt on their veracity, Aldam attempted to refute generic labels of diabolism, popery and fanaticism that would inform negative stereotypes of Quakers, by reducing them to deniable instances. At the same time, behind the circulation of printed stories, Quaker ministers worked hard to suppress actual stories of impropriety; and were privately concerned to control the behaviour of women preachers and deny stories that might 'be tattled' abroad. Thus James Nayler, publicly reputed to have abandoned his wife, reported in a letter that her visit to him in prison had been 'verie servisable' because it 'stopped many mouths'. Printed stories of Christopher Atkinson's actual adultery, the cause of some anguish in Quaker circles, were likewise subject to a skilful non-denial in print (also by Nayler): 'if ye know more, why doe you not speake the truth, but slander in secret?'[87] Some coping strategies sought privately to refute or contest damaging stories in order to discredit them among Quaker audiences and hence to fortify vulnerable members of the Quaker in-group. In 1653, the Quaker preacher Thomas Lawson was obliged to circulate a manuscript paper to deny the 'filthy things' he was alleged in print to have committed with an outspoken young Quaker woman. Lawson professed himself concerned that 'the outward minde ... looked forth at the reports of the world', and 'tatled them abroade, without any ground, but onely by heresay'.[88] Such coping strategies by Quaker authors were thus based on stigma consciousness – acute awareness of the dangers of being stereotyped – and with a range of responses that were sensitive to the proclivities of different audiences.[89] Tellingly, the Quakers' coping strategies focused purposely on the commercial context in which these hostile stereotypes were produced and disseminated. In identifying the journalists, printers and publishers responsible for the propagation of key negative stories, Thomas Aldam had clearly understood the commercial origins and interests at play in the stereotyping process and worked with it.

Sensitivity to the commercial dimensions of stereotyping is also evident in the intricate distribution strategies of key works which contested the hostile stereotyping of Quakers. In July 1660, the cartographer Richard Blome published *The fanatick history,* a hostile account of Quakers which appeared against a backdrop of openly violent assaults on Quakers and their meetings following the restoration of Charles II. *The fanatick history* incorporated a number of stereotypes of Quakers, implying they shared a heretical tradition with German Anabaptists, noting their 'blasphemous opinions', fanatic behaviour and hostility to all civil government. In doing so, Blome drew from a number of publications from the 1650s to characterise the Quakers' fanaticism, including John Gilpin's narrative and a long catalogue of Quakers 'going naked'.[90] The Quaker leader George Fox was quick to alert his co-religionists to it, and within a week a sixteen-page reply had been written and printed. The authors, Richard Hubberthorn and James Nayler, denounced Blome's work as a 'Packet of Old Lies': 'false accusations formerly written against us, which have been disproved by answers several times over'.[91] In working through Blome's accusations, Hubberthorn referred the reader to a number of Quaker pamphlets published since 1653 that had already combated negative stories about the Quakers. Other instances of fanatic or deviant behaviour were flatly denied, such as a preacher's ecstatic trembling at a meeting in Durham in 1654: 'there was no such thing, as many can witness, who was present at the Meeting'; or disowned: Mary Todd who reputedly attended a Quaker meeting 'pulling up her coats' and 'using base expressions' was rejected: 'she neither was nor is a Quaker but a Ranter, who came thither to oppose the Quakers'.[92] While the range of coping strategies was familiar, however, the dissemination of the Quaker response is informative. The *Fanatick history* was, novelly, advertised in a newsbook, and Richard Hubberthorn's response was also unusually widely disseminated, perhaps in an attempt to reach a similarly broad audience. Copies were 'given abroad in Whitehall'; others 'sould in divers shopps', and others were hawked: 'women cryes them about the streets: soe that the truth is over it'.[93] This is a rare instance of the use of hawkers and booksellers to disseminate a Quaker book, which were usually distributed discriminately by Quaker preachers and trusted booksellers. Hubberthorn's work had been printed for the bookseller Giles Calvert, whose shop was well established as a radical meeting place in London; the use of hawkers and 'divers shops' suggests a more eclectic market envisaged by Calvert and the Quakers for Hubberthorn's work. A widely advertised and defamatory work was thus responded to in kind, its dissemination shaped by knowledge of the target readership.

Locating the production and distribution of stereotyping literature within the commercial world of print helps our understanding of its role in the mobilisation of what Jason Peacey has recently called 'public politics'. As Ethan Shagan showed in relation to polemical accounts of the Irish rebellion in 1641, commercial booksellers assumed a market readership that was *already* polarised in the mounting tensions that would lead to Civil War.[94] In our growing understanding of the commercial dynamics of the market for print, it is clear that booksellers and publishers produced works and mobilised stereotypes likely to appeal to, and to reinforce, pre-established religious or political positions within markets. Printed denunciations or defences of Quakers, Ranters and their putative supporters categorised them using familiar, well-worn stereotypes that would appeal to a variety of political and religious views. The associated marketing strategies reviewed here underline both the diversity, and the prevalence, of public discussion of the radical religious sects.

Contesting stereotypes and discerning truth

As we have seen, then, Quakers acted collectively, and in concert with commercial publishers, to mobilise and control the stereotypes by which they were depicted in print. This involved contesting – sometimes disingenuously – the veracity of generic printed caricatures and stories about them, as well as counter-stereotyping their critics as 'false prophets' who were unable or unwilling to recognise the spiritual authenticity of the Quakers. These contestations and counter-accusations were not confined to printed polemical exchanges, but occurred also in public meetings between Ranter and Quaker leaders, in which the two sides argued about their respective status as true or false prophets and urged audiences to follow the light in their conscience in order to discern truth.[95] Through the 1650s, Quaker and Ranter leaders expected, and sought, public debate with each other; indeed, the degree to which Quakers appear to have routinely organised formal meetings with Ranter leaders is significant evidence that Ranters did exist and were active participants in the local religious debates. The power of Ranters over audiences in these meetings was a source of significant anxiety for Quaker leaders, as they competed directly to win over new followers. Accounts of public disputations between Quakers and Ranters are revealing of the ways in which the discernment of truth or falsehood, and thus of the spiritual authenticity of their audiences, was actively discussed in public meetings. These debates add an important dimension to our understanding of both the epistemological significance of stereotypes for radical sectaries, and of their mobilisation in contesting them.

Quaker leaders were well aware of the Ranters' formidable rhetorical skills. In late 1654 the Quaker William Dewsbury travelled to Leicestershire, anticipating a public dispute with local Ranters: when the meeting was delayed, he boasted in a letter that this was due to the Ranters' 'fearfullnes' of the Quakers. When the encounter eventually took place, Dewsbury described triumphantly how he had managed to reveal truth and silence his Ranter opponents, who included the author Jacob Bauthumley, 'the highest of them'. '[W]hen the truth was spoken to their conscience', Dewsbury explained, and 'their decaitts was layd open ... the power of the lord stayed their mouths [and] they had no power to resist', but left the meeting 'in shame and contempt'. For Dewsbury, the primary beneficiaries of this exchange were the audience: 'Frinds were much strengthened who had been bewitched'.[96] In other instances, however, Quakers were defeated by the power of Ranter rhetoric. The Quaker Henry Fell, disputing in Barbados against Joseph Salmon, a former 'ring leader of the Ranters', was stung by Salmon's deviousness, complaining he 'seems to deny Ranting outwardly', but that this was a ploy to 'deceive the hearts of the simple'. Those formerly sympathetic to the Quakers had been particularly vulnerable to Salmon's words: 'truly many are deceived by him who formerly have had a profession ... but are now drawne after this painted beast & gotten into his Image'. Salmon's skills were formidable: 'he hath gotten the forme of truth in words, the most that ever I heard', but 'soe blind and bewitched are they by him, that they nether can, nor will see him: truly he is a great enemy to ye truth'.[97]

Quakers and Ranters shared an antinomian cognitive landscape that prioritised immediate divine revelation and rejected formal learning: both worked within what McDowell has termed a 'purely inspired epistemology'.[98] This enabled both Ranter and Quaker authors to characterise the worldly learning of their educated opponents as 'carnal' in juxtaposition to their own immediate, prophetic revelation. However, in dispute with one another it became necessary to invoke language of a more immediate, apocalyptic struggle: Fell's depiction of Salmon as a 'painted beast', and of his followers as bewitched, identified Salmon's, and his audience's, inspiration as diabolical rather than divine. At stake in these meetings of course was not the contestation of the veracity of printed stereotypes but a more urgent and fundamental concern with the abilities of Quakers or Ranters to discern divine truth within the others' utterances, and thus to judge prophetic authenticity. Nevertheless, the epistemological implications of this debate are important for our assessment of the significance of stereotyping, since the discernment of truth was of existential significance to the Quakers' spirituality and their understanding of universal grace. Quakers were clear, in their printed attacks on Ranters, that the Ranters' wilful embracing of 'carnal' sin had led to apostasy and the loss of discernment. 'Once you were enlightened with the pure light, ... and the judgement within you, to have freed you from sin ... had you ... stood in the counsel of God ...', wrote Farnworth of the Ranters, but lamented instead their turn to 'fleshly joy, fleshly liberty, and fleshly pleasures'.[99] George Fox addressed Ranters in similar terms: 'you had a pure convincement, I witnesse', but this had been transformed by the Ranters into 'wantonnesse', through wilful acts of drunkenness, 'cursed speaking', 'following oaths' and 'swearing'.[100]

John Chandler, self-defined as a former Ranter turned Quaker, lamented those Ranters who previously had been 'conscious of thinking, speaking, or doing, vainly, idly, or unjustly', but who were now literally insensible to their own wrongdoing. He focused on the ephemerality, and potential for change, in their abandonment of conscience. In departing from truth, they had fallen into error 'which they *could not see at the present*' [my emphasis], and were 'unsensible thereof, by reason of their wandring minds and hearts, which brought a Vail over the Understanding, or stupified the Conscience'. For Chandler, conscience (or inner light) potentially enabled all people to recognise and denounce sin: 'Christ ... sheweth a truth to every man, which is, that he hath transgressed his Law or Light, by dark motions, words, and actions'. For Chandler, sin was not 'a fiction or fained thing in any man whatsoever, because sin is known by a Law, which Law is Light, which Light is in every man'.[101]

Within accounts such as these, Quakers argued for a significant spiritual difference between themselves and Ranters, which centred on the ability to discern truth from falsehood. This has a number of implications for our understanding of Quaker and Ranter stereotyping. First, it enabled Quaker authors to dismiss Ranters as 'worldly', carnal and unable to recognise the true prophecy of Quakers, in ways that directly recall Quaker and Ranter authors' dismissal of the 'worldly' learning of their orthodox puritan opponents. It thus enabled the Quakers, rhetorically, to reposition Ranters with the stereotypical puritan, largely predestinarian, out-group who were driven by worldly, not spiritual, guidance. Second, the anxieties of Dewsbury and Fell about their audiences' vulnerability to Ranter deceit reveal that discernment of truth and falsehood was actively and experientially discussed and contested in their preaching and public meetings. It is clear from the accounts of both Dewsbury and Fell that they sought to empower their audiences to discern and judge truth and contest falsehood and misinterpretation, and this has obvious implications for the ability of audiences to question and contest the authenticity of stereotypes. Quaker leaders were thus concerned to equip audiences with the facility to contest stereotyping and other rhetorical devices as part of public debate and proselytisation. Finally, published addresses to Ranters by Quaker authors all offered the possibility of Ranter redemption, by rejecting sin and returning to the light: this was by no means a permanent, static out-group, but temporarily 'unsensible' and thus (in ways that recall works printed by Moxon and Sparke) open to persuasion and deliverance.

The stereotyping of Quakers and Ranters offers a fruitful understanding of the diversity, fluidity and dynamism of radical religious cultures in the English Revolution. Stereotypes of Ranters were deployed polemically in a number of ways by their contemporaries, suggesting a range of political responses to their presence, from discipline and persecution to inclusion, toleration and – importantly – persuasion and debate. In this analysis Ranters did not constitute a single or static out-group, nor the fictive subject of a moral panic, but were stereotypically situated pragmatically and ideologically by different authors, discussed for implicitly different audiences or readers. Quakers and Ranters themselves were also well aware of the linguistic power of stereotyping. As agents of their own stereotyping, Ranter and Quaker authors engaged rhetorically to appropriate and subvert key stereotypes in ways that fortified their own religious identities. They also sustained long-established, ideological disputes with their opponents and putative supporters. The carefully documented records of Quaker preaching, in particular, afford access to a range of coping strategies deployed by Quaker ministers as they discussed and contested their religious identity with opponents and followers alike. The evident commercial dynamic to the use and distribution of stereotypes is evidence of a broad but complex public appetite for religious contention, and public discussions of and opposition to the shifting meanings of radical religious identities. A focus on Quaker and Ranter stereotyping has also enabled a delineation of a distinct antinomian episteme; Quaker engagement with the meanings and interpretation of stereotypes was consistent with their belief in a universal, immanent, divine presence, and they used this rhetorically in dialogue with largely Calvinist Ranter and puritan opponents in order to propagate their status as true prophets. As such, an exploration of the stereotyping of Ranters and Quakers affords a more nuanced understanding of the conduct of religious debate in the 1650s, and of a participatory public politics in which radical voices were polymorphous, oppositional and subject to persuasion. Stereotypes were deployed in ways that sought not just to caricature or isolate Ranters or Quakers as marginal eccentrics, but also to provide a *locus* for ideological mobilisation, contestation and change.

Notes

1 Ephraim Pagitt, *Heresiography, or a description of the heretickes and sectaries*, 5th edn (London, 1654), p. 136. Pagitt died in 1647 and the fifth edition appeared posthumously.

2 Pagitt, *Heresiography*, p. 143.

3 Christopher Hill, *The world turned upside down: radical ideas during the English Revolution* (Harmondsworth, 1975), pp. 236–7.

4 Hill, *World turned upside down;* J. F. McGregor and Barry Reay (eds), *Radical religion in the English Revolution* (Oxford, 1984). For the argument that

radicalism has been over-emphasised, see Conel Condren, 'Will all the radicals please lie down, we can't see the seventeenth century', in Conal Condren, *The language of politics in seventeenth-century England* (Basingstoke, 1994); Ariel Hessayon and David Finnegan (eds), *Varieties of seventeenth- and early eighteenth-century radicalism in context* (Farnham, 2011); Glenn Burgess, 'Radicalism and the English Revolution', in Glenn Burgess and Matthew Festenstein (eds), *English radicalism, 1550–1850* (Cambridge, 2007); see also my discussion: Kate Peters, 'The Quakers and the politics of the army in the crisis of 1659', *Past & Present,* 231 (2016), 98–102.

5 J. C. Davis, *Fear, myth and history: the Ranters and the historians* (Cambridge, 1986), p. 124; for discussion of Ranters as moral panic, see pp. 94–8. See also David Lemmings, 'Introduction: law and order, moral panics, and early modern England' in David Lemmings and Claire Walker (eds), *Moral panics, the media and the law in early modern England* (Basingstoke, 2009), pp. 1–17.

6 For the longevity of the Quakers, see most recently Richard C. Allen and Rosemary Moore, *The Quakers, 1656–1723: the evolution of an alternative community* (University Park, PA, 2018).

7 Kate Peters, *Print culture and the early Quakers* (Cambridge, 2005); J. F. McGregor et al., 'Debate: fear, myth and furore: reappraising the "Ranters"', *Past & Present*, 140 (1993), 155–94, at p. 161.

8 The critical response to Davis was vast. It is best summarised in two debates: J. C. Davis, 'Fear, myth and furore: reappraising the "Ranters"', *Past & Present*, 129 (1990), 79–103; J. F. McGregor et al., 'Debate: fear, myth and furore'; and J. C. Davis, 'Fear, myth and furore: reappraising the Ranters: reply', *Past & Present*, 140 (1993), 194–210. For important, more recent, scholarly responses, see the introduction to Nigel Smith, *A collection of Ranter writings: spiritual liberty and sexual freedom in the English Revolution* (London, 2014); Ariel Hessayon, 'The making of Abiezer Coppe', *The Journal of Ecclesiastical History*, 62 (2011), 38–58; Ariel Hessayon, 'Abiezer Coppe and the Ranters', in Laura Lunger Knoppers (ed.), *The Oxford handbook of literature and the English Revolution* (Oxford, 2012), 346–74; Ariel Hessayon, 'The Ranters and their sources: the question of Jacob Boehme's supposed influence', *Sciences et Techniques en Perspective*, 2nd series, 16 (2014), 77–101; Nicholas McDowell, *The English radical imagination: culture, religion, and revolution, 1630–1660* (Oxford, 2003); Nicholas McDowell, 'A Ranter reconsidered: Abiezer Coppe and Civil War stereotypes', *The Seventeenth Century,* 12 (1997), 173–205; R. C. Richardson, '"Babels of profaneness and community": the Ranter sensation in Hampshire and Wiltshire, 1649–51', *Southern History,* 36 (2014), 29–55.

9 Joad Raymond, *Pamphlets and pamphleteering in early modern Britain* (Cambridge, 2003); Jason Peacey, *Print and public politics in the English Revolution* (Cambridge, 2015); David Como, *Radical parliamentarians and the English Civil War* (Oxford, 2018); Nigel Smith and Laurent Curelly (eds), *Radical voices, radical ways: articulating and disseminating radicalism*

in seventeenth- and eighteenth-century Britain (Manchester, 2016): see the editors' introduction.

10 Mark Knights, 'Historical stereotypes and histories of stereotypes', in Cristian Tileagă and Jovan Byford (eds), *Psychology and history: interdisciplinary explorations* (Cambridge, 2014), pp. 242–67, esp. p. 245.

11 Knights, 'Historical stereotypes', pp. 242–3.

12 Smith, *Collection of Ranter writings*, pp. 14–19; Hessayon, 'Abiezer Coppe and the Ranters'.

13 McGregor, 'Fear, myth and furore', p. 159.

14 Davis, *Fear, myth and history*, pp. 107–10.

15 Kathryn Gucer, '"Not heretofore extant in print": where the mad Ranters are', *Journal of the History of Ideas,* 61 (2000) 75–95. While Gucer suggests that the Ranter opponents were broadly Presbyterian, I argue that the contestation of Ranters was broader based and involved intersections of radical and more orthodox opponents.

16 Raymond, *Pamphlets and pamphleteering,* esp. pp. 4–26, 53–97; Anna Bayman, *Thomas Dekker and the culture of pamphleteering in early modern London* (Farnham, 2016), esp. pp. 13–36.

17 Gilbert Roulston, *The Ranters bible* (London: by J. C., 1650), p. 1; *The Ranters recantation* (London: for G[eorge]. H[orton]., 1650), p. 1; *The Ranters declaration* (London, by J. C., 1650) described 'a great Company of the new Generation of Ranters', p. 2.

18 *The routing of the Ranters* (London: by B[ernard]. A[lsop]., 1650), p. 1. Clarkson, or Claxton, had written *A single eye, no darkness* (London, n.p., 1650), publication of which in June 1650 was considered by the Parliamentary committee eventually responsible for the Blasphemy Act of August 1650; Abiezer Coppe had been imprisoned in January 1650 for the publication of *A fiery flying roll* (also investigated by Parliament in the prelude to the passage of the Blasphemy Act). Coppe also knew and had written the preface to a work by Richard Coppin, *Divine teachings*, in 1649, although presumably Coppanites were followers of the flamboyant Coppe rather than Coppin. See Smith, *Ranter writings*, pp. 13–20.

19 Roulston, *Ranters recantation*, p. 1.

20 John Reading, *The Ranters ranting* (London: by B. Alsop, 1650), sig. A^{v}.

21 John Taylor, *Ranters of both sexes, male and female* (London: for John Hammon, 1651), sig. A. In a written communication Ariel Hessayon has expressed doubts over Taylor's authorship of this work and a number of other publications normally attributed to Taylor; I am grateful to Ariel Hessayon for discussing this with me.

22 For the association of woodcut title pages and marketability, see James Raven, *The business of books: booksellers and the English book trade* (London and New Haven, CT, 2007), p. 55; Raymond, *Pamphlets and pamphleteering*, p. 77. Examples of some of the woodcuts are reproduced in Davis, *Fear, myth and history*, pp. 138–203, and Hessayon, 'Abiezer Coppe and the Ranters', pp. 359–61. The following pamphlets boasted woodcut illustrations on their

title pages: *The arraignment and tryall* ([London]: by B. A., 1650); *The Ranters religion* (London: for R. H., 1650); Samuel Tilbury, *Bloudy newse from the north* (London: by J. C., 1650); *Strange newes from Newgate and the old-Baily* [London: by B. Alsop, 1651]; G. H., *The declaration of John Robins, the false prophet* (London: by R. Wood, 1651); *The Ranters monster* (London: for G. Horton, 1652); *Routing of the Ranters*; *Ranters declaration*; *Ranters ranting*; *Ranters bible.*

23 For the sexually explicit woodcuts so frequently associated with Ranters, see *Ranters declaration*; *Ranters ranting*; *Routing of the Ranters*. *The arraignment and tryall* showed Ranter meetings. *Strange newes from Newgate* carried a picture of a prison; *Bloudy newse from the North* carried an illustration depicting a brutal massacre. *The Ranters bible* carried an astrological picture and S. Sheppard, *The joviall crew* (London: for W. Ley, 1651) carried a picture of the devil riding a chariot into England.

24 *Arraignment and tryall*, sig. A; *The Ranters declaration*, sig. A; *Routing of the Ranters*, sig. A; *Ranters bible*, at p. 2 and throughout.

25 Alsop's extant 'Ranter' works are: *Routing of the Ranters; Ranters ranting* and *Strange newes from Newgate;* for Alsop as innovator, see Joad Raymond, *The invention of the newspaper: English newsbooks 1641–1649* (Oxford, 1996), pp. 33, 122.

26 Peacey, *Print and public politics*, p. 66.

27 Anthony Ascham, *The bounds and bonds of publique obedience* (London: for J. Wright, 1649); Francis Rous, *The lawfulness of obeying the present government* (London: for J. Wright, 1649).

28 John Holland, *The smoke of the bottomlesse pit* (London: for J. Wright, 1650), p. 1.

29 Holland, *Smoke of the bottomlesse pit*, p. 4.

30 Ann Hughes, *Gangraena and the struggle for the English Revolution* (Oxford, 2004), pp. 66–105.

31 Raunce Burthall, *An old bridle for a wilde asse-colt* (London: for S. Dagnall, [1650]), sig. A^{r}.

32 *Arraignment and tryall*, pp. 4–5.

33 Michael Sparke, *The narrative history of King James* (London: for M. Sparke, 1651), title page.

34 Sparke, *Narrative history*, p. 12 (i.e. sig. Bb*3^{v}).

35 Sparke, *Narrative history*, p. 8 (i.e. sig. Bb*^{v}).

36 Ian Atherton and David Como, 'The burning of Edward Wightman: puritanism, prelacy and the politics of heresy in early modern England', *English Historical Review*, 120 (2005), 1215–50, pp. 1247–9.

37 Henry Ainsworth, *The old orthodox foundation of religion* (London: to be sold by M. Spark, 1653), sig. A. For Sparke, see Cyprian Blagden, *The Stationers' Company. A history, 1403–1959* (London, 1960), pp. 131–8; Lois Spencer, 'The politics of George Thomason', *The Library*, 14 (1959), 11–27.

38 Ainsworth, *Old orthodox foundation*, sig. A2^{r}.

39 Ainsworth, *Old orthodox foundation*, sig. A2^{v}.

40 M. E. Moody, 'Ainsworth, Henry (1569–1622)', *Oxford Dictionary of National Biography* (Oxford, 2004), doi.org/10.1093/ref:odnb/240 (accessed 4 August 2017).
41 Ainsworth, *Old orthodox foundation*, sig. A.
42 I. F., *A new proclamation: or a warning peece* (London: for M. S[parke], 1653), p. 3.
43 I. F., *New proclamation*, p. 3.
44 I. F., *New proclamation*, p. 7.
45 *The Ranters creed* (London: by Ja. Moxon, 1651), sig. A^{v}–p. 1.
46 *Ranters creed*, p. 6.
47 Knights, 'Historical stereotypes', p. 246.
48 *Severall proposalls from His Excellency Sr. Tho. Fairfax: and the generall councel of the armie* [22 September 1647] (London: by Ja. and Jo. Moxon, 1647); *A moderate and clear relation of the private soldierie of Collonel Scroops and Col. Sanders regiments* (London: by Ja. and Jo. Moxon, 1648); John Lilburne, *A plea for common-right and freedom* (London: by Ja. and Jo. Moxon, 1648); *The subject's libertie set forth in the royall and politique power of England* (Rotterdam: by Ja. Moxon, 1643).
49 John Osborne, *The world to come* (London: by Ja. Moxon, 1651), sig. A2^{r}. Osborne's book took issue with Coppin's *Divine teachings* (1649) and discussed the Ranter Abiezer Coppe's work, *Some sweet sips, of some spiritual wine* (London, 1649). As mentioned above, Abiezer Coppe wrote the preface to Coppin's *Divine teachings* and the two authors clearly collaborated.
50 McDowell, 'A Ranter reconsidered,' pp. 173–205.
51 Peters, *Print culture*, pp. 91–123 and 153–92.
52 Norman Penney (ed.), *The journal of George Fox* (Cambridge, 1911), vol. 1, p. 6.
53 Bodleian Library, Clarendon State Papers 2624, MS Clarendon, vol. xx, fol. 140^{r}.
54 Anon., *The maids prophecies or Englands looking-glasse* [London, 1648]; William Batten, *The sea-mans dial* (London: n.p., 1648), p. 3; John Spittlehouse, *Rome ruin'd by White Hall* (London: 1650 [i.e. 1649]), pp. 181–2.
55 Thomas Hall, *The pulpit guarded* (London: for E. Blackmore, 1651), pp. 15 and 29. A number of Ranter authors were imprisoned in Coventry gaol in January 1650 and visited by Fox: see Hessayon, 'Abiezer Coppe and the Ranters', p. 367; Nigel Smith (ed.), *The journal of George Fox* (Harmondsworth, 1998), pp. 44–5.
56 George Fox, *An exhortation to you who contemne the power of God* [London: n.p., ?1652]; George Fox, *The trumpet of the Lord sounded* (London: for Giles Calvert, 1654), p. 7; in this paragraph I summarise a lengthier discussion in Peters, *Print culture*, pp. 99–107.
57 R[ichard] F[arnworth], *A message from the Lord to all* ([London: s.n.], 1653), p. 26; Catherine Gill, 'English radicalism in the 1650s: the Quaker search for the true knowledge' in Smith and Curelly (eds), *Radical voices*, pp. 80–4.

58 James Nayler, *The power and glory of the Lord* (London: for Giles Calvert, 1653), p. 16.
59 This tactic is similar to 'counter-stereotyping', which Morton discusses in depth in Chapter 6. Those who were prone to being accused of being 'popish' often returned the same accusation to their opponents.
60 Nayler, *Power and glory*, p. 16.
61 George Fox, *A word from the Lord* ([London: n.p.], 1654), pp. 9, 11.
62 George Baiteman, *An answer to vindicate the cause* [London: n.p., 1653], p. 13.
63 Fox, *Word from the Lord*, p. 9.
64 McDowell, 'A Ranter reconsidered'; Gill, 'English radicalism in the 1650s', also explores the rhetorical juxtaposition of worldly and spiritual learning in Quaker texts.
65 Fox, *Word from the Lord*, p. 11.
66 James Nayler, *An answer to the booke called the Perfect pharisee* [London: n.p., 1654], p. 25.
67 Jeremiah Ives, *The Quakers quaking* (London: by J. Cottrell for R. Moon, 1656), p. 3.
68 Pagitt, *Heresiography*, pp. 136–7.
69 R[ichard] F[arnworth], *A call out of false worships* [London: n.p., 1653], sig. A; R[ichard] F[arnworth], *A message from the Lord to all* ([London: n.p.], 1653), sig. A.
70 Friends' House Library, London (hereafter FHL), MS vol. 355, item 45, Richard Farnworth to Margaret Fell. For a more detailed discussion see Peters, *Print culture*, pp. 38–9. The 'litle' tracts in question are Richard Farnworth, *A brief discovery of the kingdom of Antichrist* [London: n.p., 1653]; Richard Farnworth, *A call out of false worships* [London: n.p., 1653]; Richard Farnworth, *A message from the Lord* ([London: n.p.], 1653); Richard Farnworth, *Moses message to Pharaoh* [London: n.p., 1653]; and Richard Farnworth, *A voice of the first trumpet ... together with a flying roll to the scattered and dispersed one* (London: n.p., 1653).
71 George Fox, *Saul's errand to Damascus* (London: for Giles Calvert, 1653). Other such tracts include James Nayler, *A discovery of the first wisdom from beneath* (London: for Giles Calvert, 1653), acquired in London on 25 April 1653. This is discussed and illustrated further in Peters, *Print culture*, pp. 118–23.
72 FHL, MS vol. 354, item 44, Thomas Aldam to George Fox.
73 John Gilpin, *The Quakers shaken* (Gateshead: by S[imon]. B[ulkley]., 1653), p. 3.
74 Gilpin, *Quakers shaken*, pp. 2, 3, 7, 8, 14.
75 T. Weld, W. Cole, R. Prideaux, W. Durant and S. Hammond, *The perfect pharisee under monkish holiness* (Gateside: by S. B., 1653); see p. 41 for the practice of quaking.
76 Gilpin, *Quakers shaken*; Weld et al., *Perfect pharisee*.

77 *The Quakers fiery beacon* (London: for G. Horton, 1655); *The Quakers terrible vision* (London: for G. Horton, 1655).
78 Thomas Aldam, *The searching out the deceit* ([London: n.p.], 1655), esp. pp. 3–5.
79 Edward Burrough, *Truth defended, or, certain accusations answered* [London: n.p., 1654], p. 16. See also George Fox, *To the high and lofty ones* [London?: n.p., 1655], p. 5.
80 *Certain queries and anti-quaeries, concerning the Quakers (so-called)* (London: n.p., 1653), p. 9; *The querers and Quakers cause at the second hearing* (London: by I. G. for Nath. Brooke, 1653), p. 39; the burning of ribbons by shopkeepers in Malton in the summer of 1652 was reported to George Fox in a letter by Thomas Aldam; see W. C. Braithwaite, *The beginnings of Quakerism*, 2nd edn (Cambridge, 1955), pp. 71–4.
81 *Quakers terrible vision*, sig. A, p. 5.
82 *Quakers fiery beacon*, sig. A; Donald Lupton, *The quacking mountebancke* (London: for E.B., 1655), p. 20; William Prynne, *The Quakers unmasked* (London: for Edward Thomas, 1655), p. 8.
83 Jonathan Clapham, *A full discovery and confutation of the wicked and damnable doctrines of the Quakers* (London: by T. R. and E. M. for Adonirum Byfield, 1656), p. 59.
84 Richard Baxter, *One sheet against the Quakers* (London: by Robert White for Nevil Simmons, 1657), p. 6.
85 Aldam, *Searching out the deceit*, pp. 4, 6.
86 Mark Knights, 'Historical stereotypes', p. 246.
87 FHL, MS vol. 354, item 66, James Nayler to George Fox; Nayler, *Answer to the booke,* p. 27. For an account of Quaker management of women and of their reputation more broadly, see Peters, *Print culture*, pp. 145–50.
88 FHL, MS vol. 352, items 245, 246, Thomas Lawson papers.
89 For the definition and relevant discussions see Introduction, pp. 19–21.
90 Richard Blome, *The fanatick history* (London: for J. Sims, 1660).
91 Richard Hubberthorn [and James Nayler], *A short answer to the book called the Fanatick history* (London: for Giles Calvert, 1660), title page and sig. A3[r].
92 Hubberthorn, *A short answer*, pp. 5, 9.
93 *Mercurius Publicus* (London: by John Macock, 5–12 July 1660), p. 457 (misp.; sig. Kkk); FHL, Swarthmore Transcripts, vol. 2, p. 619, Richard Hubberthorn to George Fox.
94 Ethan Shagan, 'Constructing discord: ideology, propaganda, and English responses to the Irish rebellion of 1641', *The Journal of British Studies*, 36 (1997), 4–34.
95 For the importance of discerning truth for Quakers, see Michael Birkel, 'Leadings and discernment', in Stephen Ward Angell and Ben Pink Dandelion (eds), *The Oxford handbook of Quaker studies* (Oxford, 2013), pp. 245–8.
96 FHL, MS vol. 354, item 22, William Dewsbury to George Fox.
97 FHL, Swarthmore Transcripts, vol. 2, p. 101, Henry Fell to Margaret Fell.
98 McDowell, 'A Ranter reconsidered', p. 196.

99 R. F. (i.e. Richard Farnworth), *The Ranters principles & deceits discovered* (London: for Giles Calvert, 1655), pp. 1–3.

100 Fox, *Word from the Lord*, sig. B3[r] [mispaginated p. 13].

101 John Chandler, *A seasonable word and call, to all those called Ranters* (London: for the author, 1659), p. 9.

6

Fighting popery with popery: subverting stereotypes and contesting anti-Catholicism in late seventeenth-century England

Adam Morton

Anti-popery had a paradoxical position in early modern English culture as both a pivotal point of unity and a potent mechanism of fracture. From the break with Rome into the early seventeenth century, anti-popery was a baseline ideology unifying Protestants in what they were against even if they could not agree on what they were for. Plotting the past into Revelation's *schema* defined the English church as a martyred true church persecuted by the papal Antichrist and provided post-Reformation England with a historical identity which, if not strictly 'Protestant', was vehemently anti-Catholic. Against this backdrop traits of 'Englishness' and 'Protestantism' were defined negatively – each was a binary positive of popery's absolute negative.[1] In this *schema*, Catholic acts of aggression like the Armada and the gunpowder plot were absorbed into a nascent national identity as evidence of divine favour for England, moments of insurmountable Antichristian peril foiled only by God's intervention for 'his' people.[2] During the eighteenth century, as Linda Colley has shown, this anti-popish identity was vital as the *locus* of a supranational identity which allowed the three nations to override fractures in the bedrock of the new British state.[3] Such was its power to crystallise and unify, anti-popery was frequently a clarion call of popular politics through which public opinion was mobilised behind a given cause.[4]

Yet it was precisely this clarion-call status which made anti-popery so fractious in a context where no agreement existed on what constituted the proper bounds of English Protestantism. Across the late sixteenth and seventeenth centuries, various Protestant groups – initially puritans and anti-puritans and latterly episcopal royalists and nonconformists – used anti-popery against one another, redefining what 'Protestant' encompassed by excluding their opponents from that term as 'popish'. This had severe ramifications for the Crown. What had originally been a means of defending royal supremacy following the papal Bull of Excommunication soon became an ideology with which to attack that supremacy. As Elizabeth I and the early Stuarts blocked moves for further reform, the very fact that monarchy (rather than Scripture alone) was the head of the church increasingly looked to be the problem: monarchy equated to papacy in all but name. This crypto-Catholicism, when coupled with a high-handed, 'arbitrary' style of government which protected the Stuart monarchy at the expense of Parliamentary power, was deemed to be the root of tyranny in England. As a destabilising presence, anti-popery can be seen as a vital force in both the Civil Wars and the revolution of 1688–89. Some historians would even deem it a *cause* of them.[5]

Stereotypes were vital in providing anti-popery with explanatory force and in presenting its ideology in a familiar and emotive manner. Typifying Catholics in general, and Jesuits in particular, as nefarious spectres of perfidy incessant in their intrigues against England rested upon repetition of polemical shorthands and clichés – kissing the pope's foot, Guy Fawkes's lantern and Jesuit equivocation, to name but three – entrenched in religio-political language at the point of assumption. There is a danger, however, of confusing a repetition of language and images with a repetition of meaning – a danger, in short, of seeing stereotypes as reflexive, generic and unthinking when in reality they were often restyled and reimagined by interest groups for highly specific ends.[6] Anti-popery was a form of othering – a means of defining the positive values of England's culture by pronounced and persistent attention to its 'popish' inverse. As the nature of the thing defined (Protestantism, church, sovereignty) changed according to political circumstance, so did the nature of the 'popery' used to define it.[7] Repetition of common motifs and images thus belied a complexity of application: anti-popery was not a fixed attribute reflecting static prejudice in early modern society, but a discursive form of negation through which vital religio-political issues were fought. Contrary to what much historical scholarship and social psychology asserts, this stereotype was not the result of unthinking, but inventive polemical practice.

This chapter focuses on attempts to control, subvert and dispute the use of stereotypes in late-seventeenth-century religio-political debates, complementing and developing the analysis of anti-popery that Tim Harris has outlined in the final section of Chapter 1. Four principal attributes of anti-popish stereotypes are outlined. First, it is argued that, although stereotypes' emotiveness was vital to their political appeal, they did not blinker thought and reason. Thinking beyond anti-popery and seeing through a given polemicist's deployment of it for political gain was a necessary part of being a political citizen when each side of the religio-political divide (Whig/nonconformist and Tory/episcopal royalist) used anti-popish rhetoric for decidedly contradictory ends. Thus, second, it is argued that the presence of anti-popish stereotypes in English culture was not static but acquired meaning according to the context in which they were deployed.

Superficial similarities in language (drawn from Revelations), examples (from English history) and motifs (from a polemical tradition dating from the Reformation) belie the fact that loyalists' definition of *whom* and *what* was 'popish' was radically different from that of the opposition. Controlling who applied 'popery' to whom was consequently a necessary part of political discourse, and it is arguable that the Tories' wrestling control of the term from the Whigs played a significant role in strengthening royal power in the 1680s. Building on this it is argued, third, that stereotypes are highly contested categories. As Peters has shown in her case study of Quakers in Chapter 5, disputing how the opposing party used negative stereotypes was a ubiquitous polemical practice; and, as Tim Harris and Jonathan Scott have shown, defending oneself from charges of 'popery' and redefining it to tar one's opponent was the life blood of religio-political controversy.[8] As such, anti-popery was a platform for debates about issues central to the English constitution, not a crude means of simplifying politics down to irrational fear and blind zeal as crude form of activism. Far from mere mudslinging, stereotypes here were part of a political language through which ideas were articulated, the significance of events was debated and visions of English society were propounded.

Finally, it follows that writers' efforts to contest and control stereotypes did not put an end to stereotyping itself but often caused its escalation. Late-seventeenth-century anti-popery illustrates the dialectics of stereotyping outlined in this volume more broadly. Early modern people displayed a great deal of agency and ingenuity in their use of 'popish' stereotypes and could see through a given writer or group's use of 'popery' for polemical ends. But it does not follow that they were able to step outside anti-popish patterns of thought quite so readily. The heuristic functions which stereotypes served in social life and thought made this difficult. 'Popish' stereotypes were shortcuts that made complex and evolving political processes more readily comprehensible, eased the emotional strains which accompanied religio-political strife and, by demonising opposing groups and opposing views, provided rhetorical and polemical strategies for intervening in politics.

Social psychologists now understand stereotypes to function heuristically. For much of the twentieth century psychologists believed stereotypes to be as much a cognitive flaw as a moral one – the product of unthinking. Explanations of how stereotypes about race and gender persisted so vehemently despite the individuals who held them being confronted daily with evidence which contradicted them began with the assumption that stereotypes rested on 'faulty' thinking.[9] This could emerge from a specific personality type: a prejudiced person, it was held, is so close-minded or dogmatic that their assumptions blinker them, rendering them unable to see the world 'as it is'.[10] Conversely, the subsequent generation of psychologists began to accept stereotypes as a *normal* part of cognitive practice common to everyone rather than the product of *abnormal* mental processes of certain personality types.[11] No one can see the world 'as it is', but only through the lenses of categories provided by a given culture. All views of social groups are therefore culturally conditioned (rather than individually formed) and once categories of analysis are established they became self-fulfilling: we prioritise examples or information which confirm preconditioned views of a given group.[12] Rather than 'flawed' thinking, therefore, stereotypes are normative – they are simply one type of the necessarily imperfect categories by which people evaluate the world. These categories reside in memory with certain traits attached to them according to cultural dictates – 'trees are like X, men are like Y, women are like Z' – which are recalled as we process and analyse phenomena. Prejudgement is therefore a routine part of daily life, a heuristic form of thinking which creates the illusion that the world is predictable, and recalling that the category 'minority group A' possesses certain traits is no different – cognitively speaking – from recalling that the category 'car' possesses certain traits. In both cases, these core traits might be misnomers masking the degree of variety and counter-examples which the world provides.[13]

Such approaches, however, fail to explain stereotypes' capacity to change over time. If stereotypes are stored in memory as a series of traits, how do we understand the fluidity of minority group stereotypes across the twentieth century? Psychologists have turned to group dynamics theory to answer these questions. This posits that stereotypes are the central marker of intergroup relations and change form according to the motivations of the group using them. Put simply, stereotypes define and sustain the 'us' of an in-group against the 'them' of an out-group. Individuals subordinate themselves to the group, exaggerating their similarity to the primary traits of the in-group and differences from those of the out-group by assenting to stereotypes associated with both.[14] This – as early modern anti-popery demonstrates – is a process of binary opposition by which the negative stereotype defines and valorises positive attributes associated with the in-group (Protestants in this example). This explains stereotypes' fluidity and changeability. Recent generations of social psychologists have suggested that, rather than the product of everyday cold cognition, stereotypes emerge from emotive situations and are remade according to the specific *motivation* of the group deploying them in a given context. As the social and political vantage point from which the 'other' is viewed shifts, so do the 'in-' and 'out-'group boundaries: stereotypes are modified as part of the process by which group identity is continually re-formed and contested.[15] The key point is that stereotypes are to a large degree situational but are mobilised and coordinated by a given group in response to changing political or social practices. Prejudice is therefore a representational practice through which the world is evaluated from a given vantage point at a given moment, and stereotypes are fundamental to that practice.

The popish plot and succession crisis (1678–83)

These themes will be explored through an analysis of attempts to control the 'popery' stereotype during the succession crisis of the late 1670s and early 1680s.[16] Here both sides of the political divide – understood broadly as Whigs and Tories – asserted opposing visions of what 'popery' was in an expanding news media to paint their opponents as 'popish'. The place of stereotypes as arbiters of group dynamics is highly relevant here. Party politics saw each side assert control over 'popery' because controlling the application of the stereotype was to control the centre ground of politics – by defining what was 'popish' (out) one defined what was 'Protestant' (in).

The succession crisis was driven by agitations against 'popery and arbitrary government' within the Stuart Crown nominally triggered by the conversion of Charles II's brother and heir – James, Duke of York – to Catholicism in the 1670s. The crisis stemmed from tensions surrounding the respective positions of Crown and Parliament in the English constitution, and of episcopal royalists and nonconformists in the English church, both of which had been unresolved since the Restoration settlement some twenty years earlier. Charles's increasing reliance upon heavy-handed government management under the Earl of Danby – which by stressing monarchical prerogative over Parliamentary liberty was readily interpreted as 'arbitrary' – and support of episcopal royalist uniformity over toleration of nonconformity – which by resisting calls for a broader liberty of conscience was readily interpreted as 'tyrannical' – appeared to undermine two pillars of Englishness: Protestantism and Parliamentary sovereignty. Coupled with Charles's marriage to a Catholic queen, a propensity for Catholic mistresses and repeated display of favouring Catholic France against the Protestant Dutch in his foreign policy, this increasingly appeared to be a 'popish' Crown in desperate need of reform. Jonathan Scott has demonstrated that when we consider the context of the seventeenth century more broadly – in which a resurgent Counter-Reformation Catholicism championed by Louis XIV was militantly dogmatic and advocated absolute forms of government – concerns about the threat of that Crown to its people become more understandable.[17]

The eruption of the popish plot in 1678 made these issues appear more urgent and afforded the Whig party the opportunity to lobby for the reforms it considered necessary to protect England from this 'popish' threat.[18] The farcical plot was 'discovered' by Titus Oates, who claimed that while working as a Jesuit envoy he had uncovered a Europe-wide conspiracy to murder Charles II and forcibly return England to Catholicism. Oates essentially articulated generations-old anti-popish clichés at a moment of new political tension – regicide, invasion, the black legend, martyrdom and the firing of London were all bread-and-butter stereotypes, with all but the last dating back to the mid-sixteenth century.[19] The mysterious murder of Edmund Godfrey – the magistrate who had taken Oates's depositions – gave the plot a slither of credence and led to further revelations from other 'witnesses'.[20] The subsequent convictions of Catholics accused by these 'witnesses' were the subject of a torrent of news media which, alongside petitioning campaigns and other forms of protest, were part of a very conscious use of anti-popish sentiment by the Whig party to thrust the weight of public opinion behind calls for Charles to address the need for constitutional reform.[21] The opposition was divided on what these reforms should be, but if a guiding principle existed amidst the confusion it was for a growth of Parliamentary power as the surest means of preventing arbitrary rule.[22] As Harris and Scott have shown, Charles's refusal to call Parliament – and recalcitrance in acceding to reform when it met – resulted in an increasingly partisan political culture emerging during the early 1680s.[23]

Thinking with 'popery' was a ubiquitous part of that partisan political culture. Each 'in-group' styled itself as the party with England's best interests at heart and claimed to oppose the 'popery' of the other party. Doing so necessitated redefining the 'popery' stereotype as part of controlling the central religio-political language of legitimacy. The result was the formation of two competing conspiracy theories, each of which asserted a vision of 'popery' to define a vision of the English state. First, for the Whigs/nonconformists Charles's reluctance to accede to reform made the Crown the root of the problem. This inverted a century-and-a-half-old keystone of anti-popery. Polemical justifications of royal supremacy (against papal supremacy) and English church (against the Roman church) stressed that England's Crown/church phalanx was a golden mean of moderation which provided a bulwark against 'popish' tyranny.[24] The Stuart Crown/church – it was now argued – were stalwarts of 'popery' not bulwarks against it, and only expanded Parliamentary sovereignty and toleration for nonconformists could protect England's Protestant state from their 'popery'. Second, for the Tories/episcopal royalists (who opposed reform), Whig cries of 'popery' were a ruse: using anti-popery to stir up opposition to the church and Crown was an inherently 'popish' activity because these were precisely the institutions which – according to anti-popish stereotypes – the pope and Jesuits had attacked since the Reformation. The Whigs/nonconformists were thus 'papists in masquerade' according to one contemporary slogan: people who used anti-popery to claim that they defended the Protestant state, while actually plotting against it.[25]

This Tory redefinition of 'popery' played a significant role in the Crown's resurgence in the early 1680s, which ended the succession crisis. Roger L'Estrange was the key architect of this redefinition. A vehement loyalist and Tory polemicist-in-chief, L'Estrange was incessant in combating Whig publishing to prevent the opposition from controlling public opinion.[26] Peter Hinds has shown that, on an almost daily basis, L'Estrange's publications refuted, mocked and parodied those of his rivals to claim that the Whigs – not the Crown – were the true danger to Protestant England. Contesting 'popery' was vital to this. Here, then, the anti-popish stereotype was turned upon its head and used against the very group – the hotter sort of Protestants – often deemed most effective in using it as a means of agitation. Recognising this is important. It demonstrates that, far from having thought *limited* by persistent resort to stereotypes, polemicists expected early modern audiences to be able to think beyond them as part of a routine engagement with religio-political discourse.

Stereotype v. stereotype

The collapse of licensing in 1679 triggered an unprecedented surge in printing to match the increase in publications that had occurred during the Civil Wars, with new forms of partisan publication – periodicals and newspapers chief among them – commenting on the plot and associated political developments to lobby public support. This was part of what Mark Knights has characterised as a 'crisis of representation and misrepresentation'.[27] Increasingly frequent general elections, extensive petitioning campaigns and the emergence of an increasingly informed public immersed in news spawned an increasingly representational political process: parties had to engage public opinion as the umpire of politics.[28] Misrepresentation was a by-product of this contest for public opinion which lay at the heart of party politics. As competing camps beseeched the public to judge, those parties were increasingly concerned about its ability to do so clearly in the face of a press whose mendacious capacity for misinformation was seemingly limitless. Emotive language was particularly problematic. In an environment over-saturated with a bewildering array of information and misinformation, claim and counter-claim, slogans and images crystallised opinion as totems of party positions, icons which cut through the noise of news to reify key concepts.[29] The slogans '41 is come again', 'liberty', and 'popery and arbitrary government' were highly charged and could steer public opinion, and rhetoric was routinely accused of manipulating emotions at the expense of reason.

'Popery' was a particularly acute slogan, largely because of its 150-year legacy as the great 'other' of English church and state. L'Estrange recognised its power: '[n]ow there are a sort of men, that under the Countenance of *This Plot* advance *another* of their *own*, and 'tis but the Rubbing of a Libel with a little Anti-Popery, to give it the Popular smack; and any thing else against the Government goes down Current'.[30] In the hands of the Whigs, the popish plot could blind public opinion – stereotypes provided a dangerous shorthand which manipulated the mob by preventing it from thinking: '[t]here is a kinde of *Spell* in the Word *Popery*. It transforms a *Man* into a *Beast*: And like the Great *Medicine*, it turns whatever it touches into *Plot*.'[31] Stacking up accounts of 'popery' as a miasma of unknowing would be easy. We must be wary, however, of accepting such claims at face value. There is a paradox at work in these characterisations of its power: the recognition of the problem demonstrated that it was insurmountable. L'Estrange and other authors challenged readers to see through the 'popery' stereotype even as they bemoaned their inability to do so.[32]

The problem with breaking this 'spell' was that anti-popery had been the central language of religion and politics since the Reformation. In the intervening century-and-a-half, as Peter Lake, Anthony Milton and Arthur Marotti have demonstrated, its prevalence in a dizzying array of genres had seen it woven into the fabric of English culture.[33] Despite this ubiquity, however, anti-popery was remarkably incoherent. Far from dogmatic, anti-popery was a complex interplay of arguments, narratives and images amenable to a limitless range of applications.[34] Anti-popery was thus a form of othering: a given group (royalists) defined their opponents (parliamentarians) as 'popish' to style themselves as loyal and truly Protestant, and were likely to have themselves styled 'popish' by the opposing group in another context. Aspects central to one group's 'popery' might be peripheral to another's. For Andrew Willet, writing in 1600, anti-popery was central to the English church, a means of stimulating a common identity to reunite puritans and bishops wrenched apart by the Presbyterian crisis of the previous twenty years – but for Laudians, anti-popery was the source of the Church of England's fragmentary status, a bitter ideology which explained its inability to convert recusants into a genuinely national body.[35] The puritan William Whitaker fell foul of Archbishop Whitgift when he attempted to secure the removal of the non-puritan Everard Digby from positions of influence for being 'popish'. As Lake has shown, Whitgift's 'popery' was limited to those who held communion with Rome, while Whitaker's extended to anyone who did not share his view of the English church as founded on austere Reformed Protestantism – one man's view of the Church of England required action against Digby, the other's did not.[36] Three points follow from this: first, definitions of 'popery' altered according to the political context in which the word was uttered and the vision of England's church/state it was used to define; second, it constituted a nexus of discursive materials through which groups styled themselves legitimate ('we oppose popery') and their opponents illegitimate ('they are popish'); and, third, each assertion of anti-popery was part of the struggle to control those discursive materials through which various groups hoped to sustain religio-political legitimacy. Applying stereotypes was thus an assertion of power.[37]

Thus, what constituted 'popery' was ever shifting. But being the central language of post-Reformation religio-politics meant that, even as it was recognised as destabilising, it was very difficult for a given person or group to rebut without condemning themselves to charges of being 'popish'. This was the problem facing the Tories in challenging the Whig narrative of the succession crisis which rested on the principle that the popish plot made constitutional change necessary to protect English liberties. As Charles II discovered, to resist this narrative was to be absorbed into it as part of the 'popish' problem. Consequently, rather than rejecting 'popery', Tory writers appropriated it in order to limit its capacity as a lobbying force by the Whigs. They did not reject the popish plot as a real danger which the English state must confront, but reconstructed 'popery' to include the Whigs within the plot and to call for a stronger Crown and church to deal with the threat which they posed. Tory tactics thus rested on what we in this volume have chosen to call *counter-stereotyping*.[38] Engaging with stereotypes – and challenging the public to think with them rather than simply accept them – became a necessary part of political discourse.

L'Estrange approached this in two ways. First, he limited the plot. He did not deny its existence but claimed that the trial and execution of the conspirators showed that the crisis had been met and neutered.[39] Suggesting that 'popery' was under control limited its usefulness as a stick with which the Whigs attempted to beat the regime into reform – toleration for 'true Protestant' dissenters, greater powers for Parliament and the exclusion of James from the succession. A rhetoric of reason and moderation was vital to L'Estrange's endeavour.[40] His *History of the plot* (1679), for example, appeared to present the 'facts' in a dispassionate manner but was actually a polemical rival to the various plot 'narratives' which the star witnesses had produced under the mantle of exposing popery. Avoiding those accounts' histrionics, L'Estrange presented his *History* in matter-of-fact prose to create a judicious air.[41] What appeared to be verbatim transcripts of the plotters' trials actually leaned far more heavily on sections in which the 'witnesses' under-performed, contradicted themselves, made palpably specious claims or were challenged by a rival witness or the accused. L'Estrange appeared to let the evidence speak for itself, but as readers progressed through the trials the cumulative effect of his edits was a pooling of doubt. Oates, for example, was shown as unable to recognise those whom he claimed to have witnessed conspiring – once because he was 'too tired' to see clearly, and once because the man in question had been wearing a different wig whilst plotting.[42] L'Estrange also highlighted the extent to which Oates was in the habit of suddenly remembering fresh evidence when contradicted; dozens of witnesses testified that he was abroad when he claimed to have witnessed the 'Jesuits' Consult' at which the plot was hatched.[43] The implicit question was simple: could a reasonable society really alter its constitution on such specious fears of 'popery' as these?

That L'Estrange expected his audiences to be able to grasp the sharpness of his inferences demonstrates that he assumed a high degree of political literacy.[44] Readers were to be familiar with the minutiae of the trials, to have rival accounts to hand as he unmasked their distortions and, despite L'Estrange presenting the 'popery' stereotype as a malaise on public opinion, were expected to be up to the task of seeing when those stereotypes were being employed to gull them. This often focused on minutiae. Thus, for example, L'Estrange's subtle undermining of Miles Prance, one of the chief 'witnesses' to the murder of Godfrey on whose 'evidence' three Catholics were executed in 1679. In April 1682, L'Estrange reported an incident from Prance's former career as a silversmith. In 1677 he had been contracted to make a silver antependium – a removable altar cover – for the queen's chapel. This contract included six silver screws. When the object was cleaned several years later, it was discovered that Prance has soldered silver heads onto brass screws. Peter Hinds has shown that L'Estrange made several inferences in his discussion of this incident: did this deceiving of the queen make Prance a fundamentally untrustworthy individual and, if so, was his testimony about Godfrey's murder enough evidence on which to execute a man? Had Prance gulled the public as he had gulled the queen? L'Estrange proceeded with hints and asides – these accusations were never explicit because at this moment Parliament was impeaching those who questioned the plot as 'papists' favourable to it.[45] Reminding readers that Prance had been a Catholic until his 'discovery' of Godfrey's murder was to run one stereotype into another: those who opposed 'popery' did so on evidence supplied by a 'papist'.

The second limitation which L'Estrange placed on anti-popery was to claim that Whig attempts to 'expose' the plot were actually a part of it. If the plot was under control, then attempts to browbeat the Crown with 'popery and arbitrary government' and to tar James, the king, and his queen with involvement in the plot signalled something else. This, L'Estrange claimed, was 'popery in masquerade': the use of emotive 'popery' to mask Whig/nonconformist attempts to overthrow church and state. He thus expanded the 'popery' stereotype's parameters to include those who wielded it most vocally. The Whigs/nonconformists who claimed to be the true advocates of anti-popery (and therefore to be the morally legitimate party) were actually 'popish'. History showed the papacy's chief aim was to overthrow England's Crown and church. By manipulating fears of 'popery' to call for constitutional changes which weakened the church (to the benefit of nonconformists) and the Crown (to the benefit of Parliament) the Whigs were therefore 'popish' – they used one conspiracy theory to mask their own conspiratorial lust for power.[46]

L'Estrange's narrative of the plot exemplifies this strategy. Including 'narrative' in the title was a parody of printed accounts by Oates, Bedloe and Prance which mocked the authoritative tone with which their texts accorded their fantastic inventions credence: one can only 'narrate' events which happened, and with which one is familiar.[47] L'Estrange's mockery went further. Far from undermining the plot (and therefore being 'popish' as his critics claimed) his 'narrative' was based on evidence provided by Oates – the Whigs' champion witness – asserting that 'papists' had mobilised radical Protestant actions during the Civil War and the Fifth Monarchists' revolt.[48] Groups currently using the plot as a lobbying vehicle for reform were therefore 'popish' themselves. L'Estrange (via Oates) stressed that this 'popish' use of anti-popery to stir up the populace against church and state was an old puritan trick, and current events risked replaying the descent into Civil War during the early 1640s. Then as now a run at the bishops presaged a run at the king; then as now the collapse of licensing allowed the puritans to mobilise the mob behind fears of 'popery and arbitrary government'; and then as now those puritan claims to defend the realm from 'popery' cloaked their doing the pope's work, collapsing the realm into disorder and weakening the central institutions (church and Crown) which history showed to be the best defence against Antichrist.[49] Puritanism and popery were therefore species of the same genus:

> NOW though I cannot allow it upon any *Terms* that they *help one another* by *Consent*; nothing can be plainer yet then that while they *play*, *each* of them their *Own Game*, the *One* still *leads* into the *Others hand*. If *Popery Influences schism*, *That Schism* Slides as naturally into Popery, as *Motion* from One place of *Rest* tends to *another*[.][50]

Exposing the Whigs/nonconformists – rather than church and Crown – as the true source of 'popery' undermined the stereotype's effectiveness as a weapon of oppositional politics by redefining its boundaries: styling those who used 'popery' as 'popish'.

This sophisticated mockery was certainly effective – by 1682 the Tory narrative was a dominant voice in news culture.[51] It was not, however, new. L'Estrange drew on an established polemical tradition by which one stereotype (anti-popery) was undermined by countering it with another (anti-puritanism). Anti-puritanism was as prevalent as anti-popery, a form of 'othering' by which the boundaries of church and state were contested, as Lake has shown.[52] As old as puritanism itself, it was formulated in defence of episcopacy and royal supremacy against puritan agitation in the late sixteenth century, subsequently became a feature of Jacobean and Caroline anti-Calvinist attempts to push puritans out of the establishment and was a mainstay of the defence of the English church from nonconformists during and after the Civil War – Thomas Edwards's denunciation of 'seditious' Independents and sects was typical of anti-puritanism being used to position the established church as moderate, loyal and legitimate.[53] The 'puritan' here was principally defined by two things: *popularity* – 'Calvinist' popular sovereignty in church and state was characterised as innately seditious and anti-monarchical; and *hypocrisy* – such calls for popular representation masked a power play by which the powers of those making the appeal would be enhanced. The Civil War confirmed these warnings that advocates of popular rule in the church actually lusted for popular rule in government and the endless energies against 'popery' in both masked an anti-monarchical drive for power.[54]

Like anti-popery, then, anti-puritanism was used to define orthodoxy in religious and political matters as it was understood by a given group. 'Puritan' was the negative half of a relationship which defined the positive half – 'Anglican', 'royalist' – to justify the relationship between the centre and periphery of English Protestantism in a given context.[55] Like anti-popery, anti-puritanism served a variety of polemical ends for different groups with different motivations. And, like the 'popery' stereotype, 'puritanism' was not an unthinking cloud of prejudice but a platform on which a range of other issues – barriers of church/state, the need (or not) for reform, the nature of royal authority – were debated. Formulating stereotypes of 'others' drew boundaries: 'popery' and 'puritanism' cast out persons and ideas threatening to many groups' visions of 'Protestant' England. This parallel in function drew on a parallel in language, with anti-puritanism often presented as anti-popery. L'Estrange's *Account of the growth of knavery under pretended fears of arbitrary government and popery* (1678) was a response to Andrew Marvell's *Account of the growth of popery and arbitrary government* (1677). The latter located a conspiracy for 'popery and arbitrary government' within Charles II's regime and set the agenda for how the opposition represented that regime throughout the succession crisis. L'Estrange's counter-narrative redefined 'popery' and 'arbitrary government' through classic anti-puritanism. Calls for popular government masked a cynical grasp for power; accusing the government of conspiracy was a libellous corrosion of church and state and was therefore 'popish'; and popular sovereignty was arbitrary because it rested on the inconsistent vestiges of opinion alone.[56] In short, Catholics had long conspired against the church and the Crown and this was what puritans were doing now: they were thus 'papists in masquerade'. Countering one stereotype with another was thus normal political practice. Polemic did not reflect static categories but contested those categories to attempt to control the boundaries of legitimacy in church and state.[57]

L'Estrange grounded this puritanical 'popery' historically. Stereotypes provided a coherent view of England's present by weaving elements of that past into a vision of the future. As in anti-popery, where events like the popish plot, Marian burnings or Armada were local manifestations of a longstanding historical animus – in which papal Antichrist's attempts to destroy Protestant England shaped the way in which history unfolded until the Second Coming – so in anti-puritanism recent events in English history were local manifestations of puritanism's longstanding historical animus towards monarchy and church which exposed puritanism as fundamentally and inherently un-English.[58] In *The growth of knavery and popery under the mask of Presbytery* (1678) 'puritans' were not (as they claimed) the realisation of English Protestantism fully reformed, but popish. The regicide of 1649 was the culmination of ideas originating in Calvin's Geneva, and Reformed Protestantism was therefore innately seditious.[59] The consistory was 'arbitrary' because it was subject to no one, and it was seditiously anti-monarchical because it subjected monarchy to the discipline of prelates.[60] L'Estrange traced these sentiments through a potted history of Presbyterianism, stressed how dangerously anti-monarchical its resistance theories were and interpreted puritanism's fraught relationship with the Elizabethan and Jacobean state as a sign of the former's inherently seditious nature, of which the Whigs/nonconformists were the latest manifestation.[61] 'Puritanism' was thus collapsed into 'popery' since both were forms of anti-monarchism: the former expressed this through papal claims to make and unmake kings – excommunication fomented regicide by relieving subjects of the obedience owed to their monarchs; the latter by claiming that royal supremacy over the church was tyrannical – using the Word to oppose that supremacy justified resistance to the monarchy in equally 'popish' ways.[62]

Stereotypes did not simplify politics. As a crucial language of political debate they were contested and redefined to contest the core issues of the day. 'Language' is thus perhaps a more appropriate definition than 'prejudice'. The latter implies an animus with a fixed target, but as the existence of anti-puritanism demonstrates, anti-popery had been neither uncontested nor static since the late sixteenth century. Thinking with stereotypes – rather than having thought constrained by them – was inherent in disputes over the boundaries of church and state. That anti-popery remained the language of legitimacy in religion and politics was demonstrated by its persistent use by those who wanted to control the definition of 'popery' as an effective means of political debate.

Mockery

Controlling and countering the definition of 'popery' allowed L'Estrange to focus on mocking the opposition's misuse of it. Mockery, as Quentin Skinner has shown, was well established in the rhetorical tradition.[63] It was the caustic art of studied negation. Because mockery deemed its subject unworthy of respect it was acutely damaging in an honour culture centred upon public reputation. Indeed, transgressors of gendered and moral mores – cuckolds, adulterers or shrewish women – were often subjected to punitive rituals of humiliation precisely because mockery possessed the capacity to debase and diminish.[64] This potency was captivating and problematic: captivating because by evoking pleasure, laughter afforded authors and speakers the opportunity to win over audiences and corrode their opponent; and problematic because that corrosiveness was highly dangerous if used improperly.[65] Indeed, as Alastair Bellany and Andrew McRae have demonstrated, mocking verses were a prominent and effective medium of popular politics, a means by which authority was debated and contested, respect for social betters withheld and protest against government activities solidified.[66] That seditious libel was policed by a severe legal code indicates how contentious mockery could be. Ridiculing persons of state invited disorder by eroding the ties of respect which bound the social hierarchy together.[67] It is unsurprising, then, that L'Estrange presented mockery in the Whig press as libellous and vociferously called for the state to clamp down upon it as a means of reasserting Crown control.[68] But even as he criticised his opponents' unseemly laughter, he readily engaged in it as a routine part of political practice. Here, then, is one example of what Koji Yamamoto and Peter Lake have called the dialectics of stereotyping.[69] L'Estrange's strenuous efforts to control debates hardly led to calm exchanges or de-escalation, but instead to polemical escalation and more stereotyping.

This was highly apparent in *The Observator*, L'Estrange's bi-weekly newspaper launched in 1681 to variously counter and antagonise the Whig press. Mark Goldie has shown that because its effectiveness rested upon rapid retort and the delivery of scabrous commentary on the news as this unfolded in rival newspapers, *The Observator* was little more than a cluster of animadversions which showed the Whig press to be fallacious, specious or – by undermining church and state – libellous.[70] This 'goose-quill fraternity', mocked L'Estrange, had become 'oracles of state'. *The Observator*'s incessantness earned L'Estrange the title of 'scribbler-general of Tory land' from his enemies, the 'idol' of his party. Often witty, it was rarely erudite. Vulgar, scatological and relentless in its inventive mockery, *The Observator* was overwrought, with insults and asides crammed into hectic prose which reduced politics to epithets and exclamations as L'Estrange rushed his haphazard thoughts about the day's political events to press. The energy he placed into this endeavour highlights the paradox of L'Estrange. Few loathed politics being taken down to the mob's mire more than he, but none did more to inject royalism into that mire. This was *The Observator's* stated goal: ''Tis the press that has made 'um mad, and the press must set 'em right again. The distemper is epidemical; and there's no way in the world, but by printing, to convey the remedy to the disease.' The 'madness' referred to the plot. Popery for L'Estrange was a pathological mass delusion of 'panic terrors, ecstatic raptures' and 'hypochondrines', and was reliant upon 'counterfeit' evidence, 'masquerade', 'canting' and 'vizarding' which his pen would dispel. In his hands, anti-popery became an inverted popery: a zealous creed blinkering its acolytes to their credulity, a tyranny on reason which perverted truth and natural order.[71]

Manipulating anti-popish stereotypes in this way was a crucial part of L'Estrange's polemic. His immersion in the London print trade allowed him to parody Whig anti-papal pamphlets with a rapidity which undermined them. Thus *The character of a popish successor* (1681) – in which John Phillips used a conventional anti-popish account of English history to assert that all Protestants could expect from James's accession was tyranny and bloodshed – was countered by L'Estrange's mocking *The character of a papist in masquerade* (1681) – which used the Civil War to demonstrate, conversely, that Whig/nonconformist rule posed a far greater chance of tyranny and bloodshed and was the true source of 'popery'. Similarly, *L'Estrange's sayings* (1681) – which displayed extracts from L'Estrange's writings to 'prove' his 'popish' tendencies – was speedily met with L'Estrange's *The dissenter's sayings* (1681) – which displayed anti-monarchical extracts from Whig/nonconformist texts proving them to be, like Jesuits, 'popish'. Examples could be stacked up, but the point is simple. Anti-popery was rarely left uncontested but was challenged at the moment of issue: stereotypes were not afforded the space to simply control opinion and close down thought.

In part this was because the Tories had another stereotype – the 'puritan' – with which to combat 'popery'. The stereotype of 'puritans' as zealous killjoys and/or seditious anti-monarchists was prevalent in polemic and on stage by the early seventeenth century, and anti-popish babbling was one of its key traits.[72] Vitriol bubbles out of 'puritans' like Zeal-of-the-Land Busy from Ben Jonson's *Bartholomew Fair* (1614) in incoherent ramblings made up of little more than a mishmash of clichés and generic imagery, bully-boy zealots devoid of substance.[73] L'Estrange drew on this tradition. In his satire the 'puritan' rambles against 'popery' as the motor of all traumas in recent history: 'papists' had stirred up the Civil War, had corrupted the Presbyterians who murdered Charles I and had burnt London in 1666, and so on. When asked teasingly if 'papists' had also caused the recent plague, he replies farcically: '[n]othing more likely in my judgement; for what with their Mass mumbling ... Conjurations, Incense and Holy-Water ... they have raised such a pother and sent such a foule stink among us enough to cause an infection to spread not only over the City, but the whole Nation too'.[74] Such parody forced readers to reconsider anti-popery by aping so closely stock attributes of the polemic which it mocked. The aim was to neuter the Whig's use of popery as a polemical language. Elsewhere L'Estrange was more direct. Animadversion pinned 'popery' back on the Whigs who employed it. Here is the image of the popish tyranny from Charles Blount's *An appeal from the country to the city* (1679), a tyranny which would ensue if James ascended to the throne:

> *First ... Imagine you see the whole Town in a Flame, occasioned this second time by the same Popish Malice which set it on Fire before. At the same Instant Phansie that among the distracted Crowd you behold Troops of Papists Ravishing your Wives and Daughters; dashing your little Childrens brains out against Walls, Plundering your Houses, and Cutting your Own Throats by the name of Heretick Dogs*[.]

This typical image became in L'Estrange's hands a memory of 'real' tyranny from 'Whig' rule during the Civil Wars:

> *First Imagine the whole Nation in a Flame ... by the Malice of the same Faction that embroyl'd us before; and at the same Instant, Phansy whole Droves of Coblers, Draymen, Ostlers, Quatering upon your Wives and Daughters, till ye want bread to put in your Childrens Mouths ... your Houses Rifled; your Accompt-Books Examin'd ... your Persons sent on Ship-board, transported, or thrown into nasty Dungeons ... your Throats cut, by the Name of Popish Dogs ...*[75]

Mockery was effective here because its object was so familiar, the parody echoing the stylised patterns of anti-popery to expose it as hollow. The stereotype's ubiquity rendered it pliable to inversion.

This was not frivolous. Ridicule was vital because it highlighted anti-popery's central danger: its dependency upon the separation of words and things. Because 'popery' was divorced from any concrete content it could be applied to anything/anyone which the Whigs/nonconformists desired.[76] It was therefore dangerously unstable, a 'cast of Rhetorique' which threatened order because it bound the unthinking mob in its spell and rendered them unable to perceive the Whig's mendacity: 'the *Common people* are caught just as we catch *Larks*; 'Tis but setting up a *fine Thing* for a *Wonderment*, they all flock to't ... and never leave *Flickering* about it, till the Fowler has them in the *Net*'.[77] L'Estrange's animadversions on *The character of a popish successor* highlighted this separation of words and things. He challenged its author to provide evidence for every claim about the inevitability of Catholic cruelty and arbitrary government for, as it stood, fears of 'popery' were supported by words alone rather than substance. If 'popery' was truly demonstrable, such '*Hyperboliz'd* ... Declamatory Torrent of Words' would not be necessary: '[i]t is one of the greatest Indignities that can be put upon the simplicity of a *Just Truth*, the dawbing of it with Embrodery and Flourish, and the over-doing of it'.[78] Although highly emotive, such substanceless anti-popery dissolved upon closer examination. L'Estrange thus quoted a long, furious passage from *The character* which asserted that, because a Catholic monarchy *could only* be enslaved to the pope, James's reign *could only* see martyrs at Smithfield, English law overrun and Protestantism outlawed. He deemed it hot air:

> This Passage is only the same thing over again, in a diversity of Words and Phrase. But it is well enough to answer the Ends it was intended for; the tickling of the Phansy, and the moving of a Popular Passion, without one syllable of weight to strike the Judgement ... I cannot liken it to anything better then the Gaudy Glittering Vapour that Children are used to Phansy in a Cloud. They'll Phansy *Lions, Peackocks*, in it, or what other Figures they Please; but the first Breath of Ayre scatters the Phantastique Images, and resolves the whole into its original Nothing.[79]

This 'popery' was a phantom. Accepting the stereotype was unreasonable because 'popery' here did not accord with reality: '[this] Popish Successor ... is a Figure that has no Being in Nature, but [only in the author's] own Brain'. Accepting it was to be credulous, to demonstrate that 'the very *Sound* of Popery will do the business, as well Without a Ground, as With it', that English politics was being based on fear of the *word*, not the actual *thing*.[80] In another pamphlet, L'Estrange mocked those who accepted this stereotype as reality: expecting 'papists' to look like their depiction in the fantastic graphic satires currently circulating London, his Whig character was ever watchful for 'a company of ill-looked fellows with Bags of Gun-pow[d]er and Pistols in one hand, and Daggers and long knives in the other'.[81]

Because L'Estrange was charged with being a 'papist' he was sensitive to how dangerous this separation of words and things could be. The accusation was a backhanded compliment to the success of his Tory polemic. Responding to his undermining their credibility, Oates and the other witnesses claimed to have evidence that L'Estrange was involved in the plot – painting him 'popish' tainted the legitimacy of his voice. After Parliament threatened to impeach him, L'Estrange fled London.[82] As Helen Pierce has shown, he soon became the *bête noire* of Whig street politics, caricatured as 'Towzer', the Pope's lap-dog who 'barked' at the opposition according to the dictates of his master. In 1680–1, this became a calling card of opposition politics. In a series of graphic satires 'Towzer' was mocked as the chief papal agent in England; and during the pope-burning procession of November 1681 he sat nestled on the pope's lap and was consigned to the flames alongside his master at the culmination of the festivities.[83]

L'Estrange did not simply deny the charge. His defence rested upon demonstrating that the unthinking application of the 'popery' stereotype was dangerous. A farcical dialogue between Pragmaticus and Philosophicus asked readers to consider what believing him to be 'popish' revealed about the succession crisis. How could his accusers know L'Estrange's conscience? What *evidence* supported the charge? And, given this lack of evidence, was not 'popery' here the misapplication of words to things?[84] That is, was this not – like charges of 'popery' against church and state – nonsensical? Neutering 'popery' by exposing it as meaningless, L'Estrange spun the worst possible accusation into a mockery of the accusers. Thus Pragmaticus's ridiculous response to Philosophicus's charge that L'Estrange's decades of royalism and writing against popery proved him to be no papist:

> this is wonderful strange you say, that he should be a profest enemy to the *Papists*, and yet be one himself underhand … as if the Pope could not grant a Dispensation for all this: why it is ordinarily done in such cases, and I thought you had not been so shallow as not to apprehend it … these confounded Dispensations are of a strange nature, for I have heard that by the strength of one of them a man may come to our Church, wear a Peruque and a Sword by his side, flatter and fawn upon the King, and cry God bless your Majesty, I wish you a long a prosperous Reign, and then Stab or Poison him at the first opportunity, and yet for all at last go to Heaven in a string. And I think on it a little better, might not *L'Estrange* be a Jesuite and be like enough to do some such like Prank at the long Run?[85]

The absurdity is palpable: if someone whom the Whigs styled 'popish' was demonstrably not so on the basis of decades of service to the Crown that was because the pope had granted a dispensation allowing them to dissemble during all of that time. Mockery thus highlighted danger. On this definition of 'popery', no one was safe.

Laughing at this farce relied upon being able to *see through* 'popery' as the Whigs used it. This underscores a central argument of this chapter: stereotypes here did not blinker thought but were a springboard to thinking through political issues. L'Estrange expected contesting stereotypes to be a normal part of polemical discourse. To believe that either he or the state was 'popish' was to be paralysed by public opinion rather than to exercise rational thought, to accept a stereotype rather than to question it. To this end, L'Estrange used mockery to underscore the extent to which anti-popery rested on mob rule:

> *Philo*. Then I perceive it is become now as criminal to speak well of *L'Estrange*, as to drink the Dukes Health, and all because one is supposed to be a *Papist*, and the other is so. But pray tell me one thing, supposing, though not granting *L'Estrange* to be Papist, may not a man for all that speak in his behalf, *quatenus* an honest man?
>
> *Prag*. That is a good one: An honest *Papist?* ... it is an absurdity, nay an utter impossibility. An honest man perhaps may be a *Papist*, but a *Papist* can never be an honest man: and there is the short and the long of the business pithily delivered in few words ... the *Papist L'Estrange* is a *Papist*; and whosoever speaks a good word of him is a Popeling, an Abettor of the Diabolical party, and an ill Commonwealths man.
>
> *Philo*. Acutely argued. I perceive by this you are a man of parts and perhaps can give me the reason ... why you think *L'Estrange* is a *Papist*.
>
> *Prag*. What need of any Reason, when all the Town and Country say so? sure their words may be taken without any farther Reason.
>
> *Philo*. And therefore you believe him to be a *Papist*, because he is generally reported one.
>
> *Prag*. Yes marry do I: and every good Christian ought to do the like.
>
> *Philo*. I always thought that every mans own persuasion and practice had made him of this or that Religion, and not anothers saying so: But it seems you think otherwise, and *L'Estrange* must be a *Papist*, because the people vote him one: then I say, if he be a *Papist*, they ought to be punished for being accessory to his being such, for it is evident that he was none before they talked him into it.[86]

The final gibe – that if L'Estrange was a 'papist' it was the Whig mob who made him so – was a delicious demonstration of farce undoing polemic. Here the mob is led by 'popery' into a slavishness in which anti-popery displays popery's core elements: credulity and tyranny. Mockery achieved more than highlighting such accusations' speciousness. It showed the 'popery' stereotype – rather than actual popery – to be the problem of the moment.[87]

Despite this, anti-popery could not be rejected as an ideal. It was necessary to contest its meaning precisely because it remained the centre point of religio-politics and one which it was vital to redefine as a language of Tory loyalism. *A further discovery of the plot* (1680) was typical. This refutation of charges that he was 'popish' was made all the more acidic by addressing Oates (his accuser) in a *faux*-courteous tone which used irony to say the unsayable: 'I believe the *Plot*; and *as much* of it as every *good Subject ought* to *believe*, or as any man in his *right Wits can believe*: Nay, I do so *absolutely believe* it, that, in my Conscience, *you yourself*, Doctor, do not *believe more* of it then *I do*' (i.e. not at all).[88] L'Estrange feigned an embrace of Oates as a loyal brother-in-arms by mining the myriad contradictions of Oates's 'evidence' for extracts in which their definitions of 'popery' were the same. The barb was clear: accusing me of 'popery' is to accuse yourself. L'Estrange drew attention to Oates's claims that Jesuit infiltration had inspired anti-monarchism in Scottish Presbyterians and Fifth Monarchists. As his own evidence showed 'popery' nestled amidst his biggest supporters – the nonconformists – Oates (like L'Estrange) must surely therefore see the Whigs/nonconformists as the most severe 'popish' threat to church and state.[89] Employing a centrepiece of anti-papal language – Guy Fawkes's lantern – L'Estrange savaged Oates's exposure of his own party:

> Sir, I have *Read* you, I have *Consider'd* you, and ... You have *Lighted* me into the *Vault*, where all our *Mischief* is a *Brewing*. You have shewed me not onely the Train, but *Faux himself* also (the *Master-Engineer*) *Creeping* with his *Dark Lanthern* to give *Fire* to it, and to *my Eyes*, things are as *plain*, as the *Sun* at *Noon-day*.[90]

This evoked a keystone of popular memory. Fawkes caught by divine providence about to destroy the monarchy was a visual cliché of graphic culture (see Figure 6.1).[91] Here, L'Estrange mockingly claimed Oates as the lantern exposing the chief threat to the Restoration monarchy: the Whigs. Anti-popery neutered anti-popery.

There are two central points here. First, L'Estrange understood his readers to be capable of seeing through stereotypes – anti-popery remained the primary religio-political language but controlling that language through contestation and redefinition was normal practice. Even though he clearly did not believe that the plot existed, or that 'popery' was a real issue of English politics, L'Estrange's polemics remain saturated with anti-popish language, which he appropriated in order to control. Focusing explicitly on what 'popery' actually meant, how the Whigs misused it and, by extension, how the Tory/episcopal royalist used it correctly, was central to his controlling the centre ground of opinion. Second, that the public was challenged to see beyond stereotypes tells us that they did not close thought down but

Figure 6.1 British Museum, 18,470,723.11, 'The double deliverance', featuring depictions of the Spanish Armada and the gunpowder plot (1621).

opened it up. Thus, laughing at others' credulity in accepting stereotypes was vital in making one's position appear reasonable. Indeed, mocking the farcical nature of a 'popery' discourse in which words were very definitely separate from things (that is, 'popery' was set apart from anything papist) offered L'Estrange the opportunity to bring the two back together and therefore limit anti-popery as an oppositional discourse.

This limitation centred on reintegrating 'popery' with its proper subject, the Roman Catholic church:

> Let them vent their Indignation against the *Principles* and *Practises* of the Church of *Rome*, in what Terms they please, and make *Popery* as *Odious* as they can, provided that they do not encourage *Tumults* [against church and state] and contain their *Passions* within the Bounds of *Truth* and *Justice*. If they once passe those limits ... 'tis no longer *Zeal*, but *Confederacy*[.][92]

This limited anti-popery as a political language. If 'popery' referred only to the Catholic church's doctrinal errors, it could not refer to the current Crown, Catholic princes or styles of government as the Whigs would have matters. Controlling anti-popery thus had two principal advantages. First, it positioned the Church of England – rather than the nonconformists – as the true stalwarts of anti-popery and highlighted that the church's historical alliance with the Crown was vital to its being so. It was the Church of England under the royal supremacy which had reformed itself from 'popish' error. History thus demonstrated that the church/Crown alliance was England's best safeguard against 'popery' and therefore – despite the Whigs' best efforts to separate words and things – neither institution could be 'popish'. Tory anti-popish credentials were asserted as those of the Whigs were denied.

Alongside appropriating it for Tory purposes, limiting anti-popery to a doctrinal opposition to Rome had the second polemical advantage of appearing more *reasonable*. This 'reasonable' anti-popery had a heritage in Restoration society. As Jacqueline Rose has demonstrated, polemical histories of the Civil Wars explained Charles I's execution as the result of a combination of popery and puritanism. According to these histories anti-monarchism originated in advocacy of popular sovereignty and the deposition of rulers. Here 'papists' who advocated resistance and regicide, and 'Presbyterians' who permitted resistance to and deposition of 'ungodly' rulers, were two sides of the same coin. Papal excommunication – which removed Elizabeth I's subjects from fealty – and puritan agitation – which denied her governorship over the church – amounted to the same thing. Both asserted that the people could overthrow a monarch; and both consequently made monarchy subject to *de facto* popular approval.[93] As Sir Robert Filmer noted: '[t]he main, and indeed the only point of popery is the alienating and withdrawing from subjects their obedience to their prince, to raise sedition and rebellion ... popery and popularity agree in this point'.[94] Charles I's puritan/Parliamentary 'murderers' were therefore in all actuality 'popish'. Rose has demonstrated that considerable scholarly effort was spent tying historical links between Catholicism and puritanism into one vast font of 'popish' sedition. Puritan resistance theories depended upon Catholic authors, and Catholicism and puritanism used the same propaganda methods, hot language, libels which corroded respect for the state and the stirring up of zeal amidst a credulous populace.[95] Consequently, the true defence against 'popery' was the English church's moderate Protestantism. Episcopal royalist writing became less explicitly anti-popish as its claim to be the bulwark against 'popery' increased. Where their intolerance against 'popery' was reasonable, the nonconformists' was enthusiastic and destabilising.

Resistance to the excessiveness of anti-popery should not be underestimated.[96] In a superficial sense, it seems to question anti-popery's dominance as the period's central religio-political ideology. Paradoxically, however, resistance may actually provide further evidence for that dominance as it demonstrates that even resistance to that ideology could only be asserted through ideological language. A contemporary parallel is instructive. In twenty-first-century societies, the dominance of toleration as the normative ideology forces intolerant persons to engage in its language in order to provide their positions with an air of acceptability ('I'm not racist, but ...') – the manner of dissent reinforces the grip of orthodoxy.[97] In late seventeenth-century society, the converse was true: the dominance of anti-popish intolerance meant that those who did resist it (like L'Estrange) had to voice their resistance through its language to make their positions legitimate. The key point is that contesting (and therefore controlling) the meaning of 'popery' was established polemical practice. By engaging in it L'Estrange (and other Tory authors) simultaneously limited the power of their opponent's anti-popery and asserted the morality of their own positions.

Mobilisation

'Popery' did not entail permanent demarcations between rigid 'in' and 'out' groups, but it was a stereotype which rival groups wrestled to control for specific political ends. Current research in social psychology has stressed that rather than simply *being* in a given culture, stereotypes have to be *mobilised*.[98] Far from being a *passive* product of cognition – an imperfect simplification of phenomena necessary to allow individuals to process information in a complex world – or a routine by-product of social groups who define themselves by excluding 'others', stereotypes are mobilised by one group to *do* something to another. Even a simple prejudiced stereotypical characterisation – 'ethnic minority X are stupid' – contains a rich world view: it explains reality (why ethnic minority X are socially subordinate) and responds to that reality (measures towards equality are pointless because 'they' are incapable of equality). The statement thus justifies the in-group's power as much as it *explains* the out-group's status and in doing so it intends to keep the latter in its place.[99] Stereotypes are about *doing*. They are not abstracted statements, but assertions of power deployed in specific political contexts to control the interpretation of a given moment. Thus in late-seventeenth-century England, contestation over 'popery' was the product of struggles for power between two groups: for the Whigs/nonconformists, heightened Parliamentary power and the toleration of 'true Protestant' dissenters was the surest way of resisting 'popery' in church/Crown; for the Tories/episcopal royalists, this was a malevolent, 'popish' misapplication of anti-popery against those institutions – church/Crown – best suited to protect England from 'popery'. Paradoxically, 'popery' was a viable means of sustaining existing religio-political systems (Tory/episcopal royalist) or of asserting the need for those systems to change (Whig/nonconformists). Stereotypes were mobilised in specific political contexts to justify specific political arguments. Mobilisation involves reimagining.[100]

Social scientists now frame the problem of intolerance not by asking 'why does group X hold views which are demonstrably inaccurate about group Y?' but by asking 'what do such views allow group X to *achieve*?' and 'why are such views *effective*?' Moving beyond understanding stereotypes as the product of 'flawed' thinking in individuals to view them as one means by which groups explain current social structures shows that stereotypes are bound up with issues of power and politics.[101] When stereotypes appear in historical sources, therefore, we should see them not as a reflection of uncontentious popular attitudes, but as part of a rhetorical strategy utilised at a particular moment with a particular aim. As a moral commonplace, 'popery' was often employed in argumentative contexts to assert a position, persuade an audience or defend a norm – it was a rhetorical flourish, an emotive ploy, used to achieve an end rather than a constant of popular belief.[102] Its use was promiscuous precisely because of this.

Because stereotypes are about *doing* – asserting a world view or maintaining political privilege – they are open to being resisted. Scott Sowerby has demonstrated that 'anti-anti-popery' flourished as a loyalist ideology in James II's reign. This had less to do with a decline in anti-popish sentiment than it did with a changing political context necessitating a changing polemical discourse. A Catholic king and the solidification of a Tory/episcopal royalist government meant that currents of opposition to anti-popery as a destabilising presence in English politics advocated by L'Estrange five years earlier blossomed into a full-blown rejection of the ideology in some quarters. Under James anti-anti-popery polemic offered a range of opportunities to different groups. For Tory/episcopal royalists it asserted loyalism: they – unlike the 'popish' puritans – had always supported monarchy and royal supremacy. For Whigs/nonconformists, renouncing anti-popery now had a vested interest: as James considered tolerating religious dissenters, anti-anti-popery was a language of loyalty which offered formerly rabidly anti-popish groups the opportunity to renounce any hint of dangerous zeal.[103] This was pure rhetorical practice: the abandonment of one stereotype for another as political circumstance required. As Sowerby notes: '[i]f anti-popery could be explicitly rejected and opposed, then it was not a fixed attribute that invariably dictated behaviour; rather, it seems to have been a polemical strategy that was used by certain English Protestants in pursuit of a given set of ends [and which] could be both adopted and discarded'.[104] Does this tell us that anti-popery was no more than the mere puffery of words? No: it speaks, rather, to anti-popery's ubiquity as a moral baseline with which it was necessary to engage to assert any religio-political position. The manner of that engagement – adoption or rejection – changed according to political circumstance and the aim of a given group, but the fact of the engagement remained constant.

Contradictions like these ultimately proved vital to stereotypes' vitality. We might think that early modern Protestants' ability to challenge anti-popery, the frequency with which they acknowledged that not all Catholics were malicious and their capacity to coexist in multiconfessional parishes are signs that despite the polemical bluster anti-Catholic intolerance was often moderated in practice.[105] This would be a mistake. Anti-popery was certainly an intolerance 'qualified' by positive appreciations of Catholicism. Engagement with Catholic learning and appreciation of Catholic culture was as much a factor of early modern Englishness as was anti-popery – we need only think of the Grand Tour as an aspect of 'English' gentility.[106] Curiosity and condemnation sat side-by-side: Rome was both the eternal city and the Whore of Babylon. But a contradiction is not the same as tempering. Prejudiced stereotypes are often a complex mixture of positive and negative attributes – Jews as industrious and intelligent, Black men as sexually potent. Intolerance lies in this ambivalence. Positive traits reinforce negative attitudes because they acknowledge the *potency* of the group feared, the threat 'they' pose to 'us'.[107] 'Popish' art was idolatrous because it was alluring, the Antichrist was threatening because it was so clever and Louis XIV's absolutism was terrifying because it was so successful. When the root of stereotypes is understood to be a fear of that potency, these contradictions make more sense.

Conclusion

This chapter has argued that anti-popish stereotypes were an agent of thought (rather than a barrier to it) which ultimately provided a vocabulary through which religion and politics could be debated and evaluated. That anti-popery was a representational practice which attained value in the context of its use meant authors were more than capable of thinking beyond it and expected their audiences to do so as well. Indeed, contesting an opponent's definition of 'popery' was a normal part of polemical practice, and one heightened by party politics during the succession crisis. To control what was 'popish' was to control what was 'Protestant' and thus to control the language of legitimacy. The Whigs' labelling church / Crown 'popish' and the Tories' branding the Whigs with the same label was consequently far more than trading slurs: it was to conduct a debate over fundamental issues of religion and politics – the boundaries of church, polity and constitution – through the same ideological language. As

L'Estrange exclaimed: '[t]his *Cuckoo-Song* of *Forty One, Forty One, Forty One*, over and over; were *Ill-natured* and *Ridiculous*, if the other *Cuckoo-Song of Popery and Tyranny, Popery and Tyranny* ... over and over, had not made it *absolutely Necessary*'.[108]

Examining stereotypes *in situ* is thus vital if we are to understand their potency. Stereotypes certainly *can* simplify the world and provide easy explanations for unequal majority/minority relationships, but to truly understand their persuasive force requires capturing the context of their use *and* how other groups responded to and *disputed* that use: to see stereotypes as aspects of the discursive practices necessary to sustaining ideologies. Ideologies do not exist in a vacuum and are forged through opposition and conflict rather than abstract deduction. To study stereotypes therefore requires attention to the complex interplay of use and counter-use, attack and counter-attack, by which they are at once invigorated and contained.

Seen in this way, stereotypes are ultimately assertions of power: they form a vital part of the means by which a given group controls the interpretation of political events. The succession crisis was at root a contestation between two conspiracy theories striving to control the definition of 'popery'. In this way, what historians often understand to be a 'crisis of popery and arbitrary government' in Charles II's reign could also be styled a crisis of what it meant to be 'popish'. As this chapter has demonstrated, L'Estrange's polemic rested on undermining anti-popery as a *tool* of Whig politics without rejecting it as an *ideal* of English culture. Those who did not assent to anti-popery had to appear to assent to the centre ground of acceptable intolerance – and a generations-old founding doctrine of Protestant national identity – even as they wrestled to undermine it.

Comparisons may be drawn here with modern racist groups' engagement with ideologies which they do not support. As Michael Billig has shown, such groups routinely deny that they are intolerant and, flipping the obvious accusations made against racists, attribute intolerance to their liberal opponents whilst describing their own racist positions in terms of fairness and equality. In doing so, they do not deny the language of legitimacy in Western societies – that intolerance is morally wrong – but reinforce it. Such groups thus feign embrace of an ideology (toleration) in which they do not believe because it is necessary to do so for polemical purposes, to have one's views aired and to counter expected opposition. Accusation and defence thus turn not on who has the best ideas, but on who can paint whom as intolerant: that is, who can convincingly control the normative moral language of tolerance.[109] In the late seventeenth century, the debate was equivalent if inverted. Claiming to be suitably anti-popish was necessary to rebut the political momentum gained by another group's use of anti-popery as the normative language of intolerance. In this sense early modern people were constrained by anti-popery even as they demonstrated their ability to see through and beyond it.

Notes

1 Peter Lake, 'Anti-popery: the structure of a prejudice', in Richard Cust and Ann Hughes (eds), *Conflict in early Stuart England* (New York, 1989), pp. 72–106; Anthony Milton, *Catholic and reformed: the Roman and Protestant churches in English Protestant thought, 1600–1640* (Cambridge, 1995), esp. chs 3–5.

2 Alexandra Walsham, *Providence in early modern England* (Oxford, 1999), pp. 243–66.

3 Linda Colley, *Britons: forging the nation 1707–1837* (London, 1996), ch. 1.

4 Alexandra Walsham, '"The fatall vesper": providentialism and anti-popery in late Jacobean London', *Past & Present*, 144 (1994), 36–87; David Cressy, *Bonfires and bells: national memory and the Protestant calendar in Elizabethan and Stuart England* (Stroud, 2004), esp. chs 7–9.

5 Jonathan Scott, 'England's troubles: exhuming the popish plot' in Tim Harris, Paul Seaward and Mark Goldie (eds), *The politics of religion in Restoration England* (Oxford, 1990), pp. 107–31; Anthony Fletcher, *The outbreak of the English Civil War* (London, 1981), pp. 407–19; John Morrill, 'The religious context of the English Civil War', *Transactions of the Royal Historical Society*, 5th series, 35 (1985), pp. 135–57.

6 See Adam Morton, 'A product of confession or corruption? *The common weales canker wormes* (*c.* 1625) and the progress of sin in early modern England', in Feike Dietz, Adam Morton, Lien Rogen, Els Stronks and Marc Van Vaeck (eds), *Illustrated religious texts in the north of Europe, 1500–1800* (Farnham, 2014), pp. 135–64.

7 Lake, 'Anti-popery'; Milton, *Catholic and reformed*; Frances Dolan, *Whores of Babylon: Catholicism, gender and seventeenth-century print culture* (Ithaca, NY, and London, 1999).

8 Tim Harris, *London crowds in the reign of Charles II: propaganda and politics from the Restoration until the exclusion crisis* (Cambridge, 1987), pp. 129–44; Harris, *Politics under the later Stuarts: party conflict in a divided society, 1660–1715* (London, 1993), pp. 70–1, 98–101, 122; Jonathan Scott, *England's troubles: seventeenth-century English political instability in European Context* (Cambridge, 2000), pp. 427–46.

9 My survey of developments in social psychology is indebted to Perry R. Hinton, *Stereotypes, cognition and culture* (Hove, 2000) and David J. Schneider, *The psychology of stereotyping* (New York and London, 2005), pp. 20–1, 376–87, 435–8. For the 'faulty thinking' interpretation see D. Katz and K. Braly, 'Racial stereotypes of one hundred college students', *Journal of Abnormal and Social Psychology*, 28 (1933), 280–90; Katz and Braly, 'Racial prejudice and racial stereotypes', *Journal of Abnormal and Social Psychology*, 30 (1935), 175–93.

10 T. W. Adorno et al., *The authoritarian personality* (New York, 1950); Hinton, *Stereotypes*, pp. 15–17.

11 D. T. Campbell, 'Stereotypes and the perception of group differences', *American Psychologist*, 22 (1967), 817–29; Henri Tajfel, 'Cognitive aspects of prejudice', *Journal of Social Issues*, 25 (1969), 79–97; E. J. Langer, 'Rethinking the role of thought in social interaction', in John H. Harvey, William Ickes and Robert F. Kidd (eds), *New directions in attribution research* (Hillsdale, NJ, 1978); Hinton, *Stereotypes*, pp. 20–3, 54–7; Schneider, *Stereotyping*, pp. 2–3, 10–12.

12 Hinton, *Stereotypes*, pp. 65–7.

13 Frederic C. Bartlett, *Remembering: a study in experimental and social psychology* (Cambridge, 1932); Susan T. Fiske and Shelley E. Taylor, *Social cognition* (New York, 1991); Hinton, *Stereotypes*, pp. 46–51, 65–8, 82–6; Schneider, *Stereotyping*, pp. 24–8, 150–1.

14 My comments here are indebted to Schneider, *Stereotyping*, pp. 333–63.

15 S. A. Haslam, 'Stereotyping and social influence: foundations of stereotype consensus', in R. Spears, P. J. Oakes, N. Ellemers and S. A. Haslam (eds), *The social psychology of stereotyping and group life* (Oxford, 1997), 119–43; S. Alexander Haslam et al., 'The group as a basis for emergent stereotype consensus', *European Review of Social Psychology*, 8 (1998), 203–39; Schneider, *Stereotyping*, pp. 325–8.

16 For excellent accounts see Tim Harris, *Restoration: Charles II and his kingdoms, 1660–1685* (London, 2006), chs 3–5; Mark Knights, *Politics and opinion in crisis* (Cambridge, 1994); K. H. D. Haley, *The first Earl of Shaftesbury* (Oxford, 1968).

17 Scott, 'England's troubles'.

18 For surveys of these events see John Kenyon, *The popish plot* (London, 1972); Haley, *Shaftesbury*, chs 21–30.

19 Titus Oates, *A true narrative of the horrid plot* (London, 1679); and *The discovery of the popish plot* (London, 1679); and *The King's evidence justified* (London, 1679).

20 Miles Prance, *A true narrative and discovery of several very remarkable passages relating to the horrid popish plot* (London, 1679); Miles Prance, *The additional narrative of Miles Prance* (London, 1679); William Bedloe, *A narrative and impartial discovery of the horrid popish plot* (London, 1679). On this aspect of the crisis see Alan Marshall, *The strange death of Edmund Godfrey* (Stroud, 1999).

21 John Miller, *Popery and politics in England, 1660–1688* (Cambridge, 1978), chs 8 and 9; Harris, *London crowds*, chs 5 and 6.

22 See Knights, *Politics and opinion*, chs 6–8.

23 Harris, *London crowds*, esp. chs 7 and 9; Scott, *England's troubles*, esp. ch 19. Grant Tapsell has demonstrated that this partisan culture was extended after the succession crisis when Charles II ruled without Parliament. See his *The personal rule of Charles II, 1681–85* (Woodbridge, 2007).

24 Ethan H. Shagan has urged us to be cautious in seeing moderation as a clearly definable centre ground in church and state. Rather, the rhetoric of

'moderation' was often used to assert power and control. See his *The rule of moderation* (Cambridge, 2011).

25 Miller, *Popery and politics*, ch. 9; Harris, *Restoration*, chs 4 and 5.

26 Peter Hinds, *'The horrid popish plot': Roger L'Estrange and the circulation of political discourse in late seventeenth-century London* (Oxford, 2010). All scholars working on L'Estrange are indebted to Hinds's work. See also Anne Dunan-Page and Beth Lynch (eds), *Roger L'Estrange and the making of Restoration culture* (Aldershot, 2008), esp. chapters by Mark Goldie and Peter Hinds.

27 Mark Knights, *Representation and misrepresentation in later Stuart Britain* (Oxford, 2005).

28 Mark Knights, 'London's "monster" petition of 1680', *Historical Journal*, 36 (1993), 39–67; Knights, 'London petitions and Parliamentary politics in 1679', *Parliamentary History*, 12 (1993), 29–46.

29 Knights, *Representation*, chs 5 and 6.

30 Roger L'Estrange, *The case put concerning the succession* (London, 1679), p. 37. Hinds, *Horrid popish plot*, ch. 3, pp. 303–5, 308.

31 Roger L'Estrange, *L'Estrange's narrative of the plot* (London, 1680), p. 21. See also pp. 27 and 13–18 where L'Estrange lists issues of pure folly into which 'popery' has led men in recent years. See also Roger L'Estrange, *The free-born subject: or, the Englishmans birthright* (London, 1681), pp. 8, 11.

32 For L'Estrange's use of anti-popery, see Miller, *Popery and politics*, pp. 177–9; Hinds, *Horrid popish plot*, p. 189; L'Estrange, *Case put*, pp. 2–3.

33 Lake, 'Anti-popery'; Arthur F. Marotti, *Religious ideology and cultural fantasy: Catholic and anti-Catholic discourses in early modern England* (Notre Dame, IN, 2005); Milton, *Catholic and reformed.*

34 Lake, 'Anti-popery'. See also my 'Popery, politics, and play: visual culture in succession crisis London', *Seventeenth Century* (2016), 411–49.

35 Andrew Willet, *Synopsis papismi*, 3rd edn (London, 1600). On Willet see Milton, *Catholic and reformed*, pp. 31, 47–56.

36 Peter Lake, 'The significance of the Elizabethan identification of the Pope as Antichrist', *Journal of Ecclesiastical History*, 31 (1980), 161–78.

37 Peter Lake, 'Anti-puritanism: the structure of a prejudice', in Kenneth Fincham and Peter Lake (eds), *Religious politics in post-Reformation England: essays in honour of Nicholas Tyacke* (Woodbridge, 2006), pp. 80–97.

38 See Introduction, pp. 20–1, Harris's Chapter 1, pp. 51–2 and Peters's Chapter 5, p. 163.

39 This was a recurrent aspect of L'Estrange's works. The key texts are L'Estrange, *Narrative*, pp. 4–5, 19, 20–5; *History of the plot* (London, 1679), sig. A2[r-v]; Roger L'Estrange, *An answer to the appeal from the country to the city* (London, 1679), pp. 10–23; L'Estrange, *Case put*, p. 1; L'Estrange, *Free-born subject*, p. 13; Roger L'Estrange, *A further discovery of the plot* (London, 1680), p. 6. (In subsequent notes, I will avoid repeating L'Estrange's name where citing several of his works and those of no one else.) On the *Narrative*, see Hinds, *Horrid popish plot*, pp. 163–4.

40 L'Estrange, *Case put,* pp. 18–19.

41 L'Estrange, *History of the plot*, sig. A2v.

42 L'Estrange, *History of the plot*, pp. 5–6, 10–11, 20–2, 23–4, 33–7, 39–40.

43 L'Estrange, *History of the plot*, pp. 15–16, 74–6. See also *Case put*, pp. 12–15, where L'Estrange used Oates's evidence to separate the Duke of York from the plot (and thereby undermine calls for exclusion).

44 On this reading, see my 'Intensive ephemera: the visual culture of "news" in Restoration London', in Simon Davies and Puck Fletcher (eds), *News in early modern Europe: currents and connections* (Leiden, 2014), pp. 115–40.

45 Peter Hinds, '"Tales and romantick stories": "impostures", trustworthiness and the credibility of information in the late seventeenth century' in Dunan-Page and Lynch (eds), *Roger L'Estrange*, pp. 93–100. Hinds's excellent detective work has revealed the extent to which this case caused a storm. It was discussed in *The Observator*, 1 April 1682; *The Loyal Protestant and True Domestick Intelligence*, no. 105, Thursday, 19 January 1682; *The Impartial Protestant Mercury*, no. 87, Friday, 17–21 February; *Sir Edmund Godfrey's ghost: or, an answer to Nat. Thompsons scandalous letter from Cambridge* (London, 1682); George Everett, *A second letter to Mr. Miles Prance, in reply to the Ghost of Sir Edmond-bury Godfrey* (London, 1682); *The pillory: or a dialogue betwixt Roger L'Estrange and Nat. Thompson* (London, 1682).

46 L'Estrange, *Narrative*, pp. 11, 25–7; *Case put*, pp. 4–5; *Further discovery*, pp. 23–32.

47 See L'Estrange, *Narrative*, pp. 1–2 for direct mockery of 'narratives'.

48 L'Estrange, *Narrative*, pp. 3, 5, 7–8; Hinds, *Horrid popish plot*, pp. 45–6, 97.

49 L'Estrange, *Narrative*, pp. 4–6, 11, 27–31. See esp. pp. 19–20, where L'Estrange claims not to be mocking the plot (as his critics claimed), but merely showing the Whigs to be part of it. See also Roger L'Estrange, *Dissenter's sayings* (London, 1681), sig. A3; *Case put*, pp. 27–9; Hinds, *Horrid popish plot*, p. 128.

50 L'Estrange, *Narrative*, p. 5.

51 Harris, *Restoration*, pp. 260–2.

52 Lake, 'Anti-puritanism', various; Peter Lake, 'Presbyterianism, the idea of a national church and the argument from divine right', in Maria Dowling and Peter Lake (eds), *Protestantism and the national church in sixteenth century England* (London, 1987), pp. 193–224; Peter Lake, *Anglicans and puritans? Presbyterianism and English conformist thought from Whitgift to Hooker* (London, 1988), various. See also Patrick Collinson, 'Anti-puritanism', in John Coffey and Paul Chang-Ha Lim (eds), *The Cambridge companion to puritanism* (Cambridge, 2008), pp. 19–33; Patrick Collinson, 'Ecclesiastical vitriol: religious satire in the 1590s and the invention of puritanism', in John Guy (ed.), *The reign of Elizabeth I: court and culture in the last decade* (Cambridge, 1995), pp. 150–70.

53 Thomas Edwards, *The first and second part of Gangraena* (London, 1647).

54 Lake, 'Anti-puritanism', p. 91; Nicholas Tyacke, *Anti-Calvinists: the rise of English Arminianism 1590–1640* (Oxford, 1987), pp. 27–8, 56–7, 137–9,

155–7, 236–8; Anthony Milton, *Laudian and royalist polemic in seventeenth-century England: the career and writings of Peter Heylyn* (Manchester, 2007), pp. 93–8. On popularity see Peter Lake, 'Puritanism, (monarchical) republicanism, and monarchy: John Whitgift and the "invention" of popularity', *Journal of Medieval and Early Modern Studies* (2010), 463–95.

55 This serves to remind us that Patrick Collinson's definition of puritanism as something defined in opposition to other forms of Protestantism – one half of a stressful relationship – is acutely relevant for later periods. Patrick Collinson, 'A comment: concerning the name puritan', *Journal of Ecclesiastical History*, 31 (1980), 483–8.

56 Roger L'Estrange, *Account of the growth of knavery under pretended fears of arbitrary government and popery* (London, 1678), various; Hinds, *Horrid popish plot*, pp. 192–3; Scott Sowerby, 'Opposition to anti-popery in Restoration England', *Journal of British Studies*, 51 (2012), 30; L'Estrange, *Case put*, pp. 20–1; L'Estrange, *Free-born subject*, pp. 3–5.

57 See L'Estrange, *Free-born subject*, pp. 1–2, for an explicit control of political terms.

58 I am indebted here to Lake, 'Anti-puritanism', pp. 90–2, for this interpretation.

59 Roger L'Estrange, *The growth of knavery and popery under the mask of Presbytery* (London, 1678), pp. 1–5, 42–8. Roger L'Estrange, *The character of a papist in masquerade* (London, 1681), various.

60 L'Estrange, *Growth of knavery*, pp. 5–13.

61 L'Estrange, *Growth of knavery*, pp. 13–20. This arbitrary rule was replayed in Parliament, pp. 39–42.

62 L'Estrange, *Growth of knavery*, pp. 24–5, 64–7. See also *Further discovery*, pp. 18–22.

63 Quentin Skinner, 'Hobbes and the classical theory of laughter' in his *Visions of politics*, vol. 3: *Hobbes and civil science* (Cambridge, 2002), pp. 142–76.

64 Martin Ingram, 'Ridings, rough music and the "reform of popular culture" in early modern England', *Past & Present*, 105 (1984), 79–113. Adam Morton, 'Laughter as a polemical act in late seventeenth-century England', in Mark Knights and Adam Morton (eds), *The power of laughter and satire in early modern Britain: political and religious culture, 1500–1820* (Woodbridge, 2017), pp. 107–32.

65 Skinner, 'Classical theory of laughter', various. These themes are explored in Knights and Morton (eds), *The power of laughter and satire*.

66 Alastair Bellany, 'Libels in action: ritual, subversion and the English literary underground 1603–42', in Tim Harris (ed.), *The politics of the excluded c. 1500–1850* (Basingstoke and New York, 2001), pp. 99–124; Alastair Bellany, 'Railing rhymes revisited: libels, scandals and early Stuart politics', *History Compass*, 5 (2007), 1136–79; Andrew McRae, *Literature, satire, and the early Stuart state* (Cambridge, 2004).

67 Alastair Bellany, 'A poem on the Archbishop's hearse: puritanism, libel and sedition after the Hampton Court conference', *Journal of British Studies*, 34 (1995), 137–64.

68 Examples are innumerable, but see *The committee: or, popery in masquerade* (1680); Frederick G. Stephens and Dorothy M. George, *Catalogue of political and personal satires preserved in the Department of Prints and Drawings of the British Museum* (London: British Museum, 1870–1954), 1080 (henceforth referred to as BM Satire); Roger L'Estrange, *A short ansvver to a whole litter of libellers* (London, 1680); L'Estrange, *History of the plot*, sig. A2; L'Estrange, *Case put*, pp. 6–7 and others; L'Estrange, *Account of the growth*, various.

69 See pp. 14, 115–16, 136–43, 259, 316–17, this volume.

70 Mark Goldie, 'Roger L'Estrange's *Observator* and the exorcism of the plot', in Dunan-Page and Lynch (eds), *Roger L'Estrange*, pp. 67–88; see esp. pp. 68, 72, and 76–7. My analysis in this paragraph is indebted to this excellent piece.

71 *The Observator*, 3 vols (London, 1684–7), vol. 1, issues 1, 255, 272 and 306; vol. 2, issues 53, 168 and 212; vol. 3, issues 2, 73 and 112. On the *Observator* see Hinds, *Horrid popish plot*, pp. 38–9, 60–4, 97–108, 389–97.

72 Peter Lake, *Bad Queen Bess? Libels, secret histories, and the politics of publicity in the reign of Queen Elizabeth I* (Oxford, 2016), pp. 11, 15, 33, 39–40, 105–10, 142, 190, 446–53.

73 Ben Jonson, *Bartholomew Fair* (London, 1614), 1:6, 70–82, 95–100; 3:2, 39–48, 77–87; 3:5, 27–38; 3:6, 72–4; 5:5.

74 Roger L'Estrange, *L'Estrange no papist* (London, 1681), p. 14; see also pp. 3, 12; Hinds, *Horrid popish plot*, p. 127.

75 This is from L'Estrange, *Case put*, pp. 31–3. L'Estrange transcribes the preceding block quotation faithfully, then writes this. Italics are in the original.

76 L'Estrange, *History of the plot*, preface; *Further discovery*, p. 8; *Character*, pp. 1–2, 64; *Account of the growth*, pp. 8–10, 18, 24, 52–3.

77 L'Estrange, *Character*, p. 3; see also p. 20; *Case put*, p. 3.

78 L'Estrange, *Character*, p. 2. See also Peters's Chapter 5, p. 171.

79 L'Estrange, *Character*, p. 20.

80 L'Estrange, *Character*, pp. 20–1; see also pp. 64, 69, 73–4; *Further discovery*, p. 15.

81 L'Estrange, *No papist*, p. 14; *Character*, pp. 28–9, 50–2.

82 *A letter out of Scotland from Mr. R. L. S. to his friend, H. B. in London* (London, 1681); BM Satire 1083; L'Estrange, *Further discovery*, p. 2.

83 Helen Pierce, 'The devil's bloodhound: Roger L'Estrange caricatured', in Michael Hunter (ed.), *Printed images in early modern Britain* (Aldershot, 2010), pp. 237–54; Hinds, *Horrid popish plot*, pp. 48–59, 110–11, 331–2; BM Satire 1085; *The procession: or the burning of the pope in effigie in Smithfield-rounds* (London, 1681), p. 3; L'Estrange, *No papist*, p. 17; L'Estrange, *Further discovery*, p. 10. See also Adam Morton, 'Glaring at Antichrist: printed images of the papacy in early modern England, 1530–1680', PhD thesis, University of York, 2011, ch. 3.

84 L'Estrange, *No papist*; see p. 13, where 'popery' is shown to be nothing but clichés. See also pp. 16–17 for the effect of 'popery' as a label.

85 L'Estrange, *No papist*, pp. 10–11.

86 L'Estrange, *No papist*, pp. 4–6.

87 L'Estrange, *Case put,* pp. 16–17; *Free-born subject*, pp. 20–3; *Further discovery*, p. 17; *Character*, pp. 20–1. See also *Character,* pp. 26, 49 for his discussion of Whig uses of Mary I.

88 L'Estrange, *Further discovery*, p. 2. Italics in the original.

89 L'Estrange, *Further discovery*, pp. 12–13.

90 L'Estrange, *Further discovery*, p. 14. For similar use of anti-popish tropes to 'expose' the puritans, see L'Estrange, *Dissenter's sayings*, sig. A3.

91 Samuel Ward, *The double deliverance* (1621); BM Satire 41. For the impact of this imagery on post-Reformation culture see Alexandra Walsham, 'Impolitic pictures: providence, history and the iconography of Protestant nationhood in Stuart England', *Studies in Church History*, 33 (1997), 307–28; Helen Pierce, *Unseemly pictures: graphic satire and politics in early modern England* (New Haven, CT, 2008), ch. 2.

92 L'Estrange, *Narrative*, p. 12.

93 Jacqueline Rose, *Godly kingship in Restoration England* (Cambridge, 2011), chs 1 and 3; Jacqueline Rose, 'Robert Brady's intellectual history and royalist antipopery in Restoration England', *English Historical Review*, 122 (2007), 1287–1317. I am deeply indebted to Rose's work in this section. See also John Spurr, *The Restoration Church of England, 1646–1689* (New Haven, CT, 1991), pp. 267–8. Royalism and anti-puritanism had an earlier heritage: see Peter Lake, 'Serving God and the times: the Calvinist conformity of Robert Sanderson', *Journal of British Studies*, 27 (1988), 81–116; Peter Lake with Michael Questier, *The Antichrist's lewd hat: Protestants, papists and players in post-Reformation England* (New Haven, CT, 2002), chs 12–14; Kenneth Fincham and Peter Lake, 'Popularity, prelacy and puritanism in the 1630s: Joseph Hall explains himself', *English Historical Review*, 111 (1996), 856–81.

94 Robert Filmer, *Patriarcha and other writings*, Johann P. Sommerville (ed.) (Cambridge, 1991), pp. 132–3, quoted in Rose, 'Robert Brady', p. 1289.

95 Rose, 'Robert Brady', pp. 1292–1301. Older works also used the equation of popery and Presbyterianism. See Peter Heylin, *Aerius redivivus* (London, 1670). On this text see Milton, *Laudian and royalist polemic*, pp. 204–15. Richard Bancroft, *Dangerous positions and proceedings* (London, 1593) traced sedition from the Presbyterians through Scottish writers to Geneva, the strategy employed by L'Estrange in *Growth of knavery*, pp. 5–23. This was typical of anti-puritanism. See Henry Foulis, *The history of wicked plots and conspiracies* (London, 1662) and George Hickes, *The spirit of popery speaking out of the mouths of phanatical Protestants* (London, 1680).

96 On this point, see Sowerby's excellent 'Opposition to anti-popery', pp. 26–49.

97 Margaret Wetherell, 'The prejudice problematic', in John Dixon and Mark Levine (eds), *Beyond prejudice: extending the social psychology of conflict, inequality and social change* (Cambridge, 2012), pp. 158–78, esp. pp. 168–72.

98 My comments here are indebted to Stephen Reicher, 'From perception to mobilization: the shifting paradigm of prejudice' in Dixon and Levine (eds), *Beyond prejudice*, pp. 27–47, esp. pp. 30–8.

99 Reicher, 'From perception to mobilization', pp. 31–2.

100 This emphasis on reuse leading to reimagining is a common way of understanding culture among early modern historians. See Roger Chartier, *The cultural uses of print in early modern France*, trans. Lydia G. Cochrane (Princeton, NJ, 1987); Roger Chartier, *Cultural history: between practices and representations*, trans. Lydia G. Cochrane (Ithaca, NY, 1988); Michelle O'Callaghan, '"Thomas the scholer" versus "John the sculler": defining popular culture in the early seventeenth century', in Matthew Dimmock and Adrian Hadfield (eds), *Literature and popular culture in early modern England* (Aldershot, 2009), pp. 45–56.

101 Reicher, 'From perception to mobilization', p. 35.

102 This emphasis on 'doing' has a direct point of contact with studies of early modern polemic and discourse through speech act studies. The crucial work here has been produced by Quentin Skinner. See his 'Seeing things their way', 'Meaning and understanding in the history of ideas' and 'Interpretation and the understanding of speech acts' in his *Visions of politics*, vol. 1: *Regarding method* (Cambridge, 2002), pp. 1–8, 57–89, 103–27.

103 Sowerby, 'Opposition to anti-popery', pp. 26–49.

104 Sowerby, 'Opposition to anti-popery', p. 28.

105 These themes are explored in Alexandra Walsham, *Charitable hatred: tolerance and intolerance in England 1500–1700* (Manchester, 2006); Nadine Lewycky and Adam Morton (eds), *Getting along? Religious identities and confessional identities in early modern England – essays in honour of Professor W. J. Sheils* (Farnham, 2012); C. Scott Dixon, Dagmar Freist and Mark Greengrass (eds), *Living with religious diversity in early-modern Europe* (Aldershot, 2009).

106 Anthony Milton, 'A qualified intolerance: the limits and ambiguities of early Stuart anti-Catholicism', in Arthur F. Marotti (ed.), *Catholicism and anti-Catholicism in early modern English texts* (Basingstoke, 1999), pp. 85–115.

107 Social psychologists have much to say about this. See Reicher, 'From perception to mobilization', pp. 36–8; Peter Glick and Susan T. Fiske, 'An ambivalent alliance: hostile and benevolent sexism as complementary justifications for gender inequality', in Dixon and Levine (eds), *Beyond prejudice*, pp. 70–88.

108 L'Estrange, *Free-born subject*, p. 16.

109 Michael Billig, 'The notion of "prejudice": some rhetorical and ideological aspects', in Dixon and Levine (eds), *Beyond prejudice*, pp. 139–57.

7

'We do naturally ... hate the French': francophobia and francophilia in Samuel Pepys's *Diary*

David Magliocco

In the summer of 1666, Samuel Pepys recorded the following social event in his diary:

> Thence to my Lord Bellasyse by invitation, and there dined with him and his lady and daughter; and at dinner there played to us a young boy, lately come from France, where he had been learning a year or two on the viallin, and plays finely. But impartially, I do not find any goodness in their ayres (though very good) beyond ours.[1]

Like so many entries, this brief passage prompts various lines of inquiry. This chapter pursues just one of these: Pepys's engagement with 'Frenchness'. It argues that this engagement was structured by two powerful but contradictory stereotypes. On one hand, French things, people and France itself were identified with excess, or the absence of moderation.[2] In such cases, a national identity was constructed, if often only implicitly, in relation to a stereotyped French 'other'. At the same time, France, French things and, more equivocally, the French themselves were habitually identified with contemporary notions of distinction.[3] Here, the same constellation of places, things and people was used to construct and differentiate a cosmopolitan social identity. In other words, Pepys embraced a series of contradictory stereotypes, invoking different aspects of them depending on contexts. These conflicting stereotypes were bolstered by, and in turn buttressed, other social representations – relating to gender, class, religion and age – that were central to contemporary constructions of both 'self' and 'other'. This chapter is primarily expository in ambition. It uses a single source, Pepys's diary, to examine the production and reproduction of specific stereotypes within a circumscribed milieu and at a particular conjuncture, deploying theoretical insights from social psychology. At the same time, it is also intended as a historiographical intervention, challenging the accepted representation of English attitudes towards the French in the opening decades of the Restoration.

Transnational turn, social psychology and Restoration England

A study of national stereotypes might seem peculiar, even perverse.[4] The historiographical imperative of the last two decades has, after all, been 'the enlargement of scale and broadening of perspective': a concerted effort, that is, to escape from what one practitioner has aptly termed 'methodological nationalism'.[5] Consequently, the recommended measure of scholarly inquiry is now anything but national. This *trans*national turn has certainly been welcome. Indeed, this chapter is indebted to this scholarship, incorporating its questions, methodology and vocabulary, and attentive to its shortcomings, particularly the failure to properly consider countervailing forces of repulsion and resistance. This is manifested in an inattentiveness to politics and to the question of power more generally. To their credit, historians of transnationalism are aware of these problems. Patricia Clavin, for instance, has commented on the 'tendency ... to present transnational encounters as consistently progressive and co-operative'.[6] Likewise, Peter Burke has admitted, historians are typically more inclined than their host populations to celebrate what he terms 'cultural hybridity'.[7] It is undoubtedly desirable that historians avoid writing ethnocentric histories, by which I mean something quite different from the very real need for transnationally informed histories of ethnocentrism – with all their associated stereotypes and stereotyping practices. As such, this chapter is conceived as continuation and critique of the transnational project.

Aping these wider historiographical developments, national stereotypes remain decidedly *outré* in the more restricted field of Restoration history. Indeed, since the Second World War British historiography as a whole might be characterised as a rejection – more and less successful – of the earlier whig narrative of English, i.e. national, exceptionalism. More recently, as Mark Knights has noted, early modern historians have concentrated their collective energies on religious and gender identities, a feature replicated elsewhere in this collection.[8] Again, the object of inquiry here should not be taken as criticism of such scholarship. Nevertheless, the lack of interest in national stereotypes is still surprising. Firstly, the late seventeenth century was a critical juncture in the evolution of the Westphalian system. During this period, national identities took on added weight alongside the double helix of institutional form and interstate system. Next, the Restoration itself witnessed a tectonic shift in the national imaginary: the Hispanophobia that had characterised the previous century being displaced by a Francophobic disposition that extended well into the nineteenth century – and, arguably, continues to this day in the 'Little Englander' form which fuelled anti-European Union sentiment during the 2016 British referendum on Brexit and beyond.[9]

Amongst Restoration historians, Steven Pincus is the exception to the rule. He has argued that English 'public opinion' was anti-Dutch in the 1660s before turning anti-French in the 1670s.[10] This was a consequence of shifting judgements upon which of these nations aspired to 'universal monarchy': a construct based, in his account, on 'political economy'. Pincus's reading of public opinion is based primarily on printed material circulating in a world of coffee houses, taverns and similar institutions: that is, within a Restoration public sphere. While not rejecting Pincus's position wholesale, this chapter takes a different approach to this problem and reaches different conclusions. In place of 'political economy' and 'public opinion', it examines national stereotypes through the concepts of 'distinction' and 'moderation'. Discussions of the former, influenced by the work of Pierre Bourdieu, have proliferated across the social sciences and humanities over the last two decades.[11] In comparison, the uptake of 'moderation' has been quite limited. Yet, as Ethan Shagan has shown, this was a keyword in the early modern period.[12] While his study covers considerable ground, it does not explicitly address the role of moderation in constructing national identity and difference. Besides being attentive to seventeenth-century thought and practice, the benefits to this approach are twofold. First, viewing national stereotypes through these twin lenses highlights their connections with the other stereotypes – and stereotyping practices – that collectively shaped early modern society. Second, this approach spans the divide between the public and private spheres – wherever this happens to be drawn – recognising the connections between ideas and practices in each realm.

Like the other contributions in this collection, this chapter is also intended as an exercise in that most faintly praised of activities, interdisciplinary investigation. For most historians of early modern Britain 'theory' is a four-letter word. This chapter proceeds from an earlier premise that theoretical awareness sharpens empirical analysis (and vice versa). The goal, as Caroline Bynum has commented, is to write history in such a way that 'theory is not merely present [but] enables insights of sophistication and subtlety'.[13] This chapter utilises the conceptual tools and interpretative insights developed by social psychologists. This intellectual debt explains the preference for the terms 'stereotype' and 'stereotyping' rather than the more familiar vocabulary of 'identity'.[14] Historians have recently become aware of the possibilities presented by this interdisciplinary encounter. In part, this simply reflects common interests.[15] More importantly, however, each field offers the other the means to address pressing methodological problems. For historians, social psychology's insistence on the social and political (and not merely cognitive) aspects of stereotypes serves as an antidote to the discursive orientation of much cultural history. Specifically, social psychology provides historians with the intellectual resources to examine the social construction of such representations – to *de*naturalise them – whilst remaining attentive to their very real political effects.[16] Finally, since intellectual exchange should benefit both parties to the transaction, this enquiry is also intended as a contribution to an ongoing historicist turn within social psychology. It is hoped that the empirical detail within this study will be of use to social psychologists interested in what Sandra Jovchelovitch has termed the 'long standing psychological problem [of] apprehending time in its lived and experiential dimension' – or, put more simply, history.[17] As such, this investigation is a response to Vlad Glăveanu and Koji Yamamoto's recent call for 'bridge-building' between the two disciplines.[18]

This chapter draws the bulk of its evidence from a single source, Samuel Pepys's diary. The limitations of the case study form require little by way of elaboration. The specificities of time, location and individual subjectivity necessarily restrict the applicability of any findings. Whilst acknowledging the costs of this approach, they should not be overstated. Firstly, the resulting restrictions can be more positively construed as richly textured temporal and spatial contexts. Indeed, as a source, Pepys's diary addresses Martin Daunton's insistence that, '[the] transnational turn should be complemented by a concern for localities'.[19] Likewise, Mary Fulbrook and Ulinka Rublack have countered that the supposed radical subjectivity of the 'self' is greatly overstated. In reality, the 'self' that Pepys narrates is undeniably 'social'.[20] In fact, using the diary has clear benefits in this case. Specifically, it provides an unrivalled account of the conjunction of the private and the public in at least two senses: first, by marrying action and reflection, and second, by chronicling both the public sphere and domestic life. It does so, moreover, in, at times, remarkable, and, elsewhere, mundane, but, above all, exhaustive detail. Consequently, when taken together, the conceptual structure, the subject matter and the referential density of the diary offer rich terrain for unearthing what Jovchelovitch has termed the 'apparently ordinary and inconsequential'. Here, she argues, we can begin to unpack 'the modalities of thinking [and] the behaviours and imaginations' that constitute the social practices of stereotyping.[21] Indeed, it is hardly far-fetched to reimagine Pepys as a proto-social psychologist, providing an exhaustive field report on the 'social objects' or 'common sense' of his day, albeit one whose own social representations are now themselves subject to historical analysis.

Frenchness in Pepys's *Diary*

A preliminary question: why Frenchness? After all, this encounter is just one subset of a larger set encompassing people, objects and practices from around the world that Pepys recorded in his diary. Persians and Turks, Russians and Swedes, Dutch and Germans, French, Spaniards and Italians rubbed shoulders with Englishmen, Irishmen and Scotsmen (and women). Similarly, he recorded in his journals foreign objects as diverse as parmesan cheese, 'a brave turkey carpet', chocolate, Spanish books, a 'parti-coloured Indian gown', a 'very fine African mat', French pornography, Dutch yachts and a west African baboon.[22] Various cities, countries and regions – from China and Africa to the Americas – were the subjects of everyday and more rarefied discussion.[23] This diversity of interactions has been reflected in recent early modern research. Accordingly, historians have tended to look either closer to home or further afield. The 'archipelagic turn' has, thus, focused on connections and interactions between Ireland, Scotland and England (the last of these taken to encompass Wales).[24] In the latter case, Atlantic, imperial and global historians have investigated the importance of much wider frames of reference. To be sure, there have been contrary voices. Pincus and Jonathan Scott, for instance, have insisted on the centrality of an alternative, triangular, English-French-Dutch axis: a contact zone marked by emulation as much as antagonism.[25] Nonetheless, if, historically, French national markers were one such grouping among many, historiographically they have receded into the background. Focusing on Frenchness, then, requires something by way of justification.

First some numbers.[26] The terms 'France', 'French' and 'Frenchman' (but never 'Frenchwoman') occur 495 times in the *Diary*.[27] By contrast, the terms 'Holland', 'Hollander', 'Dutch' and 'Dutchmen' occur in 585 places, or a little under 20 per cent more often (see Table 7.1).[28] The greater incidence of terms relating to the Dutch should come as no surprise, since the English and Dutch fought the Second Anglo-Dutch War in this period. When this factor is accounted for, the picture is materially altered. Outside the period of conflict (1664–7), there are 248 references to the nexus of French terms but just 118 to the Dutch – more than twice as many references to the former than the latter. The relative incidence of French/Dutch

Table 7.1 Incidence of French/Dutch national markers in Pepys' *Diary*

	1660	1661	1662	1663	1664	1665	1666	1667	1668	1669	Total
France/ French	38	37	26	62	42	41	42	122	59	26	495
% of total	8	7	5	13	9	8	9	25	12	5	101
Holland/ Dutch	36	8	21	23	126	106	90	145	18	12	585
% of total	6	1	4	4	22	18	15	25	3	2	100

Source: See note 26.

markers is put into wider perspective, however, when compared to other nations and nationalities. Notwithstanding Pepys's well-known interest in Spanish cultural production, terms relating to the other great power in western Europe occur just 153 times in total. Closer to home, various cognate terms for Scotland and the Scottish appear just 85 times; the equivalent Irish terms, 104; whilst the Welsh elicited comment on a mere 17 occasions. Similarly, the American colonies, bar passing comments on naval actions in the Caribbean, barely registered at all.

Clearly, quantitative exercises of this nature have their limitations. It is not suggested here, for instance, that Pepys recorded anything like the absolute totality of his encounters with the national constellations that these terms – French, Spanish, Irish, etc. – signify. His diary was not a comprehensive record of his lived experience in this – or any other – respect.[29] Nor is it assumed that Pepys marked every encounter with a foreigner or foreign object that he did record in his diary with the appropriate national signifier. For instance, the famous Dutch-born artist Sir Peter Lely, whose studio Pepys visited on a number of occasions, is identified simply as 'the painter Lilly'.[30] This measure is, at best, then, a rough-and-ready indicator of the absolute presence of the foreign 'other' in Pepys's social world. The real value of these diary data points lies, instead, in what they reveal about Pepys's spatial imaginary. Their presence is suggestive of how these national clusters of place, practices, products and people impressed themselves on Pepys's edited textual consciousness: that is, as a quantification of the qualitative. With these caveats in mind, two conclusions may be ventured. Firstly, these findings confirm, for Pepys's represented experience, the paramount significance attached to a triangular Anglo-French-Dutch relationship – and the diminished importance of 'archipelagic' and Atlantic spatial configurations.[31] Secondly, allowing for the impact of the Anglo-Dutch War, Pepys recorded the cluster of terms relating to the French/France far more frequently than any other national grouping.

Francophile *habitus*: prestige, taste and cosmopolitanism

In both the representational space of the diary and the social world it recorded, Pepys and his contemporaries were predisposed to identify French products and practices with prestige, taste and learning. The French 'things' present in the *Diary* took many forms: clothes, wigs, prints, fricassees, the French language, heroic drama, among others. If the technical quality of such 'products' – material and cultural – was undoubtedly important, it was, nonetheless, what Arjun Appadurai terms their 'semiotic virtuosity' that was critical.[32] Thus understood, an object or thing is 'no longer just a product or a commodity, but signs in a system of signs of status ... devices for reproducing relations between persons'.[33] Alexandra Shepard has recently argued that social identity in early modern England 'was rooted in the possession of moveable estate' – things. This, she adds, 'made for the regular scrutiny of the goods people owned'. These 'forms of reckoning', as she terms them, were not restricted to elites but 'articulated throughout the social scale'.[34] In Pepys's hierarchical, status-conscious world, French things, French people and even France itself were incorporated into critical processes of individual self-fashioning and social stratification: that is, in the formation of social stereotypes and stereotyping practices.

Pepys's first reference to France sets the tone for the entire diary. Thus, whilst serving with the fleet dispatched to collect Charles II from his Continental exile in 1660, he noted '[t]his afternoon I first saw France ... with which I was much pleased'.[35] Thereafter, Pepys repeatedly expressed his desire to visit France. In February 1661, for example, perhaps prompted by an afternoon reading 'some little French romances', Pepys noted that he and his wife Elizabeth 'did please ourselves talking of our going into France'.[36] In this respect, Pepys was wholly unremarkable. The same year, he noted, 'I dined with my Lord, and then with Mr. Shepley and Creed (who talked very high of France for a fine country)'.[37] Creed's comments, and the discussion itself, exemplify the attraction that France exerted over the metropolitan middling classes.[38] It also crossed religious affiliations. Younger members of the related Crew and Mountagu families, parliamentarian in the Civil Wars and puritan in sympathy, travelled to France (and beyond) in the diary period. Pepys's travel plans, thus, corresponded to an established practice amongst early modern English elites. This nascent 'grand tour' functioned, *inter alia*, as a means for the Restoration 'gentleman' to acquire the cultural capital deemed appropriate to his station.[39] Overseas travel was thus intimately linked to domestic display. Francis Osborne, one of Pepys's favourite authors, whilst generally sceptical of its merits nonetheless admitted that travel, '*advanceth Opinion in the world*, without which Desert is useful to none but it self'.[40]

The acquisition of other languages – and, by the Restoration, French in particular – was a ubiquitous justification for foreign travel. Hence, Osborne argued that '*French* is the most useful, *Italian* and *Spanish* not being so fruitful in Learning'.[41] Pepys did make use of his knowledge of French in his official capacity.[42] Such linguistic competence was not solely a professional requirement, however: it was also a sociocultural marker. Consequently, fluency in French could become a matter of competitive social display. On one such occasion, Pepys compared his own linguistic prowess with that of his colleague, Sir William Penn, noting: '[a]fter supper Mr. Pen and I fell to discourse about some words in a French song my wife was saying, "*D'un air tout interdict*," wherein I laid twenty to one against him which he would not agree with me, though I know myself in the right as to the sense of the word, and almost angry we were, and were an hour and more upon the dispute'.[43] Whilst fuelling in-group competition, linguistic facility also demonstrated and reinforced social stratification. Sandwich and Pepys at times conversed in French before the former's servants. On one such occasion, Sandwich disclosed the politically sensitive news of Anne Hyde's pregnancy.[44] Here, French served as an oral equivalent to Pepys's use of shorthand in his diary: a convenient means for elites to manufacture domestic secrecy. The wisdom of this strategy is, however, called into question by a quite extraordinary incident recorded later in the diary. In 1664, Pepys noted that, on his deathbed, his brother, Thomas, 'did talk a great deal of French very plain and good'.[45] Unlike his brothers Samuel and John, Thomas Pepys had not received advanced education, and how he acquired his knowledge of French remains unclear.[46] Regardless of how he came to possess this capacity, his recourse to French at this most existential of moments suggests a surprising social depth, at least within London, to some basic familiarity with the French language. This linguistic *imperium*, or 'Francosphere', extended spatially as well as socially. While in the United Provinces in 1660 to collect Charles II, Pepys discovered that 'every body of fashion' among the natives spoke French.[47] Consequently, he found the Dutch admiral Lord Opdam's lack of French remarkable.[48]

The prestige afforded to France as a country and to the French language extended to French cultural products and practices. This was especially true of what, at one time, would have been termed 'high culture'. Thus, in his professional capacity, Pepys was a regular visitor to Whitehall, where he listened appreciatively to the French music and, often, the French musicians that Charles II favoured over their domestic counterparts.[49] As the quotation that opened this chapter demonstrates, such performances took place in both private and public venues. Likewise, Pepys's frequent trips to the capital's theatres exposed him to the vogue for rhymed-heroic drama, a French genre that had accompanied the Stuarts back from their European exile.[50] At a less exalted level, he acquired numerous French books. He read these at home with his wife Elizabeth and, more visibly, with friends and acquaintances. Pepys was, for instance, an early reader of De Bussy's *Histoire amoureuse des Gaules* – a work that Kate Loveman has recently described as a 'touchstone of fashionable and cultured reading in England'.[51] Interestingly, in a will he made in 1660, he stipulated that his French books should be left to Elizabeth.[52] Moreover, books, French or otherwise, were not owned just to be read but to be displayed. The high symbolic value attached to French works is confirmed by their prominent position in the library Pepys bequeathed to his *alma mater*, Magdalene College.[53] A good selection of foreign, but especially French, books helped Pepys project himself as a discerning reader: elite, educated and wealthy.[54] It was altogether appropriate, then, that this collection was fashioned according to the precepts laid out by the French 'librarian', Gabriel Naudé.[55] French prints performed a similar function. Pepys was an admirer of Robert Nanteuil, eventually owning no less than forty-seven of his prints.[56] In the period covered by the *Diary* his collection included portraits of Louis XIV and the latter's chief minister, Colbert. Prints of France were displayed at Pepys's home – a domestic feature intended to impress select publics.[57] By the end of the diary, Pepys was using his greater wealth and influence to secure French books and prints at source.[58]

As Fernand Braudel recognised many years ago, 'costume everywhere is a persistent reminder of social position'.[59] Osborne advised his readers to '[w]ear your *Cloaths neat*', warning them to '*spare all other ways rather than prove defective in this*'.[60] Pepys, a tailor's son, clearly agreed. On one occasion, after purchasing a new cloak-and-suit ensemble, he noted 'I must go handsomely, whatever it costs me, [as] the charge will be made up in the fruit it brings'.[61] In this respect, Pepys seems to have been typical. Recent research has revealed the considerable economic investment in clothing in the early modern period by women and men alike, and across the social spectrum.[62] Outer clothing was amongst the most conspicuous items of early modern consumption, visibly signalling internal cultural dispositions as much as material wealth. Within this field of social display, French clothing – or French styles – occupied a privileged position. In 1669, the commentator Edward Chamberlayne stated that '[f]or *Apparel* or *Clothing* the *French Mode* hath been generally used in *England* of late years'.[63] Early in the *Diary*, Pepys marvelled at Sandwich's hugely expensive French-tailored suit, purchased at the incredible cost of £200, for Charles II's coronation (his annual salary after the Restoration was £250).[64] Sandwich's revelation of the price tag identifies this item as a Restoration 'Veblen good' *par excellence*.[65] 'Taste-makers' at court – like Sandwich on this occasion – performed what Appadurai has termed a 'turnstile' function, prompting cultural diffusion and social emulation across wider segments of Restoration society.[66] As with books and prints, Pepys was acquiring clothes directly from France for Elizabeth by the end of the period recorded in his diary.[67] He himself was an early adopter of the Restoration vogue for wigs: a product and practice imported from the court of Louis XIV.[68] He experimented with various locally made models before finally settling on one made by a French artisan resident in London – an indication itself of English demand for 'authentic', fashionable French apparel.[69] The social stakes involved in such affectations could be high. Pepys was at first acutely sensitive to responses to his new accessory. The reward, however, merited the risk. In 1667, Pepys noted: 'I to church, and with my mourning [clothes], very handsome, and new periwigg, make a great shew'.[70] In this manner, the timely adoption of French fashions helped form recognisable social stereotypes, lending visible and legible prestige in the everyday competition over social status.

This desire for French 'things' extended to French cuisine. In 1668, after eating at the Covent Garden house of his fellow royal officer, but social superior, Thomas Chicheley, Pepys noted '[a] *very fine* house, and a man that lives in *mighty great fashion*, with all things in a *most extraordinary manner noble* and *rich* about him, and eats in the French *fashion ... and mighty nobly served* with his servants, and *very civilly*; that I was *mighty pleased* with it: and good discourse'.[71] Here, French food constituted an integral part of a 'fashionable' lifestyle. As Thomas Cohen and Elizabeth Cohen have noted, in addition to displaying the host's cultural credentials, such social events were the occasion for forging social bonds.[72] French wine served the same functions. Thus, somewhat earlier in the *Diary*, Pepys noted 'with Sir J. Cutler and Mr. Grant to the Royall Oak Tavern ... where Alexander Broome the poet was ... and here drank a sort of French wine, called Ho Bryan, that hath a good and most particular taste that I never met with'.[73] As in the examples above, the diarist's favourable experience of a material object was mediated by the social context. At the time, Pepys's status was beneath those of Cutler, a city-merchant-*cum*-politician, and the courtier-poet, Brome. Pepys's appreciation of the wine, whilst no doubt genuine, was shaped by the company and setting in which he drank it.[74] This association extended to the most quotidian items. In 1665 Pepys attended a meeting of the Royal Society where French bread was afforded the *imprimatur* of the nation's authoritative 'scientific' body.[75] As in the twenty-first century, appreciation of French gastronomy signalled both the consumer's economic status and their cultural capital.[76] This was not simply a matter of French food tasting good, but of good 'taste'.

Finally, the diary also records numerous encounters with French people. Certainly, as will be discussed below, not all such interactions were positive. Many, however, were. They occurred in locations ranging from domestic spaces to the various institutions of the public sphere. Closest to home, Elizabeth's fluency in French clearly enhanced her status. As noted above, the Pepys' common appreciation of French culture was not restricted to the household. Loveman has shown how Elizabeth displayed her superior knowledge of fashionable French romances in other social settings.[77] These sociable gatherings formed an integral part of the couple's strategy for their mutual advancement. Here, Elizabeth assumed the role of 'cultural mediator': converting her facility in the French language and awareness of French literature into cultural capital. Outside the home, such prestige was most likely to accrue to those French 'cultural entrepreneurs' who congregated around the court and other cultural spaces of polite London. This is evident in a variety of culturally charged but otherwise mundane interactions. In the summer of 1661, Pepys heard a Frenchman play 'the Gittar, most extreme well' at George Mountagu's chamber; two years later he shared a coach with the Royal Physician's wife Mrs Clarke's 'Frenchman (who sings well)'; in 1667, he noted seeing 'a Frenchman ... one Monsieur Prin, play on the trump-marine, which he do beyond belief'.[78]

The French person most often recorded in the diary, however, is an altogether more exalted figure: Louis XIV. His pre-eminence within this textual universe is unrivalled by any other foreign figure. His presence as both the subject of everyday talk and object of domestic display serves as a reminder of the unstable boundary between cultural and political interactions in the early modern era.[79] As Burke demonstrated, the 'fabrication' of Louis's 'greatness' was the central concern of an array of cultural institutions and associated actors, including the musician Lully and the engraver Nanteuil.[80] Such French cultural production was intended to promote the 'soft power' of France, as a nation, and the image of its ruler Louis XIV. Moreover, Louis's influence extended to such items of everyday luxury as periwigs. As noted above, Pepys was an avid consumer of the products of this French cultural-political complex. His observation, at the end of 1663, that the 'great talk is the designs of the King of France ... and all the Princes of Europe have their eye upon him', neatly encapsulated England's peripheral position in an emerging transnational system centred on Louis and France.[81]

In Pepys's social world, then, France and French things were routinely associated with notions of prestige, taste and cosmopolitanism. These attributes extended to those people – French or not – who mediated these cultural transactions. To realise the full social value of this cultural investment, it had to be recognised by one's peers. Thus, clothes and wigs had to be worn, French spoken, French books read, French prints had to be displayed, French food and wine had to be consumed – and all before appropriate, and appreciative, audiences. This involved the internalisation of prevalent notions of 'taste', and their externalisation through social performance. These performances, in turn, extended from intimate domestic settings to the capital's various public spaces. In Pepys's world, French products and cultural practices were, thus, incorporated into discursive stereotypes and stereotyping practices that shaped critical processes of identity formation and social differentiation. If these interactions were initially the result of *cultural* exchange, the effects were also *social* and *political*. Certainly, French goods and practices did not exercise anything like a complete monopoly in Shepard's 'culture of appraisal'.[82] Instead, they shared these qualities and functions with other products and practices, both foreign and domestic: ownership of Dutch paintings, drinking coffee and chocolate, familiarity with classical texts and reading natural philosophy, to name but a few. However, as Pascale Casanova has pointed out, within the early modern *trans*national economy of national prestige, French things had the highest exchange value.[83] The Restoration pursuit of distinction, then, involved the public adoption of what, following Bourdieu, might be termed a Francophile *habitus*.

Francophobia and practices of moderation

Restoration London, then, was an exemplary transnational space and the *Diary* itself an invaluable record of the phenomenon Rodgers has recently termed 'cultures in motion'.[84] Pepys, like many of his contemporaries, appears to have generally experienced these cultural transactions as a form of gain. This, however, was neither his nor his contemporaries' only response. As Tim Harris's Chapter 1 has noted above in relation to English attitudes towards the Scots, it was possible for early modern men and women to entertain both positive and negative stereotypes about the same group of people, highlighting certain of their features depending on the context.[85] Indeed, many people, including those most intimately involved in cultural mediation with the French, were uneasy about the evidently unequal terms of exchange, and at the resultant transformation of native, 'English' identities.[86] This anxiety was shaped by, sustained and expressed in the form of negative stereotypes of Frenchness. These social representations were, in turn, contained within the central structural binary of moderation and excess – with the French, and Frenchness more generally, attached to the latter, negative pole. Unpacking the coexistence of such contradictory attitudes – what social psychologists would call *cognitive polyphasia* – now allows us to shed fresh light on English attitudes to the French.[87]

'Moderation', as Shagan has recently argued, was a central organising concept in post-Reformation England and, indeed, Renaissance Europe as a whole.[88] In Shagan's account, the English increasingly valorised what they identified as 'moderate' behaviour in this period. He thus notes, 'worldly virtue was achieved when the moderation of people's urges, passions or appetites produced a middle way between excess and deficiency'. Ultimately based on Aristotelian notions of virtue, 'moderation' was 'at the centre of virtually all ethical writings in early modern England'.[89] 'Moderation', on this account, was double-edged: it involved the exercise of self-control whilst justifying the imposition of coercive constraints on those who were incapable of such self-government. 'Moderation', moreover, operated across a whole range of discursive fields: religion and politics, gender and generational relations, and the social hierarchy.[90] In each instance, those groups that successfully laid claim to the mantle of 'moderation' occupied the central normative position, whilst those identified as lacking in this respect were, with more or less success, marginalised. 'Moderation', then, serves as a key to Renaissance claims to normativity, both as a term in public discourse and as a guide to everyday practice. Phrased somewhat differently, such discursive practices were responsible for forming and sustaining the stereotypes and stereotyping practices that structured early modern society. Pepys's own internalisation and externalisation of negative stereotypes of the French – as a form of 'common sense' and set of everyday practices – are representative of a prevalent Francophobic *habitus*.

The mildest manifestation of this Francophobic *Angst* was cultural equivocation. Literary scholars have long identified this as a characteristic of Restoration cultural production. Hume and Love, for instance, have noted that John Dryden's 'view of France and the French is always conflicted ... [he] resists, apes, envies, and filches from the French'.[91] The quotation that opened this chapter demonstrates that such anxieties were not restricted to the producers and products of 'high culture' but, instead, percolated down through Restoration society. When Pepys, for example, noted hearing a Frenchman play the guitar, he immediately undermined his praise by adding 'though at the best methinks it is but a bawble'.[92] These comments express widespread unease at what was evidently experienced as a musical centre–periphery relationship. These concerns, moreover, were not restricted to the field of cultural production. In 1661, arriving at a friend's home, Pepys discovered 'a Frenchman, a lodger of hers ... just as I came in was kissing my wife, which I did not like'. His subsequent comment, 'though there could not be any hurt in it', carries less conviction.[93] Three years later, Pepys recorded the rumoured rape of an English woman, 'her husband being bound in his shirt, they both being in bed together, it being night, by two Frenchmen, who did not only lye with her but abused her with a linke'.[94] In these cases, fear of the national 'other' was linked to gendered anxieties about domestic patriarchy and, by extension, social order. Fears of excessive French influence extended to politics and religion. As the diary progressed, these were increasingly linked, and more so still in the years that followed its conclusion.[95] While Pepys was generally sceptical of plots, whether 'papist' or 'fanatic', after the Dutch (and therefore Protestant) victory on the Medway he recorded widespread anger 'that we are bought and sold, and governed by Papists, and that we are betrayed by people about the King, and shall be delivered up to the French'.[96] In his account, these anxieties often coalesced on the court as an institution, and the persons of the Queen Mother, Henrietta Maria and James, Duke of York in particular. If Henrietta Maria served as a proxy for the French 'other', the Duke of York represented the unduly 'Frenchified' English self. Interestingly, despite England's being at war with the United Provinces for a good part of the period covered, Pepys registers no comparable concerns regarding the Dutch. Fears of the French and of Frenchness thus extended from the domestic sphere to the public realm and, as these latter examples demonstrate, was linked to anxieties regarding patriarchal authority.[97]

These anxieties about cultural exchange took the form of disciplinary national stereotypes. Pepys recorded an everyday example that occurred during a routine trip on the Thames with his professional and social superior, Sir William Coventry. Pepys subsequently noted, 'he told me the passage of a Frenchman through London Bridge, where, when he saw the great fall [i.e. violent current around the wide bridge piers], he begun to cross himself and say his prayers in *the greatest fear* in the world, and soon as he was over, he swore "Morbleu! c'est *le plus grand plaisir* du monde"'. To indicate he had understood the moral of the story – or had got the joke – Pepys then added, '[this] being the most like a French humour in the world'.[98] A little under a year earlier, another entry provides a further example of such Francophobic stereotypes. The context on this occasion was an armed confrontation on the streets of London between the households of the Spanish and French ambassadors. Observing the beaten French, Pepys commented that 'there is [*sic*] no men in the world of a *more insolent* spirit where they do well, nor before they begin a matter, and *more abject* if they do miscarry, than *these people*'. For good measure, he added, 'we do *naturally* all ... hate the French'.[99] For all their differences, these two entries share important characteristics. First, they each carry out the same cognitive operation. The ascribed behaviour of a single Frenchman, or small sample of them, was extrapolated to the French as a nation. Next, the alleged characteristics revealed in these incidents were not, in themselves, deemed remarkable. Instead, they embodied collective and commonplace assumptions. Finally, the structural form this stereotype took was a lack of moderation – although described here, in the negative sense, as a propensity to excess. As explicit statements of national stereotypes go – Francophobic or otherwise – they are also unique within the *Diary*.

This almost deafening silence in an account spanning nearly a decade is less damaging than it might at first appear, however. The reason lies in Pepys's use of the concept of moderation in his stereotyping of the French. Admittedly, 'moderate' and its various cognate terms are not keywords in the Pepysian lexicon – at least if measured quantitatively. They are used sparingly, and typically operate as value-neutral modifiers.[100] Occasionally, however, there is a clearer normative sense to Pepys's usage of these words. The diarist, for example, considered the alderman and goldsmith, Sir Robert Vyner, 'a very moderate man': an indication of approval.[101] The Conventicle Bill, by contrast, was deemed 'too devilish a severe act … beyond all moderation', by the diarist's cousin, the MP Roger Pepys.[102] The underlying concept of 'moderation', nonetheless, saturates Pepys's prose and guided his day-to-day practice. Pepys attempted, with mixed success, to moderate his own behaviour – be it illicit sexual activity, excessive drinking, compulsive play-going or his rampant bibliophilia.[103] Thus, in autumn 1663, Pepys wrote, 'to Westminster Hall, thinking to meet Mrs. Lane, which is my great *vanity* … but I must *correct* it'.[104] He took equally, if not more, seriously his role as a 'moderator' of others' behaviour – whether his wife's, his relations', his clerical assistants' or his servants'. This often took the form of physical violence. After beating his personal servant Wayneman Birch, he told Birch's sister Jane 'how much I did *love* the boy … and how much it do concern [me] to *correct* the boy … or else he would be undone'.[105] While the notion of affectionate violence may now jar, there is no reason to suspect Pepys of being disingenuous on this occasion.[106] His actions, nonetheless, were undeniably self-interested. Pepys occupied the dominant 'moderate' position in an array of hierarchical relationships that *collectively* structured his own world, and early modern society more generally. At the same time, his practice of moderation, of himself as much as others, was a response to deep-seated anxieties about his personal authority and public reputation: a condition characterised by Mark Breitenberg as 'anxious masculinity'.[107] 'Moderation' of self and others, then, was of equal and central importance to Pepys in his exercise of domestic and public authority. As such, it represented an essential aspect of Restoration 'common sense', shaping Pepys's thought and directing his actions.

It is hardly surprising, then, that Restoration public discourse was populated by 'immoderate' Frenchmen. It was the ubiquity of this stereotype that provided the shared social meaning of Coventry's anecdote and Pepys's French diplomats. In an exact echo of Pepys's assessment of the French diplomats, a jest book from 1666, for example, noted that '[the French] are brave fellows at a first On-set, begin an action like thunder, and end it in a smoke, at the first encounter more than men, in the close thereof less than women'.[108] Likewise, the French were routinely depicted on the Restoration stage as cowardly braggarts. James Howard's 1666 play, *The English monsieur*, which Pepys attended and enjoyed in 1666, and again in 1668, featured a pair of boastful, but ultimately craven, French tailors in its comic subplot.[109] Robert Hume has noted that Restoration plays were 'highly … conventional, imitative and repetitive'. The deployment of a variety of recognisable stereotypes – 'stock characters' – was an important element of this proven formula.[110] The same national stereotype was pervasive in the various printed 'characters' of different nations that were published at the time. Shepard has noted that the authors of these works dealt in a common stock of derogatory stereotypes that were immediately recognisable to their audience.[111] Their appeal, then, lay in the situational or topical treatment of the stereotype in question, not its general contours.

Certainly, early modern English authors across a range of genres identified specific characteristics with particular nations. Osborne, for instance, warned overseas travellers against 'the external Levity of France, Pride of Spain, and Treachery of Italy'.[112] These individual characterisations of the French, Spanish and Italians were entirely conventional, and would have been immediately familiar to his readership – including his admirer, Pepys. Yet, notwithstanding their specificity, each of these national 'others' was negatively characterised by excess. Thus, in *The character of Spain*, published in 1660, the anonymous author stated that '[the Spanish] have a saying of the French ... Their first onset manifests them more then men, but their last less then women. But they [i.e. the French] to requite their kindness, have an ill-favor'd saying of them, *That the Spaniards in point of true active valor, are but bearded women.*'[113] There is a strict homology between Coventry's stereotypical Frenchman and these, quite literally, 'caricatured' Frenchmen and Spaniards. This commonality across generic forms testifies to the working of a structural template, as opposed to any evidence-based analysis of the French – or indeed other nationalities. This confirms the following observation by Wolfgang Wagner and other social psychologists: the 'resulting trope [i.e. stereotype] is not "correct"' – at least not in any rigorous empirical sense – rather, '[i]t is just good to think with'.[114] If the foreign 'other' – French, Spanish, Italian or whomsoever – was laughably or alarmingly excessive, the English were, at least implicitly, reassuringly moderate.

The problem with this comforting conclusion was the all too visible evidence of wholesale cultural borrowing. Accordingly, the desire to contain the French 'other' was also directed at the English 'self'. Excessive Francophobia was routinely caricatured in the stereotype of the 'Frenchified' fop.[115] This figure ridiculed the lack of 'moderation' evident in pervasive Francophile affectations, of the sort outlined in the previous section. For instance, alongside its comical French tailors, *The English monsieur* featured an affected, and ridiculous, Francophile Englishman, the unimaginatively named 'Mr Frenchlove'.[116] This stereotype was not, however, restricted to theatrical representations: he was also a stock figure of travel literature and, as the Restoration progressed, political polemic. John Evelyn for instance, one of the leading cultural brokers of this period, mocked his compatriots' emulation of French fashion in the suggestively titled *Tyrannus*. One 'Frenchified' contemporary was, Evelyn noted, 'a silken thing which I spied walking through *Westminster Hall*, that had as much Ribbon on him as would have plundered six shops, and set up a twenty Country Pedlers: All his body was dres't like a May-Pole'. For Evelyn, sartorial tyranny had serious consequences: 'when a Nation is able to impose, and give laws to the habits of another', he added, 'it has (like that of Language) proved a Fore-runner of the spreading of their Conquests'.[117] The location of this English abomination, Westminster Hall, is suggestive of the political element in this seemingly cultural anxiety. As Rublack has shown, such connections between national habit and national *habitus* were a Renaissance commonplace.[118] The Frenchified fop, however, was not merely a discursive trope, but a flesh-and-blood figure that could be encountered on the capital's streets. In 1664, for instance, after meeting the future Quaker leader William Penn, newly returned from France, Pepys noted 'I perceive something of *learning* he hath got, but a great deal, if not too much, of the *vanity* of the French *garb* and *affected* manner of *speech* and *gait*'. Ventriloquising a familiar complaint, he added 'I fear all real profit he hath made of his travel will signify little'.[119] Penn's embodiment of cosmopolitan values and affect, so evident in Pepys's own clothing, diction and deportment, was now the subject of destructive, and entirely formulaic, criticism. For all its comedic effect, then, the Frenchified fop embodied genuine unease over cultural emulation and national domination. Across these same genres, the fop faced a similarly stereotypical counterpart: the culturally circumscribed 'country gentleman' – in *The English monsieur*, 'Mr Wellbred' and 'Mr Comely'.[120] The affected and, to some, excessive cosmopolitanism of London, and specifically the court, was contrasted with a more authentic and moderate 'country'. In the case of the Frenchified fop, the Francophile urbane–rustic cultural binary was transformed into a Francophobic affected–authentic national configuration.

Such hostile stereotypes shaped encounters, everyday and extraordinary, with the French 'other'. These interactions often took coercive form: Shagan's moderating practices transposed onto the field of national identities. As is well known, xenophobia was a common complaint of travellers to early modern England. To be sure, such dislikes were not confined to the French. The Tuscan visitor Lorenzo Magalotti claimed that Londoners 'were proud, arrogant and uncivil to foreigners', before qualifying this by adding 'especially the French'.[121] Admittedly, this was not always the case. By contrast to Magalotti, the Dutch visitor William Schellinks's stay appears to have passed without trouble.[122] Ironically, Pepys himself was subjected to just such a xenophobic microaggression during a visit to the Chatham dockyard. He was, he recorded, woken in the middle of the night by a man 'calling me "French dogg" twenty times, one after another; and I starting, as if I would get out of the bed, he fell a-laughing as hard as he could ... I asked him what he meant: he desired my pardon for that he was mistaken, for he thought ... that it had been Salmon the Frenchman, with whom he intended to have made some sport'.[123] In other cases, the foreignness of those involved in these interactions may not have been the cause of the confrontations. Given the pervasiveness of negative stereotypes, however, it seems likely that it was an aggravating factor. In Pepys's journal, this is clearest in the encounter, noted earlier in this section, when the French ambassador's followers clashed with their Spanish counterparts on the streets of London. On this occasion, civic ritual took a distinctly carnivalesque turn, with the French subjected to a humiliating barrage of brickbats and insults.[124] As social historians have shown, 'crowd actions' typically took on recognisable and legible form.[125] The aim of such practices, according to this scholarship, was the public punishment of deviant behaviour, the reinforcement of shared values and the restoration of 'appropriate' power relations – in this case between the English and the French. As so often in Pepys's diary, the extraordinary reconnected with the everyday, and the public with the private. Thus, on returning home, Pepys noted that he 'vexed' Elizabeth by 'pleading' for the Spanish. The patriotic 'moderation' of French excess in the public sphere, thus, seems to have presented an opportunity for the anxious husband to practise some patriarchal 'moderation' in the domestic sphere on his part-French wife.[126]

Conclusion

In Pepys's *Diary* and the social world that it exhaustively but selectively recorded, national stereotypes and stereotyping practices took place in a transnational cultural space. This space was populated by people, practices and products from numerous parts of the world. In the resulting economy of national difference, however, Frenchness was distinguished, at least in Pepys's account, by its quantitative incidence and qualitative value. It was habitually associated with prestige by Pepys and his contemporaries – from across the social and ideological spectrum – and appropriated in both individual strategies of self-fashioning and collective processes of social stratification. If the former might seem primarily cultural, the latter serve as a reminder that cultural distinction is always implicated in social reproduction. These positive stereotypes of Frenchness were pervasive in discourse and shaped everyday practices in public and private settings alike. The resulting Francophile *habitus* was internalised in notions of good taste, and externalised, *inter alia*, in reading, speech, dress and dining, as well as in more recognisably aesthetic choices. This cultural formation and its associated practices positioned England, like other European cultures, in a French-dominated transnational space. At the same time, the obvious implication of national inferiority provoked countervailing cultural tendencies that sought to assert English parity – or even superiority. In these cases, Frenchness was, instead, characterised by excess. Its opposite, moderation, structured a variety of domains of normative difference and justified coercive regimes and practices. Accordingly, this hostile stereotype shaped interactions in both public and private settings. This equation of Frenchness with excess underpinned a habitual Francophobe disposition amongst Pepys and his compatriots. Expressed in a variety of textual genres and public performances, it shaped Restoration 'common sense' and informed everyday interactions. As Pepys shows, these countervailing stereotypes coexisted at the individual and collective levels; their balance, at any moment, was determined by the local and national context. While at one level routine, even automatic, they were also subject to conscious manipulation. This understanding of dispositions towards French things, people and France itself complicates the existing understanding of 'public opinion' in this period articulated most forcefully by Pincus. To be sure, Restoration attitudes towards France and the French were shaped by political economy, print publication and coffee house discourse. Such attitudes however were much more complex than is suggested by the schematic account of the shift from the anti-Dutch to the anti-French positions. As we have seen, both positive *and* negative stereotypes about the French coexisted during the Restoration period. These operated in private as well as public settings, and were incorporated into social practices as well as political discourse. Different approaches are now needed if we want to assess the rising hostility against the French. How did latent prejudices against the French come to be mobilised in the 1670s? How was Francophile *habitus* sidestepped in decision-making in general and in the formation of diplomatic policies in particular? Who controlled the meanings of the Frenchness and swayed public opinion? What psychologists have called cognitive polyphasia and its evolution can thus be studied in concrete historical settings. Pursuing these questions, historians would be able to engage with social psychologists and political scientists interested in the role of ethnocentrism in the making of current foreign policies. Closer to home, studying the politics of stereotyping as advocated in this chapter would also enable us to bring closer together cultural history with political history and the history of imperial rivalry in late seventeenth-century England.

Notes

1 Samuel Pepys, *The diary of Samuel Pepys*, eds Robert Latham and William Matthews (11 vols, London, 1666; 1971–83), vol. 7, p. 171.

2 See Ethan H. Shagan, *The rule of moderation: violence, religion and the politics of restraint in early modern England* (Cambridge, 2011).

3 See Pierre Bourdieu, *Distinction: a social critique of the judgement of taste*, trans. Richard Nice (Cambridge, MA, 1984).

4 This chapter was substantively completed before the 2016 UK referendum on European Union membership and the US presidential election the same year.

5 Bernard Bailyn, 'Preface', in David Armitage and Michael Braddick (eds), *The British Atlantic world, 1500–1800* (Basingstoke, 2002), pp. xiv–xx, p. xvii; Kenneth Pomeranz, 'Presidential address: histories for a less national age', *American Historical Review*, 119 (2014), 1–22, p. 2.

6 Patricia Clavin, 'Defining transnationalism', *Contemporary European History*, 14 (2005), 421–39, p. 424. For a general discussion of this issue, see Helmut Reimitz, 'From cultures to cultural practices and back again: a German afterword', in Daniel T. Rodgers, Bhavani Raman and Helmut Reimitz (eds), *Cultures in motion* (Princeton, NJ, 2014), pp. 270–8.

7 Peter Burke, *Cultural hybridity* (Cambridge, 2009), pp. 1–12, esp. pp. 5–7.

8 Mark Knights, 'Historical stereotypes and histories of stereotypes', in Cristian Tileagă and Jovan Byford (eds), *Psychology and history: interdisciplinary explorations* (Cambridge, 2014), pp. 242–67, esp. pp. 250–1.

9 Ali Meghji, 'Towards a theoretical synergy: critical race theory and decolonial thought in Trumpamerica and Brexit Britain', *Current Sociology* (2020), 1–18, pp. 9–11. For an informative analysis of representations in newspapers, see Steven Woodbridge, '"Little Englander": some thoughts on a contested label', *History@Kingston* blog (2 February 2020), https://historyatkingston.wordpress.com/2020/02/02/little-englander-some-thoughts-on-a-contested-label/ (accessed 5 May 2021).

10 Steven C. A. Pincus, *Protestantism and patriotism: ideologies and the making of English foreign policy, 1650–1668* (Cambridge, 1996), esp. pt 3, and Steven C. A. Pincus, 'From butterboxes to wooden shoes: the shift in English popular sentiment from anti-Dutch to anti-French in the 1670s', *The Historical Journal*, 38 (1995), 333–61.

11 For a succinct summary of Bourdieu's critical term, see Loïc Wacquant, 'A concise genealogy and anatomy of *habitus*', *The Sociological Review*, 64 (2016), 64–72.

12 Shagan, *Moderation*, various.

13 Caroline Walker Bynum, 'Perspectives, connections and objects: what's happening in history now?', *Daedalus*, 138 (2009), 71–86, p. 76.

14 For a helpful discussion on the overlap between these concepts in social psychology, see Michael Pickering, *Stereotyping: the politics of representation* (Basingstoke, 2001), ch. 3.

15 Knights, 'Historical stereotypes', p. 254.

16 For similar criticism relating to distinct fields of early modern scholarship, see Noah Millstone, 'Historicising common sense', *Integrative Psychological and Behavioral Science*, 46 (2012), 529–43, esp. p. 535, and Karen Harvey and Alexandra Shepard, 'What have historians done with masculinity? Reflections on five centuries of British history, *circa* 1500–1950', *Journal of British Studies*, 44 (2005), 274–80, p. 276.

17 Sandra Jovchelovitch, 'Narrative, memory and social representations: a conversation between history and social psychology', *Integrative Psychological and Behavioral Science*, 46 (2012), 440–56, p. 440.

18 Vlad Glăveanu and Koji Yamamoto, 'Bridging history and social psychology: what, how and why', *Integrative Psychological and Behavioral Science*, 46 (2012), 431–39.

19 Martin Daunton, 'The future direction of history', *History Workshop Journal*, 72 (2011), 222–39, p. 235.

20 Mary Fulbrook and Ulinka Rublack, 'In relation: the "social self" and ego-documents', *German History*, 28 (2010), 263–72. See also Steven Shapin, 'The sciences of subjectivity', *Social Studies of Science*, 42 (2012), 170–84.

21 Jovchelovitch, 'Narrative, memory', p. 441.

22 On parmesan, see Pepys, *Diary*, vol. 7, p. 274; the Turkey carpet, *Diary*, vol. 1 (1660), p. 232; chocolate, *Diary*, vol. 1, p. 179; Spanish books, *Diary*, vol. 6 (1665), p. 332; the Indian gown, *Diary*, vol. 4 (1663), p. 391; the 'African mat', *Diary*, vol. 7, p. 167; French pornography, *Diary*, vol. 9 (1668–9), pp. 21–2; Dutch yacht, *Diary*, vol. 2 (1661), p. 120; west African baboon, *Diary*, vol. 2 (1661), p. 160.

23 For instance, on China, see Pepys, *Diary*, vol. 9, pp. 17–18 and 22; Africa, *Diary*, vol. 3 (1662), p. 298, vol. 4 (1663), p. 363 and vol. 5 (1664), p. 274; the Americas, *Diary*, vol. 2 (1661), p. 56 and vol. 8 (1667), p. 426.

24 See J. G. A. Pocock, 'British history: a plea for a new subject', *The Journal of Modern History*, 47 (1975), 601–21.

25 Pincus, *Protestantism and patriotism*; Jonathan Scott, *England's troubles: seventeenth-century English political instability in European context* (Cambridge, 2000).

26 All figures are compiled from the nineteenth-century transcription by H. B. Wheatley. The main shortcoming of this edition was its excision of material that the transcriber, a Victorian clergyman, deemed offensive to his readers. Since this largely related to Pepys's bodily movements and sexual transactions, these errors and alterations are deemed immaterial for this chapter's purposes. On this transcription, see *Diary*, vol. 1, pp. xc–xcvi.

27 These figures have been adjusted for misleading entries. For instance, of the sixty-eight entries with the stem 'Turk*' eighteen refer to Pepys's consumption of poultry, including 'four great turkeys' in *Diary*, vol. 6 (1665), p. 338.

28 I have included the terms 'States General' and 'United Provinces'.

29 I consider 'false positives', i.e. acts of misrecognition or deliberate deceit on Pepys's part, immaterial to this data set.

30 For Sir Peter Lely, see Pepys, *Diary*, vol. 3, pp. 112 and 230.

31 Pincus, *Protestantism and patriotism*; Scott, *England's troubles*.
32 On the issue of quality, see Frank Trentmann, 'Materiality in the future of history: things, practices, and politics', *The Journal of British Studies*, 48 (2009), 283–307, p. 289. For the relationship between practical and aesthetic qualities, see Ulinka Rublack, 'Matter in the material Renaissance', *Past & Present*, 219 (2013), 41–85, p. 62 and generally. On the semiotic quality of 'things', see Arjun Appadurai, 'Introduction: commodities and the politics of value', in Arjun Appadurai (ed.), *The social life of things: commodities in cultural perspective* (Ann Arbor, MI, 1986), pp. 3–63, esp. p. 38.
33 Appadurai, 'Introduction', pp. 25 and 45.
34 Alexandra Shepard, *Accounting for oneself: worth, status and the social order in early modern England* (Oxford, 2015), pp. 1 and 36.
35 Pepys, *Diary*, vol. 1, p. 105; for a similar entry, see *Diary*, vol. 1, p. 163.
36 Pepys, *Diary*, vol. 2, p. 35. Pepys, along with Elizabeth and his brother-in-law Balty, finally visited France in 1669.
37 Pepys, *Diary*, vol. 2, p. 33.
38 Although Creed, like his master Sandwich, and indeed Pepys, was already distancing himself from his earlier religious affiliation. In fact, Francophilia may have constituted an aspect of this self-refashioning.
39 For a concise overview of the Grand Tour, see James Buzard, 'The Grand Tour and after (1660–1840)', in Peter Hulme and Tim Youngs (eds), *The Cambridge companion to travel writing* (Cambridge, 2002), pp. 37–52.
40 Francis Osborne, *The works of Francis Osborn Esq* (1673), p. 55, original emphasis.
41 Osborne, *Works*, p. 68.
42 Pepys, *Diary*, vol. 1, pp. 131 and 153.
43 Pepys, *Diary*, vol. 6, p. 223.
44 Pepys, *Diary*, vol. 1, pp. 260–1.
45 Pepys, *Diary*, vol. 5, pp. 86–7.
46 Latham notes that the form and extent of Thomas Pepys's education is unknown, but adds it was likely 'nothing very thorough': 'Pepys, Thomas', in Pepys, *Diary*, vol. 10 (companion volume), p. 324. His knowledge of French may have been related to his profession as a tailor.
47 Pepys, *Diary*, vol. 1, p. 139.
48 Pepys, *Diary*, vol. 1, p. 142.
49 For an exemplary treatment of music in the *Diary*, see 'Music': Pepys, *Diary*, vol. 10, pp. 258–82.
50 Robert D. Hume, *The development of English drama in the late seventeenth century* (Oxford, 1976), p. 28.
51 Kate Loveman, *Samuel Pepys and his books: reading, newsgathering, and sociability, 1660–1703* (Oxford, 2015), p. 123.
52 Pepys, *Diary*, vol. 1, p. 90.
53 Loveman, *Books*, ch. 9, esp. p. 251. See Robert Latham (ed.), *Catalogue of the Pepys library at Magdalene College Cambridge* (7 vols, Woodbridge, 1978–83), vol. 1: *Printed books*.

54 On the presentation of Pepys's collection, see Loveman, *Books*, pp. 46–7.
55 Gabriel Naudé, *Instructions concerning erecting of a library*, trans. John Evelyn (London, 1661).
56 Pepys, *Diary*, vol. 9, p. 427, n. 1.
57 Pepys, *Diary*, vol. 4, p. 320.
58 For such shipments, see Pepys, *Diary*, vol. 9, p. 427. Pepys's funding of the 'grand tour' of his nephew and heir, John Jackson, came with a list of book purchases attached; see Loveman, *Books*, p. 191.
59 Fernand Braudel, *Civilization and capitalism, 15th–18th century*, trans. Siân Reynolds (3 vols, New York, 1979–84), vol. 1, p. 311.
60 Osborne, *Works*, p. 14.
61 Pepys, *Diary*, vol. 5, p. 302.
62 Eleanor Hubbard, *City women: money, sex, and the social order in early modern London* (Oxford, 2012), p. 175.
63 Edward Chamberlayne, *Angliae Notitia* (1669), p. 24.
64 Pepys, *Diary*, vol. 2, p. 83; Loveman, *Books*, p. 8.
65 Thorstein Veblen, *Theory of the leisure class* (New York, 1899).
66 Appadurai, 'Introduction', pp. 31–2.
67 Pepys, *Diary*, vol. 9, pp. 450–1.
68 Pepys and John Creed visited a wig-maker the very same day he discovered that the Duke of York and the king planned to adopt this fashion: Pepys, *Diary*, vol. 4, p. 360.
69 For 'Robins' see Pepys, *Diary*, vol. 8, p. 211; for another French wig-maker see Pepys, *Diary*, vol. 9, p. 334.
70 Pepys, *Diary*, vol. 8, p. 139.
71 Pepys, *Diary*, vol. 9, p. 112; emphasis added.
72 Thomas V. Cohen and Elizabeth S. Cohen, 'Postscript: charismatic things and social transaction in Renaissance Italy', *Urban History*, 37 (2010), 474–82.
73 Pepys, *Diary*, vol. 4, p. 100.
74 On the intersubjective formation of both sensory taste and subjective 'taste', see Shapin, 'Subjectivity'.
75 Pepys, *Diary*, vol. 6, p. 48.
76 For wine as a source of cultural capital see Pepys, *Diary*, vol. 6, p. 151.
77 Loveman, *Books*, ch. 5.
78 Pepys, *Diary*, vol. 2, p. 142; vol. 4, p. 142; vol. 8, p. 500. *Tromba marina*, or trumpet marine, is a single-stringed wind instrument.
79 See, for instance, Kevin Sharpe and Peter Lake, 'Introduction', in Kevin Sharpe and Peter Lake (eds), *Culture and politics in early Stuart England* (Basingstoke, 1994), pp. 1–20; Timothy C. W. Blanning, *The culture of power and the power of culture: old regime Europe 1660–1789* (Oxford, 2003).
80 Peter Burke, *The fabrication of Louis XIV* (New Haven, CT, 1994).
81 Pepys, *Diary*, vol. 4, p. 439.
82 Shepard, *Accounting for oneself*, p. 2.
83 Pascale Casanova, *The world republic of letters*, trans. Malcolm DeBevoise (London, 2007), esp. ch. 2. To avoid charges of Eurocentrism, the claim for the

pre-eminent value of French things should perhaps be restricted to European transnational space.

84 Daniel T. Rodgers, 'Cultures in motion: an introduction', in Rodgers, Raman and Reimitz (eds), *Cultures in motion*, pp. 1–19.

85 Chapter 1, pp. 45–6 above.

86 The term English is placed in quotation marks in this instance to make clear that this was not an essential quality but, rather, the product of a historical and contested construction.

87 On cognitive polyphasia, see Introduction, p. 21. William Cavert's Chapter 8 also explores the striking coexistence of what he calls 'the earnest and the derisive' modes of 'anti-urban stereotype'. See pp. 249–51 below.

88 Shagan, *Moderation*; see also Shepard's longer list: 'rational *self-government*, thrift, *moderation*, strength, courage, and fortitude', Alexandra Shepard, 'Manhood, patriarchy, and gender in early modern history', in Amy E. Leonard and Karen L. Nelson (eds), *Masculinities, childhood, violence: attending to early modern women and men* (Newark, NJ, 2010), pp. 77–95, esp. p. 83, emphasis added.

89 Shagan, *Moderation*, p. 35.

90 See also Alexandra Shepard, *Meanings of manhood* (Oxford, 2003).

91 Robert D. Hume and Harold Love (eds), *Plays, poems, and miscellaneous writings associated with George Villiers, Second Duke of Buckingham* (Oxford, 2007), vol. 1, p. 251.

92 Pepys, *Diary*, vol. 2, p. 142.

93 Pepys, *Diary*, vol. 2, p. 10.

94 Pepys, *Diary*, vol. 5, p. 58. By contrast, when Pepys's sometime mistress Doll Lane complained that a Dutchman 'pulled her into a stable [and] did tumble her and toss her', Pepys dismissed her allegations, complacently claiming 'elle hath suffered me to do any thing with her a hundred times': Pepys, *Diary*, vol. 8, p. 323.

95 For the connection between French influence and 'popery' in this period, see John Miller, *Popery and politics in England 1660–1688* (Cambridge, 1973).

96 Pepys, *Diary*, vol. 8, pp. 269–70, emphasis added.

97 On the relationship between patriarchal concerns in the home and the state, see Rachel Weil, *Political passions: gender, the family and political argument in England 1680–1714* (Manchester, 1999).

98 Pepys, *Diary*, vol. 3, p. 160, emphasis added.

99 Pepys, *Diary*, vol. 2, pp. 188–9, emphasis added.

100 For instance, Pepys, *Diary*, vol. 4, p. 89; vol. 6, p. 273; vol. 8, p. 59; vol. 9, p. 260.

101 Pepys, *Diary*, vol. 6, p. 108.

102 Pepys, *Diary*, vol. 4, pp. 159–60.

103 On Pepys's 'bibliophilia', see Loveman, *Books*, pp. 35–9.

104 Pepys, *Diary*, vol. 4, p. 316. See also *Diary*, vol. 8, p. 344.

105 Pepys, *Diary*, vol. 3, p. 66, emphasis added. See Pepys, *Diary*, vol. 2, pp. 206–7; Pepys, *Diary*, vol. 4, pp. 7–8 and 109.

106 For the related notion of 'charitable hatred', see Alexandra Walsham, *Charitable hatred: tolerance and intolerance in England, 1500–1700* (Manchester, 2006).
107 Mark Breitenberg, *Anxious masculinity in early modern England* (Cambridge, 1996). I am grateful to Dr Tim Reinke Williams for directing me to this work.
108 Anon., *Poor Robin's character of France* (1666), p. 9.
109 James Howard, *The English monsieur* (1674). See Pepys, *Diary*, vol. 7, p. 401 and vol. 9, p. 155.
110 Hume, *Drama*, p. 30. As Bridget Orr's Chapter 9 suggests, however, stock characters in late seventeenth- and eighteenth-century plays 'frequently reveal[ed] a degree of significant divergence from their models', thereby demonstrating 'a powerful individuating effect'. See Chapter 9, p. 266 below.
111 On the early modern 'character' genre, see Shepard, 'Manhood, patriarchy and gender', p. 80.
112 Osborne, *Works*, p. 54.
113 Anon., *The character of Spain* (1660), p. 17. Note also the gendered nature of the national stereotype.
114 Wolfang Wagner et al., 'Theory and methods of social representations', *The Asian Journal of Social Psychology*, 2 (1999), 95–125, at p. 100.
115 In contemporary discourse, 'Frenchified' also meant the 'French pox', i.e. venereal disease.
116 Howard, *The English monsieur.*
117 I. E. [John Evelyn], *Tyrannus, or the mode: in a discourse of sumptuary laws* (1661), pp. 11 and 4. Evelyn's reference to 'Country Pedlers' suggests how metropolitan fashions disseminated into the provinces.
118 Ulinka Rublack, *Dressing up: cultural identity in Renaissance Europe* (Oxford, 2010), ch. 4.
119 See Pepys, *Diary*, vol. 5, p. 257, emphasis added. See also *Diary*, vol. 4, p. 58.
120 Howard, *The English monsieur.*
121 Quoted in Pepys, *Diary*, vol. 2, p. 188, n. 4.
122 Maurice Exwood and Hans L. Lehmann (trans. and eds), *The journal of William Schellinks' travels in England, 1661–1663* (London, 1993).
123 See Pepys, *Diary*, vol. 4, pp. 226–7; i.e. Soulemont, a clerk working for Sir George Carteret, the Navy Treasurer; see 'Soulemont, [Solomon]' in *Diary*, vol. 10, p. 400.
124 See Pepys, *Diary*, vol. 2, pp. 186–9.
125 The classic statement of the 'legibility' of such crowd actions is Edward P. Thompson, 'The moral economy of the English crowd in the eighteenth century', *Past & Present*, 50 (1971), 76–136. For the Restoration, see Tim Harris, *London crowds in the reign of Charles II* (Cambridge, 1987).
126 See Pepys, *Diary*, vol. 2, p. 189.

8

'Sin and sea coal': smoke as urban life in early modern London

William Cavert

In the early 1720s Daniel Defoe revelled in the view of stunning mansions along the Thames. This sight, he insisted, was quite new, 'much more than our ancestors, even of but one age ago, knew anything of'. They were adorned with fashionable gardens and with buildings that appeared, to the viewer passing along the river, truly magnificent. No European capital could compete with such a collection of grandeur; 'in a word', Defoe wrote, 'nothing can be more beautiful'. Given their beauty it was remarkable that these stunning buildings were not homes at all, but merely villas intended only for occasional retreats. Those who were citizens used them merely for brief breaks 'from the hurries of business, and from getting money, to draw their breath in a clear air'. After such breaks they inevitably 'return to smoke and dirt, sin and seacoal (as it was coarsely expressed) in the busy city'.[1]

This 'coarse expression', the city of London as defined, equally and reciprocally, by its 'sin and sea coal' is, at first consideration, surprising coming from an author like Defoe whose career was so metropolitan. To represent London through its environment, and in particular through the air pollution arising from its unique consumption of mineral coal, was not unusual. Early modern London, as was widely known and noted, was fuelled by thousands of fires that dirtied its air and gave it a characteristic atmosphere. 'The joys of London are full of smoke', wrote one diplomat in the 1630s, a conclusion to which many other inhabitants and visitors agreed during the seventeenth and eighteenth centuries.[2] But to link this environment to sin seems to suggest either that urban air pollution was already considered deeply immoral centuries before the emergence of environmental politics, or that the entirety of urban society could be marked as materially and morally dirtied. This could be expected from a figure like Pope or his many imitators who, during the eighteenth century, championed the moral superiority of a countryside free from the greed and ambition of the city. But Defoe was both a native Londoner and perhaps the period's most active chronicler and embodiment of urban life. While there were indeed many ways – political, legal, medical and aesthetic – that early modern people objected to London's smoky air, they did not yet frame urban dirtiness as a sin against pristine nature.[3] Nor did Defoe despise his native city. Rather, something else is going on in this passage, something that allowed a writer to gesture towards the proposition that urban society was inherently sinful, and yet also to avoid the anti-urban implications of this suggestion. We cannot do justice to Defoe's proposition unless we now move firmly beyond the analysis of stereotyping and ensuing polemical escalation developed in the previous chapters, and enter into the discussion of irony, subversion and knowing acceptance.

As London's population grew tenfold from the mid-sixteenth to the mid-eighteenth centuries, its inhabitants, visitors and governors wrestled with what to make of its evolving physical spaces and social dynamics. There existed a classical tradition denigrating urban life, drawing on literary traditions celebrating the pastoral and the georgic as well as a distinct but easily assimilated Christian tradition that denounced urban vices like greed and vanity. Against these, there emerged during the seventeenth century a contrary position that celebrated cities in general, and London in particular, as civilised and urbane, the economic heart of a commercial society and the political capital of a powerful monarchy. This chapter, however, examines a more ambivalent and less polemical approach to urban life, one that could use anti-urban rhetoric even as it ignored, mocked and undermined it. Throughout the seventeenth and eighteenth centuries London's dirt, and specifically its dirty air, was associated with a broad range of moral failures said to be specific to, or at least most widely found in, Britain's capital. But this assimilation of the moral into the material, summarised most memorably for contemporaries in the phrase 'sin and sea coal', was evoked surprisingly often in texts that offered not criticism of urban pollution and urban manners, but rather an attitude of acceptance or even celebration of both.

Stereotypes and rhetorical escalation

One of the most important features of stereotypes during the early modern period, and perhaps more generally, was the way that they allowed their holders to accept and yet marginalise information that would seem to challenge or invalidate them. One's Catholic friends could be good neighbours and earnest Christians, but this did nothing to blunt the danger thought to be posed by 'popery'.[4] Many Londoners during the years around 1600 probably joined in the ridicule of the hypocritical, schismatic and subversive puritans depicted on the stage and in the pulpit, and yet respected the learning and piety displayed by some godly ministers.[5] Stereotypes of women as weak and yet also dangerous were immensely powerful and enduring, regardless of how much strength real women displayed.[6] Stereotypes, both then and now, are able to withstand such contradiction, to divide up the world into meaningful *schemas* despite indications that there exist exceptions. People seem to be able to hold strong stereotypical views in the face of abundant evidence that they do not adequately explain all of the evidence. The very idea of a stereotype perhaps even presupposes this sort of inadequacy; a belief not opposed by much contrary evidence would hardly be called a stereotype at all.

The study of stereotypes, then, is in large part an attempt to understand how people manage information that is contradictory or multivalent. One scholar has even claimed that all communication involves a representation of difference, implying that stereotypical representations, especially as polemical interventions in ongoing conversations, are always already aware of opposing positions and are actively trying to marginalise or defeat them.[7]

One approach to explaining this has been to stress that people are able to lay aside stereotypes when they do not work, but without rejecting them entirely. Studying the interplay of stereotype and social interactions, psychologists distinguish between a stereotype's activation and its application. That is, they note that it is common for people to hold a stereotypical view of a group, but not to apply this view in particular cases until and unless that application helps accomplish a goal.[8] Here it may be useful to consider Alex Gillespie's claim that almost all communication implies a recognition of opposing views and possibilities. If one says that Catholics are dangerous, for example, this is only worth saying as part of an attempt to navigate a world in which there exist other very different positions, such as the claim that Catholics are in fact members of the one true church, or that they can be good neighbours, or that all Christians should just get along. Much communication – and this probably applies to most statements invoking or defending stereotypes – is explicitly polemical, a self-conscious attempt to negate, defuse or silence alternate positions. Gillespie describes a separate but similar style of representing difference, in which there is not one polemical target but rather a marketplace of possibilities, all of which challenge the speaker's position. In both cases, the act of communicating is part of a conversation in which other possibilities are always in play, at least implicitly and sometimes quite explicitly.[9]

Stereotypes, from these perspectives, are not blinders that prevent people from perceiving reality but, rather, useful tools allowing actors to navigate a complex world. Their holders are not brainwashed by destructive lies; rather, they retain a great deal of agency, the power to consider whether and to what extent various stereotypes are useful in specific situations. This dynamic could, as shown by Adam Morton's Chapter 6, lead to polemical escalation and increasing division, as struggles for power make stereotypical explanations of an opposing group's dangerous motives and goals seem useful, both intellectually and strategically. But this focus on choice and agency also opens up the possibility that – given the right circumstances and contexts – stereotypes can become unthreatening and not prone to producing violence, even when they have not been formally rejected or disproven. People can hold stereotypes that they do not, in practice, apply.[10]

Stereotypes of early modern London and its inhabitants

Stereotypes of spaces and the communities they contain may more often lie dormant in this way than do images of political, religious or ethnic groups. Early modern London was both a physical space – the walled city and its extramural suburbs – and also a political community – the chartered Corporation of London with its institutions and privileges.[11] The coherence of Londoners as a meaningful group, however, was undercut by several factors. First, the legal and political borders of the city were not entirely clear, as its many livery companies enjoyed privileges and jurisdictions that often extended for miles outside the civic boundary, even as the city itself had limited powers over activities within sight of its boundaries.[12] Additionally, citizenship, in London as elsewhere, was a political status that neither demanded nor necessarily arose from residence within the city.[13] Most people living in London, including almost all of its children, women, the poor, middling tradesmen and recent immigrants, were not citizens. Moreover, many who were citizens spent a great deal of their time in homes outside the city, in country houses or suburban villas or travelling for business.[14] During the early modern period sprawling urban growth prompted no important revision of civic jurisdiction, leaving the vast majority of metropolitan residents during the seventeenth and eighteenth centuries outside the governance of the Lord Mayor, aldermen, and subordinate officers. Finally, the capital's population was highly transient, with both the poor and the elite moving in and out frequently.[15] This is far easier to track for the rich who increasingly lived in the West End, of course, and whose time was split between Westminster and other western suburbs and their provincial residences.

In short, who *was* a Londoner was no more clear to contemporaries than it has become to historians. The habits, practices, prejudices and agendas associated with the capital city, therefore, could be understood more as temporary modes than as permanent identities. Following from and furthering this, metropolitan London was never unified around any political agenda or interest to the extent that many other groups were. There was arguably less incentive to apply urban stereotypes, therefore, less to be gained from polemical escalation. There were certainly active stereotypes of London and Londoners, but their weaker political purchase made them, in many contexts, less likely to lead to exclusion and violence than to mockery and satire.

Representations of London and its inhabitants buttress the claim by social psychologists that stereotypes are efforts to navigate a marketplace of multiple, competing interpretations. Paul Slack has argued that London's image gradually improved over the course of the seventeenth century, as a discourse of urban sin and vanity was gradually supplanted by the celebration of growth, circulation, trade, demographic expansion and civility.[16] This change, however, was never complete and was achieved in the face of powerful anti-urban rhetoric that argued – in various ways, for many purposes and in different genres – that London worsened more problems than it solved.[17] Indeed while Slack's chronology usefully illuminates some innovative ways to praise the city and its contribution to the public good, it continues to be true across the seventeenth century that praise and blame were often difficult to disentangle. Commentators of various kinds stressed the dangers of wealth becoming greed, or of grand new buildings effacing existing urban structures and the familiar identities they perpetuated, or of trade and circulation leading to disease and contamination. Indeed, the attractions of improvement often appeared less significant than the dangers of unbridled greed and exploitation, the anxieties that, as Koji Yamamoto has shown, made critiques of early capitalism coalesce around the figure of the 'projector'.[18]

The anti-urban position, as Slack and others suggest, drew on ancient models and ideals, both classical and Christian, that saw city life as too worldly, greedy, corrupt and immoral. But these sources resonated in part because they could contribute to a living, urgent ideology closely connected to rapid social and political change.[19] This is evident, in particular, in King James I's regime's repeated attempts to limit the growth of metropolitan London, whose population had tripled under Elizabeth and continued to grow rapidly throughout his reign. This led to a series of social problems, as urban expansion produced over-crowding, insalubrious buildings and districts, and a fear that urban masses were undisciplined, masterless and criminal. Bridewell, deportation and other forms of policing and discipline were thought appropriate for the poor, but London's growth also presented problems that could not be addressed by such means.[20] Much of the population growth, especially to the west of the city of London itself, was driven by the immigration of elites, who presented social problems of a very different kind. According to the king these people rightly belonged in the country, governing the provinces, dispensing hospitality, spending money and generally maintaining social and political order there.[21]

James I asserted that while the effects of excessive elite residence in the capital were social and political, the causes of this practice were moral. In his Star Chamber speech of 1616, he claimed that 'one of the greatest causes of all gentlemen's desire, that have no calling or errand, to dwell in London, is apparently the pride of the women ... because the new fashion is to be had nowhere but in London. And here, if they be unmarried, they mar their marriages, and if they be married, they lose their reputations, and rob their husband's purses.' Living in London was the height of feminine and effeminate luxury, the kind of 'idle foreign toy' that was unknown under 'the old fashion of England'.[22] James further amplified this gendered critique in a poem dated 1622, which was addressed to 'ye women that do London love so well, whom scarce a proclamation can expel'. The king here again assumed the (somewhat unlikely) voice of the moralist, advising women to shun urban temptation, 'for save some few here that are full of grace, the world hath not a more debauched place'. He repeats the social benefits gained by the gentry living and spending in the provinces ('thence your revenues rise, bestow them there') but emphasises the moral benefits accruing to individual women who choose honest, clean and economically sustainable country life for themselves and their grateful family. The political and the moral are fused, both depending on women's ability to choose the upright virtue of country life: 'waste not golden days/In wanton pleasures which do ruinate/Insensibly both honour, wealth, and state'. All of the agency here is feminine; husbands simply follow their wives' lead. After forty-eight lines addressing women, the poem ends with two lines directed to the husbands: 'and you good men, it's best you get you hence/Lest honest Adam pay for Eve's offence'.[23] Urban expansion, for King James, was both consequence and cause of moral failure, especially a feminine love of vanity, consumption, novelty and display.[24]

Early Stuart 'characters', stereotypical representations of social types, described the 'plain country-fellow' and the 'country gentleman' as avoiding the city, exactly as King James asserted they ought to do. Yet this only contributed to their unworldliness and ignorance. The plain country fellow in John Earle's *Micro-cosmographie* knows nothing beyond his fields, crops and animals. He is dirty and smelly, devoid of worthwhile conversation, has no awareness of public events, and lacks independent judgement. Connected to all of this, he only ever goes to London to pursue a law case at Westminster, and when there is entirely out of place.[25] Similarly, Thomas Overbury's 'country gentleman' is non-urban and indeed anti-urban. Nothing less than a subpoena can force him to be in the city at all, and while there he stares at everything, becomes the victim of every thief and is ridiculous at court. He is ridiculed here for being what King James would have him be: uncorrupted by urban manners and desires, an earnest country JP and landlord who thinks about farming and the kingdom's laws rather than metropolitan fashions.[26] But this does not save him from censure, as the countryman's occasional and unavoidable visits to London expose him as a hick whose rejection of the city is based not on wisdom but on ignorance.

By the 1620s such representations of London had developed several features that would, in the coming decades, become key components of references to its dirty air. There was a general moral critique of the city as greedy, lustful and obsessed with fashion and consumption, either because of the intrinsic sins of its citizens or because residing there fostered such tendencies in the gentry. There was also, however, a recognition that occasional trips to the capital were essential for anyone who owned land or participated in national politics. Some moderate level of familiarity with England's metropolis was therefore necessary, and the countryman who lacked this, or who was blindly prejudiced against London's reasonable centrality, was hardly any better than the foppish slaves of urban fashion. The appropriate response to extreme love of urban novelty, consumption and desire was not to be a rural hermit, but rather to achieve a moderate and moderated appreciation for the city and its contribution to trade and governance.[27]

Representations of urban pollutions, moral and environmental

During the reign of Charles I this moral critique of London came to be associated with its distinctively smoky air. Sir Richard Fanshawe's poem, 'An ode, upon occasion of His Majesties proclamation in the year 1630. Commanding the gentry to reside upon their estate in the country', celebrates the king and his reign, stressing the peace resulting from wise governance. The 'gentry' are yet again directed away from London, with the reasonableness of this command now described through a mingled description of urban dirt and dishonesty:

> Nor let the Gentry grudge to go
> Into those places whence they grew,
> But think them blest they may do so.
> Who would pursue
> The smoky glory of the Town,
> That may go till his native Earth,
> And by the shining Fire sit down
> Of his own hearth,
> Free from the griping Scriveners Bands,
> And the more biting Mercers Books'
> Free from the bait of oiled hands
> And painted looks?[28]

Greedy scriveners, debts owed for fashionable dress and unnaturally adorned bodies here are at home in the smokiness of the city. The claim that only the 'purer air' of the country could make its real virtues as much a 'rage' as those of the city leads Fanshawe to expect a new Virgil to celebrate properly the 'benefits' of the gentry's return to the country. Thus the gendered critique of an effeminate city remains in the attention to the city's 'bright beauties' with their 'painted looks', as does the broader claim that both the social order and individual virtue benefit from a de-urbanised elite. What has changed in this familiar language is that it has become expressed, in part, through the material dirtiness that was peculiar to London. The 'smoky glory' was false and vain, a bar to true contentment found in the pastoralised countryside.

This is the earliest example I have found of what became a poetic commonplace during the later seventeenth and eighteenth centuries, the use of smoke to quickly and effectively invoke a familiar critique of urban immorality. Soon others followed. William Davenant, as will be discussed below, used urban smoke in this way during the 1630s. After the Restoration Alexander Brome published an earlier poem regretting London's 'smoke, and sin, and business'. Both Francis Kinnaston and, most influentially, Sir John Denham's 'Cooper's Hill', associated London's coal smoke with urban business, worry and desire.[29]

Such critiques are earnest, drawing on the classical pastoral tradition and innumerable sermons and devotional literature denouncing those sins that were particularly (though certainly not exclusively) located in the city. But the seriousness of this poetic representation of city life was often mocked or undermined, especially on the stage. Characters who were unrepentant urbanites and embraced the negative stereotypes that accompanied that status were aware of these tropes, but were hardly persuaded by them. Plays themselves were, arguably, conservative and conventional in that such immorality was usually unrewarded or temporary. For the town-dwellers ('cits') themselves, however, there was a great deal of fun to be had in mocking and subverting the moral critique of city life as they persisted in celebrating themselves as rakes, dissemblers or frauds.

London's coal smoke was as useful a metaphor to those scorning the anti-urban critique as it was to those embracing it. In a scene early in Henry Glapthorne's 1635 comedy *The lady mother* a young cit travelling in the country, Crackby, happily proclaims himself to be most at home with, indeed positively to glory in, many of the same moral failures denounced by the capital's enemies. He acknowledges that London is especially prone to 'sickness', that it is full of greed and fraud, that it is a place of dissipation where customers pay high prices for unwholesome food and drink, where young men imitate French fashions and affectations and where young women are sexually available. All of these urban stereotypes are invoked quickly and efficiently, in only a few sentences, and all in the service of explaining to his friend, Captain Suckett, why the country has changed his usual manner. He is 'dejected' and 'bashful' and hence unable to 'attack the local women', as Suckett puts it in an extended military/sexual metaphor. Crackby is literally out of his element, 'metamorphised' by the country air.[30] Writing at a time when urban coal smoke was attacked by Charles's regime as both ugly and unhealthy, Crackby longs to be in his 'native city air again, within the wholesome smell of seacoal'.[31] This celebration of urban air signals what follows, a comic inversion of the standard urban critique that becomes an embrace of urban living. London, Crackby states, is indeed the home of debauchery, greed and illness. And yet there is nowhere he would rather be.

The difference between the earnest and the derisive uses of this anti-urban stereotype derived less, at least in some cases, from an author's real position than from the demands of genre. William Davenant, for example, was capable of deploying coal smoke as a symbol for urban life in both modes. Writing in the 1630s, his poem 'The Queen, returning to London after a long absence', opens by asking Londoners,

> How had you walked in mists of sea coal smoke,
> Such as your ever teeming wives would choke,
> (False sons of thrift!) did not her beauties light,
> Dispel your clouds, and quicken your dull sight?

Though most of the poem develops the theme of the Queen's ability to dispel smoke and engender flowers, both real and metaphorical, it is clear that citizens have deserved to suffer because they are entirely, and unrepentantly, 'false', 'distrustful', greedy and ungrateful.[32] Davenant is not here interested in the gendered and sexualised critique of urban desire, but he does use the image of London's smoky air to stress the dull, narrow and covetous sensibilities of its citizens. This is a version of the courtly critique of the citizens' city as a place lacking in nobility because it is dominated by the base passions of businessmen.

Davenant offers a very different critique in *The first days entertainment at Rutland-House*, in which representatives of London and Paris list the other city's failures as they defend their own supremacy. According to the Parisian, London suffered from a pervasive failure of social and architectural decorum, as different types of people, like different orders of buildings and urban spaces, were mixed together in an illegible jumble that effaced their true natures and meanings. Dirty air in spaces that should exude nobility and grandeur were part of this hopeless disorder; 'here a Palace, there a Wood-yard, here a Garden, there a Brew-house. Here dwells a Lord, there a Dyer, and between both *Duomo Comune*'.[33] This last, a common house or brothel, is the supreme example of this lack of decorum, a place in which base desires lead to the mixtures of social groups (men and women, noble and poor) that should be distinguished. In a closing song brewers and dyers, both trades commonly associated with heavy smoke emissions, are blamed for the fact that '*London* is smothered with sulpherous fires;/Still she wears a black hood and cloak,/Of Sea-coal smoke'.[34] Urban smoke here reinforces not only urban greed and lust, but also disordered spaces and an indistinct social order. This smoky city is squalid and uncivil, governed by a general failure of self- and public governance. In both *Rutland-House* and 'The Queen returning to London' Davenant used urban smoke as a vehicle to critique urban society and its cultural and political failures. This is a similar authorial position, and a similar critique of urban squalor and mercantile greed, to that which Peter Lake and Koji Yamamoto identify in Ben Jonson's work in Chapter 4. For Jonson and for this portion of Davenant's *oeuvre*, there is a cluster of urban sins that are being critiqued from a moral high ground.

In two plays written during the 1630s, however, Davenant offered characters who embraced urban smoke as symbols of their own urban sins with little hint of regret. In his successful 1633 comedy *The wits*, a young gentleman expresses surprise at seeing Sir Morglay Thwack, a 'rich old knight' from northern England newly arrived in London's streets, ''mongst so much smoke, diseases, law, and noise'.[35] Thwack, however, immediately reveals himself to be very different from the stereotypically virtuous but gullible country gentleman. Unlike that 'character', Thwack is in London to embrace its vices entirely, to outdo the citizens in their characteristic urban sins of fraud and greed. He plans to extract money from Londoners, specifically from rich widows, never paying for anything while milking them for everything they are worth. The plot is in the tradition of Ben Jonson, a clever series of frauds depicting a city almost entirely corrupt, a place where wealth, credit, social position and power can be conjured using nothing but artifice and theatrical deceit. In the end, of course, such schemes fail and are either punished or prompt a conversion to virtue. But for most of the play Thwack is unrepentant, entirely comfortable amidst the smoke and associated urban sins. Here, as also in his *Newes from Plymouth*, Davenant used coal smoke to invoke a city defined by the urban sins of greed and fraud.[36] In the latter play the association between urban sin and coal smoke focuses on high city prices and resulting social mobility, as greedy city tradesmen leave their 'smoky habitation in the town' to usurp gentlemen's manor houses in the country. Here urban greed is asserted as a slander, while in *The wits* it is openly boasted of by the greedy themselves. In both cases, for Davenant London means specifically the City and its mercantile citizens, whose defining sins are economic. For Glapthorne, as for Fanshawe,

London was a more ambiguous space, including not only the walled City but also perhaps the developing town of the West End, and for both writers the city's sins were sexual as well as economic. For all these authors, however, coal smoke offered a convenient way to summarise a familiar set of urban sins which, already by the 1630s, could be denounced by virtuous poets but also celebrated by characters with whom audiences may well have identified and sympathised.

'Sin and sea coal'

By the Restoration there were multiple modes through which to criticise London smoke, including legal, political and medical readings of the urban environment, all of which, in their various ways, tended to avoid seeing smoke as an aspect of urban sin. The most famous denunciation of London's smoke, John Evelyn's 1661 tract *Fumifugium*, did associate it with the revolution and the need to expiate the sins of the republican regime. But he focused not on metropolitan London in general, nor even on the hotbeds of religious and political radicalism in the city, but on the greed of a few 'tradesmen' like brewers who, he claimed, caused most of the city's smoke. *Fumifugium*, moreover, was less focused on denouncing urban sins than it was on reforming and improving the urban environment. It was a project rather than a sermon. Charles II's regime showed some sympathy with Evelyn's agenda, approaching smoke as a governmental rather than a moral problem.[37]

While the association between urban sin and smoke could be ignored, after 1660 it also became increasingly useful for a variety of literary and dramatic purposes. The key text which did the most to synthesise the variety of pre-Civil War representations of urban immorality and dirtiness was Thomas Shadwell's 1672 comedy *Epsom-Wells*. A bit more than a decade after Evelyn wrote, when the excitement and possibility of the monarchy's restoration had long since faded, the play memorably consolidated many of the strands of existing anti-urban, anti-smoke stereotypes.

Its action was set at the newly fashionable spa in Surrey but was nevertheless very much about London: about Londoners outside London, about how the country differed from London and about whether the country could offer a moral counterweight to boring and greedy citizens, their dishonest wives and the witty gentlemen of the town, all of whom were primarily interested in opportunities for non-marital sex. In contrast to these representatives of the capital, the play offered Justice Clodpate (i.e. 'Earthhead'), an embodiment of Overbury's country gentleman. Clodpate is a landowner inordinately proud of his service to his county, of his status as a gentleman and pillar of local order; above all else, however, he is defined by his absurd hatred of anything and everything connected to the capital. 'That damned town of London', was, for him, 'damned', 'odious' and 'Sodom'. Clodpate's London is the home of all vices, 'pride, Popery, folly, lust, prodigality, cheating knaves, and jilting whores; wine of half a crown a quart, and ale of twelve pence, and what not'. He is a stereotype of an ignorant, parochial Englishman, characterised in large part through his own ready and uniformed acceptance of other stereotypes, including the mingled dangers of the French, of popery and of court culture.[38] London, he thought, was a city of pleasure, but its pleasures were monstrous:

> to sit up drunk till three a clock in the morning, rise at twelve, follow damned French fashions, get dressed to go to a damned play, choke your selves afterwards with dust in Hyde Park, or with sea coal in the town, flatter and fawn in the drawing room, keep your wench, and turn away your wife, Gods-ooks.[39]

Clodpate's hatred of London is so excessive, so based on mere prejudice, that he immediately plans to marry a young woman simply because she hires a fiddler to sing a song beginning 'Oh, how I abhor/The tumult and smoke of the town'.[40] This equivalence between London's physical dirt and its moral and political corruption is nicely summarised in one of his first lines, when he calls London 'that place of sin and sea coal' – a line that summarises his reasons for hating the city and that proved to be memorable for some of Shadwell's audience.[41] The play makes it quite clear that Clodpate's position is to be laughed at rather than piously embraced. Two of his interlocutors marvel at his 'inveterate' hatred of London, adding that Clodpate 'is such a villain' that he observes the anniversary of the City's burning in 1666 as a 'festival'. In contrast to his praise of the country's 'good horses, good dogs, good ale', they return a toast to London's 'good wine, good wit, and good women'. They point out to him that his fears are exaggerated and proceed to make his invectives the basis for their own witty mockery.[42] Shadwell's urban audiences were more likely to side with these men or with the witty Lucia, who shocks Clodpate with her preference for the city's wit, culture, and excitement. 'There is no life but in London', she claims, and further dismisses Clodpate's celebration of country air by concluding that 'there's fresh air in a wilderness, if one could be content with bears and wolves for her companions'.[43] *Epsom-Wells* was a popular play, seen by King Charles II and revived throughout the decades after its first performance in 1672, and it was therefore very well positioned to embed a phrase like 'sin and sea coal' into the culture and conversation of England's play-going and play-reading elites.

After *Epsom-Wells* the phrase 'sin and sea coal' is used in a knowing, playful, referential way that presumes familiarity with, but an ironic distance from, Clodpate's hypocritical equation of the city with sin. In the minor 1693 play *The wary widow*, for example, a libertine named Scaredevil opens with a speech in which the phrase is used to summarise rakish urban pleasures that the speaker plans unwillingly to abandon:

> How empty this town is grown since this unlucky war. I have traversed the streets, and have not met with one of my acquaintance. The playhouses are silent, the bowling greens abandoned, not a vizor stirring in the mall. I have beat it on the hoof quite through the City, ransacked our old quarters and rendevouz and cannot start one honest fellow to communicate my thoughts with, nor so much as a whore roving about to pick up coach hire. Well, if this wicked lewd town continues under so strict a discipline and reformation, it will be high time to bid adieu to this scene of sin and seacoal, and trudge down to my last reserve of country friends.[44]

In another contemporary play a character similarly declares his intention to 'renounce the follies of the town ... [to] forsake this hole of sin and sea coal'. In both cases, however, the renunciation is highly unconvincing and fleeting.[45] In both, a language of righteous and moralising anti-urbanism is invoked only to be subverted, or indeed, mocked. Scaredevil never planned to renounce sin, did not leave the town, did not repent or get punished. Clodpate had meant what he said, but he too was mocked, in his case by the economy of the play itself, in which he ends up marrying a woman who he calls 'a Londoner, and consequently a strumpet'.[46] In all three of these plays, then, we are presented with a discourse in which London's coal burning and consequent smokiness is equated with, or stands for, specifically urban sins. These sins, moreover, are to be avoided by avoiding urban life and the urban environment itself. But this language is never convincing. It gestures towards a moral that the play neither endorses nor explicitly counters. One final publication from the 1690s offers an exception that confirms this trend. A brief tract, which presents itself as a true account but reads like a burlesque comedy, describes a 'rampant vicar' who decides to travel to, rather than from, the capital of 'sin and sea coal'. The vicar, in this story, chooses London precisely because of his debauched morals.[47]

The tone of these plays is light-hearted and perhaps a little cynical, with the text presuming that the audience laughs with rather than at these libertines. Unlike the Jonson plays assessed by Lake and Yamamoto, these texts allowed audiences to dismiss those who were overly concerned by urban greed, desire and dirt. Unlike the stereotypes related to popery and Quakers discussed by Kate Peters and Adam Morton, in which victims fiercely contested the meaning and the applicability of stereotypes, here what is called *stigma consciousness* in this volume did not lead to contestation. Instead, by about 1700, 'sin and sea coal' represented the physical and moral dangers of the urban environment, as well as its inhabitants' self-aware choices to endure or even to embrace those same dangers.

This was the freight carried by the phrase in November of 1712 when it was deployed in its most enduringly famous and influential way in the pages of *The Spectator*. The narrator informed readers of the ambivalent news that his friend, 'the gay, the loud, the vain Will Honeycomb, who had made Love to every great Fortune that has appeared in Town for above thirty years together, and boasted of Favours from Ladies whom he had never seen, is at length wedded to a plain Country Girl'.[48] It is crucial here that Honeycomb's transformation has already occurred when the narrator describes it, and its completeness is signalled by the new formality with which Honeycomb informs his London friends of his marriage and the associated denunciation of a rakish urban life.

Honeycomb, in a letter to *The Spectator's* narrator, gestures towards this bundle of changes through the metaphor of urban smoke. 'I question not but you, and the rest of my acquaintance, wonder that I, who have lived in the smoke and gallantries of the town for thirty years together, should all on a sudden grow fond of a country life.' Only an accident brought him down to his estates, without which 'I had still been immersed in sin and sea coal'. Honeycomb's readers, here, are presumed not to need it explained what 'sin and sea coal', 'smoke and gallantries' have to do with each other, why urban air should imply the pursuit of non-marital sex.[49]

By the time he writes to us, however, that is all in the past. Now he 'can scarce forbear filling my letter with breezes, shades, flowers, meadows, and purling streams'. The new wife 'charms me wonderfully' precisely because she is the opposite of London women:

> She is born of honest parents, and though she has no portion, she has a great deal of virtue. The natural sweetness and innocence of her behaviour, the freshness of her complection, the unaffected turn of her shape and person, shot me through and through every time I saw her, and did more execution upon me ... than the greatest beauty in town or court.

With such a virtuous wife and healthful country estate, 'it shall be my business hereafter to live the life of an honest man, and to act as becomes the master of a family'.[50] Such honesty here is not merely the absence of urban vices; it is their opposite.

Indeed, Honeycomb's future life is primarily described through such negation, but this is ambiguous. He had recently observed a 'tribe of fashionable young fluttering coxcombs', but rather than express disgust at their frivolity or immorality, Honeycomb reflects that he had grown too old to behave in such ways himself anymore. 'For I may now confess my age to thee, I have been eight and forty above these twelve years.'[51] It is clear that he has enjoyed himself and perhaps wishes he could remain a 'young fluttering coxcomb'. His choice of rural virtue over sin and sea coal is conditional on his own inability to successfully enjoy the 'smoke and gallantries' of the town anymore. Perhaps because of this, *The Spectator* drops hints that there are troubles ahead. The opening Latin epigram glosses Honeycomb's marriage as an 'incongruous' match', and anyone who knew their Horace would have suspected that Honeycomb's innocent, virtuous wife would soon make him a cuckold.[52]

These then, are the stakes of Honeycomb's deployment of the phrase 'sin and sea coal'. For Honeycomb, as for Shadwell and other late-Stuart writers, the phrase describes the totality of a certain kind of polite but immoral town life, and it is used at moments of transition, usually when that life is being denounced or renounced, but occasionally also when it is embraced. Honeycomb, of course, is not a country bumpkin like Clodpate, and his renunciation of urban pleasure is knowing and self-aware, born of the maturity and perhaps fatigue of advancing age rather than an absolute moral stance against sexual profligacy and associated modes of consumption and sociability. Honeycomb has tasted this life, indeed seems to have lived it fully for decades while treating his estates as merely a source of income. But if he does not adopt Clodpate's unthinking raillery, he still, in the end, accepts his equation of urban smoke and an immoral lifestyle as well as his simple distinction between the dirty, libertine town and the virtuous, innocent and healthy country. Honeycomb's acceptance of this conventional anti-urban rhetoric is knowing, ironic and world-weary, but it is not critical. This ironic anti-urbanism is what Raymond Williams called, in another context, 'the literary means by which this trick can be played, noticed, and still win'.[53] But this trick – an urbanite deploying a rhetoric of moral/material urban corruption – only wins for Honeycomb. The broader universe of *The Spectator* itself continues to celebrate a version of urban politeness that sidesteps the implications of Honeycomb's choice. Honeycomb, then, uses sea coal smoke to gesture towards a reading of urban life stressing its libertinism and shallowness, a reading which *The Spectator* itself does not directly challenge but does sidestep, insofar as the entire weight of its project is to stress that the town was in fact something quite different and better, a realm of politeness and interpersonal commerce that was not sinful but virtuous.[54]

Through the popularity of Shadwell's comedy, and even more through the vast and enduring influence of *The Spectator*, 'sin and sea coal' came to invoke, for the eighteenth century's literate classes, a moralised rhetorical distinction between London and the country. 'Sin and sea coal' was an immediately legible invocation of this vision, a shorthand summary of a stereotypical urban lifestyle. It came quickly to Daniel Defoe's pen in the

1720s as he described London citizens leaving behind a pleasant suburban retreat and returning to their urban routine. It was similarly used even during the 1680s by Walter Yonge, who wrote to John Locke that of course the air of a country garden would be more welcome than joining in a planned trip to 'that sink of sin and sea coal'.[55] Throughout the eighteenth century the phrase was used by a variety of authors who shared a need to invoke a stereotypical reading of London life without necessarily endorsing it. It was useful to Hannah More in 1782 when she celebrated an excursion from the city into the pure air of Hampton.[56] It was quoted ironically by a dissipated aristocrat in the Duchess of Devonshire's 1779 novel *The sylph*, when he complained of 'languishing for sin and sea coal', by which he meant that he was anxious to return to the city despite the clear moral superiority of the country. Indeed, that was the problem; '[y]our mere good kind of people are really insipid sort of folks; and as such totally unsuited to my taste'.[57] In 1782 the Duchess's political rival William Pitt the Younger used the same phrase in a spirit of ironic detachment, though not of dissipated mockery, in a letter to his friend William Wilberforce.[58] For all of these authors, 'sin and sea coal' gestured nicely towards a familiar set of stereotypes regarding urban life. It was a phrase that hinted at a point without needing to fully defend it, in part because the moralised anti-urban rhetoric associated with a character like Clodpate was so flawed.

The point here, however, is not that such visions were inaccurate, but that their very inaccuracies matter as evidence of how this culture chose to understand and represent itself. As this volume examines from several perspectives, stereotypes do cultural work, they help explain and order the world, in part because they *are* oversimplifications and distortions. This approach to categorising the city as greedy and dirty and the country as materially and morally clean was useful. It was, like Lake's description of the ideology of anti-popery, 'a way of dividing up the world between positive and negative characteristics, a symbolic means of labelling and expelling'.[59] The country vision of urban immorality did do this, but with a crucial difference in tone. Whereas Lake's divines were busy determining how England might please God, and in so doing what constituted legitimate political authority and the limits of political allegiance, neither *The Spectator* nor less *Epsom-Wells* claimed such stakes. Unlike many cases of stereotyping studied in this volume, the above representations of urban sin and dirt did not escalate towards increasing division and violence.

The anti-urban language described here could certainly have political implications, but the generic conventions of comedic theatre allowed it to be voiced in ambiguous and subversive ways. Audiences and readers could dismiss Clodpate as a fool, and therefore remain untouched by his invective, or they might, like Honeycomb, recognise some truth in the suggestion that urban manners and air were comparably polluted. If so, they might remain cynically aware of their sinful environment without any particular concern, or they might resolve to achieve a retreat into rural virtue at some point in the future. The implications of living in a sinful environment thus might be either disregarded or contained. Within the comedic world of a play both were possible, as rakes could achieve unconvincing and seemingly superficial conversions. Thus whereas the dialectic between Protestant and papist increased the potential for violent conflict, the similarly structured distinction between clean rural virtue and dirty urban sin could much more easily be used for playful appropriation, sly subversion and ironic penitence.

In other genres this could be taken more seriously. Many bad eighteenth-century poems, even if they did not use the precise phrase 'sin and sea coal', found smoke a useful metaphor through which to denounce urban luxury. Richard Savage's 1735 poetic praise of Queen Caroline, for example, listed the interconnected problems that she manages to solve. She invites, wrote Savage, people away 'from city smoke and noise,/ Vapours impure, and from impurer joys;/From various evils, that, with rage combin'd,/Untune the body, and pollute the mind'.[60] A more conventional example of the eighteenth-century poetry of rural retirement began 'Farewell, the smoky town! Adieu/Each rude and sensual joy;/Gay, fleeting pleasures, all untrue,/That in possession cloy'.[61] In poems like this, generic conventions preclude the playfulness found in comedic drama, and the proper response to urban pollution is flight rather than resignation, scorn or personal renewal rather than laughter. Despite these differences in tone, however, the city is the same kind of symbol in both genres. In both cases the city is equated with sin, and in both cases the possibility that one might actually choose urban worldliness, indeed the plain fact that hundreds of thousands did make that choice, is an ever-present problem.

We have, then, a metaphor for urban life that can be either serious or playful, earnest or mocking, moralising or libertine. What varied was context, as literary genres or social situations altered the situations within which this stereotype could be deployed, and therefore what power and meaning it could have. What was at stake in references to 'sin and sea coal' was the extent to which true virtue was compatible with an urban, materialist and commercial society. These were and perhaps are a crucial set of questions. What was not immediately at stake, however, in such discussions of urban dirtiness were power or violence. The stereotype of the sinful and dirty city existed, but its power was restricted in two ways. First, in plays like *Epsom-Wells* it was always represented as an insufficient representation of reality, a reading of London and Londoners that was quite clearly partial and prejudiced. A claim by a character like Clodpate that London contained nothing more than 'pride, Popery, folly, lust, prodigality, cheating knaves, and jilting whores' was clearly not entirely true. There was, then, an early modern awareness that the anti-urban position expressed in this way was a stereotype, a flawed but powerful claim about a complex world. It was premised upon, was a response to, a set of alternative visions that saw the city as something quite different.[62] Contrary to the claim that perceptions of the city shifted during the seventeenth century from negative to positive, the uses of 'sin and sea coal' suggest how the nature and meaning of urban life remained unresolved through the early modern period (and beyond).

Second, the anti-urban stereotype was not so much defeated by its internal tensions as it was contained by its social and political context. While there may be structural similarities to other stereotypes, the claim that London was home of 'sin and sea coal' differed because it did not address, at least not in the context of post-Restoration England, fundamental political issues like who would wield power, how communities should be formed and who might acquire wealth. The stereotype remained available to those who needed it, but such needs tended to be ironic and mocking rather than polemical and aggressive. This stereotype, then, did not contribute to increasing social tension or political division, it did not cause people to fight their neighbours or kill their enemies. Instead, its influence was subtler and more gradual. It contributed to a nagging and persistent sense that urban growth and economic improvement had regrettable but perhaps inevitable costs, environmental as well as social and moral.

Notes

1 Daniel Defoe, *A tour thro' the whole island of Great Britain*, intro. G. D. H. Cole (London, 1968), vol. 1, pp. 165, 167, 169.

2 Sir Thomas Roe to Sir John Finet, 24 October 1631, in *Calendar of State Papers, domestic series, of the reign of Charles I. Addenda: March 1625 to January 1649* (London, 1897), p. 419.

3 William Cavert, *The smoke of London: energy and environment in the early modern city* (Cambridge, 2016).

4 Classic discussions of anti-popery include John Miller, *Popery and politics in England, 1660–1688* (Cambridge, 1973); Peter Lake, 'Anti-popery: the structure of a prejudice', in Richard Cust and Ann Hughes (eds), *Conflict in early Stuart England: studies in religion and politics, 1603–1642* (New York, 1989), pp. 72–106; Anthony Milton, *Catholic and reformed: the Roman and Protestant churches in early Protestant thought, 1600–1640* (Cambridge, 2002).

5 Key discussions of anti-puritan stereotypes and representations include Peter Lake with Michael C. Questier, *The Antichrist's lewd hat: Protestants, papists, and players in post-Reformation England* (New Haven, CT, 2002), chs 12–15; Lake, 'Anti-puritanism: the structure of a prejudice', in Kenneth Fincham and

Peter Lake (eds), *Religious politics in post-Reformation England: essays in honour of Nicholas Tyacke* (Woodbridge, 2006), pp. 80–97; Patrick Collinson, *Richard Bancroft and Elizabethan anti-puritanism* (Cambridge, 2013); Milton, *Catholic and reformed.*

6 Studies of gender roles and stereotypes of women include Laura Gowing, *Domestic dangers: women, words, and sex in early modern London* (Oxford, 1999); Sara Mendelson and Patricia Crawford, *Women in early modern England, 1550–1720* (Oxford, 2000). But, somewhat contrary to gender norms, London's women were actively engaged in social life and commerce, for which see Eleanor Hubbard, *City women: money, sex, and the social order in early modern London* (Oxford, 2012); Tim Reinke-Williams, *Women, work and sociability in early modern London* (New York, 2014).

7 Alex Gillespie, 'Social representations, alternative representations and semantic barriers', *Journal for the Theory of Social Behaviour*, 38 (2008), 375–91.

8 Ziva Kunda and Steven J. Spencer, 'When do stereotypes come to mind and when do they color judgment? A goal-based theoretical framework for stereotype activation and application', *Psychological Bulletin*, 129 (2003), 522–44.

9 This is a reading of Gillespie's categories of 'polemical' and 'emancipated' representations of alterity. He also offers a third category, 'hegemonic' representations, which are 'completely devoid of alternative representations'. This seems a doubtful category, especially since the example he offers, individualism, seems to be the subject of an implicit critique in his own description of it.

10 Since stereotypes are usually seen as negative or potentially damaging, this possibility has encouraging implications. However, it also means that stereotypes can lie dormant until they are called upon, as in the case of one who never seems to hold – and perhaps does not even perceive themself to hold – a stereotype, but then deploys it readily when changing conditions make it useful.

11 For tensions between city as community and city as space across early modern Europe, see Richard Kagan, '*Urbs* and *civitas* in sixteenth- and seventeenth-century Spain', in David Buisseret (ed.), *Envisioning the city: six studies in urban cartography* (Chicago, 1998), pp. 75–108; Yair Minztker, *The defortification of the German city, 1689–1866* (Cambridge, 2012).

12 On the evolving relationships between the livery companies and the growing metropolis, see Joseph Ward, *Metropolitan communities: trade guilds, identity, and change in early modern London* (Stanford, CA, 1997); Ian Anders Gadd and Patrick Wallis (eds), *Guilds, society, and economy in London, 1450–1800* (London, 2002).

13 On the process of becoming a citizen see Steve Rappaport, *Worlds within worlds: structures of life in sixteenth-century London* (Cambridge, 1989). For some of those excluded from citizenship, see Jacob Selwood, *Diversity and difference in early modern London* (Farnham, 2010). For urban citizenship's roles in local and national politics, see Phil Withington, *The politics of commonwealth: citizens and freemen in early modern England* (Cambridge, 2005).

14 Elizabeth McKellar, *Landscapes of London: the city, the country, and the suburbs, 1660–1840* (New Haven, CT, 2013).

15 Hubbard, *City women*, stresses the experience of young women in domestic service; Cavert, *Smoke of London*, argues that mobility was a key strategy for those bothered by ill health, urban pollution and associated complaints.
16 Paul Slack, 'Conceptions of the metropolis in seventeenth-century England', in Peter Burke, Brian Harrison and Paul Slack (eds), *Civil histories: essays presented to Sir Keith Thomas* (Oxford, 2000), pp. 161–80; Paul Slack, *The invention of improvement: information and material progress in seventeenth-century England* (Oxford, 2015), pp. 142–53.
17 Key collections exploring varying interpretations of urban growth include Lena Cowen Orlin, *Material London, ca. 1600* (Philadelphia, PA, 2000); Paul Griffiths and Mark Jenner (eds), *Londinopolis: essays in the social and cultural history of early modern London* (Manchester, 2000); Julia F. Merritt (ed.), *Imagining early modern London: perceptions and portrayals of the city from Stow to Strype, 1598–1720* (Cambridge, 2001); Deborah Harkness and Jean E. Howard (eds), *The places and spaces of early modern London*, special issue of the *Huntington Library Quarterly* 71 (2008).
18 Koji Yamamoto, *Taming capitalism before its triumph: public service, distrust, and 'projecting' in early modern England* (Oxford, 2018).
19 The relationships between classical literary traditions and urban expansion are explored by Ken Hiltner, *What else is pastoral? Renaissance literature and the environment* (Ithaca, NY, 2011). The key survey of literary representations of early modern London remains Lawrence Manley, *Literature and culture in early modern London* (Cambridge, 1995).
20 Ian Archer, *The pursuit of stability: social relations in Elizabethan London* (Cambridge, 1991); Paul Griffiths, *Lost Londons: crime, change, and control in the capital city 1550–1640* (Cambridge, 2008); T. G. Barnes, 'The prerogative and environmental control of London building in the early seventeenth century', *California Law Review* 58 (1970), 1332–63; Cavert, *Smoke of London*, pp. 48–54.
21 Felicity Heal, *Hospitality in early modern England* (Oxford, 1988).
22 Johann P. Sommerville (ed.), *King James VI and I: political writings* (Cambridge, 1994), p. 226. Spellings have been modernised here and in other quotations.
23 James Craigie (ed.), *The poems of James VI of Scotland*, 2 vols (Edinburgh, 1958), vol. 2, pp. 178–81, printing BL MS Egerton 923, fol. 21^{r}–^{v} and Add. MS 28,640, fol. 126^{v}–127.
24 For a similar, though far more sympathetic, account of how women, fashion, shopping and luxury contributed to the development of early modern London, see Linda Levy Peck, *Consuming splendour: society and culture in seventeenth-century England* (Cambridge, 2005).
25 John Earle, *Micro-cosmographie: or, a peece of the world discouered* (1628, STC/780:10), see under 'A plaine country fellow'.
26 Thomas Overbury, *New and choise characters, of seuerall authors together with that exquisite and unmatcht poeme, The wife* (1615, STC/1732:25), see under 'Countrey-gentleman'.
27 As Chapters 7 and 10 by David Magliocco and William Bulman suggest, virtuous moderation served as a powerful yardstick with which to diagnose

moral deviance and religious excess, and hence to stereotype Christian and non-Christian others. See pp. 229–36, 294–9. For attempts to incorporate urban growth and social change into prevailing models of moderation, see Joshua Scodel, *Excess and mean in early modern English literature* (Princeton, NJ, 2002), esp. ch. 4; Ethan H. Shagan, *The rule of moderation: violence, religion and the politics of restraint in early modern England* (Cambridge, 2011), esp. ch. 6.

28 Sir Richard Fanshawe, 'An ode, upon occasion of His Majesties proclamation in the year 1630. Commanding the gentry to reside upon their estate in the country'. In H. J. C. Grierson and G. Bullough (eds), *The Oxford book of seventeenth century verse* (Oxford, 1938), p. 450.
29 Cavert, *Smoke of London*, pp. 204–5.
30 Henry Glapthorne, *The lady mother* (Malone Society, 1958), pp. 8–9.
31 For politicised responses to London smoke during the 1620s and 1630s, see Cavert, *Smoke of London*, ch. 4; William M. Cavert, 'The environmental policy of Charles I: coal smoke and the English monarchy, 1624–40', *Journal of British Studies* 53 (2014), 310–33.
32 William Davenant, *Madagascar; with other poems* (1638), E1[r]–E2.
33 William Davenant, *The first days entertainment at Rutland-House* (1657), p. 53.
34 Davenant, *The first days entertainment*, p. 85.
35 William Davenant, *The vvitts A comedie, presented at the private house in Blacke Fryers, by his Majesties servants*, 2nd edn (1636, STC/6309), sig. B4[v].
36 *The works of Sir William Davenant, Kt.* (1673; Wing/207:09) (3rd pagination, 2).
37 John Evelyn, *Fumifugium: or, the inconveniencie of the aer and smoak of London dissipated* (1661).
38 Thomas Shadwell, *Epsom-Wells* (1673, Wing 296:13), pp. 5–7.
39 Shadwell, *Epsom-Wells*, p. 7.
40 Shadwell, *Epsom-Wells*, p. 43.
41 Shadwell, *Epsom-Wells*, p. 6.
42 Shadwell, *Epsom-Wells*, pp. 5–7.
43 Shadwell, *Epsom-Wells*, pp. 19–20.
44 Henry Higden, *The wary widow* (1693, Wing/1060:16), p. 1.
45 James Carlile, *The fortune-hunters, or, two fools well met a comedy* (1691, Wing/410:08), p. 67.
46 Shadwell, *Epsom-Wells*, p. 177.
47 *The new Westminster wedding or, the rampant vicar* (1693; Wing (CD-ROM, 1996)/P61), p. 1.
48 *Spectator*, ed. Donald F. Bond, 5 vols (Oxford, 1965), vol. 4, p. 390.
49 *Spectator*, vol. 4, p. 390.
50 *Spectator*, vol. 4, pp. 390–1.
51 *Spectator*, vol. 4, p. 391.
52 *Spectator*, vol. 4, p. 390. 'Sic visum Veneri; cui placet impares/Formas atque animos sub juga ahenea/Saevo mittere cum joco.' 'So Venus decrees, who finds it amusing to join incongruous bodies and minds beneath her metal yoke.' Horace,

Ode 33 in David Mulroy, trans., *Horace's odes and epodes* (Ann Arbor, MI, 1994), pp. 93–4. In the full ode, the word 'adultero' immediately precedes the quotation selected by *The Spectator*.

53 Raymond Williams, *The country and the city* (London, 1985), p. 64.

54 On the culture of urbane politeness see Lawrence Klein, *Shaftesbury and the culture of politeness: moral discourses and cultural politics in early eighteenth-century England* (Cambridge, 1994); Markku Peltonen, 'Politeness and Whiggism, 1688–1732', *Historical Journal* 48 (2005), 391–414; Brian Cowan, *The social life of coffee: the emergence of the British coffeehouse* (New Haven, CT, 2005), ch. 8.

55 Walter Yonge to John Locke, 10 November 1686, in E. S. de Beer (ed.), *The correspondence of John Locke. In eight volumes* (Oxford, 1978) vol. 3, p. 67.

56 William Roberts, *Memoirs of the life and correspondence of Mrs. Hannah More* (New York, 1834), vol. 1, p. 140, and a similar letter at p. 176.

57 [Georgina Spencer Cavendish, Duchess of Devonshire], *The sylph* (1779), pp. 24, 28; a similar usage appears in *Sophronia: or, letters to the ladies* (1761; 1775 edn), p. 58.

58 A. M. Wilberforce (ed.), *Private papers of William Wilberforce* (London, 1897), p. 4. Other letters using the phrase include: Hester Chapone to Rev. Burrows, 22 September 1764, in *The works of Mrs Chapone*, vol. III. *Life and posthumous works* (London, 1807), p. 163; Elizabeth Montagu to the Duchess of Portland, 6 December 1783, in Historical Manuscripts Commission, *Calendar of the manuscripts of the Marquis of Bath, preserved at Longleat, Wiltshire* (1904), vol. 1, p. 351.

59 Lake, 'Anti-popery', p. 74.

60 Richard Savage, 'The volunteer laureate. A poem on Her Majesty's birth-day, 1734–5. No. IV', *The works of Richard Savage, Esq.* (London, 1778), vol. 2, p. 229.

61 *The canary bird or, gentlemen and lady's polite amusement* (1760), p. 21.

62 Gillespie, 'Social representations'.

9

Laboratories of subjectification: characters and stereotypes in late Stuart and Georgian theatre

Bridget Orr

The 'stereotype' is a category elaborated by Walter Lippmann which migrated many years ago from twentieth-century American sociological discourse into humanities disciplines. Although invoked by literary scholars interested in analysing conventional characterisations in terms of gender, race, religion, ethnicity, class and sexual orientation, reliance on the term has been limited because the reductive and coercive dimensions of the stereotype are not only suspect in themselves but often seem too crude to illuminate the more subtle and ambiguous effects of literature and performance. Undoubtedly the most influential repurposing of the category in literary scholarship is Homi Bhabha's mobilisation of the term in his much-republished essay 'The other question: stereotypes and colonial discourse', a foundational text in post-colonial scholarship.[1] Bhabha's essay identifies the stereotype as the master trope of colonial discourse, a rhetorical strategy intended to create subject nations through rendering people knowably, visibly 'other', constructing populations of 'degenerate types' on the basis of racial origin to justify conquest. Bhabha is concerned with the processes of subjectification enabled by stereotyping rather than identifying the positive or negative valences of images, but he also shows how the apparent fixity of stereotypes is repeatedly transgressed by differences which reveal the limits and instability of colonial discourse and thus the possibilities of subversion and resistance.

Bhabha's work is illuminating in thinking about the later Stuart and Georgian theatre as a central location in the construction of colonial discourses facilitating the continuous expansion of imperial power in this period. At the same time, however, it is important to bear in mind that the stereotype is not the only rhetorical category the primary function of which was to establish fixed, knowable and visible subjects. The early modern European theatre inherited from Greek and Roman drama a range of figures known as stock characters, including the jealous patriarch, the bombastic soldier, the naive rustic and the cunning slave.[2] As with the stereotype, these characters' fixity serves to underscore their essentialising function as representative embodiments of particular social and sexual types. Chapters in this volume have shown the remarkable degree to which early modern men and women contested negative stereotyping to which they were exposed. Here I wish to argue that frequently theatrical stock characters themselves reveal a degree of significant divergence from their models, a process that not only has a powerful individuating effect but serves to underscore the role of performativity in subject formation on and off the stage. Notwithstanding the views of Romantic critics, whose fetishism of Shakespeare as the creator of characters with unique and complex individual personalities we have inherited, the universal dependence of early modern theatre on stock types serves as a reminder that subjectification *per se*, not just that of colonial subjects, depends on our being cast in gendered, raced, classed and sexual roles from our first appearance in the *theatrum mundi*. One of the greatest fascinations of theatre is witnessing the process by which individuation is constructed through characterological deviation from a normative role, thereby offering a model and a commentary on the processes of self-fashioning in which we are all imbricated. The proliferation of stereotypes in late Stuart and Georgian plays can be seen not as a sign of an aesthetic defect but as offering a particularly rich series of case studies revealing the workings of social casting and the ensuing negotiations that lie at the heart of this volume.

The importance of stock types and stereotypes in late seventeenth- and eighteenth-century drama arises in part from the theatre's dependence on a series of particular genres, all of which employed predictable figures. Manners comedies, comedies of intrigue, sentimental comedy, heroic tragedy and she-tragedy all deployed character types with which contemporary spectators were fully familiar. The theatre largely depended on an equally familiar set of play texts which formed a stable repertory, in which certain stock parts were frequently performed by particular actors. The genres themselves both encoded social, political and cultural tensions, such as anxieties over companionate marriage or the rise of the 'monied interest', and were shaped by the capacities and theatrical skills of charismatic performers. Within this largely stable and predictable theatre system, new kinds of character emerged by virtue of their contrast with or development of well-known types.

Theatre as laboratory of subjectification

When late eighteenth-century critics and scholars looked back at Elizabethan and Jacobean drama, they saw characters – larger-than-life protagonists like Lear, Macbeth, Hamlet, Richard III and Prospero but also such memorable figures as Falstaff, Malvolio, Iago, Jacques and Beatrice.

So compelling were such figures that they bred a new form of dramatic scholarship, practised by scholars like William Richardson and critics like William Hazlitt, which explored the complexities and ambiguities of these inimitable persons. Richardson's *Essays on Shakespeare's Dramatic Characters* (1812) went through many editions and provided a powerful model of analysis that focused on figures whose lifelikeness Richardson ascribed to Shakespeare's unique ability to channel the feelings animating his creations, as 'the Proteus of the drama'.[3] Richardson believed that Shakespeare created characters through the imaginative inhabitation of their passions, in contrast to a dramatist such as Pierre Corneille who, he believed, simply (and infinitely less plausibly) 'describes' them from a thoroughly external perspective. In a challenging test case, moreover, Richardson explored what he saw as Shakespeare's originality in creating characters who exhibit 'national' characteristics, including in this category Jews, Africans, Scots, Irish and Frenchmen. He argued that no ancient comic dramatist, from Aristophanes to Plautus, produced stock characters determined by 'nation' and compared Shakespeare favourably with recent and contemporary playwrights who specialised in the recuperation of such figures, notably sentimental dramatist Richard Cumberland. Richardson argued that Shakespeare anticipated his successors by making his 'national characters' sympathetic individuals rather than the more usual 'aggregate of all the individuals that belong to one race or community'.[4] He observes that 'National Manners – of Jews, of Negroes, of Frenchmen; of Scotsmen and of Irishmen have with great success, employed the exertions of contemporary, or modern, ingenuity' but mostly, he emphasises, the effect of such representations is deliberately and degradingly 'ludicrous'. 'It is only with writers of superior merit, that we have such judicious discrimination as we feel illustrated in the Fluellen of Shakespeare, the Jew, and Colin MacLeod, of Cumberland',[5] he remarks, explaining that Fluellen, like Shylock and Othello, are representations of individuals who 'are not to be despised'.[6]

Richardson's attempt to harmonise Shakespeare's invention of stock types based on race, community or nation, whose later deployment he acknowledged was generally hostile, with his admiration for the dramatist's individuation of particular figures such as Fluellen, articulates a contradiction he cannot fully resolve. If Shakespeare was responsible for extending stock characterisation to invent figures primarily defined by race, ethnicity, nationality or religion, he had a crucial role in transforming a venerable staple of European comic drama into Bhabha's colonialist stereotype, a trope intended to define, degrade and rule. From this perspective, however persuasive their reality effect as individuated dramatic personae, characters such as Othello, Shylock and indeed Fluellen might be considered as no more than racist projections.

Is there a way through this problem? Northrop Frye came at the issue of stock type and individuation from a robustly formalist perspective that suggests a proleptic awareness of more recent formulations of subjectification as a general social process. Writing in 1953, with an impatient contempt for historicist critics of Shakespeare who read his plays primarily in terms of contemporary political reference, Frye argued that the playwright's characterisation was not shaped to refer to current political figures but was governed primarily by dramatic necessity.[7] Shakespeare, he claimed, used precisely the same cast of stock types who had populated drama for the last two and a half thousand years. He was not a different kind of dramatist to his peers – he was simply better, using 'the same formulas, but in a much more subtle, complex and unpredictable way'. Frye went on to write:

> It is because he can get every ounce of dramatic effect out of his situation that Shakespeare's characters seem so wonderfully lifelike. I am not trying to reduce them to stock types but I am trying to suggest that the notion of an antithesis between the lifelike character and the stock type is a vulgar error. All Shakespeare's characters owe their consistency to the appropriateness of the stock type which belongs to their dramatic function. That stock type is not a character but it is as necessary to the character as a skeleton to the actor who plays it.[8]

Frye's brilliant *aperçu* – that it is the variations and play on or difference from the stock character which creates the effect of lifelikeness or individuation – is consonant with modern accounts of subject formation that argue that we are all 'called' into a given social role. One famous formulation of this process is provided by Louis Althusser's theory of interpellation, in which we are 'hailed' into our subject position. Althusser identified families, schools and churches as 'ideological state apparatuses' that call us into being even before we are born, identifying us as, for example, Catholic, female, working-class.[9] A more recent version of this view is articulated by Judith Butler in *Gender Trouble*, in which she argues that we are cast as gendered, raced subjects within a heteronormative matrix that requires us to perform a given identity from our infancy.[10] In both these accounts, individuals do not express a deep interior personhood but are cast from birth in roles that many find onerous, even imprisoning, as in the case of those who reject their initial gender assignment. Stock types and stereotypes can thus be seen not just to encode specific ideological presumptions (about gender, sexuality, religion, class, ethnicity and so on) but, more importantly, to be a point of departure from which subjectification is established and (sometimes) contested.

One of the most significant dimensions of theatre is that the constructedness and conventionality of subject formation – dependent on a communal willingness to subject ourselves to shared fantasy in accepting artificial identities – is so acutely modelled by the experience of performance and of spectatorship. Audiences of early modern plays knew everyone in the dramas they watched had a conventional role, but theatrical texts and performers took great delight both in undermining and underscoring the arbitrary and fictitious nature of that imaginative presumption, not least through metatheatrical commentary. For all their overt polemical and ideological purposes, early modern theatres can be seen as laboratories of subjectification, in which the audience might witness elite men and rebellious women, revolting slaves and vengeful bastards exhibiting a refusal to accept their assigned roles and attempting to assert other particular or chosen forms of identity.

Later Stuart and Georgian plays: case studies

The theatre of the Elizabethan and Jacobean periods has been privileged by late twentieth-century scholars, who emphasised the institution's peculiar capacity to provoke reflection on the intrinsically social nature of subject formation, with *Hamlet* as Exhibit A.[11] This is not unconnected to the idolisation of Shakespeare's virtuoso characterisation of Hamlet by Romantic writers, who regarded Restoration and eighteenth-century theatre as inferior to the theatre of the late sixteenth and early seventeenth centuries. Late eighteenth-century commentators did name-check more recent theatrical figures, such as the Plain Dealer Manly, Sir Fopling Flutter, Captain MacHeath and the Fair Penitent Calista but these characters failed to generate the same depth of fascination as their predecessors. They were prominent because they were exemplary – they were recognisable as models and as types – they were imitable, sometimes most improperly so. William Cooke reports that magistrate Sir John Fielding, Henry Fielding's half-brother, 'once told the late Hugh Kelly', on a successful run of *The Beggar's Opera*, 'that he expected a fresh cargo of highwaymen in consequence at his office'. Upon Kelly's being surprised at this, Sir John assured him 'that ever since the first representation of this piece, there had been, on every successful run, a proportionate number of highwaymen brought to the office'.[12] Shakespearian avatars appear to have been harder to detect.

Differences between early modern and long eighteenth-century dramaturgy have generally been used to denigrate the latter, although the explanations for the inadequacy of Georgian theatre differ. To the question 'Why there are so few good modern Comedies?' William Hazlitt replied '[w]e are deficient in Comedy, because we are without characters in real life', arguing that by the early nineteenth century strong personalities had been reduced to 'spectators, not actors in the scene'.[13] After some brilliant gleams in the Restoration, the literary quality of theatre is regarded as declining while the power and prestige of the performer waxed in the Ages of Betterton, Barry, Quin, Cibber, Clive, Garrick, Siddons, Kemble, Jordan and Kean. The Elizabethan Age was the age of the dramatist, but the eighteenth century was the age of the actor. Even scholars of the period, such as Allardyce Nicoll writing in the 1950s, viewed eighteenth-century dramaturgy as largely valueless: 'with respect to the stage, the eighteenth century was in many ways a period of decay and disintegration ... perhaps the greater the oblivion that could fall on the dramatic productivity of those years, the better'.[14] In the 1970s and 1980s, more sophisticated explanations of this gloomy narrative were articulated by critics such as David Marshall, Richard Sennett and Jean-Christophe Agnew. In their accounts, as social personalities became more performative, dramatic personalities lost their representative power and theatrical writing gave way to forms better suited to express individual subjectivity, such as the novel.[15] Theatrical and performative metaphors were crucial in defining identity and relationships, but these critics uniformly agree that drama as a form and theatre as an institution degraded in the eighteenth century.

These judgements have come under pressure over the last two decades, in part because scholars take a more expansive view of the cultural significance of celebrity performance and partly through a recuperative attitude to eighteenth-century dramaturgy. Joseph Roach has argued that the theatre became the site of quasi-religious enchantment in an increasingly secular age, with theatrical stars the focus of devotional fan cults that still inform contemporary psychology.[16] He has also explored the ways performers were able to invest their roles with a sense of psychological depth, easier in the case of Shakespeare's brilliant characterisation but still possible with the threadbare scripts of late Georgian tragedy. Stereotypes enter our discussion in this context. Felicity Nussbaum has shown that actresses modelled adventurous forms of identity that laid the ground for new kinds of female selfhood. On the dramaturgical side, Lisa Freeman has suggested that the stage provided a powerful model of character – one situationally and socially inflected, shaped by generic constraints and expectations but powerfully resonant just the same – that rivalled the attractions of the mode of subjectivity supposedly articulated in the emergent form of novelistic fiction, complex interiority.[17] Freeman's argument is particularly suggestive for our purposes in that her stress on the way generic expectations shaped character types understood by actors and audiences alike meant a particularised character could emerge when created as a complex variant of a familiar figure. Freeman also reminds us that, along with the subtleties generated by the play on generic expectations, audience familiarity with aspects of the actors' and actresses' reputations and offstage lives frequently inflected both the delivery and the reception of their performances, reducing a sense of theatrical character as 'natural' but enforcing a belief in its existence as a complex, legible series of surfaces.

Further, during the eighteenth century, particularised dramatic stereotypes often assumed an extraordinary auratic power, generating multiple textual and dramatic representations as characters were appropriated by other writers and imitators, moving well beyond their original scene of production. An excellent example is Tony Lumpkin, Oliver Goldsmith's cunning yokel in *She Stoops to Conquer* (1773). Lumpkin is an utterly familiar stock type, the *agroikos* or rustic first named in Aristotle's *Nicomachean Ethics* and occurring frequently in ancient and early modern comedies. Although often simply a foil to more intelligent urban or higher-status characters, eighteenth-century rustics increasingly provided vertical invaders from the city with a run for their money in plays such as Charles Johnson's *The Country Lasses* (1715), George Lillo's *Silvia; or, the Country Burial* (1730) and John Burgoyne's *The Lord of the Manor* (1787). Goldsmith's Lumpkin is not the hero of the comedy but he dominates its action, successfully tricking all the apparently wittier and more sophisticated characters and ending by achieving his own emancipation from paternal authority. Crucially, his successful trickery is not that of the cunning servant (another stock type) but depends on his use of local knowledge, an ability to predict urban presumption and exploit outsider ignorance of local topography. Goldsmith's unsentimental but affectionate reworking of the country bumpkin in Lumpkin underscores his attachment to country life, the endangerment of which he mourns in the poem *The Deserted Village* (1770) at the same time as attacking the vices of commercial empire.

Lumpkin is a powerful example of the kind of character who generated spin-offs, prequels, sequels and fan lit in Georgian culture. The initial expectations for *She Stoops to Conquer* were low, but the casting was widely regarded as turning the play into a hit, with an initial run of twenty nights, a more-than-respectable figure given that authors were relieved if their plays ran for three nights and gave them a 'Benefit', the evening's takings. Recalling the initial run in 1803, 'The pic nic' remarked that 'the part of Tony Lumpkin was assigned to Quick and if we may compare great things to small, Booth gained no more fame in Cato than Quick in Tony'.[18] But the play became a repertory staple on the basis of its dramaturgy as much as its star performers, with Richard Sheridan including a rustic role (Bob Acres) in *The Rivals* (1775) two years later and Lumpkin himself reappearing in a successful farce by the prolific Irish comedian John O'Keeffe, called *Tony Lumpkin in Town* (1778). Commentary on the farce underscores the characterological continuity between Tony's two outings, with one reviewer remarking that Lumpkin 'appears still more of a country savage than he is drawn by Dr Goldsmith' while another expresses admiration for his sardonic commentary on 'macaronis', fashionable dandies whose excessive preoccupation with dress disturbed contemporary assumptions about masculinity.[19] In O'Keeffe's play, Lumpkin expands into a protagonist whose boisterous physicality and rhetorical 'savagery' enforces rather than delegitimating a conventional rustic critique of urban masculinity at a time when war with the American colonies put a premium on male aggression rather than politeness.

Proliferating national and ethnic stereotypes on stage

Tony Lumpkin's success provides a provocative example of the continuing theatrical and cultural power of stock types in eighteenth-century theatre, challenging the assumption that a shift towards a proliferation of stereotypical characters in drama from the late seventeenth century forward is a sign of dramatic debility. After all, as Chapters 2, 3 and 4 by Peter Lake and Koji Yamamoto have shown, Elizabethan and early Stuart plays also contained (and often invented) a range of stock types including the alchemist, the puritan and the projector, which firmly engaged with the advent of the Protestant Reformation, commercialisation and state formation. Looking at the rise and adoptions of the phrase 'sin and sea coal' in plays across the seventeenth century, William Cavert's Chapter 8 has shown that Caroline and post-Restoration plays both exhibited subtle acknowledgement (and even knowing acceptance) of urban sins of commercial consumption and sexual promiscuity. Thus, one should exercise caution when contrasting early Stuart and later Stuart plays. But it is certainly the case that, from the Restoration forward, predictable stereotypes are easily identifiable in dominant genres such as manners comedy or the heroic play, as stock types become even more emphatic than in earlier seventeenth-century drama. The comedy of manners is likely to include a (possibly reforming) rake; a witty heroine who may be a coquette (together conceived of as a 'gay couple'); a fop (a sexual and sartorial fool); a rattle (a talkative fool); a pert maid; and a pair of ageing, often inappropriately desirous, guardians, male and female, who act as blocking agents. A heroic play will include an ungoverned ruler, a Herculean hero, a domineering virago and a virtuous and pacific virgin. An Ottoman ruler in a heroic play is likely to be despotic, with at least one cruel and fanatical pasha or vizier, and his harem will likely include women of great passion, ambition and cunning.[20]

City comedies and comedies of intrigue expand the range of stereotypes, often along spatial as well as class and vocational lines. Easily gulled merchants and clownish country squires were joined by flotillas of navy officers with their own maritime argot, such as Ben in William Congreve's *Love for Love*; during the period leading up to the Act of Union in 1707, 'North Britons' or Scots proliferated in comedy, sometimes becoming the romantic lead. The expansion of trade and colonial activity introduced new comic types such as nabobs and planters, and the latter part of the period saw multiple iterations of cunning servants of African origin. The stage Irishman was a fixture from the appearance of Teague in Sir Robert Howard's *The Committee* (1672) forward.

A major factor in this proliferation of national and ethnic stereotypes is the increasing awareness that the theatre served as the mirror of the nation. Although the Restoration and eighteenth-century theatres were commercial operations, they were objects of intense interest to successive monarchs and governments and functioned self-consciously as arenas of interstate cultural rivalry. The enthusiasm of Charles II, in particular, for French dramatic genres and performance practices ignited a long-running debate over the extent to which English theatre was being infiltrated and at worst debauched by foreign influences. Under attack by champions of neoclassical decorum, the irregularity and excess of the English repertoire was frequently defended by reference to the peculiar political constitution of the British Isles, with its unparalleled degree of liberty. From this point of view, Shakespeare's highly individuated characters could be seen as consonant with his idiosyncratic dramatic structures, the latter's untrammelled mixture of low mirth, intense pathos and violence a striking (and to some Continental critics, savage) travesty of proper theatre. From the point of view of many English critics, however, Shakespeare's lack of decorum was held to reflect a native soil that encouraged imaginative originality and force.[21]

Michael Ragussis has been particularly interested in tracing the emergence of what he calls the multiethnic spectacle on the Georgian stage, noting that dramatic characters frequently embodied negative ethnic stereotyping but arguing also that audiences and dramatists often actively resisted offensive representations.[22] In his account, the stage was a space in which the circulation of stereotypes was contested. One of his several striking examples of such incidents is the success of the Jewish community in driving Thomas Dibdin's anti-Semitic *Family Quarrels* off the stage in 1802. But while there were some successful interventions in shutting offensive plays down, many such plays remained in the repertoire. Further, even when stock types of ethnicity, gender or religion were deliberately revised along 'positive' lines (as in the cases William Richardson cites), usually the resulting character still incorporated stereotypical features. Such 'individuated' figures thus remained in a kind of characterological prison insofar as their theatrical representation reiterated a particular ethnicity or religion or gender or class or occupation as the fundamental and inescapable ground of personhood. Perhaps it was in response to this proliferation of typology in characterisation (and casting) that Samuel Foote – known as the 'English Aristophanes' – achieved such success in dramatising and performing versions of real, identifiable people through the 1750s, 1760s and 1770s. A poor actor of repertory parts, Foote made a fortune imitating real people – including, bizarrely, a certain Mr Apreece who begged Foote to put him on stage – and changed his mind after a wave of humiliating notoriety that made his personal affectations a city-wide laughing-stock.[23] The dangers of such a career course were made plain when the Duchess of Kingston, in retaliation for his caustic depiction of her in *A Trip to Calais* (1775), not only had the play refused a licence but caused Foote's prosecution for sodomy and his premature death.[24]

Negotiating stereotypes: actresses, 'gay couples' and playwrights

Foote's unhappy experience suggests that generalised caricatures were safer than mimicry but the proliferation of dramatic stereotypes after 1660 has a lengthy back story. As we have noted, stock types that originated in Greek and Roman plays re-emerged in early modern English dramaturgy but their recirculation in *commedia dell'arte* also contributed to Spanish, Italian and French comedies that influenced Restoration English dramatists whose royal patrons had enjoyed such plays in exile. Thus, a turn to neoclassical and Continental dramatic models stuffed with stock characters, encouraged by royal patronage, combined with an ever more expansive spectatorship interested in seeing emergent kinds of social types to generate the stereotypical turn. These developments in taste aside, there remains the larger question of the extent to which new habits of thought and discourse which privileged categorical and systematic ways of thinking about peoples and cultures also reshaped the terms in which human difference might be represented and performed.[25]

To turn from the general to the particular is, however, to be reminded of the importance of individual performers and writers in this larger process. The most striking change in late seventeenth-century theatre is the advent of the actress. It is perfectly apparent that having 'real, beautiful women' on stage altered dramaturgy. The exploitation of female performers' sexual allure is obvious in the huge expansion of breeches parts, with over eight hundred created between 1660 and 1714 and an equally striking proliferation of 'couch scenes' (such as Desdemona being discovered in bed).[26] Increasingly women *en deshabille* were presented as victims of violence as well as seduction – in a notorious scene from Mary Pix's *Ibrahim the*

Thirteenth Emperor of the Turks (1696) the heroine Morena is shown bleeding and dishevelled after being wounded and raped, and Elkanah Settle's *The Conquest of China* (1676) ended with a pile of raped and murdered women on stage. Obviously, both these scenes not only emphasise women's corporeal vulnerability to male power but reinscribe stereotypical English assumptions about the violence to which women were presumed vulnerable in 'oriental' states. Sometimes however, women dramatists invoked such orientalist stereotypes of hyper-masculine despotic oppression to question English presumptions that their own gender order was superior to that of the Asian world, Delarivier Manley's *Almyna* (1703) being a case in point. Here, the text makes full use of the orientalising stereotypes of a harem setting populated by murderous mutes armed with strings. Importantly, however, the heroine's rational discourse reforms the hitherto ungoverned sultan. Her eloquent attacks on the degrading effects of miseducation and enclosure are as pertinent to the position of Englishwomen as to Arabians.[27]

While the advent of women actors as a class created new theatrical possibilities, particular performers were also strikingly influential in shaping dramatic stereotypes. An obvious example of this is the establishment of the 'gay couple', often described as the most important innovation in Restoration comedy.[28] While the pairing of a witty rakish hero and an equally articulate heroine had precedents in plays by Shakespeare, Richard Brome and James Shirley, it became a recurring element in comedy of this period and can be traced to the brilliance of Nell Gwyn in partnership with Charles Hart. From their first appearance as the anti-Platonic lovers in James Howard's *All Mistaken* (1665) audiences were highly enthusiastic about these partners who agreed to be 'as mad as we please'. Plays with similar couples – James Howard's *The English Monsieur* (1674) and Richard Rhodes' *Flora's Vagaries* (1663) – were revived to be played by Hart and Gwyn; the second Duke of Buckingham, George Villiers adapted John Fletcher's *The Chances* (1682) to provide a free-spirited role for Gwyn and in 1667 John Dryden wrote Florimell in *Secret Love* for Gwyn with Hart as her Celadon. *Secret Love* was followed by *An Evening's Love* (1668), George Etheredge's *She Would if She Could* (1668), Thomas Shadwell's *Epsom-Wells* (1672) and many others.

While Nell Gwyn's personality and reputation were crucial in the establishment of the witty heroine as a favoured stereotype, the gay *ingénue* outlived Gwyn herself. Further, a crucial dramatic element of manners comedy, the proviso scene in which the lovers mutually recognise the difficulties of marriage and try to safeguard freedom and commitment, points us to reasons beyond performative charisma in the popularity of these comic types. In a context in which the importance of love within marriage and a greater degree of equality between spouses were increasingly debated, often in terms that invoked contract theory, it is hardly surprising that spirited and independent heroines demanding greater freedom within marriage were popular.[29] It is also important to remember that the English increasingly thought of their irregular drama – and their comedy in particular – as reflective of the peculiar liberty they enjoyed in the political realm, so the freedom of thought, speech and conduct demonstrated by the witty heroine were also markers of a superior, more generous gender order, against which the confinement of women in Latin Europe and the Orient was implicitly and explicitly defined.

While Gwyn played a crucial role in the development of the madcap heroine, as Elizabeth Howe has shown, two pairs of tragic actresses were central to Restoration tragedy's repeated use of contrasting women locked in erotic rivalry. First Rebecca Marshall and Elizabeth Boutrell and then Elizabeth Barry and Anne Bracegirdle played chaste and gentle characters contrasted with figures of ungoverned passion. Marshall and Boutrell's initial pairing in William Joyner's *The Roman Empress* (1670) was followed by appearances in Dryden's *The Conquest of Granada* (1670), where Marshall played the wicked Lyndaraxa and Boutell the loving and virtuous Benzayda. These castings were followed by roles as the corrupt Poppea and the pure Cyara in Nathaniel Lee's *The Tragedy of Nero* (1674), the passionate Berenice and the pious Clarona in Crowne's *The Destruction of Jerusalem* (1677) and, most successfully, as Roxana and Statira in Lee's *Alexander the Great* (1677). The last play became a fixture of the repertoire and the rival queens Roxana and Statira were later played by Barry and Bracegirdle. In their pairing, Bracegirdle always played the innocent virgin, whether cast as Barry's rival, daughter or friend, while Barry, who excelled in tragedy, played the passionate 'darker woman' in plays including Congreve's *The Mourning Bride* (1697), William Mountford's *The Injur'd Lovers* (1688), John Bancroft's *King Edward III* (1690), Delarivier Manley's *The Royal Mischief* (1696) and Charles Hopkins' *Boadicea* (1697), among others.

These contrasted parts and casting, reiterating highly stereotypical characterisations of women as angelic or vicious, drew not just on ancient traditions of misogyny but on the sexual reputations of the actresses concerned: while Barry had a vivid personal life, Bracegirdle, 'the Diana of the Stage', was famously pure – on one occasion being sent £1,000 by a group of aristocratic male fans to celebrate her chastity. Barry's warmer reputation combined with her skill to inspire Thomas Otway, Thomas Southerne and Nicholas Rowe in their creation of the 'she-tragedy', a genre that departed from the heroic mode to focus on the sufferings of a victimised and sexually exploited woman. The debt these playwrights felt to Barry is succinctly stated in Southerne's dedication of the hugely successful *The Fatal Marriage* (1694): 'I made the Play for her part and her part has made the Play for me'. Elizabeth Howe argues that such was Barry's charisma and skill, she generated a new type of heroine – sexually passionate and unchaste but still deeply sympathetic, thus deconstructing the fundamental binary of female identity between virgin and whore – examples being Angelica in Aphra Behn's *The Rover* (1677) and Southerne's *The Maid's Last Prayer* (1693).[30]

Howe's virtuoso demonstration that plays inspired by actresses contributed hugely to modifying stereotypical assumptions in female roles is a crucial insight for the broader argument of this chapter. In real life, as on stage, influential actresses, when coupled with matching stories, helped challenge existing gender stereotypes while giving rise to new ones.

In other words, although the parts for women in drama after 1660 still drew on stock types, the range of those types expanded and female characters acquired new complexity. In discussing Shakespeare's characterisation of Imogen (from *Cymbeline*), Hazlitt remarks that '(Imogen) is only interesting herself for her tendency and constancy to her husband. It is the peculiar excellence of Shakespeare's heroines, that they seem to exist only in their attachment to others. They are pure abstractions of the affections.'[31] Hazlitt's admiration for these cipher-like figures is highlighted by his dissent from Colley Cibber's rather different estimate of the situation:

> Cibber, in speaking of the early English stage, accounts for the want of prominence and theatrical display in Shakespear's [*sic*] female characters from the circumstance, that women in those days were not allowed to play the parts of women, which made it necessary to keep them a good deal in the background. Does not this state of manners itself, which prevented them from exhibiting themselves in public, and confined them to the relations and charities of domestic life, afford a truer explanation of the matter? His women are very unlike stage-heroines; the reverse of tragedy queens.[32]

While overtly arguing against Cibber's suggestion that the presence of women actors changed female characterisation, citing different social customs as a cause of their previous uniformity and marginality, Hazlitt nonetheless implicitly acknowledges that female performance has reshaped women's parts by generating 'stage-heroines' and 'tragedy queens'. Distasteful and artificial he may have found them, yet such figures crowded the stage. But the quarrelsome and passionate virago was by no means the only heroine in town: the late seventeenth-century 'she-tragedies' were not populated by strident, squabbling 'rival queens'. Laura Brown has argued persuasively that the deeply feeling, tortured heroines of pathetic tragedies such as the eponymous heroine of Rowe's *Tragedy of Jane Shore* (1703) provided a model for the new-style protagonists of eighteenth-century domestic fiction, anticipating the creation of characters with a complex interiority we associate now with subjective depth and individuality – the very antithesis of the stock type.[33]

It is also important to bear in mind that the new characterisation of women in both serious and comic drama was informed by ethnic, religious and cultural stereotypes: in plays depicting the clash between 'the Crescent and the Cross', for example, generally the gentle figures of female virtue were Christian and the passionate viragos were Muslim. But again, ethnic and religious stock characters of both genders were often very deliberately reshaped: some women writers (such as Manley) remodelled viragos as embodiments of female rebellion. Tolerationist dramatists writing in the first half of the eighteenth century, such as John Hughes, also scrambled the characterisation of male and female Muslims alike in such plays as *The Siege of Damascus* (1718) and *Zara* (1736), both highly successful texts that presented Muslim characters as tolerant, rational and humane.[34] These latter modifications were driven by the dramatists' desire to mount enlightened, Whiggish arguments against bigotry, not by the availability of particular performers. Reshaping stereotypes required new writing as well as new performers.

Shaping and reshaping Jewish characters

The shared, alternating capacity of performer and dramatist to shape and reshape stereotypes is nowhere more apparent than in the extended oscillation in the eighteenth-century theatricalisation of Jews. In 1741, Charles Macklin appeared as Shylock in a version of *The Merchant of Venice*. Macklin is still credited, along with Garrick, with introducing a new, more naturalistic style of acting to the Georgian stage.[35] His performance as Shylock established not only a new mode of acting but a new version of the character. Shylock was previously played as a comic figure indebted to the *commedia dell'arte* tradition, most famously by Thomas Doggett. By contrast, Macklin prepared for the role through participant observation. As George Colman and Thomas Bonnell commented in *The Connoisseur* in 1754, 'he made daily visits to the centre of business, the 'Change, and the adjacent Coffee-houses; that by a frequent conversation with "the unforeskinned race" he might habituate himself to their air and deportment'.[36] He researched Jewish costume in Venice, discovering that Jews habitually wore red hats, and he pored over Josephus's *History of the Jews*, noting down high points in his commonplace book. He did not share his plans for his ambitious revisionist interpretation of the part with his fellow actors, who were as amazed as the audience by the overwhelming power of his performance. For the rest of the eighteenth century – up until Edmund Kean's equally revolutionary sympathetic reinterpretation in 1814 – Macklin's Shylock *was* 'the Jew of Venice'. This performance emphasised the most negative aspects of Jewish stereotyping: avarice, cruelty and vengefulness. The performance was so terrifying that George II was said to find it impossible to sleep after seeing it while one young man fainted when Macklin approached Bassanio with his knife ready to slice off the infamous pound of flesh. The German traveller Georg Christoph Lichtenberg, who witnessed Macklin's performance in 1775, had no doubt the performance was anti-Semitic, commenting 'the sight of this Jew is more than sufficient to awaken at once in the best-regulated mind all the prejudices of childhood against this people'.[37]

There is no more powerful instance of an actor's entrenchment of a stereotype on the eighteenth-century stage. But Macklin's performance did not go unanswered. Picking up the enlightened project of toleration initiated by Hughes and Aaron Hill, in 1794 dramatist Richard Cumberland expanded his mission to rebuke 'national reflections' and 'to do away with old prejudices; and to rescue certain characters from the illiberal odium to which custom has marked them'.[38] Having already rehabilitated the West Indian and the Irishman in *The West Indian* (1771) and the Scot in *The Fashionable Lover* (1772), Cumberland created a play, *The Jew*, in which Sheva, the title character, serves as the moral centre, educating and disciplining an unprincipled English merchant and rescuing needy Christians. The play was extremely successful and generated an enormous amount of public discussion.

Michael Ragussis credits Cumberland's play with softening the hardened anti-Semitism of Macklin's Shylock, not just through recording the enthusiastic contemporary reception but by analysing the play's commentary on the constitutive power of stereotypes. When Sheva is unveiled as a secret benefactor, not only the audience but the character himself is confused by the removal of his disfiguring persona. At the moment that Sheva is able to 'present' himself rather than be 'represented', Ragussis suggests, 'he finds it impossible to recognise himself in the praise of others', still trapped in the negative stereotypes of anti-Semitism.[39] This moment is another heightened reminder that identity is constituted through the repetitive re-enactment of an enforced social role, through interpellation and performance. An egregious mask might be forced onto an individual by a hostile society but, however disfiguring, it becomes an element of social personality that cannot simply or easily be removed.

Other scholars, such as Jean Marsden, regard *The Jew* with much greater scepticism, arguing that Sheva's unmasking simply recasts him as a secret sharer in Christianity. In this account, the Jew's recuperation made the

English audience feel complacently proud of their peculiarly tolerant and humane culture without causing any real questioning of prejudice.[40] But it is suggestive to consider that when William Hazlitt wrote in praise of Edmund Kean's equally revolutionary, because sympathetic performance of Shylock in 1814, he suggested that the brilliance of the role lay in its revelation of the way a brutalised person may become themselves an agent of aggression.

Theatre historians concur that Kean's revisionary interpretation of Shylock reflected his own bitter experience as an outcast, illegitimate, poor and perpetually insecure.[41] Whatever its sources, Kean's performance remains culturally and politically significant for the way in which it effectively sidelined Macklin's previously dominant interpretation, creating a complex and nuanced figure who served as a *locus* of sympathy rather than revulsion and fear. Like Macklin, Kean did not draw attention to his wholesale revision of the role in rehearsal and his performance, although initially poorly attended, fell on London audiences like a thunderclap. Deliberately using a style of acting the fluency and careful shading of which stood in contrast with that of his rival John Philip Kemble, Kean invested Shylock with an explosive feeling that, as Judith Page summarises, reinvented the character, challenged the Venetian stereotype of Jewishness and redefined the play as a romantic comedy. Page persuasively suggests that Kean's performance of Shylock not only drew on a new cultural veneration for ambiguity and empathy but points to a potential parallel with Mary Shelley's creation of Frankenstein's monster, in which the creator of monstrosity recognises that being characterised as malign by a scornful world actually generates disfigurement.

Accounts of Kean's transformational recreation of Shylock place a good deal of stress on his presumed identification with another 'outsider'. This understandable but perhaps problematic impulse to identify the player with the played recurs with Charles Macklin, a peculiarly fascinating figure in this context because he not only reiterated stereotypes as a performer and writer but also tried to modify them. His reworking of the stage Irishman in *Love à la Mode* (1758) is commonly reckoned to be the most successful rehabilitation of the figure, achieving wide popularity in its presentation of the Hibernian hero as a noble, brave and successful lover, even as he created a series of repellent Scotsmen in the forms of Sir Archy MacSarcasm and Sir Pertinex Macsycophant in *The Man of the World* (1785). There is no agreement over the extent to which the dramatic modification of the Irishman diminished prejudice but one of the most intriguing recent lines of argument on this issue points out that extant frames of analysis may be inadequate precisely because they are themselves entangled in stereotypical thinking. David O'Shaughnessy argues that it is wrong to think of Macklin as a 'mutilated Irishman', a perpetually angry Hibernian other raging against English oppression, pointing out that Macklin's extraordinary career – including an incident in which he killed a fellow actor in the green room by pushing a cane into his eye in a dispute about a wig – has made it easy to characterise him as a stock figure himself. This has prevented us from recognising the extent to which he was involved in the prosperous, intellectually and politically sophisticated circles of enlightened Irish in London. Thinking about Macklin as a committed Whig, well read in the Commonwealth classics of Algernon Sidney and James Harrington, with a wide variety of affiliations with affluent, not marginal, fellow Irish beyond the theatre, suggests his mobilisation of stereotypes – as in the case of his Scotophobic depiction of Sir Archy MacSarcasm – may be more strategic and contingent than it initially appears, servicing a Whig critique of corruption rather than expressing ethnic hatred.[42]

The genres that thrived in Restoration and eighteenth-century English theatre deployed highly conventional stock types, often modified or joined by new kinds of character who reflected changing social, economic and political realities. For much of the last three centuries, scholars and critics have denigrated this period of theatre by comparing its characterisation to that of Shakespeare and finding it artificial, predictable and narrow in comparison with the Bard's creation of memorable individuals. Such assessments fail to recognise not just the palpable richness of particular characters in eighteenth-century dramaturgy but also the larger fascination of the theatre system in which they played their parts. When we track the development of female characterisation in the Restoration, it becomes obvious that 'real, beautiful women', both players and playwrights, actively modified stock types and stereotypes, considerably expanding the repertoire of roles for women both onstage and off. Dramatists were equally concerned with generating or modifying new versions of familiar figures by creating civil Muslims, men of feeling, benevolent Jews and heroic Irishmen. More subtly, the theatre of the long eighteenth century used its dependence on stock types and stereotyping to model the process of differentiation from norms by which individuality is in general achieved, as characters emerge as complex variants of familiar social and dramatic roles. And in certain instances, the theatrical interrogation of and departure from stereotype revealed the intense brutality of subjectification in a hierarchical, intolerant and imperialist society.

Notes

1 Homi K. Bhabha, 'The other question: the stereotype and colonial discourse', in K. M. Newton (ed.), *Twentieth-century literary theory: a reader* (London, 1997).

2 See Erich Segal, *Roman laughter: the comedy of Plautus*, 2nd edn (New York and Oxford, 1987).
3 William Richardson, *Essays on Shakespeare's dramatic characters: with an illustration of Shakespeare's representation of national characters, in that of Fluellen*, 6th edn (London: printed for Samuel Bagster, 1812), p. 31.
4 Richardson, *Essays on Shakespeare*, p. 377.
5 Richardson, *Essays on Shakespeare*, p. 393.
6 Richardson, *Essays on Shakespeare*, p. 393.
7 Northrop Frye, 'Characterization in Shakespearian comedy', *Shakespeare Quarterly*, 4 (1953), 271–7.
8 Frye, 'Shakespearian comedy', p. 277.
9 Louis Althusser, 'Ideology and ideological state apparatuses (notes towards an investigation)', in *Lenin and philosophy and other essays*, trans. Ben Brewster (New York, and London, 1971).
10 Judith Butler, *Gender trouble: feminism and the subversion of identity* (New York, and London, 1990).
11 For influential discussions, see Catherine Belsey, *The subject of tragedy: identity and difference in Renaissance drama* (London, 1985; 2014); Jonathan Dollimore, *Radical tragedy: religion, ideology and power in the drama of Shakespeare and his contemporaries* (Chicago, 1984; Durham, NC, 2004); and Christopher Pye, *The vanishing: Shakespeare, the subject and early modern culture* (Durham, NC, 2000).
12 William Cooke, *Memoirs of Charles Macklin* (London: James Asperne, 1806), p. 64. Articulating one of the most ancient anti-theatrical fears, Cooke is emphatic about the ill effects of the 'lower orders' watching the play and 'having (their) ambition whetted to rise in a superior style': p. 63.
13 William Hazlitt, 'On modern comedy', in *The collected works of William Hazlitt*, eds A. R. Waller and Arnold Glover, intro. W. E. Henley (12 vols, London, 1902), vol. 1, pp. 10, 12.
14 Allardyce Nicoll, *A history of English drama, 1660–1900*, vol. 2, *Early eighteenth century drama*, 3rd edn (Cambridge, 1952), pp. 1–2.
15 See Richard Sennett, *The fall of public man* (New York, 1977); Jean-Christophe Agnew, *Worlds apart: the market and the theater in Anglo-American thought 1550–1750* (Cambridge, 1986); and David Marshall, *The figure of theater: Shaftesbury, Defoe, Adam Smith and George Eliot* (New York, 1986).
16 Joseph Roach, *It* (Ann Arbor, MI, 2007).
17 Felicity Nussbaum, *Rival queens: actresses, performance and eighteenth-century British theater* (Philadelphia, PA, 2013) and Lisa A. Freeman, *Character's theater: genre and identity on the eighteenth-century stage* (Philadelphia, PA, 2002).
18 'The pic nic', *The Theatre*, London: Issue 2 (15 January 1803), 49.
19 'Short account of Tony Lumpkin', *The Universal Magazine*, 62:434 (June 1778), 367–8.
20 English depictions of Ottoman Muslims are discussed in William J. Bulman's Chapter 10.

21 For discussions of these issues, see Michael Dobson, *The making of the national poet: Shakespeare, adaptation and authorship, 1660–1769* (Oxford, 1992); Bridget Orr, *Empire on the English stage, 1660–1714* (Cambridge, 2001) and Freeman, *Character's theater*.

22 Michael Ragussis, *Theatrical nation: Jews and other outlandish Englishmen in Georgian Britain* (Philadelphia, PA, 2010).

23 For a discussion of this episode, see Jane Moody, *Illegitimate theatre in London, 1770–1840* (Cambridge, 2000).

24 For a recent account of this unhappy story, see Matthew J. Kinservik, *Sex, scandal, and celebrity in late eighteenth-century England* (New York, and Basingstoke, 2007), pp. 177–92.

25 The classic account of this development is Michel Foucault, *The order of things: an archaeology of the human sciences* (New York, 1970; French original, 1966). See also Anthony Pagden, *The Enlightenment and why it still matters* (New York, 2013).

26 For the first and fullest discussion of this process, see Elizabeth Howe, *The first English actresses: women and drama, 1660–1700* (Cambridge, 1992). Many of my examples below are drawn from Howe.

27 For discussion of orientalist dramatic stereotypes, see Orr, *Empire on the English stage*.

28 For the inaugural account, see John Harrington Smith, *The gay couple in Restoration comedy* (Cambridge, MA, 1948). See also Howe, *First English actresses*, which reveals how important the actress was to the development of this staple of Restoration characterisation.

29 For a feminist assessment, see Carole Pateman, *The sexual contract* (Cambridge, 1988); for audience concerns, see David Roberts, *The ladies: female patronage of Restoration drama, 1660–1700* (Oxford, 1989).

30 See Howe, *First English actresses*, chs 3, 6.

31 Hazlitt, 'Cymbeline', in *Collected Works*, vol. 1, p. 180.

32 Hazlitt, 'Cymbeline', in *Collected Works*, vol. 1, p. 180.

33 Laura Brown, *English dramatic form, 1660–1760: an essay in generic history* (New Haven, CT, 1981).

34 For fuller discussion, see Bridget Orr, *British Enlightenment theatre: dramatizing difference* (Cambridge, 2019), pp. 60–112.

35 See William Worthen Appleton, *Charles Macklin: an actor's life* (Cambridge, MA, 1960).

36 *The Connoisseur* (31 January 1754).

37 Georg Christoph Lichtenberg, *Lichtenberg's visits to England: as described in his letters and diaries,* trans. and ed. Margaret L. Mare and William Henry Quarrell (New York, 1938), p. 40.

38 The phrase is taken from another play, by George Colman: 'Prelude', in *New hay at the old market: an occassional drama, in one act* (London: printed by W. Woodfall for T. Cadell and W. Davies, 1795), no page.

39 Ragussis, *Theatrical nation*, p. 117.

40 Jean I. Marsden, 'Richard Cumberland's *The Jew* and the benevolence of the audience: performance and religious tolerance', *Eighteenth-Century Studies*, 48 (2015), 457–77.

41 See, for example, Judith W. Page, '"Hath not a Jew eyes?": Edmund Kean and the sympathetic Shylock', *Wordsworth Circle* 34 (2003), 116–19.

42 David O'Shaughnessy, '"Bit, by some mad Whig": Charles Macklin and the theater of Irish enlightenment', *Huntington Library Quarterly*, 80 (2017), 559–84.

10

From Reformation to Enlightenment in post-Civil War orientalism

William J. Bulman

The Enlightenment has long been taken to have employed stereotyping in order to distinguish and define itself. Traditional historiography identifies a series of stereotypes that served as foils for the Enlightenment's commitment to philosophy and secular liberalism. First the impostor and the priest, and later the oriental despot, became regular targets of critique. This expanding range of targets is taken to match up with the Enlightenment's emergence as a species of political and religious radicalism and its evolution into a programme of domestic and colonial governance. Since the 1980s, however, the notion that the Enlightenment was inherently opposed to Christianity, emancipatory in its early stages and only later corrupted by an alliance with state power has slowly lost all credence. Today even many of the most strident and learned exponents of the traditional view, such as Jonathan Israel, grudgingly admit the existence of a Christian Enlightenment, even if they consider it backsliding and disastrous.[1]

Less ideologically loaded renderings of the Enlightenment are now readily available.[2] But they have not yet incorporated an understanding of Enlightenment stereotyping that is consistent with a recognition that the Enlightenment took Christian, authoritarian and imperialist forms from the beginning. This chapter extends our understanding of the origins and nature of the English Enlightenment's stereotypical repertoire by exploring its links to religious conformism, orientalism and colonial expansion. The discussion is focused on the later Stuart period but extends into the later eighteenth century. Its primary aim is to clarify how the politics of stereotyping related to popery and puritanism (discussed above by Harris, Lake, Peters and Morton) were transformed and deployed in Enlightenment depictions of societies outside western Europe, and in particular the Ottoman empire. This was one way in which post-Reformation stereotypes enjoyed wide currency well beyond the end of the seventeenth century, lending themselves, on new frontiers, to discovery, edification, polemics and propaganda.[3]

The Restoration era was a crucial moment in the transition from Renaissance and Reformation to Enlightenment in England. The emergence of Enlightened stereotypical discourse is one of many clear indicators. Two of the most important post-Reformation polemical discourses – anti-puritanism and anti-popery – were central to the development of early Enlightenment forms of stereotyping that had potentially universal application.[4] The post-Civil War universalisation of anti-popery has already been observed by a number of historians. Steve Pincus, for instance, has documented the partial shedding of the theological content of popery and universal monarchy in international politics. After the Restoration, these two terms became so ideologically and referentially capacious that they were applied to a variety of the English state's alleged enemies – most importantly, to France and the Netherlands. Popery and universal monarchy obviously no longer necessarily referred exclusively to the pope, to monarchies or even to Catholics. Instead, they signified the seeking of universal dominion and the actions that conduced to it. They could be applied both to Catholic tyrannies and to Protestant republics.[5]

Mark Goldie and Justin Champion have observed similar developments in their examinations of connections between English religious politics and the early Enlightenment. In the later Stuart period, they have shown, Christianity in general was described as an imposture for the first time, at least in England. Around the same time a new Whig term of abuse, 'priestcraft' (apparently coined by James Harrington, a republican proponent of civil religion, in 1657), became a central slogan of the English Enlightenment. Priestcraft was, in Goldie's words, 'popery universalized'. All religious leaders, the logic went, had a tendency to behave in a manner once specifically associated with the pope and his priestly minions. 'Priests' abused the unwarranted power they exerted over ordinary people in order to realise their own political ambitions or solidify their empires. In the process, they threatened both true religion and civil stability.[6]

There are, however, at least three things we have yet to appreciate about the emergence of a universal typology of religious corruption in the Restoration period. The currently available narrative reflects the remnants of Whiggery and insularity present in much recent work on later Stuart England. An expansive, early Enlightenment understanding of religious and political imposture and corruption was embraced by a far wider portion of the English elite than simply the Whigs and their republican predecessors. In the Restoration era this understanding was commonplace among both Stuart absolutists and Anglican persecutors. Secondly, the absolutist and conformist variants of this discourse were above all characterised not by a universalised anti-popery but rather by a universalised anti-puritanism. Thirdly, the early Enlightenment's new, secularised language of religious and political deformity was confined neither physically nor referentially to Europe. As England entered into an increasingly complex and intense engagement with the early modern Islamic empires and their Muslim, Jewish, pagan and Christian populations, these populations became central sites for the development of Enlightenment discourses of priestcraft and despotism that incorporated the languages of both anti-popery and anti-puritanism. Servants of the Restoration English empire, who led England's engagement with the Islamic empires, fashioned the emergent stereotypes of the early Enlightenment while promoting their political, economic and religious agendas abroad.

As this all suggests, there is in fact a direct historical relationship between post-Reformation stereotyping and modern British orientalism. This relationship cannot be understood simply by supposing that the universalist stereotypes of the English Enlightenment emerged exclusively from the discourse of anti-popery. This supposition inevitably leads one to over-emphasise the foundational, central role of enemies of the Church of England in the English Enlightenment. Moreover, historical treatments of general developments in early modern Europeans' political thinking about the Islamic empires exhibit similar tendencies for similar reasons. They have yet to take adequate account of the crucial shifts in orientalist discourse that resulted from the employment of post-Reformation, intra-Protestant stereotyping and led to distinctive, Enlightened forms of political thinking about non-Christian religions and societies.[7] The later seventeenth century is the moment at which the relationship between universalised forms of post-Reformation stereotyping and Enlightenment depictions of non-Christian religions and societies crystallised.[8]

This chapter maintains that any plausible account of the transformation of religious stereotyping that occurred in later Stuart England must recognise the primacy of civil stability and the centrality of conformist Anglicanism in the early Enlightenment. It must also place the English religious stereotyping examined throughout this volume in its European and global contexts. This perspective first allows us to see that both anti-puritanism and anti-popery, directed against multiple targets in different ways by figures of varying ideological affinities, provided the basis for an Enlightenment language of religious corruption that was employed both domestically and abroad. Second, this perspective exposes the fact that the constellation of Enlightenment stereotypes with roots in post-Reformation polemic was hardly limited to the languages of priestcraft and imposture. It was equally constituted by the languages of enthusiasm and fanaticism. Third, this perspective illuminates the fact that conformist and Tory elements were just as instrumental in the emergence of the notions of priestcraft and imposture as their religious and ideological opponents were. After all, as Noel Malcolm has recently made clear, the discourse of imposture, both originally and in its early incarnations, was largely employed by establishment figures.[9]

Finally, and most importantly, this perspective allows us to explain how the universalisation of post-Reformation stereotyping occurred: not simply by means of intra-English stereotyping but also by the application of stereotypes that originally developed within intra-Christian contexts to all the known religions of the world. In other words, the post-Reformation languages of religious corruption were not artificially or philosophically universalised by a radical clique. They were empirically universalised in an intellectual culture that was still relentlessly historical in orientation by writers of a wide variety of ideological orientations.

All these correctives emerge simultaneously if we take a close look at the learned writing of the travelling historians and orientalists of England and its empire. These men – servants of the trading companies, the church and the Crown – were immersed in the historical culture of the late Renaissance and the early Enlightenment. They used this background to craft scholarly reports on the Islamic empires, their inhabitants and the history of Eastern religions. They operated within a political culture of counsel, propaganda and information management. Historical scholarship conceived in this milieu was inherently rhetorical and ideological, but it simultaneously adhered to the latest methodological standards for uncovering 'matters of fact'. It was founded upon an assumption that both the wise management of politics and religion in these empires, and the instability, decline and excesses of the same polities, yielded important lessons for English statesmen and churchmen who sought to manage better their dominions within and without the British Isles, to conduct foreign policy and to convert Jews, pagans and Muslims to Christianity. The late humanist, global understanding of the Republic of Letters that these men had internalised dictated that useful knowledge about the histories of Asia and Africa was to be sought from the non-European inhabitants of these continents, their literary traditions and their public records.[10]

It should be clear already that the orientalist works under study in this chapter are selected from a much smaller body of texts and authors than the one famously surveyed by Edward Said from the late eighteenth century onwards. They were at least in part historical works, whether they described the ancient past or the contemporary world. They featured both performances of erudition and appeals to wider bodies of educated readers, in varying proportions. They were normally intended as works of political counsel. This meant that in an ostensible effort to aid the ongoing work of the imperial state or the church they provided sustained analyses of particular Islamic empires. The polemics surrounding Said's *Orientalism* do not provide a reliable guide to such works because of the dichotomy they establish between scholarship and the exercise of power. Said, of course, was well aware that many orientalist texts improved the accuracy of Western understandings of Islamic societies, praised these societies in important ways and drew comparisons between the laudable characteristics of the East and the West. He was also largely uninterested in these facts and, in isolation, none of these facts is of any importance to the present chapter either.[11] The orientalist histories of the later Stuart period never dwelled exclusively on either difference or critique. They probed common ground and regularly praised the political and religious wisdom of non-Europeans. But this chapter is concerned more generally with the fact that oriental scholarship and writings derived from it – whether plentiful or deficient in factual veracity – were without exception important political resources.

As a result, these works' content was fundamentally determined by their utility and legibility for Europeans. That criterion of utility could lead and did lead to a body of writing that varied significantly in its content and ideological orientation. Depending upon what activities it was meant to motivate or guide, the utility of any given orientalist text could rest upon varying doses of inaccuracy and accuracy, sophistication and simplicity, likeness and difference, native informants and armchair erudition. This is why the stereotyping described below is best appreciated as a practice of both analysis and critique. While the particular geographical and demographic foci of the later Stuart orientalist texts under examination here varied enormously, the likenesses and continuities between them are equally important. Orientalism, when applied to any particular part of the Islamic empires, was both ideologically multivalent and intended to mobilise political activity with recourse to either counsel or propaganda and polemic.[12]

From Renaissance and Reformation to Enlightenment

Civil and natural religions were the usual antidotes to religious violence prescribed by the writers of the early Enlightenment. These religions of peace were typically described not in philosophical treatises but in historical narrations and descriptions. These histories tended not to be positive in nature because early Enlightenment writers largely followed their late humanist predecessors in assuming that religions of purity and order were best described by reference to their opposites. The writing of histories of religion had been spurred and motivated by confessional conflict, missionary zeal and imperial aggression since the sixteenth century. Catholics and Protestants identified idols, superstitions and other forms of corruption on a global scale – among fellow Christians and unbelievers, in the past and in the present, and at home and abroad. Employing techniques developed in the late Renaissance and Reformation, they gradually assembled a global history of religious imposture, conspiracy and ignorance. Yet the terrestrial causes of error did not exclusively consume their attention until the later seventeenth century. It was at this point that they were first able to describe the universal features of religious corruption without recourse to theology or demonology. Eastern religions, in particular, had traditionally been derided with primary reference to their diabolical origins.[13]

English developments were variants within a pan-European process. From Elizabeth's reign onwards, the most important discourses employed for diagnosing and narrating religious corruption – anti-popery and anti-puritanism – slowly became universalised in both their content and range of application. Before the end of the sixteenth century, anti-popery's ambit had been extended beyond Protestant polemics against Continental Catholicism and its alleged English remnants. As suggested by Harris, conformist divines in the reigns of Elizabeth I and the early Stuarts regularly tarred the behaviour and political thinking of *puritans* with the brush of anti-popery. From the moment this was first done in the 1570s, the claim that puritanism was popish became an element of the broader discourse of anti-puritanism.[14] Lengthy, derisive descriptions of puritan theology, ecclesiology, pastoral work and piety claimed to reveal the hypocrisy, libertinism, theatricality, delusion, divisiveness and sedition of the godly.[15] At the same time, anti-puritans brought anti-popery itself into contestation by espousing points of practice and doctrine that other Protestants viewed as popish. And by the early Jacobean period, the enemies of popery were indulging in detailed comparisons between popery and paganism. They were also expanding their analytical gaze by turning their attention to the more obviously political and international dimensions of Catholicism. Now Catholic princes joined the pope as the great architects and masterminds of popery: all were would-be universal monarchs. As these comparative practices developed, anti-popery and anti-puritanism came to draw on a humanist discourse of superstition.[16] This helped them slowly to separate from their theological moorings and their original polemical triggers.

The widening scope of English anti-popery and anti-puritanism thus contributed to a development of even greater scale: the use of scholarly tools developed in the late Renaissance and the Protestant and Catholic Reformations to fashion the characteristically anthropological understanding of religion that typified the Enlightenment. Erudite Christians in early modern Europe possessed a range of techniques for diagnosing religious corruption that were ancient in origin. Historians and antiquarians on both sides of the Reformation divide used these tools to furnish accounts of idolatry, superstition and other types of error. They observed these deformities among fellow Christians as well as among the pagans of antiquity and contemporary Asia, Africa and America. The crucial transformation in this documentation of corruption occurred in the later seventeenth century. Some scholars decided no longer to interpret idolatry and other instances of religion gone wrong with recourse to theology and demonology. Instead, they moulded the ancient understanding of superstition into a sociological model of religion. This ultimately allowed Voltaire in 1764 to dismiss the term 'idolatry' as useless and pejorative.[17]

This development occurred on three main fronts: confessional polemic, antiquarian treatises on ancient religion and travellers' accounts of Europe's new worlds. Scholars working in each area were driven by confessional, missionary and imperial goals. Utilising the techniques of late humanist historical criticism, they identified dynamics common to Christianity and other religions, both ancient and contemporary.[18] The fecundity of this comparative style of inquiry was clear enough in England by the early seventeenth century that in 1613 popery could be identified among the Native Americans of Virginia who, according to Samuel Purchas, accepted the doctrine of the immortality of the soul. This doctrine was the foundation for their popish belief that works on Earth determined eternal rewards and punishments. Even the immortality of the soul itself was supported by popish argumentation: the Native Americans, Purchas wrote, 'tell tales of men dead and revived again, much like to the popish legends'.[19]

Like his Catholic contemporaries, Purchas mostly examined modern paganism through an ancient lens. But the utility of comparing modern paganism to Catholicism was still compelling. By the middle of the seventeenth century, other English Protestants had become so accustomed to applying anti-popery and anti-puritanism to the study and the criticism of non-Christian religions that this method rivalled ancient frames of reference in its importance. Especially in printed works that sought readerships somewhere between the scholarly and the middling and saw confrontation with corrupt religion as an unavoidable consequence of expansion, the discourses of popery, puritanism, enthusiasm, idolatry, superstition and priestcraft mingled constantly. At this point, they resembled a single, voluminous stream of historical knowledge more than they resembled separate traditions or discourses. In this form they were capable of yielding a typology of corruption and imposture. The Civil War was the crucial moment when this universalisation of anti-popery and anti-puritanism began to accelerate in England. Learned writers of all ideological stripes quickly developed a preoccupation with identifying the mechanics of religion gone wrong and the sources of political instability, whether populist or authoritarian. The conflicts among these writers were for the most part not intellectual in nature. Instead, commentators differed over which groups in English society were engaging in the sorts of behaviour that everyone knew hazarded another decade of devastation and extremism.[20] Anti-popery and anti-puritanism were among their most important analytical and polemical tools.

Sir Paul Rycaut on the Greek church and the Ottoman empire

My focus here will mostly be on English treatments of Islam, even though scholars working in the late seventeenth and eighteenth centuries described a variety of religions practised in the Islamic empires – including Judaism, Zoroastrianism, Hinduism and Christianity – as popish, puritanical, priest-ridden and conducive to tyranny. While anti-popery and anti-puritanism were only thoroughly universalised after the Civil Wars, some of the earliest humanistic travel writing dealing with Asian religion described Islam and the Islamic empires as popish and puritanical. Examples include the first extensive ethnographic text to emerge from the East India Company's activities in South Asia, the chaplain Edward Terry's *A voyage to East-India*. Mostly written in the 1620s but published in 1655, this book was rife with analysis of the popery and puritanism of Islam.[21]

In general, though, these were isolated developments prior to the restoration of the monarchy. By that time, those who sought to endorse their own particular version of a Protestant *via media* certainly had a developed stereotypical vocabulary at their disposal. One example would be Samuel Pepys, discussed by Magliocco in Chapter 7. These writers most commonly described religious corruption as popery, puritanism, fanaticism, enthusiasm or imposture. Again, by the Restoration period these stereotypical discourses were already and commonly being applied to multiple groups. Popery need not be Catholic, puritanism could assume many different, errant Protestant forms, fanaticism could be found in a variety of groups, enthusiasm was taken to be an all too widely shared trait and imposture crossed the Catholic–Protestant divide.[22] Yet while these discourses were generalised, they were hardly universal, since they still referred overwhelmingly to corrupt forms of Christianity.

The terrain quickly began to shift, however. This transition is most clear in the writings of those who directly served England's empire in the Mediterranean world.[23] These establishment figures also allow us to correct the bias that results from studying the universalisation of post-Reformation discourse solely from the perspective of freethinkers and republicans. The central portion of this chapter will explore the full contours of the early Enlightenment universalisation of anti-popery and anti-puritanism by paying close attention to the writing of one Mediterranean traveller, Sir Paul Rycaut. Rycaut was perhaps the pre-eminent English travelling historian of his day, and his works were crucial sources for many later Enlightenment writers, including Pierre Bayle, Montesquieu and the *philosophes*.[24] He is primarily known as a diplomat, consul and secretary who spent over a decade living in the Ottoman empire and became a member of the Royal Society. The relationship between his scholarly pursuits and his religious views, however, has been largely ignored. Like so many of the most talented orientalists of his day, Rycaut was a Tory Anglican conformist with (it appears) some Laudian inclinations in matters of piety. This structured the way he wrote about Islam and the Ottoman empire, but it also influenced his treatment of Greek Christianity.[25]

In the irenic and ecumenically minded preface to his *Present state of the Greek and Armenian churches* (1679), Rycaut attacked both Catholics and radical Protestants. He blamed 'the extreme ambition of the Roman Jesuitical clergy on the one side, and the too hot and blind zeal of some Pharisaical professors on the other', who dared to 'penetrate into the decrees of predestination, dispute the manner of the Holy Ghost's procession, and dive into the mysteries of Holy Trinity, and secrets of the eucharist', for the rift between the Roman and Protestant churches.[26] His irenicism, however, was no 'latitudinarianism': instead it seems to have been the sort of irenicism characteristic of so many Laudians, which very often entailed serious interest in union with Eastern Christianity.[27] In the same preface, Rycaut praised Greek Christians for how 'they are startled and affronted at the sentence of excommunication, how strict and frequent some are in their confessions, how obedient and submissive to the censure and injunction of the priest; which certainly do evidence some inward tenderness of conscience, and dispositions toward being edified'.[28] When speaking of England, while he lauded the 'daily lectures we hear from our pulpits' and the comparably wide access to Scripture in England, in order to compare his home country partially favourably with Greece, he immediately moved on to add that, for the most part, these Reformed traditions of active preaching and familiarity with the Word among the laity only 'serve to render us more blind, or perverse', because they had led English Christians to forget more essential traditions.[29] 'Who is it that values the excommunication of a bishop, or other ecclesiastical censures?', he complained, implying that his countrymen cared little for these processes.[30] 'Who accounts of vigils and fasts according to the institutions of the universal, and of their own church? Or weighs the private instructions of a priest, who is the monitor of his soul?' Here, Rycaut said, even conforming Anglicans were often guilty of a laxity that they would themselves describe as 'the characteristical point of a phanatick'.[31]

Rycaut went on to attack the arrogance of those who considered these institutions of 'the clergy's power' unnecessary. While these critics of the ministry believed 'that they are better instructed than to be guided by their priests or to stand in awe of the condemnation of a supercilious prelate', it was in fact the case that the 'humble and submissive' layman who was 'willing to be instructed' was 'a better Christian'.[32] Rycaut made a pointed argument for the restoration of priestly confession in the Church of England

and went on to expressions of nostalgia for the days of William Laud's dominance.[33] He speculated that had Cyril, a patriarch of Constantinople who published a rigorously Calvinist confession of faith in 1631, at that time 'spent some time in England, and there observed that purity of our doctrine, and the excellency of our discipline, which flourished in the beginning of the reign of King Charles the Martyr, and viewed our churches trimmed and adorned in a modest medium, between the wanton and superstitious dress of Rome, and the slovenly and insipid government of Geneva', he would have 'entertained a high opinion of our happy Reformation' and drawn 'a pattern whereby to amend and correct the faults of the Greek church'.[34]

Rycaut was not only something of an anti-Calvinist, as these excerpts make clear, but also a virulently anti-Catholic writer and politician. He detested Europe's aspiring universal monarch, Louis XIV.[35] Even so, in his most famous work, *The present state of the Ottoman empire* (1667), Rycaut warned against European elites' obsession with the French potential for universal monarchy because it distracted them from the Ottomans. Europe's governors were utterly mistaken in taking the Turks to be ignorant barbarians. This European ignorance was in his view partly responsible for the success of Ottoman aggression in European territories. The Habsburgs, in particular, made foolish peace treaties with the Ottomans because the Habsburg emperor was preoccupied by the French. Rycaut's description of Ottoman government was similar to his description of French government, but his normative judgement differed. He argued that tyranny was appropriate and prudent for a state constituted in the way the Ottoman regime was. Both the Turks and the French had embraced Justinian's notion of absolute rule. This was appropriate, Rycaut argued, for any state seeking universal dominion.[36] In his mind, the powerful link between popery and universal empire knew no religious or national boundaries.

For the purposes of this chapter, however, it is more important to appreciate the religious side of Rycaut's application and universalisation of stereotypes of Reformation-era lineage, and to consider his exploration of the political consequences of religious corruption. Rycaut described Islam in the Ottoman empire with recourse to the languages of both anti-puritanism and anti-popery. It was not, of course, that he was unaware of the fundamental differences between the Christian and Ottoman religions and empires, but that he used his understanding of Catholic institutions and puritan habits to guide his analysis of Islam at numerous points. Popish and puritan doctrines, ceremonies and political strategies, he argued, enabled the expansion and relative stability of the Ottoman empire.

Like adherents of Rome, Rycaut said, the Turks 'conceive that the civil law came as much from God, being delivered by their Prophet, as that which immediately respects their religion, and came with the same obligations of injunctions to obedience'.[37] Here the Ottomans mimicked the imperialist scheming of the Prophet himself, who 'made his spiritual power as large as his temporal'.[38] In the Ottoman dominions 'the dignity and authority of infallible determinations' in religious matters was granted to the mufti, 'the principle head of the Mahometan religion or oracle of all doubtful questions in the law'.[39] While the mufti was never contradicted on matters of doctrine, he was usually not a source of civil instability because 'his election is solely in the Grand Signior' and his judgements were regularly used to add religious legitimacy to the sultan's rulings.[40] In any case where the sultan could not procure the ruling he wanted, 'the mufti is fairly dismissed from his infallible office, and another oracle introduced, who may resolve the difficult demands with a more favorable sentence'.[41] Here Rycaut was describing Ottoman policy in terms of an understanding of popery appropriate to the second half of the seventeenth century, when pontifical claims for political superiority rang hollow, dependent as they often were upon Spanish or French cooperation. The mufti aimed not to protect the original intent of the Qur'an, but to adjust its authoritative meaning to imperial imperatives. 'Though they preach to the people the perfection of their Qur'an, yet the wiser hold, that the mufti hath an expository power of the law to improve and better it, according to the state of things, times and conveniencies of the Empire', Rycaut wrote. 'Their law was never designed to be a clog or confinement to the propagation of faith, but an advancement thereof, and therefore to be interpreted in the largest and farthest fetched sense, when the strict words will not reach the design intended.'[42] As in Catholicism, Rycaut suggested, honest exegesis had been sidelined in favour of evangelical and political strategy.

The materiality of Islam also mirrored that of Catholicism. 'The Turks are very magnificent in their mosques and edifices directed to the service of God', Rycaut wrote, 'and not only in the buildings, but the endowments of them, with a revenue which records the memory of the donor to all posterity and relieves many poor who daily repeat prayers for the souls of such as who died with a persuasion that they have need of them after their decease.' This belief was common despite the fact that it could not be linked to the contents of the Qu'ran.[43] Ottoman piety was in many senses a potent combination of the excesses of puritans and papists. 'The Turks', Rycaut continued, 'are certainly a very cleanly people in their exterior manner of living, as in their washings relating to their holy exercises and duties, they are very precise and superstitious; some of them believing that the very water purifies them from the foulness of their sins, as well as from the uncleanness of their bodies.'[44]

In his description of Ottoman religion, Rycaut also regularly described Ottoman ecclesiastical organisation as many would have described the

Roman. Imams, for instance, were to be understood as 'parochial priests'.[45] He emphasised what he called the prevalence of 'monasteries and orders of religious men' or 'friars' among the Ottomans. These units included the Sufi orders. He explained this with reference to Muhammad's supposed borrowing from Christianity. Nevertheless, he said, there was little evidence of Muslim religious orders prior to the early Ottoman era. This contradicted Ottoman claims that they were coeval with Muhammad. The Ottoman counterparts to Catholic religious orders joined those orders in attributing miracles to the founders of their traditions. The Ottoman monks, he wrote, 'incline to a pretended mortification and strictness of life, to poverty, and renunciation of the world's enjoyments, according to the devotion of Christians a thousand years past'.[46] The best-known inhabitants of the 'Mahumetan convents', the dervishes, 'pretend to great patience, humility, modesty, charity and silence, in presence of their superior or others ... They profess poverty, chastity, and obedience, like Capuchin friars or other orders of St. Francis.' Some dervishes, he claimed, 'exercise some kind of legerdemain, or tricks, to amuse the minds of the common people; and some really apply themselves to sorceries and conjurations by help of familiar spirits'.[47] Indeed, members of many orders were masters of priestcraft: 'notable sophisters and hypocrites, their secrets they reveal to none but those of their own profession, by which means they are able to cheat those of other religions'.[48] All the orders, in their monkery, also practised various extremes of asceticism and hermitry. Many monasteries had a patron 'saint' or master whom they honoured, and to whose tombs thousands made pilgrimage.[49]

What struck Rycaut most of all about Ottoman Islam, however, was its puritanism. Like Oliver Cromwell and Muhammad, the Ottomans built their empire on a false providentialism. They attributed military success to divine favour. Anyone who died in battle with infidels, they claimed, would be saved. 'The same argument', Rycaut pointed out, 'in the times of the late rebellion in England, was made use of by many, to entitle God to their cause, and make him the author of their thriving sin, because their wickedness prospered.'[50] The structure of Ottoman religious institutions also recalled the Cromwellian church. Rycaut noted that the mufti 'hath no jurisdiction over the imams, as to the good order or government of the parishes, nor is there any superiority or hierarchy as to rule amongst them; every one being independent and without control in his own parish'. This ecclesiastical form, he noted, 'may not unaptly seem to square with the Independency in England, from which original pattern and example our Sectaries and Phanatick Reformers appear to have drawn their copy'.[51]

The likenesses between Ottoman Islam and puritanism extended to doctrine. Continuing to survey Ottoman beliefs about providence and predestination, Rycaut noted that 'the doctrine of the Turks in this point seems to run exactly according to the assertion of the severest Calvinists; and in proof hereof their learned men produce places of Scripture, which seem to incline to the same opinion'.[52] Because Turks 'are of the opinion that every man's destiny is wrote on his forehead', their soldiers were ready 'to throw away their lives in the most desperate attempts', and they were taught not to fear the plague.[53] Some were such strict predestinarians that they denied the notion of human will and contended that even the smallest human action was divinely determined.[54] From time to time these opinions had led to antinomianism. A Muslim, some Ottomans claimed, 'though guilty of the grossest sins, is not punished for them in this world, nor receives his absolution or condemnation after death'. Puritanical Turks believed too that 'as impiety with the true belief shall never be punished, so piety and good works proceeding from a false and erroneous faith, is of no validity or power conducing to the fruition of the joys of paradise'. 'To these', Rycaut wrote, 'may not improperly be compared some sectaries in England, who have vented in their pulpits that God sees no sin in his children, and that the infidelity of Sarah, being of the house of the faithful, is more acceptable to God, than the alms, prayers and repentance of an erroneous believer without the pale and covenant of grace.'[55] In addition, many Ottomans had made a fetish of their spiritualism, arguing in their condemnation of the dervishes that 'the Qur'an expressly forbids all devotion and service to God with music'. Therefore, 'in calling their people to prayers, they use no bells'.[56]

In Rycaut's view, Ottoman Islam also exhibited, like puritanism, an inherent tendency towards a proliferation of conventicles and sects that often hatched rebellion. Some sects were politically acquiescent. They were careful never to 'derogate from the authority of their governors, or produce factions or disturbances of state'. In the Ottoman empire, unlike England, there was no automatic movement from heterodoxy to sedition.[57] 'These modern times', however, 'have produced other sects among the Turks, some of which seem in part dangerous, and apt to make a considerable rupture in their long continued union; when time changes and revolutions of state shall animate some turbulent spirits, to gather soldiers and followers under these doctrines and other specious pretences.'[58]

Ottoman disunity mirrored the fissiparous nature of puritanism. The main 'separatist' grouping in the empire disagreed amongst themselves so thoroughly on how properly to understand the equity and unity of God that they 'divided into two and twenty sects, which are maintained with that passion on all sides, that every party accuses his opposites of infidelity', spurred on in their division by 'wrangling sophisters'.[59] Members of one such group were

> of a melancholy and Stoical temper, admitting of no music, cheerful or light discourses, but confine themselves to a set gravity ... They are exact and punctual in the observation of the rules of religion ... In short, they are highly pharisaical in all their comportment, great admirers of themselves, and scorners of others that conform not to their tenets, scarce according them a salutation or common communication.

Others 'observe the law of Mahomet in divine worship with a strictness and superstition above any of the precisians of that religion', but because of their extremely low estimation of men's capacity for understanding the divine, they 'hold it unlawful to adjoin any attributes to God'.[60] These Ottoman separatists mirrored the divisive and hypocritical social practices of the godly in England. Many of the religious orders also engaged in a series of enthusiastic and mystical practices.[61] Another 'sort of fanaticks' of an antinomian stripe 'pretend to religion' by means of 'libertinism and looseness in their conversation'.[62] Indeed, 'fools and frantick people' had long 'been had in honor and reverence amongst the Turks, as those whose revelations and enthusiasms transported [them] out of the ordinary temperament of humanity'.[63]

Similarly, in the early empire, there appeared 'a sort of phanatick Mahometans which at first met only in congregations under pretence of sermons and religion, appeared afterwards in troops armed against the Government of the Empire'. These revolutionaries saw that 'broaching a new sect and religion' and 'persuading the people to something contrary to the ancient Mahometan superstition' was the best way to 'raise sedition' and civil war. Their leader, Rycaut reported, 'vented doctrines properly agreeing to the humor of the people, preaching to them freedom and liberty of conscience and the mystery of revelations'. He 'used all arts in his persuasions, with which subjects used to be allured to a rebellion against their prince', and the main weapon of these religious rebels was preaching. All this, Rycaut noted, showed 'that the name of God's cause, revelations, liberty and the like, have been old and common pretences and delusions of the world, and not only Christians, but infidels and Mahometans have wrote the name of God on their banners, and brought the pretence of religion into the field to justify their cause'.[64]

The presence of (in Rycaut's estimation) well over seventy sects in Ottoman Islam suggested to him that England was to be acquitted 'from the accusation of being the most subject to religious innovations'.[65] The Ottoman spectacle of sectarian proliferation was attributable to 'superstitious and schismatical preachers', and thus to popery and puritanism.[66] 'We might proceed', he wrote, 'to recite as many sects as there are towns or schools in the empire, every one of which some pragmatic preacher or other have always started a new opinion, which can never want disciples.' It was as if 'the diversity of opinions in Turkey is almost infinite'.[67] Every prospective sectmaster 'who was but a form above a meer pedagogue, and reads a few books of the Arabian fables, esteems himself of mean account, if by some singular opinions which he instils in his disciples, he distinguishes not his gymnasium from the common and inferior schools'.[68] In this way, Rycaut thought not simply about Islam and Ottoman Islam in general, but about division *within* Islam, in terms of Christian religious corruption.

Some of the Ottoman sects even seemed popish in certain respects. The adherents of one rejected the doctrine of predestination, 'affirming that everyone is a free agent, from whose will as from the first principle all good and bad actions flow and are derived, so that as with just reason God crowns man's good works with the rewards of bliss and felicity; so on the other side justly punished his evil actions in the world, and in the next to come'.[69] Others argued 'that a man fallen into any great or mortal sin, is put into the condition of a desertor of his faith; and though he be a professor of the true belief, shall yet without recovery forever be punished in hell'.[70] Still others adopted a doctrine approaching that of purgatory, believing that 'whosoever hath but the weight of an atom remaining in his heart of faith, shall in due time be released from the fiery torments; for which cause some sects among the Turks use prayers for the dead'.[71] At a final extreme, some sectarians, 'though Mahometans in profession, seem yet to run contrary to the stream and general consent of all its professors who give themselves commonly the title of enemies and confounders of idolatry', because their men could be found 'commonly worshipping the sun, and the women the moon, and others the Arctic pole'.[72] In the variety of Ottoman Islam Rycaut saw reflected nearly every form of religious corruption familiar to Christians.

The eighteenth century

Rycaut's histories had counterparts among the writings of East India Company and Church of England servants working in South Asia during the later Stuart era. Between 1696 and 1702 the physician John Fryer, the chaplain John Ovington and the ambassador William Norris all composed or published historical accounts that followed a pattern established by English scholars of the Ottoman and Moroccan empires. The Mughal world, they argued, was a theatre of popery, puritanism, priestcraft and despotism.[73]

The author of the most vivid account of the three, Fryer, spent nearly a decade serving the East India Company in the Safavid and Mughal empires between 1672 and 1682. He published his *New account of East-India and Persia* in 1698. It described Hinduism as idolatry supported by the priestcraft of the Brahmins and the enthusiasm of monks, saints, pilgrims and ascetic impostors.[74] Fryer was, however, far more interested in Islam. The Mughals were 'of a more puritanical sect' of Islam than the Persians, he said. He had witnessed the florid piety of Mughal 'conventiclers' and other hypocritical holy men, who professed strict religious observation but practised licentiousness. He had also observed a recent crackdown on most religious holidays by 'a religious bigot of an emperor', Aurangzeb, who believed that such holidays gave 'opportunity' to unbelievers 'to think Musslemen favor the lewd worship of the heathens'. In this way 'the jollity and pomp of the heathens is much allayed by the puritanism and unlimited power of the Moors', Fryer claimed. Even among the Persians Fryer encountered 'such strict puritans, that if they meet a Christian, Jew, or Banyan, and by chance his garment brush against him, they hye them home, shift and wash, as if they had been defiled with some unclean thing, a dog or hog; undervaluing all but their own sect, as if there were no holier creatures in the world'. Yet the Muslims of Persia and India were not wholly without popery. Some of them indulged in 'guardian angels', a 'sacramental wafer' placed in the tombs of the dead, 'petitions' for the dead, superstitious saints' tombs, rosary beads, prelacy and the worship of the Prophet. Islam, Fryer argued, was perfectly outfitted for bolstering tyrannical empire in Persia and south Asia. But in its more puritanical forms, it could also prompt rebellion.[75]

The connections between post-Reformation and orientalist stereotypes are equally obvious in accounts of Islam in general and the Ottoman empire in particular that appeared in the early eighteenth century. The literary figure and projector Aaron Hill, who lived in the Ottoman empire for four years with his relative Lord Paget, the English ambassador in Constantinople, exemplified this continuity. His *Full and just account of the present state of the Ottoman empire* (1709) rehearsed nearly all the supposed likenesses between Islam and both Catholicism and puritanism found in earlier works.[76] Even the more learned and less hostile introductory material in George Sale's 1734 English translation of the Qu'ran noted both the extremism and the political utility of early Islamic beliefs in 'absolute election and reprobation'. Sale also observed that such tenets spawned politically disruptive heresies of free will.[77]

The movement from post-Reformation to Enlightenment, or from anti-popery and anti-puritanism to anti-priestcraft and anti-enthusiasm, solidified in the second half of the eighteenth century. In writings on South Asia, for example, explicit references to either Catholicism or radical Protestantism became rarer and rarer. It is the disappearance of these clues that has obscured the deep roots of Enlightenment orientalism in post-Reformation historical scholarship and led historians to assume that this form of orientalism was invented by French philosophers. Some writers on the Ottoman empire continued in the tradition of Hill and his predecessors. In his *Observations on the religion, law, government, and manners of the Turks* (1768), Sir James Porter observed 'enthusiasm' and 'religious tyranny' that appeared to be Muslim forms of Pelagianism and monasticism.[78] Alexander Dow, an historian of South Asia, was keen to emphasise that Islam was 'perfectly calculated for despotism', since Muhammad 'enslaved the mind as well as the body'. One ingredient of Mughal mind control, according to Dow, was the doctrine of 'absolute predestination', which had led to absolute docility in Muhammad's followers and in more recent times pacified the subjects of Muslim tyrants. Latter-day Muslim antinomians, Dow claimed, trust 'the whole to Providence' and make 'God agent in [their] very crimes'.[79]

During the early period of East India Company rule in Bengal, however, Islam drew less attention than Hinduism. Writings on Hindu religion mostly relied upon the stereotypical language of priestcraft. The deist J. Z. Holwell, in an effort to unearth a 'pure' and ancient Hinduism, documented the corruption of contemporary Indian religion in an Enlightenment idiom that exhibited traces of Reformation polemic. He blamed the corruption of 'the simple doctrines of Bramah' on the Brahmins, 'the laity thus being precluded from the knowledge of their original scriptures'. Some Brahmins, like imagined pre-Reformation proponents of vernacular Bible translations, were concerned about such attempts 'to enslave the laity'. This, Holwell said, caused the first schisms within Hinduism. At this juncture a set of pseudo-scriptures, the Vedas, were invented by the reformers, adding another layer of corruption. 'Priestly power' predominated everywhere. Civil authorities recognised that political stability was threatened by princes' dependence on religious experts and the 'sacerdotal slavery' those experts fostered among ordinary people. Holwell asserted that entire families and households were being turned into 'machines' by the Brahmins living amongst them. The haze of superstition and slavery in which they found themselves predisposed Hindus to submit to 'the yoke of Mahommedan tyranny', itself a providential punishment for the desecration of their once pure, native religion.[80] Other writers echoed Holwell's fundamentally anti-popish commentary on scriptural control, government of the mind, schism and ritual superstition.[81] Warren Hastings, for one, likened Brahmin 'spiritual discipline' to 'the religious order of Christians in the Romish Church'.[82] Holwell, however, had also linked Hinduism to puritan enthusiasm and fanaticism, which was most obvious in Hindus' devotion to *sati*.[83] In the end this Enlightenment portrait of Hinduism was a combination of the stereotypical discourses of puritanical enthusiasm and popish libertinism and performativity. In a vivid example of the combination, Dow described mendicant philosopher enthusiasts who made use of pilgrimages, self-flagellation and erudition to render their order 'more revered among the vulgar'.[84]

The process at work in all these texts was in one sense a classic case of what some social psychologists call 'anchoring'.[85] These writers were themselves seeking to understand non-Christian religions with reference to familiar categories of analysis and critique, and in their writings they provided this same form of intelligibility and largely pejorative understanding for their patrons and readers. It is also clear, however, that this process was strategic in its relation to domestic English politics. These commentaries on other religions were also clearly intended to serve as coded commentaries on the English scene. Both processes encouraged the emergence of universal stereotypes. The extension of anti-puritanism and anti-popery to Islamic contexts implied the cross-cultural applicability of core concepts of religious corruption that could be grafted onto fuller descriptions of particular societies and religions. The use of Islamic history as a parallel for English history encouraged much the same thing. The new vocabulary of priestcraft, imposture, enthusiasm and fanaticism simply rendered explicit the effect of ceaseless historical comparison. Only by adopting a global perspective and eschewing liberal and secularist assumptions can we begin to unravel the startling agility, function and persistence of stereotyping in the early Enlightenment, early modern orientalism and post-Restoration public discourse.

Notes

1 Jonathan I. Israel, *Enlightenment contested: philosophy, modernity, and the emancipation of man, 1670–1752* (Oxford, 2006).

2 For examples and fuller bibliography see William J. Bulman and Robert G. Ingram (eds), *God in the Enlightenment* (Oxford, 2016); J. G. A. Pocock, *Barbarism and religion* (6 vols, Cambridge, 1999–2015); David Sorkin, *The religious Enlightenment: Protestants, Jews, and Catholics from London to Vienna* (Princeton, NJ, 2008); Jonathan Sheehan, *The Enlightenment Bible: translation, scholarship, culture* (Princeton, NJ, 2005).

3 For the wide range of functions served by post-Reformation stereotypes, see the two final sections of this chapter and pp. 15–25 above.

4 This chapter cannot discuss similar uses of non-Christian religions in earlier Protestant polemics against Catholics and radical Protestants, but a convenient and excellent discussion of European uses of Islam and the Ottoman empire is available in Noel Malcolm, *Useful enemies: Islam and the Ottoman empire in Western political thought, 1450–1750* (Oxford, 2019), pp. 76–103.

5 Steven Pincus, *Protestantism and patriotism: ideologies and the making of English foreign policy, 1650–1668* (Cambridge, 1996).

6 Justin Champion, *The pillars of priestcraft shaken: the Church of England and its enemies, 1660–1730* (Cambridge, 1992); Mark Goldie, 'Priestcraft and the birth of Whiggism', in Nicholas Phillipson and Quentin Skinner (eds), *Political discourse in early modern Britain* (Cambridge, 1993), pp. 209–31.

7 These developments can be incorporated within the general account available in Malcolm, *Useful enemies*. This work, in its treatment of the late seventeenth and eighteenth centuries, tends to emphasise more radical currents of thought and (accordingly) to see 'orthodox' accounts as fundamentally unchanged from earlier periods.

8 A more complete account of this process can be found in William J. Bulman, *Anglican Enlightenment: orientalism, religion and politics in England and its empire, 1648–1715* (Cambridge, 2015); William J. Bulman, 'Enlightenment and religious politics in Restoration England', *History Compass*, 10 (2012), 752–64; William J. Bulman, 'Publicity and popery on the Restoration stage: Elkanah Settle's *The Empress of Morocco* in context', *Journal of British Studies* 51 (2012), 308–39; William J. Bulman, 'From anti-popery and anti-puritanism to orientalism', in Jason Peacey (ed.), *Making the British empire, 1660–1800* (Manchester, 2020), pp. 56–76.

9 Malcolm, *Useful enemies*, esp. p. 32.

10 Bulman, *Anglican Enlightenment*, ch. 3.

11 Edward Said, *Orientalism* (New York, 1978), p. 55. Opposing viewpoints include Joan-Pau Rubiés, *Travel and ethnology in the Renaissance: South India through European eyes, 1250–1625* (Cambridge, 2000); and Robert Irwin, *For lust of knowing: the orientalists and their enemies* (New York, 2007).

12 Generally similar approaches to various periods include Alexander Bevilacqua, *The republic of Arabic letters: Islam and the European Enlightenment* (Cambridge, MA, 2018); Michael S. Dodson, *Orientalism, empire, and national culture: India, 1770–1880* (New York, 2007), pp. 1–17; Suzanne Marchand, *German orientalism in the age of empire* (Cambridge, 2009), pp. xvii–xxxiv; Malcolm, *Useful enemies*.

13 Bulman, *Anglican Enlightenment*, pp. 115–16.

14 See esp. pp. 20, 51–2, 189–90, 192, 194, 196–200 above.

15 Here 'anti-puritanism' refers to critiques of puritans, Presbyterians, dissenters, Independents and sectarians. On anti-puritanism before the Civil War, see Chapters 2 and 4 written and co-authored by Peter Lake. See also Peter Lake, *Anglicans and puritans? Presbyterianism and English conformist thought from Whitgift to Hooker* (London, 1988); Peter Lake with Michael Questier, *The Antichrist's lewd hat: Protestants, Papists and players in post-Reformation England* (New Haven, CT, 2002), pp. 521–78; Patrick Collinson, 'Ecclesiastical vitriol: religious satire in the 1590s and the invention of puritanism', in John Guy (ed.), *The reign of Elizabeth I: court and culture in the last decade* (Cambridge, 1995), pp. 150–70; Patrick Collinson, 'Ben Jonson's *Bartholomew Fair*: the theatre constructs puritanism', in David L. Smith, Richard Strier and David

Bevington (eds), *The theatrical city: culture, theatre and politics in London, 1576–1649* (Cambridge, 1995), pp. 157–69; Alexandra Walsham, '"A glose of godlines": Philip Stubbes, Elizabethan Grub Street and the invention of puritanism', in Susan Wabuda and Caroline Litzenberger (eds), *Belief and practice in Reformation England* (Aldershot, 1998), pp. 177–206; Peter Lake, 'Anti-puritanism: the structure of a prejudice', in Kenneth Fincham and Peter Lake (eds), *Religious politics in post-Reformation England* (Woodbridge, 2006), pp. 80–97; Peter Lake, 'Puritanism, (monarchical) republicanism, and monarchy; or John Whitgift, antipuritanism, and the "invention" of popularity', *Journal of Medieval and Early Modern Studies*, 40 (2010), 463–95.

16 For an example of this three-node analysis see, e.g., Oliver Ormerod, *The picture of a puritane* (London, 1605) and *The picture of a papist* (London, 1606). For broader accounts see Anthony Milton, *Catholic and reformed: the Roman and Protestant churches in English Protestant thought, 1600–1640* (Cambridge, 1995); Lake, *Anglicans and puritans*; and Peter Lake, 'Anti-popery: the structure of a prejudice', in Richard Cust and Ann Hughes (eds), *Conflict in early Stuart England: studies in religion and politics 1603–1642* (London, 1989), pp. 72–106.

17 Joan-Pau Rubiés, 'Theology, ethnography, and the historicization of idolatry', *Journal of the History of Ideas*, 67 (2006), 571–96; Carlos Eire, *War against the idols: the reformation of worship from Erasmus to Calvin* (Cambridge, 1986); Peter Harrison, *'Religion' and the religions in the English Enlightenment* (Cambridge, 1990); Sabine MacCormack, *Religion in the Andes: vision and imagination in early colonial Peru* (Princeton, NJ, 1991); Anthony Pagden, *The fall of natural man: the American Indian and the origins of comparative ethnology* (Cambridge, 1984); Rubiés, *Travel and ethnology in the Renaissance*; Peter N. Miller, *Peiresc's Europe: learning and virtue in the seventeenth century* (New Haven, CT, 2000); Martin Mulsow, 'Antiquarianism and idolatry: the *Historia* of religions in the seventeenth century', in Gianna Pomata and Nancy G. Siraisi (eds), *Historia: empiricism and erudition in early modern Europe* (Cambridge, MA, 2005), pp. 181–210.

18 See Donald R. Kelley, *Foundations of modern historical scholarship: language, law, and history in the French Renaissance* (New York, 1970); Anthony Grafton, *What was history? The art of history in early modern Europe* (Cambridge, 2007); Markus Völkel, *'Pyrrhonismus historicus' und 'fides historica': die Entwicklung der deutschen historischen Methodologie unter dem Gesichtspunkt der historischen Skepsis* (Frankfurt am Main, 1987).

19 Samuel Purchas, *Purchas his pilgrimage* (London, 1613), pp. 948–9. This was an edited and abridged version of Thomas Hariot, *A brief and true report of the new found land of Virginia* (London, 1588), p. 26.

20 Bulman, *Anglican Enlightenment.*

21 Edward Terry, *A voyage to East-India* (London, 1655), pp. 261, 271–2, 281–3, 290, 292, 309, 440. See also Henry Lord, *A display of two forraigne sects in the East Indies* (London, 1630).

22 On fanaticism and enthusiasm see anon., *A breife description or character of the religion and manners of the phanatiques in generall* (London, 1660); Meric Casaubon, *A treatise concerning enthusiasme* (London, 1654).
23 For numerous other examples and a discussion that partly overlaps with the content of this chapter, see Bulman, *Anglican Enlightenment*; Bulman, 'From anti-puritanism and anti-popery to orientalism'; Bulman, 'Publicity and popery on the Restoration stage'. For additional, related, primary materials see Lancelot Addison, *The first state of Mahumedism* (London, 1678); Lancelot Addison, *West Barbary* (Oxford, 1671); Lancelot Addison, *The present state of the Jews* (London, 1675); Francis Osborne, *Politicall reflections on the government of the Turks* (London, 1656).
24 On Rycaut's biography see Sonia P. Anderson, *An English consul in Turkey: Paul Rycaut at Smyrna, 1667–1678* (Oxford, 1989).
25 Anderson, *English consul*, pp. 259–60, 269.
26 Paul Rycaut, 'The preface', *The present state of the Greek and Armenian churches* (London, 1679).
27 Anderson, in *English consul*, p. 20, appears to mistake such professions of irenicism for liberalism when she makes a series of misleading and undocumented references to Rycaut's 'passionate belief in religious toleration'.
28 Rycaut, 'The preface', *Greek and Armenian churches*, sig. a2^{r}.
29 Rycaut, 'The preface', *Greek and Armenian churches*, sig. a2^{r}.
30 Rycaut, 'The preface', *Greek and Armenian churches*, sigs a2^{r-v}.
31 Rycaut, 'The preface', *Greek and Armenian churches*, sig. a2^{v}.
32 Rycaut, 'The preface', *Greek and Armenian churches*, sig. a3^{r}.
33 Rycaut, 'The preface', *Greek and Armenian churches*, sig. a3^{v}–a4^{v}.
34 Rycaut, 'The preface', *Greek and Armenian churches*.
35 See e.g. Anderson, *Rycaut*, p. 269.
36 Paul Rycaut, *The present state of the Ottoman empire* (London, 1667), sig. a2^{v} and Book I, esp. pp. 6–8; Justinian, *Institutes*, Book 2, title 17, p. 8.
37 Rycaut, *Ottoman empire*, p. 97.
38 Rycaut, *Ottoman empire*, p. 104.
39 Rycaut, *Ottoman empire*, pp. 97, 105.
40 Rycaut, *Ottoman empire*, pp. 105–6.
41 Rycaut, *Ottoman empire*, p. 106.
42 Rycaut, *Ottoman empire*, pp. 106–7.
43 Rycaut, *Ottoman empire*, p. 112. See also p. 129.
44 Rycaut, *Ottoman empire*, p. 158.
45 Rycaut, *Ottoman empire*, pp. 108, 112, 114.
46 Rycaut, *Ottoman empire*, pp. 135–6.
47 Rycaut, *Ottoman empire*, pp. 135–9.
48 Rycaut, *Ottoman empire*, p. 144.
49 Rycaut, *Ottoman empire*, pp. 142–5, 147–50.
50 Rycaut, *Ottoman empire*, p. 105. See also pp. 115–16.
51 Rycaut, *Ottoman empire*, p. 109.
52 Rycaut, *Ottoman empire*, p. 115.

53 Rycaut, *Ottoman empire*, p. 116.
54 Rycaut, *Ottoman empire*, p. 126.
55 Rycaut, *Ottoman empire*, p. 126.
56 Rycaut, *Ottoman empire*, p. 138.
57 Rycaut, *Ottoman empire*, pp. 128, 135.
58 Rycaut, *Ottoman empire*, p. 128.
59 Rycaut, *Ottoman empire*, p. 123.
60 Rycaut, *Ottoman empire*, p. 130.
61 Rycaut, *Ottoman empire*, pp. 135–43.
62 Rycaut, *Ottoman empire*, p. 145.
63 Rycaut, *Ottoman empire*, p. 150.
64 Rycaut, *Ottoman empire*, p. 116.
65 Rycaut, *Ottoman empire*, p. 127. See also p. 135.
66 Rycaut, *Ottoman empire*, p. 123.
67 Rycaut, *Ottoman empire*, p. 135.
68 Rycaut, *Ottoman empire*, p. 128.
69 Rycaut, *Ottoman empire*, p. 125.
70 Rycaut, *Ottoman empire*, p. 126.
71 Rycaut, *Ottoman empire*, p. 126.
72 Rycaut, *Ottoman empire*, p. 132.
73 John Ovington, *A voyage to Suratt in the year 1689* (London, 1696); John Fryer, *A new account of East-India and Persia* (London, 1698); Sanjay Subrahmanyam, 'Frank submissions: the Company and the Mughals between Sir Thomas Roe and Sir William Norris', in H. V. Bowen, Margarette Lincoln and Nigel Rigby (eds), *The worlds of the East India Company* (Woodbridge, 2002), pp. 69–96, p. 89.
74 Fryer, *New account of East-India and Persia*, pp. 32, 44, 102–3, 159, 180.
75 Fryer, *New account of East-India and Persia*, pp. 92–6, 102, 107–10, 143–4, 194–6, 249, 259, 348–9, 357, 361, 367, 387.
76 Aaron Hill, *A full and just account of the present state of the Ottoman Empire* (London, 1733 edn), pp. 37–42, 45, 47–9, 51, 54–6, 58–60. See also Thomas Shaw, *Travels, or observations relating to several parts of Barbary and the Levant* (Oxford, 1738).
77 George Sale, *Koran, commonly called the Alcoran of Mohammed* (London, 1795 edn), vol. 1, pp. 137–8.
78 James Porter, *Observations on the religion, law, government, and manners of the Turks* (London, 1771 edn), pp. 12, 17, 31–2, 40–1.
79 Alexander Dow, *A history of Hindostan* (3 vols, London, 1768–72), vol. 3, p. xvii.
80 J. Z. Holwell, 'Chapters on "The religious tenets of the Gentoos"', in P. J. Marshall (ed.), *The British discovery of Hinduism in the eighteenth century* (Cambridge, 1970), pp. 57–60.
81 Alexander Dow, 'A dissertation concerning the Hindoos', in Marshall (ed.), *British discovery of Hinduism*, pp. 109–10, 119; Charles Wilkins, '"The translator's preface", from the *Bhagvat-Geeta*', in Marshall (ed.), *British discovery of Hinduism*, pp. 192–5; Robert Orme, *Historical fragments of the Mogul empire*

(London, 1805), p. 432; Robert Orme, *A history of the military transactions of the British nation in Indostan* (London, 1763), p. 3; Luke Scrafton, *Reflections on the government of Indostan* (London, 1770), pp. 5–6.

82 Warren Hastings, 'Letter to Nathaniel Smith', in Marshall (ed.), *British discovery of Hinduism*, p. 186.

83 Holwell, 'Chapters on "The religious tenets of the Gentoos"', in Marshall (ed.), *British discovery of Hinduism*, pp. 91–2; Dow, 'Dissertation concerning the Hindoos', in Marshall (ed.), *British discovery of Hinduism*, p. 116; Nathaniel Brassey Halhead, '"The translator's preface" to a code of Gentoo laws', in Marshall (ed.), *British discovery of Hinduism*, pp. 149, 170; J. Z. Howell, 'A dissertation on the metempsychosis of the Bramins', *A view of the original principles, religious and moral, of the ancient Bramins* (London, 1779), p. 7.

84 Dow, 'Dissertation', pp. 117–18.

85 Serge Moscovici, *Psychoanalysis: its image and its public* (Cambridge, 2008), esp. pp. 17–18; Serge Moscovici, 'Notes toward a description of social representation', *European Journal of Social Psychology*, 18 (1988), 211–50; Serge Moscovici, 'The phenomenon of social representations', in Robert Farr and Serge Moscovici (eds), *Social representations* (Cambridge, 1984), pp. 3–70.

Coda: The dialectics of stereotyping – past and present

Sandra Jovchelovitch, Koji Yamamoto and Peter Lake

This volume brings together a series of pilot studies that collectively can be taken as a point of departure for exploring the striking pervasiveness of stereotypes in early modern England. Drawing on case studies of the period, it shows that stereotypes are more than cognitive shortcuts and distorted beliefs expressing the errors of people who are prejudiced, irrational and limited in their understanding. In these studies, historical actors are not passive agents waiting to be impressed by prejudices and preconceptions derived from popular culture or from dominant (yet often erroneous) ideologies. Rather, the opposite: the chapters collected here emphasise the contested and practical character of stereotyping as a key psychological and social practice in the making of history. Stereotypes, yesterday as today, are best understood in the context of argumentative social practices that underlie intergroup interactions, interests and representations of the world.

From the path-breaking historical research of Patrick Collinson, Alexandra Walsham, Mark Knights and Peter Lake, among others, we already know that stereotypes were often mobilised in early modern polemical and political contexts, where negotiations of power and identity were central driving processes.[1] Thanks to this scholarship, we also know that stereotypes were not only depictions of the groups they were trying to represent but also, and importantly, rich descriptors of the people holding and using them. Yet such case studies have hitherto been undertaken in relative isolation. Perhaps it is due to this isolation and lack of comparison that stereotyping has been conceived mainly as a process inherently harmful to society and that appeals to reason would be sufficient to contain their escalation. Arguably, this has made it difficult to appreciate the striking persistence of stereotyping, indeed the near impossibility of removing stereotypes from social interactions.

This coda gives us the opportunity to emphasise how the historical evidence presented here sheds light on stereotyping processes themselves. It also offers a chance to take further our conversation on the synergies between social psychology and history.[2] Social and cognitive psychologists have provided much of the ammunition for approaching stereotypes as 'bad thinking' – forms of rigid, over-generalised and therefore simplistic cognitions that are intrinsically linked to prejudice and other forms of intergroup bias.[3] Most research in the field has been elusive about social and historical contexts, remaining firmly grounded in the assumption that stereotypes are based on individual cognitive processes that over-emphasise differences between and similarities within groups. From this perspective, stereotypes represent social groups as homogeneous and by the very same process erase the individuality of members – everyone in an out-group becomes 'stereotypically' the same.[4] Yet, it was not always thus and it would be wrong to conclude that all social psychology has been reductive in its approach to stereotyping. If anything, historical evidence, as presented in this volume, will fuel the hope once expressed by Robert M. Farr that social psychologists will become more conscious of the historicity of social-psychological phenomena.[5]

The pilot studies in this volume contribute to a recasting of the analysis of stereotyping towards a wider understanding of the problem and its consequences. Starting from the ground up, these studies build a rich and thick description of stereotyping processes that offers a welcome opportunity to rethink the concept through social and historical lenses. These studies shift our point of departure from a focus on stereotypes as a form of erroneous representation of (and about) out-groups to *practices of stereotyping* in early modern England – how stereotypes were forged, ignored, disseminated, eventually contested and even co-opted, with far-reaching repercussions for the people and societies involved. In prompting this shift, they also enable a reappraisal of the theoretical fatalism that has conceived all categorisation and stereotyping as a direct and inevitable pathway to prejudice and discrimination towards out-groups.[6] And given how much domestic and international politics in the twenty-first century has turned out to be profoundly affected by stereotypes, reappraising their impact in the early modern period may have unexpected political and practical resonances today.

Engaging with early modern case studies

Stereotypes in early modern England were never simply an amalgam of prejudice and ideology. As shown by Tim Harris (Chapter 1), stereotypes of the Scottish or the Irish were often invoked in polemical contexts in order, for example, to undermine a particular policy or isolate an opponent from moderate groups. In this tactical mobilisation, stereotypes were often 'false composites', mixing different characteristics (say, about Scots) that would never be found in a single individual. Harris shows that such polemical uses conditioned political debates and influenced the unfolding of political crises. Such false composites, fuelled by prejudice, could be invoked in order to promote and justify riots.[7] In this context of political mobilisation, the 'falseness' of stereotypes was more than a false construction; rather, it was deployed creatively as a purposeful and meaningful move driven by political, economic and social interests.

In addition to the importance of polemical mobilisation in understanding their deployment, stereotypes went well beyond prejudice and the stigmatising of subordinate out-groups. As Peter Lake (Chapter 2) has revealed, they could be purposefully brought into being by an out-group. The stereotype of the puritan was in fact brought into print by the godly reformers themselves, who argued that if a thoroughgoing Protestant Reformation had not materialised, it was because their neighbours refused cooperation by accusing the godly of being hypocritical 'puritaines'. Thus defenders of the ecclesiastical status quo and their attack dogs did not invent the term 'puritan' to stigmatise the religious minority. Rather, the character first appeared in print when puritan preacher George Gifford used it to explain the relative failure of his own camp's reformist agenda and to type his critics as profane and ultimately crypto-papists. If we apply the language of social psychology, then the puritan stereotype was first used by the religious out-group to explain its own marginality. Only later was it co-opted by the in-group in order to stigmatise the out-group.

Stereotypes also had comic potential. In their analysis of the Jonsonian characters of the puritan and the projector, Peter Lake and Koji Yamamoto (Chapter 4) have demonstrated that post-Reformation England was profoundly affected by religious politics in response to puritans' call for further reform and by the fiscal exactions perpetrated by projectors close to the royal court. To that extent, laughing at a puritan's hypocrisy on stage and dismissing a projector's scheme as mere fantasy driven by greed served as anxiety displacement for Jonson's audience and offered comforting comic relief, which lessened the magnitude of the problems involved, even as it exposed their nature. Similar comic potential has been ably explored by William Cavert's study of 'sin and sea coal' (Chapter 8). There we find that, instead of caricaturing the threat of metropolitan environmental hazard, those who accepted the anti-urban polemic and detested metropolitan 'sin and sea coal' were parodied as gullible country gentlemen so naive as to swallow other kinds of stereotype, such as those about popery and courtly life. These early modern contemporaries were thus capable of creatively using the power of stereotypes as satire to colour knowledge, shape value and influence behaviour (see also Chapters 7 and 10, by David Magliocco and William Bulman). Stereotypes performed a number of distinct, if related, functions, and their societal implications were not always negative.

What emerges from the evidence provided by the studies in this volume is that stereotypes were not monolithic signs of prejudice but instead had a variety of heuristic functions in the religious, political, social, economic and epistemic spheres. Stereotypes provided frames for discovering abuses and thereby offered a rallying point for participatory politics (see Yamamoto and Lake, Chapters 3 and 4). In addition, national and religious stereotypes profoundly shaped the construction of individual identity (as shown in Chapter 9 by Bridget Orr), and also the production of knowledge about non-Christian faiths (as demonstrated by Bulman in Chapter 10).

Underlying these various *uses* of stereotypes is the question of agency, a topic which has been most fully explored by Kate Peters and Adam Morton in their discussion of responses to stereotyping (Chapters 5 and 6). Through Peters's case study of Ranters and Quakers, we have learned about the remarkably wide range of coping strategies in response to the threat of being stereotyped, such as mounting coordinated responses, demanding concrete proof, avoiding stereotyped behaviours and challenging stereotypes in face-to-face debates. These are historical examples that could be readily compared to the strategies deployed today by Muslim women in Scotland or young Black youth living in the *favelas* of Brazil.[8] As in Morton's discussion, even Sir Roger L'Estrange's appeal to his readers' reason and impartiality was an integral part of his polemics against the nascent Whig party intent upon excluding the Catholic heir from the English throne. As Harris has noted in Chapter 1, counter-stereotyping has a long pedigree. Results of modern fieldworks suggest that counter-stereotyping continues to this day, fuelling the responses of contemporary actors dealing with issues as diverse as urban marginalisation and contradictory stigmatised identities.[9]

Substantive findings from these studies are threefold. First, they show the linkage between the symbolic content of stereotypes and their social realisation. Thus when specific notions are invoked in polemic contexts, their symbolic content is activated to galvanise support and denigrate enemies (see Chapters 1, 5 and 6 by Harris, Peters and Morton). It is in the context of highly charged religious and political debates that we find appeals to readers' reason and impartial judgement. If readers were to use their reason as expected, they would be taking a clear side, say in the battle against the succession of the Catholic James II. The symbolic appeal to reason is not a matter of precise or imprecise cognition, but instead is deeply connected to argumentative and polemical intergroup interactions that betray their own political, socially purposive reason.

Second, stereotypes do not easily go away because even those denying and contesting particular stereotypes use them, often drawing on the same and/or other stereotypes. Once activated, stereotypes become ideas circulating and used in the public sphere, as reservoirs of meaning that can be mobilised to produce an effect that is not only psychological but also social and political. Thus, and significantly, the effort to contest stereotypes and even bring them under control did not cause stereotyping to cease. Instead, Chapters 6 and 1 by Morton and Harris show that contestation over stereotypes often accelerated, rather than attenuated, the circulation of related stereotypes, which accounts for their resilience and continuous endurance in minds and society.

Third, and linked to the above, the collective engagement with stereotypes did not lead to their reduction because of their multiple heuristic functions. Stereotypes were deployed to incite laughter and displace anxiety, but they could also be taken up and turned around to facilitate political judgement, promote civil political participation and even escalate conflicts. These findings take us back to what makes stereotypes a plural, polyphasic and contested cognitive form, expressive of the flexibility and openness of the human cognitive toolkit, and of their vital role in the social and political life of given communities. Stereotypes are representations integral to the dynamics of social life and contestations over power and knowledge, which explains why they do not easily go away.[10]

Implications for social psychology and sociology

The studied attention to historical instantiations of stereotyping as a relational and dynamic process recasts and expands psychologists' understanding of stereotypes in substantive ways. First, it debunks the standard assumption that stereotypes are a direct pathway to prejudice, a shortcut deviating from rational and precise social thinking, an excessive generalisation or, as Gordon Allport originally put it in 1954, 'an exaggerated belief associated with a category'.[11] These findings combine to show that stereotypes are not just perceptions gone amiss, but rather a relational process of sense-making and meaning development through which social actors act purposefully in social fields. Seen as a battle over representations, there is nothing of the 'cognitive miser' in either historical or contemporary practices of stereotyping.[12] These socio-cognitive practices are integral to processes of social representation, condensing and by the same token expanding social categories, symbolically creating and transforming people, relations and objects in time and context.[13] This volume has documented the remarkable extent to which early modern men and women, far from being irrational, were capable of mobilising stereotypes and disputing their validity in a variety of contexts. This not only debunks commonly held assumptions (among social scientists) that social thinking in pre-modern Europe was riddled by irrational and homogeneous beliefs that went uncontested, but also contributes to a reappraisal of the elements of agency and mobilisation that pertain to the dynamics of stereotyping in other historical periods.[14]

An exploration of the wide variety of mobilisation strategies, as well as the broad consequences that follow such mobilisations, emphasises the social mode of the realisation of stereotypes and lends support to long-standing arguments that sought to decouple stereotyping from the inevitability of prejudice.[15] Most psychology research on categorisation, stereotypes and prejudice assumed that if stereotyping is integral to categorisation and all stereotyping is prejudiced, then human thinking is by definition prejudiced and therefore misguided and deficient. The evidence presented here unsettles such direct and linear equalisations and the reduction of stereotypes to prejudice. It points instead to a variety of functions stereotypes fulfil in social life, corroborating understandings that emphasise the view of stereotypes as rhetorical, polyphasic and argumentative representations, dependent on the concrete uses to which they are put.[16]

Of course, it would be both incorrect and politically undesirable to deny that stereotypes can lead to prejudice towards out-groups and create falseness in representing people and events. But if we want to understand why this type of symbolic content was and still is produced, then it is vital that we unpack its underlying societal processes rather than relying on a reductive psychological approach that naturalises deficit and irrationality in human cognition. Seen as only prejudice, the cognitive, social and historical dynamics of stereotypes are reduced to a deficit, which trickles all the way backwards to the understanding of social thinking itself and exonerates social psychologists from the more arduous task of investigating stereotypes as they are embedded in social and historical contexts.

A second key contribution of this volume is to demonstrate the futility of trying to eradicate stereotypes. Instead, the essays collectively show the importance of understanding how and why they come about and documenting in detail how they present in a different era, so that this knowledge can also inform the present. This careful historiography shows that stereotypes are better understood as symbolic and social processes collectively mobilised and negotiated. Such collective capacity to engage with stereotypes hardly freed actors (and society) from stereotyping. Rather, efforts to cope with stereotypes (say, of popery or urban degeneration) paradoxically ensured greater currency for the very same stereotype and/or ended in circulating another set of stereotypical representations (e.g. of those ignorant country gentlemen who hated the urban vices rampant in London to such a point that it became comic). These early modern case studies reveal the profound difficulties that society encounters when seeking to control, contain or eradicate stereotypes. This is not surprising given the centrality of stereotypes to human thinking, society and culture. In his classic work on the topic, Henri Tajfel suggested that stereotypes lie at the centre of common sense, everyday knowledge and understanding.[17] For Serge Moscovici, they are a function of social representations and equally central to the symbolic environments humans construct to organise and make sense of the world, events and people.[18] Because they are extended from the mind and body into practices of communication and intergroup relations, they are embedded in both micro-scale contestations of power and macro-processes of institutional and historical development.

The historical analysis presented in this volume enables us to highlight important social psychological insights that continue to be elusive to many strands of social psychology and more broadly social science research. The first is that stereotypes are cultural and symbolic tools circulating in the social world; they live and grow in the interactions between minds, anchored and objectified in narratives, artefacts and social practice. Once produced, they become available as relatively stable templates of signification (*stereo+types*) that permeate social fields carried by a diversity of cultural and commercial media; these, however, make them susceptible to the dynamics of representational change.[19] Thus, very often combating particular stereotypes – whether intentionally or unintentionally – leads to the production and mobilisation of the same or other stereotypes, which entangles relative stability in social change. Even if modern political activists combat one stereotype and its adverse impacts – say, those about immigrants or religious minorities – the very same effort might reinforce other stereotypes (about bigotry and homophobia) and in the process reinforce the stereotype of (say) working-class people as ill-educated consumers of biased news. As symbolic tools and relational practices, stereotypes pertain to a collective dynamic that goes beyond individual minds. They circulate in social worlds to be used, contested and transformed by everyone and everywhere.

Also worth highlighting is that stereotypes express our human, all-too-human emotions, interests and passions. The social science literature – relating to ill-health, disability, race and stigma – often discusses how to cope with and ultimately reduce stereotypes.[20] However, as resources for sense-making, stereotypes are guided by emotional and social motivations, as documented throughout this volume. They draw on reasons of which accuracy in cognition is but one and not always the most important. Negative motivations are part of human psychology and a permanent possibility inscribed both in our development and our modalities of relating to each other. The complete eradication of stereotypes, and even prejudice, is more desire than factual possibility.[21]

Since stereotyping has been studied nevertheless as the opposite of reasoned cognition, it is not unfair to ask whether this was psychology's attempt to accomplish the project of modernity. (Here, Steven Pinker's work serves as an exemplary demonstration of psychology's infatuation with the modern dream of a pure and cold cognition.)[22] Much psychology saw the 'education of reason' just as modernity did: a journey towards a cognition free of irrationality, the distortions, prejudices and 'religious superstitions' that were supposedly typical of the pre-modern world.[23] In this project, the role of psychologists would be to detect and diagnose residual errors so that the world becomes a better place. However, psychology itself has demonstrated that reason has never quite managed to free itself from the embodied and emotional mind *homo sapiens* evolved or from the social, cultural and historical contexts in which this mind is always already located.[24]

Finally, an important third expansion suggested by the essays in this volume is the theoretical contribution to the dynamics of intergroup relations that will be of interest to social scientists, especially sociologists and social psychologists. Most works in social psychology discuss how stereotypes help dominant 'in-groups' to forge their group identity by creating stereotypes of lesser 'out-groups'. Early modern case studies enable us to broaden our perspective through careful documentation of how stereotyping divided, as much as united, communities. This is most clearly seen in the case of religious stereotypes such as anti-puritanism and anti-popery. Anti-popery could be used by insurgent minorities to assault and change the structures of power in church and state. Crucially, those accused of popery could also return the accusation, denouncing those minorities to be acting on popish principles. The same might also be said to be true of anti-puritanism because, in the hands of the defenders of the ecclesiastical status quo, it enabled them to defend the current power structure and their own places within it, while more locally it enabled subordinate groups to critique and ridicule those puritan elites who had seized local power and were using it to impose various types of further reformation.

Stereotyping has played a vital role not only in areas such as religious disputes and political crises, but also in the pursuit of enlightened knowledge and natural philosophy. Not only do stereotypes reflect cultural assumptions, but also they actively shape culture, condition political conduct and influence debates and the course of events. In this sense, they offer a set of shared references that operate as social representations building common ground.[25] How exactly this common ground was used depended on the dynamics of the immediate situation; on who was doing what to whom, and why. The mobilisation of stereotypes was then, as now, a rich and dynamic relational process in which both tactical actions and emotive experiences were at stake. Such processes of stereotyping and ensuing contestation have the power to draw and redraw the boundaries between 'us' and 'them', creating, dividing and re-creating communities. The historical evidence on the ways in which all social groups use stereotyping to divide as well as unite communities unsettles conceptions of neat and clear-cut boundaries between in-groups and out-groups as well as the assumed homogeneity of any one in-group.

This is a question that lies at the core of social psychological investigation, but which has only partially been addressed in the classical literature on stereotypes. As Michael Billig rightly observes, Tajfel's theory of intergroup relations was above all a theory of group freedom because at its centre we can find an examination of the pathways through which social groups construct and escape social identities, using agency to resist and transform negative representations held by others.[26] Arguably, social creativity in the reconstruction of stereotypes and prejudiced representations was perhaps more important for Tajfel than conforming to the in-group and adjusting one's own identity accordingly, which is not entirely surprising in a man who survived the horrors of the Second World War. Stereotypes are not just cognitive generalisations of out-groups, but contain in themselves powerful particularisations of subgroups *within* the in-group.[27] Research in social psychology today has robustly corroborated these insights, showing how identity negotiations appropriate and subvert stereotypical representations so as to reposition groups and individuals in social fields.[28] This can be seen for example in the ways young Muslim Scottish women use stereotypes of the veil to redefine not only what the veil itself is but also who they are, appropriating representations built by out-groups to recast their Muslim identity and to project what they want to be in the public sphere.[29] Manipulating stereotypes creatively can serve the purposes of those being stereotyped and, through the subtle appropriation of representations of others, redefine power imbalances and misrecognised identities.[30] Here, stereotypes are meaningful symbolic constructions, devices for sense-making and regulating both the presentation and social representation of selves in everyday life and contested political arenas, as Erving Goffman once studied.[31] Early modern historical actors did not simply lump together a group of people around a homogeneous group signifier but used stereotypes as reservoirs of meaning to be deployed within and across social groups. Just as it was with our early modern predecessors, human communities today continue to draw on particular stereotypes in order to redefine and creatively transform them.

By documenting practices of stereotyping and studying their repercussions, we are invited to reappraise both the surprising human agency over particular stereotypes, and simultaneously the disturbing resilience of stereotyping as a mode of human interaction across centuries. This is what this volume has tentatively called the *dialectics of stereotyping*. Documented here in detail are individual and collective efforts to control stereotypes – by asking for concrete proof, disputing the validity of what was being attributed to them, contesting the validity of stereotypes and more. Yet in this agentic process of resistance and contestation early modern men and women often found themselves mobilising and reproducing stereotypes themselves, thereby perpetuating practices of stereotyping as modes of divisive social interaction. As the debates over Brexit and the 2016 elections in the United States have shown in the early twenty-first century, we have scarcely been able to overcome the trap of this dialectical process. Future studies of stereotyping in past and present societies can now take this work as a point of departure and start raising new questions.

Civic implications

We would like to end the volume by reflecting on implications for civil societies on both sides of the Atlantic and in Eurasia. Contributions to this volume do point to the sheer difficulty of eradicating stereotyping itself. These implications, we suggest, are not trivial. In the politics of the present, the politics of stereotyping has been pursued in all directions and can easily get out of control. Many forms of gender-, race- and age-based stereotype are being developed and deployed today as prejudice to stigmatise and discriminate against, not merely bodies of opinion, attitudes or policies, but social groups who are identified as the main carriers or supporters of those opinions, attitudes and policies. As attempts to understand, explain or act upon reality, these twenty-first-century stereotypes display disturbing similarities to the politics of stereotyping found in early modern case studies.

Unless we choose to learn from history and try to think and act differently, it seems that political debates today risk becoming (as they did in the early modern past) a peculiarly vicious form of identity politics played out on highly commercialised platforms, driven by a series of claims and counter-claims about whose stereotypes are true and whose false, whose are malign and whose benign. Given the contemporary format of the virtual public sphere, it may be the case that the dialectics of stereotyping identified in early modern England have set in with a vengeance. The growth of the participatory Web 2.0 and new media signals a new psychology in the contemporary public sphere, where connectivity and interconnectedness have become widespread and individuals and organised communities hold a new freedom to produce and distribute content. This unbounded and hyper-connected public space has also become more fragmented, lonely and paradoxically homogeneous. As the recent term 'echo chamber' reminds us, the new self-centred controls of the networked public sphere are conducive to rigidifying the boundaries of in-groups while at the same time decreasing the exchanges and exposure to different opinions that enable differences to be negotiated and overcome.[32] The speed and immediacy of online communications, facilitated by powerful corporations with as-yet under-regulated global influence – Google, Facebook, Twitter and Tik Tok among others – make the politics of stereotyping particularly acute and the possibility of containing and controlling its prejudiced forms much more elusive than previously expected.

While the significance of modern technologies cannot be overplayed, the dangers of repeating and accelerating a divisive politics of stereotyping are also to be found at the very core of our human psychology and social relations. The work reported here shows that stereotypes can be more than prejudice and discriminatory cognition; and that they endure and persist in our public spheres. Working through what they mean and learning from the past is essential for avoiding what has been frequently described as the 'return of the repressed', a resurgence of those darker, divisive, prejudiced motivations that do not go away and remain with us as a past that does not pass, a compulsion to repeat. Only a wiser, wider and dialogical rationality will be able to treat these undercurrents as part of itself. If anything, the capacity of rational individuals or society to contain and control the other side of reason relies on a more nuanced and historical understanding of the stereotyping process and a commitment to just and inclusive public spheres. Like democracy, the reduction and management of negative stereotypes seems to be one of the unfinished projects of our time. This requires expanded theory and proper understanding of the collective mobilisations that make and unmake all stereotyping, including prejudiced ones. Anyone committed to such a project has much to learn from the past.

Notes

1 See Patrick Collinson, 'Ben Jonson's *Bartholomew Fair*: the theatre constructs puritanism', in David L. Smith, Richard Strier and David Bevington (eds), *The theatrical city: culture, theatre, and politics in London, 1576–1649* (Cambridge, 1995), pp. 157–69; Patrick Collinson, 'Ecclesiastical vitriol: religious satire in the 1590s and the invention of puritanism', in John Guy (ed.), *The reign of Elizabeth I: court and culture in the last decade* (Cambridge, 1995), pp. 150–70; Alexandra Walsham, '"The fatall vesper": providentialism and anti-popery in late Jacobean London', *Past & Present*, 144 (1994), 36–87; Alexandra Walsham, *Providence in early modern England* (Oxford, 1999); Mark Knights, *Representation and misrepresentation in later Stuart Britain: partisanship and political culture* (Oxford, 2004); Peter Lake, 'Anti-popery: the structure of a prejudice', in Richard Cust and Ann Hughes (eds), *Conflict in early Stuart England: studies in religion and politics, 1603–1642* (London,

1989), pp. 72–106; Peter Lake, 'Anti-puritanism: the structure of a prejudice', in Kenneth Fincham and Peter Lake (eds), *Religious politics in post-Reformation England: essays in honour of Nicholas Tyacke* (Woodbridge, 2006), pp. 80–97.

2 Vlad Glăveanu and Koji Yamamoto, 'Bridging history and social psychology: what, how and why', *Integrative Psychological and Behavioral Science*, 46 (2012), 431–9; Sandra Jovchelovitch, 'Narrative, memory and social representations: a conversation between history and social psychology', *Integrative Psychological and Behavioral Science*, 46 (2012), 440–56; Mark Knights, 'Taking a historical turn: possible points of connection between social psychology and history', *Integrative Psychological and Behavioral Science*, 46 (2012), 584–98; Mark Knights, 'Historical stereotypes and histories of stereotypes', in Cristian Tileagă and Jovan Byford (eds), *Psychology and history: interdisciplinary explorations* (Cambridge, 2014), pp. 242–67.

3 For reviews and discussion, see James L. Hilton and William von Hippel, 'Stereotypes', *Annual Review of Psychology*, 47 (1996), 237–71; Serge Moscovici, 'The coming era of representations', in Jean-Paul Codol and Jacques-Philippe Leyens (eds), *Cognitive analysis of social behavior* (The Hague, 1982); Michael Billig, 'Prejudice, categorization and particularization: from a perceptual to a rhetorical approach', *European Journal of Social Psychology*, 15 (1985), 79–103. For more recent work see Lasana T. Harris, 'Leveraging cultural narratives to promote trait inferences rather than stereotype activation during person perception', *Social and Personality Psychology Compass*, 15 (2021), doi: /10.1111/spc3.12598.

4 For an evaluation of this work and the entire recasting of the problem, see Michael Billig, 'Henri Tajfel's "Cognitive aspects of prejudice" and the psychology of bigotry', *British Journal of Social Psychology*, 41 (2002), 171–88.

5 Robert M. Farr, *The roots of modern social psychology: 1872–1954* (Oxford, 1996).

6 Billig, 'Prejudice, categorization and particularization'.

7 Brodie Waddell, 'The Evil May Day riot of 1517 and the popular politics of anti-immigrant hostility in early modern London', *Historical Research*, 94 (2021), 713–35.

8 Nick Hopkins, 'Dual identities and their recognition: minority group members' perspectives', *Political Psychology*, 32 (2011), 251–70; Sandra Jovchelovitch, Maria Cecilia Dedios Sanguineti, Mara Nogueira and Jacqueline Priego-Hernández, 'Imagination and mobility in the city: porosity of borders and human development in divided urban environments', *Culture & Psychology*, 26 (2020), 676–96.

9 For sociological works, see David Harvey, *Rebel cities: from the right to the city to the urban revolution* (London and New York, 2013); James Holston, 'Insurgent citizenship in an era of global urban peripheries', *City & Society*, 21 (2009), 245–67; Loïc Wacquant, *Urban outcasts: a comparative sociology of advanced marginality* (Cambridge, 2007). For psychological studies, see Sandra Jovchelovitch and Jacqueline Priego-Hernández, *Underground sociabilities: identity, culture and resistance in the favelas of Rio de Janeiro* (Brasilia, 2013);

Celestin Okoroji, Ilka H. Gleibs and Sandra Jovchelovitch, 'Elite stigmatization of the unemployed: the association between framing and public attitudes', *British Journal of Psychology*, 112 (2021), 207–29; Wolfgang Wagner, Ragini Sen, Risa Permanadeli and Caroline Howarth, 'The veil and Muslim women's identity: cultural pressures and resistance to stereotyping', *Culture & Psychology*, 18 (2012), 521–41; Amena Amer and Caroline Howarth, 'Constructing and contesting threat: representations of white British Muslims across British national and Muslim newspapers', *European Journal of Social Psychology*, 48 (2018), 614–28.

10 Sandra Jovchelovitch, 'Introduction to the classic edition', in Sandra Jovchelovitch, *Knowledge in context: representations, community and culture*, classic edn (Abingdon, 2019).

11 Gordon W. Allport, *The nature of prejudice* (Cambridge, MA, 1954).

12 Compare Jovchelovitch, 'Introduction' and Billig, 'Henri Tajfel's "Cognitive aspects of prejudice"'.

13 Martin W. Bauer and George Gaskell, 'Towards a paradigm for research on social representations', *Journal for the Theory of Social Behaviour*, 29 (1999), 163–86.

14 Glăveanu and Yamamoto, 'Bridging history and social psychology'; Bronach C. Kane, *Popular memory and gender in medieval England: men, women and testimony in the church courts, c. 1200–1500* (Woodbridge, 2019).

15 Billig, 'Prejudice, categorization and particularization'; Penelope J. Oakes and S. Alexander Haslam, 'Distortion v. meaning: categorization on trial for inciting intergroup hatred', in Martha Augoustinos and Katherine J. Reynolds (eds), *Understanding prejudice, racism, and social conflict* (London, 2001), 179–94.

16 Margaret Wetherell and Jonathan Potter, *Mapping the language of racism: discourse and the legitimation of exploitation* (New York, 1992); Wolfgang Wagner and Nicky Hayes, *Everyday discourses and common sense: the theory of social representations* (Basingstoke, 2005); Martin W. Bauer and George Gaskell, 'Social representations theory: a progressive research programme for social psychology', *Journal for the Theory of Social Behaviour*, 38 (2008), 335–53.

17 Henri Tajfel, *Human groups and social categories: studies in social psychology* (Cambridge, 1981).

18 Serge Moscovici, *Social representations: explorations in social psychology*, ed. Gerard Duveen (Cambridge, 2000).

19 Paula Castro, 'Legal innovation for social change: exploring change and resistance to different types of sustainability laws', *Political Psychology*, 33 (2012), 105–21; Jovchelovitch, 'Introduction'.

20 For example, see Miriam Heijnders and Suzanne Van Der Meij, 'The fight against stigma: an overview of stigma-reduction strategies and interventions', *Psychology, Health & Medicine*, 11 (2006), 353–63; Claude M. Steele, *Whistling Vivaldi: how stereotypes affect us and what we can do* (New York, 2010).

21 Sandra Jovchelovitch, *Knowledge in context: representations, community and culture*, 1st edn (London, 2007).

22 Steven Pinker, *Enlightenment now: the case for reason, science, humanism, and progress* (New York, 2018). For a historian's critique, see Peter Harrison, 'The enlightenment of Steven Pinker', *ABC Religion and Ethics*, www.abc.net.au/religion/the-enlightenment-of-steven-pinker/10094966 (accessed 6 June 2021).
23 Jean Piaget, *Sociological studies*, ed. Leslie Smith (London, 1995).
24 Ontogenetically, another human being must become involved for a human infant to become a person and that is where the contradictory complexities of the relational sphere probably start. See Michael Tomasello, *Becoming human: a theory of ontogeny* (Cambridge, MA, 2019); Ivana Marková, *The dialogical mind: common sense and ethics* (Cambridge, 2016).
25 Moscovici, *Social representations*; Jovchelovitch, 'Introduction'.
26 Billig, 'Henri Tajfel's "Cognitive aspects of prejudice"'.
27 Billig, 'Prejudice, categorization and particularization'.
28 Caroline Howarth, '"So, you're from Brixton?": the struggle for recognition and esteem in a stigmatized community', *Ethnicities*, 2 (2002), 237–60; Jovchelovitch and Priego-Hernández, *Underground sociabilities*.
29 Nick Hopkins and Ronni Michelle Greenwood, '*Hijab*, visibility and the performance of identity', *European Journal of Social Psychology*, 43 (2013), 438–47.
30 Amer and Howarth, 'Constructing and contesting threat'; Amena Amer, 'Between recognition and mis/nonrecognition: strategies of negotiating and performing identities among white Muslims in the United Kingdom', *Political Psychology*, 41 (2020), 533–48; Madeleine Chapman, 'Veil as stigma: exploring the role of representations in Muslim women's management of threatened social identity', *Journal of Community & Applied Social Psychology*, 26 (2016), 354–66; Sandra Jovchelovitch, 'Peripheral groups and the transformation of social representations: queries on power and recognition', *Social Psychology Review*, 1 (1997), 16–26.
31 Erving Goffman, *The presentation of self in everyday life* (Edinburgh, 1956).
32 Jovchelovitch, 'Introduction'; Matteo Cinelli, Gianmarco De Francisci Morales, Alessandro Galeazzi, Walter Quattrociocchi and Michele Starnini, 'The echo chamber effect on social media', *Proceedings of the National Academy of Sciences*, 118 (2021), doi: 10.1073/pnas.2023301118.

Index

Notes: 'n.' after a page reference indicates the number of a note on that page. Literary works can be found under authors' or publishers' names unless anonymous. Page numbers in *italic* refer to illustrations.

EU authorised representative for GPSR:
Easy Access System Europe, Mustamäe tee 50,
10621 Tallinn, Estonia
gpsr.requests@easproject.com

www.ingramcontent.com/pod-product-compliance
Ingram Content Group UK Ltd.
Pitfield, Milton Keynes, MK11 3LW, UK
UKHW041309190726
13851UKWH00002B/18

* 9 7 8 1 5 2 6 1 1 9 1 3 1 *